O'Burr

Becoming a Master Student Athlete

Doug Toft
Contributing Editor

Karl P. Mooney
Faculty Advisor

Houghton Mifflin Company   Boston   New York

Publisher: Patricia A. Coryell
Senior Sponsoring Editor: Mary Finch
Development Editor: Shani B. Fisher
Editorial Associate: Andrew Sylvester
Senior Project Editor: Cathy Labresh Brooks
Composition Buyer: Sarah Ambrose
Art and Design Manager: Jill Haber
Manufacturing Manager: Karen Banks
Marketing Manager: Elinor Gregory
Marketing Assistant: Evelyn Yang

College Survival
2075 Foxfield Drive, Suite 100
St. Charles, IL 60174
1-800-528-8323
collegesurvival@hmco.com

Cover credit: Cover image © Robert Schoen Photography;
Alan Thornton/Getty Images

Photo and illustration credits:

p. xii: (swimmer) Image100/Wonderfile, (girl eating apple) RubberBall/PictureQuest, (woman at computer) PhotoDisc/PictureQuest, (woman using weight machine, handing off baton) Comstock Images, (graduate) Ryan McVay/PhotoDisc Green/Getty, (sitting man with book) PNC/PhotoDisc Red/Getty, (mortarboard) Thinkstock/Getty, (collage) Walter Kopec; pp. 3–7: Catherine Hawkes/Cat & Mouse Design; p. 9: © David H. Wells/Corbis; p. 11: Comstock Images; p. 12: PhotoDisc; pp. 14–15 (all): PhotoDisc; p. 17 (faces): PhotoDisc, (inset background): Photomondo/PhotoDisc Red/Getty, (collage): Walter Kopec; p. 18: © Elektra Vision: AG/ PictureQuest; p. 20 (refresh button): © Royalty Free/Corbis, (illustration): Walter Kopec; pp. 22, 25: Walter Kopec; p. 27 (collage): Walter Kopec; p. 33: Comstock Images; p. 34 (top): AP/Wide World Images, (bottom): Fotosearch; p. 35: Catherine Hawkes/Cat & Mouse Design; pp. LSI-5, LSI-8: Walter Kopec; pp. 38-39: Walter Kopec; p. 45: (man): PhotoDisc, (lightbulbs): ComstockKLIPS, (collage): Walter Kopec; p. 49: courtesy of Ken Procaccianti; p. 50: Mathiesl/Getty; pp. 53, 54, 55, 56: Walter Kopec; p. 58: Walter Kopec; p. 61: Walter Kopec; p. 65 (monitor with notes): Janice Christie/PhotoDisc Green/Getty Images, (illustration): Walter Kopec; pp. 68, 69, 70, 71: C Squared Studios/PhotoDisc Green/Getty Images; p. 72: (woman's face, clock, trash can): PhotoDisc, (gears, baseball, "Rush" stamp): ComstockKLIPS, (collage): Walter Kopec; p. 73: (woman's face, clock, folders): PhotoDisc, (gears, stoplight): ComstockKLIPS, (hammock): Artville, (collage): Walter Kopec; pp.74, 75, 76: Walter Kopec; p. 77: Ryan McVay/PhotoDisc Green/Getty Images; p. 80: (piggy bank): Duncan Smith/PhotoDisc Green/Getty Images, (burning bill): Don Farrall/PhotoDisc Green/Getty Images, (illustration): Walter Kopec; p. 83: Comstock Images; p. 84: Don Farrall/PhotoDisc Green/Getty Images; p. 87: © Bettmann/Corbis; p. 88: Digital Vision/Getty; p. 90: PhotoDisc; p. 91 (all): PhotoDisc; p. 92 (all): Walter Kopec; pp. 95: Brand X Pictures/Alamy; p. 96: (windmill) Digital Vision/Getty, (shark) Digital Vision/Getty, (illustration) Walter Kopec; p. 100: (door): Photospin, (illustration) Walter Kopec; p. 103: PhotoDisc Blue, (illustration) Walter Kopec; p. 104: © Franco Vogt/Corbis; p. 107: © Duomo/Corbis; p. 108: Corbis/Royalty Free; p. 110, 111, 112, 113, 114: (images): PhotoDisc, (collage) Walter Kopec; p. 115: (frame) PhotoDisc; p. 117: Stockbyte; p. 120: Stockbyte; p. 124: (monitor/keyboard) PhotoDisc, (illustration) Walter Kopec; p. 127: © Bettmann/Corbis; p. 128: Brand X Pictures/Alamy; p. 130: (eye) PhotoDisc; p. 133: (ear) PhotoDisc; p. 137: (brain) Brand X Pictures/Alamy, (eye, ear) PhotoDisc, (collage) Brian Reardon; p. 139: Walter Kopec; p. 145: Corbis/Royalty Free; p. 146: PhotoDisc Royalty Free/Fotosearch; p. 149: © Bettmann/Corbis; p. 150: Comstock Images; p. 152: Gaetano Images Inc./Alamy; p. 156: Image Source/Royalty Free/Fotosearch; p. 157: Image Source/Royalty Free/Fotosearch; p. 161: Brand X Collection/Wonderfile; p. 166: Alamy; p. 168: © Elektra Vision/AG/PictureQuest; p. 170: Corbis Royalty Free/Fotosearch; p. 173: © Duomo/Corbis; p. 174: PhotoDisc; p. 180: Catherine Hawkes/Cat & Mouse Design; pp. 181-182: (chess pieces) PhotoDisc, (illustration) Brian Reardon; pp. 183, 184: AP Photo/Jim Mone; p. 187: (images) PhotoDisc, (collage) Walter Kopec; p. 195: © Digital Vision; p. 196: Image 100 Royalty Free/ Fotosearch; p. 199: © Bettmann/Corbis; p. 200: EyeWire (PhotoDisc)/ Fotosearch; p. 202: (images) EyeWire, Corbis, PhotoDisc, (collage) Walter Kopec; p. 205: (images) EyeWire, Corbis, PhotoDisc, (collage) Walter Kopec; p. 206: (both) Able Stock; p. 208: PhotoDisc; p. 209: Brand X (X Collection)/Wonderfile; p. 213: Comstock/Fotosearch; p. 214: PhotoDisc/Fotosearch; p. 218: PhotoDisc/Fotosearch;

(continued on page 332)

Printed in the U.S.A.

Library of Congress Control Number: 2004113722
Student Edition ISBN: 0-618-49323-9

2 3 4 5 6 7 8 9 – WC – 09 08 07

advisory board

brief table of contents

introduction   Making Transitions   1

chapter 1   First Steps   18

chapter 2   Planning   50

chapter 3   Memory   88

chapter 4   Reading   108

chapter 5   Notes   128

chapter 6   Tests   150

chapter 7   Thinking   174

chapter 8   Communicating   200

chapter 9   Diversity   230

chapter 10   Technology   250

chapter 11   Health   272

chapter 12   What's Next?   302

table of contents

Making Transitions

Master Student Map   xii
On your mark . . .   1
This book is worth $1,000   2
Exercise #1: **Textbook reconnaissance**   2
Get the most out of this book   3
Exercise #2: **Commitment**   4
The Discovery and Intention Journal Entry system   5
Go! And rewrite this book   6
Discovery and Intention Statement guidelines   7
Journal Entry #1: Discovery Statement   8
Making the transition to higher education   9

Mastering transitions   10
Connect to resources   11
Get to know the organizations that govern college
    athletics   12
Journal Entry #2: Discovery Statement   13
Ways to change a habit   14
Following instructions   15
Power Process: Discover what you want   16

1   First Steps

Master Student Map   18
First Step: Truth is a key to mastery   19
Journal Entry #3: Discovery/Intention Statement   19
If you skipped the Introduction . . .   20
Exercise #3: **Taking the First Step**   21
Exercise #4: **The Discovery Wheel**   22
Journal Entry #4: Discovery/Intention Statement   26
Textbook reconnaissance, take two   26
The Master Student   27
The value of higher education   31
Practicing Critical Thinking #1   32
Learning by seeing, hearing, and moving: The VAK
    system   33
Learning styles: Discovering how you learn   35
    Learning Style Inventory   LSI-1
    Interpreting your Learning Style Graph   LSI-2

    Scoring your Inventory   LSI-3
    Learning Style Graph   LSI-5
    Cycle of Learning   LSI-6
Journal Entry #5: Discovery/Intention Statement   LSI-7
    Balancing your preferences   LSI-8
Using your learning style profile to succeed in school   37
The magic of metacognition   38
Academic skill vs. athletic skill   39
Claim your multiple intelligences   40
Attitudes, affirmations, and visualizations   41
Motivation   42
Power Process: Ideas are tools   44
Put It to Work   46
Quiz   47
Learning Styles Application   48
Master Student Profile: Ken Procaccianti   49

2 Planning

Master Student Map   50
You've got the time   51
Journal Entry #6: Discovery/Intention Statement   51
Exercise #5: **The Time Monitor/Time Plan process**   52
Journal Entry #7: Discovery Statement   57
Developing your game plan: Setting and achieving goals   57
Balancing athletics and academics   59
Exercise #6: **Get real with your goals**   60
The ABC daily to-do list   61
Planning sets you free   62
Strategies for scheduling   63
The seven-day antiprocrastination plan   65
More ways to stop procrastination   66
Practicing Critical Thinking #2   67
25 ways to get the most out of now   68

Keep on going?   69
Remember cultural differences   71
Time management for right-brained people (. . . or what to do if to-do lists are not your style)   72
Exercise #7: **Master monthly calendar**   74
Gearing up: Using a long-term planner   75
Exercise #8: **Create a lifeline**   76
Financial planning: Meeting your money goals   77
Take charge of your credit card   80
Exercise #9: **Education by the hour**   81
Power Process: Be here now   82
Put It to Work   84
Quiz   85
Learning Styles Application   86
Master Student Profile: Greg Louganis   87

3 Memory

Master Student Map   88
Take your memory out of the closet   89
Journal Entry #8: Discovery/Intention Statement   89
The memory jungle   90
20 memory techniques   92
Exercise #10: **Use Q-cards to reinforce memory**   96
Notable failures   97
Exercise #11: **Remembering your car keys—or anything else**   98
Journal Entry #9: Discovery Statement   98
Keep your brain fit for life   98

Remembering names   99
Mnemonic devices   100
Practicing Critical Thinking #3   101
Exercise #12: **Be a poet**   101
Power Process: Love your problems (and experience your barriers)   102
Put It to Work   104
Quiz   105
Learning Styles Application   106
Master Student Profile: Dot Richardson   107

4 Reading

Master Student Map   108
Muscle Reading   109
Journal Entry #10: **Discovery/Intention Statement**   109
How Muscle Reading works   110
Phase one: Before you read   111
Phase two: While you read   112
Five smart ways to highlight a text   113
Phase three: After you read   113
Reading fast   115
Exercise #13: **Relax**   116
When reading is tough   117

Journal Entry #11: **Discovery Statement**   118
English as a second language   119
Reading on the road   120
Practicing Critical Thinking #4   121
Power Process: **Notice your pictures and let them go**   122
Put It to Work   124
Quiz   125
Learning Styles Application   126
Master Student Profile: **Jim Abbott**   127

5 Notes

Master Student Map   128
The note-taking process flows   129
Journal Entry #12: **Discovery/Intention Statement**   129
Observe   130
Journal Entry #13: **Discovery/Intention Statement**   132
What to do when you miss a class   132
Record   133
Review   137
Journal Entry #14: **Discovery Statement**   138
The instructor gameplan   139
When your instructor talks fast   140

Taking notes while reading   141
Exercise #14: **Revisit your goals**   142
Get to the bones of your book with concept maps   143
Practicing Critical Thinking #5   143
Power Process: **I create it all**   144
Put It to Work   146
Quiz   147
Learning Styles Application   148
Master Student Profile: **Billie Jean King**   149

6 Tests

Master Student Map   150
Disarm tests   151
Journal Entry #15: **Discovery/Intention Statement**   151
What to do before the test   152
Cooperative learning: Studying with people   154
Ways to predict test questions   155
Journal Entry #16: **Intention Statement**   155
What to do during the test   156
Words to watch for in essay questions   158
The test isn't over until . . .   159
Integrity in test taking: The costs of cheating   160
Have some fun!   160

Let go of test anxiety   161
Journal Entry #17: **Discovery/Intention Statement**   163
Exercise #15: **20 things I like to do**   163
Overcoming math and science anxiety   164
8 reasons to celebrate mistakes   166
Practicing Critical Thinking #6   167
Power Process: **Detach**   168
Put It to Work   170
Quiz   171
Learning Styles Application   172
Master Student Profile: **Mia Hamm**   173

7 Thinking

Master Student Map   174
Critical thinking: A survival skill   175
Journal Entry #18: **Discovery/Intention Statement**   175
Becoming a critical thinker   177
Attitudes of a critical thinker   179
Finding "aha!": Creativity fuels critical thinking   180
Tangram   180
Ways to create ideas   181
Uncovering assumptions   183
Ways to fool yourself: Six common mistakes in logic   184
Gaining skill at decision making   185
Four ways to solve problems   186
"But I don't know what I want to do": Choosing a
   major   187

Majors for the taking   189
Exercise #16: **Make a trial choice of major**   189
Solving math and science problems   190
Asking questions   191
Exercise #17: **Explore emotional reactions**   192
Journal Entry #19: **Discovery/Intention Statement**   192
Exercise #18: **Translating goals into action**   192
Practicing Critical Thinking #7   193
Power Process: **Find a bigger problem**   194
Exercise #19: **Fix-the-world brainstorm**   195
Put It to Work   196
Quiz   197
Learning Styles Application   198
Master Student Profile: **Oscar Robertson**   199

8 Communicating

Master Student Map   200
Communicating creates our world   201
Journal Entry #20: **Discovery/Intention Statement**   201
The communication loop   202
The communication loop: Listening   202
The communication loop: Sending   204
Five ways to say "I"   204
Communicating with coaches and with instructors:
    Bridging the cultures of athletics and academics   206
Journal Entry #21: **Discovery/Intention Statement**   207
Staying cool in the spotlight: Coping with high visibility
    and the media   208
The fine art of conflict management   209
Networking—communicating to create your future   210
Communicating for powerful workplace teams   211
You deserve compliments   211
Hazing   212
Exercise #20: **Write an "I" message**   212

Relationships can work   213
Relationships change   213
7 steps to effective complaints   214
Criticism really can be constructive   214
Exercise #21: **V.I.P.s (very important persons)**   215
Three phases of effective writing   216
Phase One: Getting ready to write   216
Phase Two: Writing a first draft   217
Phase Three: Revising your draft   218
Giving credit where credit is due: Avoiding the high cost
    of plagiarism   220
Writing and delivering speeches   221
Practicing Critical Thinking #8   223
Power Process: **Employ your word**   224
Put It to Work   226
Quiz   227
Learning Styles Application   228
Master Student Profile: **Sheryl Swoopes**   229

9 Diversity

Master Student Map   230
Living with diversity   231
Journal Entry #22: **Discovery/Intention Statement**   231
Diversity is real—and valuable   232
Communicating across cultures   234
Overcome stereotypes with critical thinking   236
Students with learning disabilities: Ask for what you
    want   237
Dealing with sexism and sexual harassment   238
We are all leaders   240

Journal Entry #23: **Discovery/Intention Statement**   242
Journal Entry #24: **Discovery Statement**   242
Practicing Critical Thinking #9   243
Power Process: **Choose your conversations and your
    community**   244
Put It to Work   246
Quiz   247
Learning Styles Application   248
Master Student Profile: **Dat Nguyen**   249

10   Technology

Master Student Map   250
Technology, satisfaction, and success   251
Journal Entry #25: **Discovery/Intention Statement**   251
Connect to cyberspace   252
Overcoming technophobia   253
Finding what you want on the Internet   254
Thinking critically about information on the Internet   255
Using technology to manage time and money   256
Ways to waste time with your computer   257
Write e-mail that gets results   258
Becoming an online learner   259

Exercise #22: **Evaluate search sites**   260
Exercise #23: **Staying motivated with technology**   261
Staying up-to-date with technology   261
Library—the buried treasure   262
Exercise #24: **Revisit your goals, take two**   264
Practicing Critical Thinking #10   265
Power Process: Risk being a fool   266
Put It to Work   268
Quiz   269
Learning Styles Application   270
Master Student Profile: Rick Hansen   271

11   Health

Master Student Map   272
Thinking about health   273
Journal Entry #26: **Discovery/Intention Statement**   273
Take care of your machine   274
Your machine: Fuel it   275
Prevent and treat eating disorders   275
Your machine: Move it   276
Your machine: Rest it   277
Your machine: Observe it   278
Your machine: Protect it   279
Journal Entry #27: **Discovery/Intention Statement**   279
Stay up-to-date on STDs   282
Men, consider your health   283
The experts recommend—seven dietary guidelines   284
Developing self-esteem   285
Emotional pain is not a sickness   287
Suicide   288

Alcohol, tobacco, and drugs: The truth   289
Getting high—the costs for student athletes   289
Some facts . . .   290
Exercise #25: **Addiction: How do I know . . .?**   291
Seeing the full scope of addiction   292
Journal Entry #28: **Discovery Statement**   293
Warning: Advertising can be dangerous to your health   294
Journal Entry #29: **Discovery/Intention Statement**   294
Practicing Critical Thinking #11   295
Power Process: Surrender   296
Put It to Work   298
Quiz   299
Learning Styles Application   300
Master Student Profile: Wilma Rudolph   301

Master Student Map 302
Now that you're done—begin 303
Journal Entry #30: **Discovery/Intention Statement** 303
"... use the following suggestions to continue ..." 304
Exercise #26: **Do something you can't** 305
Transferring to another school 306
Career planning: Begin the process now 308
Twenty-five transferable skills 310
Exercise #27: **Recognize your skills** 311
Jumpstart your education with transferable skills 312
Use the SCANS reports to discover your skills 313
Use résumés and interviews to "hire" an employer 314
Cruising for jobs on the Internet 315
Journal Entry #31: **Intention Statement** 315
Contributing: The art of selfishness 316

Service learning: The art of learning by contributing 317
Practicing Critical Thinking #12 318
Exercise #28: **Plan for sophomore-year success** 319
Define your values, align your actions 320
One set of values 321
Exercise #29: **The Discovery Wheel—coming full circle** 322
Journal Entry #32: **Discovery/Intention Statement** 325
Exercise #30: **This book shouts, "Use me!"** 325
Power Process: Be it 326
Put It to Work 328
Quiz 329
Learning Styles Application 330
Master Student Profile: John Wooden 331

Photo and Illustration Credits 332
Endnotes 332
Index 334

INTRODUCTION
Making Transitions

why
the Introduction matters . . .

You will acquire learning strategies to make a smooth and successful transition to the world of higher education and the new demands of collegiate athletics.

what
is included . . .

On your mark . . .
Get the most out of this book
The Discovery and Intention Journal Entry system
Discovery and Intention Statement guidelines
Making the transition to higher education
Connect to resources
Ways to change a habit
Power Process: "Discover what you want"

how
you can use this Introduction . . .

Discover a way to interact with books that multiplies their value.
Use writing to translate personal discoveries into powerful new behaviors.
Connect with people and organizations that can support your success in academics and sports.

As you read, ask yourself
what if . . .

I could use the ideas in this Introduction to master any transition in my life?

Change and growth take place when a person has risked himself and dares to become involved with experimenting with his own life.

HERBERT OTTO

The human ability to learn and remember is virtually limitless.

SHEILA OSTRANDER AND LYNN SCHROEDER

On your mark...

The purpose of this book is to help you make a successful transition to higher education by setting up a pattern of success that will last throughout your college experience and the rest of your life. You become convinced of the value of an athletic practice regimen when you realize its benefits during competition. In the same way, you are more likely to use the ideas in this book when you are convinced that you have something to gain. That's the reason for this introduction—to persuade you to step up to the starting line and use this book actively.

Before you stiffen up and resist this sales pitch, remember that you already have this book in your hands. You bought it. Or perhaps it was provided as a part of your athletic scholarship. In either case, here's what's in it for you.

Pitch #1: You can save money now and make more later. Start with money. Your college education is one of the most expensive things you will ever buy or earn if you are receiving an athletically related scholarship. Typically, it costs students $30 to $70 an hour to sit in class. Unfortunately, many students think their classes aren't worth even 50 cents an hour.

As a master student, you control the value you get out of your education, and that value can be considerable. The joy of learning aside, college graduates make more money during their lifetimes than their nondegreed peers.[1] The income advantage you gain through higher education could total over half a million dollars. It pays to be a master student.

Pitch #2: You can rediscover the natural learner in you. Joy is important, too. Think of the exhilaration you feel when you win an athletic contest or achieve a personal best performance. You lift yourself to a level that is higher than ever before by disciplined practice. As you become a master student, you will learn to gain knowledge in a similar way—by discovering the joyful, natural learner within you.

Many athletes are great natural students. They quickly master complex skills, such as gymnastic routines, and they have fun doing it. For them, learning is a high-energy process involving experimentation, discovery, and sometimes injury. Then comes school. For some students, drill and drudgery replace discovery. Learning can become a drag. You can use this book to reverse that process and rediscover what you knew from your athletic experience—that laughter and learning go hand in hand.

Sometimes learning takes effort, especially in college. As you become a master student, you will learn many ways to get the most out of these efforts.

Pitch #3: You can choose from hundreds of techniques. *Becoming a Master Student Athlete* is packed with hundreds of practical, nuts-and-bolts techniques. And you can begin using them immediately. For example, during the textbook reconnaissance on page 2, you can practice three powerful learning techniques in one 15-minute exercise. If you doze in lectures, drift during tests, or dawdle on term papers, you'll find ideas in this book that you can use to become a more effective student.

Not all of these ideas will work for you. That's why there are so many of them in *Becoming a Master Student Athlete*. You can experiment with the techniques. As you discover what works, you will develop a unique style of learning that you can use for the rest of your life.

Pitch #4: You get the best suggestions from thousands of students. The concepts and techniques in this book are here not because learning theorists, educators, and psychologists say they work. They are here because tens of thousands of students from all kinds of backgrounds have tried them and say that they work. These are people who dreaded giving speeches, couldn't read their own notes, and fell behind in their course work. Then they figured out how to solve these problems. Now you can use their ideas.

Pitch #5: You can learn about you. The process of self-discovery is an important theme in *Becoming a Master Student Athlete*. Throughout the book you can use Discovery and Intention Statements for everything from organizing your desk to choosing long-term athletic and academic goals. Studying for an organic chemistry quiz is a lot easier with a clean desk and a clear idea of the course's importance to you. You're more likely to meet your athletic goals when you develop an organized off-season training plan that meets your personal needs. You benefit in academics and athletics when you engage in the process of self-discovery.

Pitch #6: You can use a proven product. The first ten editions of *Becoming a Master Student* have proved successful for hundreds of thousands of students. In schools where it was widely used, the dropout rate decreased as much as 25 percent, and in some cases, 50 percent. Students with successful histories have praised the techniques in this book. This edition has been fine-tuned to address the unique concerns of student athletes.

Pitch #7: You can learn the secret of student success.
If this sales pitch still hasn't persuaded you to use this book actively, maybe it's time to reveal the secret of student success. (Provide your own starter gun or referee whistle here.) The secret is—that there are no secrets. Perhaps the ultimate formula is to give up formulas and keep inventing.

The strategies and tactics that successful students use are well known. You have hundreds of them at your fingertips right now, in this book. Use them. Modify them. Invent new ones. You're the authority on what works for you.

However, what makes any technique work is commitment—and action. Without them, the pages of *Becoming a Master Student Athlete* are just 2 pounds of expensive mulch. Add your participation to the mulch, and these pages are priceless. ◪

exercise 1

TEXTBOOK RECONNAISSANCE

Before you engage in any competition, you survey the playing field. You can use the same strategy in your courses. Start becoming a master student this moment by doing a 15-minute "textbook reconnaissance." Here's how.

First, read the table of contents. Do it in three minutes or less. Next, look at every page in the book. Move quickly. Scan headlines. Look at pictures. Notice forms, charts, and diagrams. Don't forget the last few pages in back, which include extra copies of planning forms that you might find useful.

A textbook reconnaissance shows you where a course is going. It gives you the big picture. Whether the setting is athletic or academic, brains work best when going from the general to the specific. Getting the big picture before you start makes it easier to recall and understand details later on.

Before an athletic event, your coaches provide you with information that you can use to scout the opposition. You determine what you can do to gain an advantage during the upcoming contest. Scouting a textbook will work even better if, as you scan, you look for ideas you can use to your advantage. When you find one, write the page number and a short description of it in the space below. If you run out of room, just continue your list on a separate sheet of paper. Or use Post-it Notes to flag the pages that look useful. You could even use notes of different colors to signal priority, such as green for ideas to use right away and yellow for those to apply later. The idea behind this technique is simple: It's easier to learn when you're excited, and it's easier to get excited about a course if you know it's going to be useful, interesting, or fun.

Remember, look at every page, and do it quickly. And here's another useful tip for the master student: Do it now.

Page number   *Description*

_____

_____

_____

_____

_____

_____

Get the most out of this book

1 Rip 'em out. The pages of *Becoming a Master Student Athlete* are perforated because some of the information here is too important to leave in the book and some your instructor might want to see. For example, several exercises in this book ask you to list some important things you want to get out of your experiences in college. To keep yourself focused, you could rip these pages out and post them on your bathroom mirror or some other place where you'll see them several times a day.

You can reinsert the pages later by sticking them into the spine of the book. A piece of tape will hold them in place.

2 Skip around. You can use this book in several different ways. Read it straight through. Or pick it up, turn to any page, and find an idea you can use. Look for ideas you can use right now. For example, if you are about to choose a major or are considering changing schools, skip directly to the articles on these topics in Chapters Seven and Twelve, respectively.

3 If it works, use it. If it doesn't, lose it. You would not use a workout regimen that fails to improve your performance on the field. If there are sections of the book that don't apply to you at all, you can use the same strategy. Skip them—unless, of course, they are assigned. Then see if you can gain value from these sections anyway. When you are committed to getting value from this book, even an idea that seems irrelevant or ineffective at first can turn out to be a powerful tool.

4 Put yourself into the book. Sports psychologists believe that athletes who are able to visualize themselves performing well in challenging moments in their sport will have a better chance of coming out on top. As you read about techniques in this book, create your own scenarios, starring yourself in the title role. For example, when reading through Exercise #1: "Textbook reconnaissance," picture yourself using this technique on your world history textbook.

5 Listen to your peers. Throughout this book you will find Student Voices, short features that contain quotations from students who used *Becoming a Master Student* to promote their success. As you dig into the following chapters, think about what you would say if you could add your voice to theirs. Look for tools and techniques that can make a huge difference in your life.

6 Own this book. As an athlete you know you feel most likely to be successful when you are using your own equipment. It just feels better than something that you borrow. The same idea applies to using this book. Right now, make this book part of your own academic equipment. Put your name, address, and related information on the inside cover, and don't stop there. Determine what you want to get out of your total college experience and create a record of how you intend to get it. Every time your pen touches a page in this book, you move closer to mastery of learning.

7 Do the exercises. Coaches realize that learning often works best when it involves action. You have to swing at the ball to make contact and get a hit. Action also makes this book work. To get the most out of an exercise, read the instructions carefully before you begin. These exercises invite you to write, touch, feel, move, see, search, ponder, speak, listen, recall, choose, commit, and create. You might even sing and dance. To get the most out of this book, do most of the exercises. More important, avoid feeling guilty if you skip some. By the way, it's never too late to go back and do the ones you skipped.

8 Practice critical thinking. Throughout this book are Practicing Critical Thinking activities. Their purpose is to reinforce contemplation and problem solving. Note that other elements of this text, including the exercises and Journal Entries, also promote critical thinking.

9 Learn about learning styles. Check out the Learning Styles Application in each chapter. These exercises are included to increase your awareness of your preferred learning styles and to help you explore new styles. Each application will guide you through experiencing four specific modes of learning as applied to the content of the chapter. The modes can be accessed by asking four basic questions: *Why? What? How?* and *What if?* You'll find more details in the Learning Styles Inventory in Chapter One.

10 **Navigate through learning experiences with the Master Student Map.** You can orient yourself for maximum learning every time you open this book by asking those same four questions. That's the idea behind the Master Student Map included on the first page of each chapter. Eventually, you'll be able to use the four-part structure of this map to guide yourself in effectively learning anything in your academic pursuits, your athletic efforts, or your career.

11 **Link to the Web.** Throughout this book, you'll notice reminders to visit the Web site for *Becoming a Master Student Athlete*:

mastterstudent.college.hmco.com

Check regularly for articles, online exercises, and links to other useful Web sites.

12 **Sweat the small stuff.** Look for sidebars— short bursts of words and pictures placed between longer articles—throughout this book. In athletic competition, the smallest details can have a huge impact on the final outcome. In the same way, these short pieces might offer an insight that transforms your experience of higher education. Remember this related point: Shorter chapters in this book are just as important as longer chapters.

13 **Take this book to work.** With a little tweaking in some cases, you can apply nearly all of the techniques in this book to your career. For more details, see the Put It to Work articles in each chapter. Use them to make a seamless transition from success in courses and sports to success on the job.

14 **Get used to a new look and tone.** This book looks different from traditional textbooks. *Becoming a Master Student Athlete* presents major ideas in magazine-style articles. You will discover lots of lists, blurbs, one-liners, pictures, charts, graphs, illustrations, and even a joke or two.

Even though this book is loaded with special features, you'll find some core elements. For example, the two pages that open each chapter include a "lead" article and an introductory Journal Entry. And at the end of each chapter you'll find a Power Process, Put It to Work article, chapter quiz, Learning Styles Application, and Master Student Profile—all noted in a toolbar at the top of the page.

Note: As a strategy for avoiding sexist language, this book alternates the use of feminine and masculine pronouns. ▧

COMMITMENT

As an athlete, you know that commitment to a goal involves active participation. The same goes for your academic life. This book is worthless unless you actively participate in its activities and exercises. One powerful way to begin taking action is to make a commitment. Conversely, without commitment, sustained action is unlikely, and the result is again a worthless book. Therefore, in the interest of saving your valuable time and energy, this exercise gives you a chance to declare your level of involvement up front. From the choices below, choose the sentence that best reflects your commitment to using this book. Write the number in the space provided at the end of the list.

1. "Well, I'm reading this book right now, aren't I?"
2. "I will skim the book and read the interesting parts."
3. "I will read the book and think about how some of the techniques might apply to me."
4. "I will read the book, think about it, and do the exercises that look interesting."
5. "I will read the book, do some exercises, and complete some of the Journal Entries."
6. "I will read the book, do some exercises and Journal Entries, and use some of the techniques."
7. "I will read the book, do most of the exercises and Journal Entries, and use some of the techniques."
8. "I will study this book, do most of the exercises and Journal Entries, and use some of the techniques."
9. "I will study this book, do most of the exercises and Journal Entries, and experiment vigorously with most of the suggestions in order to discover what works best for me."
10. "I promise myself to get value from this book, beginning with Exercise #1: 'Textbook reconnaissance,' even if I have to rewrite the sections I don't like and invent new techniques of my own."

Enter your commitment level and today's date here:

Commitment level _____   Date _____

If you selected commitment level 1 or 2, you might consider passing this book on to a friend. If your commitment level is 9 or 10, you are on your way to terrific success in school. If your level is somewhere in between, experiment with the techniques and learning strategies in this book. If you find that they work or if this is a required text for a course, consider returning to this exercise and raising your level of commitment.

The Discovery and Intention Journal Entry system

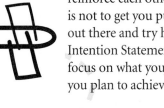

One way to become a better student is to grit your teeth and try harder. There is another way. Using familiar tools and easily learned processes, the Discovery and Intention Journal Entry system can help increase your effectiveness by showing you how to focus your energy.

The Discovery and Intention Journal Entry system is a little like flying a plane. Airplanes are seldom exactly on course. Human and automatic pilots are always checking positions and making corrections. The resulting flight path looks like a zigzag. The plane is almost always flying in the wrong direction, but because of constant observation and course correction, it arrives at the right destination.

A similar system can be used by all students. Most Journal Entries throughout this book are labeled as either Discovery Statements or Intention Statements. Some are Discovery/Intention Statements. Each Journal Entry will contain a short set of suggestions that involve writing.

Through Discovery Statements, you can assess "where you are" academically and athletically. These statements are a record of what you are learning about yourself as a student—both strengths and weaknesses. Discovery Statements can also be declarations of your goals, descriptions of your attitudes, statements of your feelings, transcripts of your thoughts, and chronicles of your behavior.

Sometimes Discovery Statements chronicle an "aha!" moment—a flash of insight that results when a new idea connects with your prior experiences, preferred styles of learning, or both. Perhaps a solution to a long-standing problem suddenly occurs to you, or a life-changing insight wells up from the deepest recesses of your mind. Don't let such moments disappear. Capture them in Discovery Statements.

Intention Statements can be used to alter your course. They are statements of your commitment to do a specific task or take a certain action. An intention arises out of your choice to direct your energy toward a particular goal. While Discovery Statements promote awareness, Intention Statements are blueprints for action. The two processes reinforce each other. The purpose of this system is not to get you pumped up and excited to go out there and try harder. Rather, Discovery and Intention Statements are intended to help you focus on what you want to accomplish and how you plan to achieve your goals.

→ Go! And rewrite this book

Some books should be preserved in pristine condition. This isn't one of them.

Something happens when you interact with your book by writing in it. *Becoming a Master Student Athlete* is about learning, and learning is an active pursuit, not a passive one. When you make notes in the margin, you can hear yourself talking with the author. When you doodle and underline, you can see the author's ideas taking shape. You can even argue with the author and come up with your own theories and explanations. In all of these ways, you become a coauthor of this book. You rewrite it to make it yours.

While you're at it, you can create symbols or codes that will help when reviewing the text later on, such as "Q" for questions or exclamation points for important ideas. You can also circle words to look up in a dictionary.

Remember, if any idea in this book doesn't work for you, you can rewrite it. Change the exercises to fit your needs. Create a new technique by combining several others. Create a technique out of thin air!

Find something you agree or disagree with on this page and write a short note in the margin about it. Or draw a diagram. Better yet, do both. Let creativity be your guide. Have fun.

Begin rewriting now.

The Journal Entry process is a cycle. First, you write Discovery Statements about where you are now and where you want to be. Next, you write Intention Statements about the specific steps you will take to get there. Then you follow up with Discovery Statements about whether you completed those steps and what you learned in the process, followed by more Intention Statements, and so on. Sometimes a statement will be long and detailed. Usually, it will be short—maybe just a line or two. With practice, the cycle will become automatic.

While Discovery Statements promote awareness, Intention Statements are blueprints for action. The two processes reinforce each other.

Don't panic when you fail to complete an intended task. Straying off course is normal. Simply make the necessary corrections. Miraculous progress might not come immediately. Do not be concerned. Stay with the cycle. Use Discovery Statements to get a clear view of your world and what you want out of it. Then use Intention Statements to direct your actions. When you notice progress, record it.

The following statement might strike you as improbable, but it is true: It often takes the same amount of energy to get what you want in college as it takes to get what you *don't* want. Sometimes getting what you don't want takes even more effort. An airplane burns the same amount of fuel flying away from its destination as it does flying toward it. It pays to stay on course.

You can use the Discovery and Intention Journal Entry System to stay on your own course and get what you want. Consider the guidelines for Discovery and Intention Statements that follow, and then develop your own style. Once you get the hang of it, you might discover you can fly.

Discovery and Intention Statement guidelines

Discovery Statements

1 Record the specifics about your thoughts, feelings, and behavior. Thoughts include inner voices. We talk to ourselves constantly in our heads. When internal chatter gets in the way, write down what you are telling yourself. If this seems difficult at first, just start writing. The act of writing can trigger a flood of thoughts.

Thoughts also include mental pictures. These are especially powerful. Picturing yourself flunking a test or losing a match is like a rehearsal to do just that. One way to take away the power of negative images is to describe them in detail.

Also notice how you feel when you function well. Use Discovery Statements to pinpoint exactly where and when you learn most effectively.

In addition, observe your actions and record the facts. If you spent 90 minutes chatting online with a favorite cousin instead of reading your anatomy text, write about it and include the details, such as when you did it, where you did it, and how it felt. Record your observations quickly, as soon as you make them.

2 Use discomfort as a signal. When you approach a daunting task, such as a difficult accounting problem, notice your physical sensations—a churning stomach, perhaps, or shallow breathing or yawning. Feeling uncomfortable, bored, or tired is common among student athletes as the time for a competition approaches. Skilled athletes coach themselves to stick with it and remember that they can handle the discomfort just a little bit longer. When you apply this strategy to other challenges, you will be rewarded.

You can experience those rewards at any time. Just think of a problem that poses the biggest potential barrier to your success in college. Choose a problem that you face right now, today. (Hint: It might be the thing that's distracting you from reading this article.) If you have a lot of emotion tied up in this problem, that's even better. Write a Discovery Statement about it.

3 Suspend judgment. When you are discovering yourself, be gentle. Suspend self-judgment. If you continually judge your behaviors as "bad" or "stupid" or "galactically imbecilic," sooner or later your mind will revolt. Rather than put up with the abuse, it will quit making discoveries. For your own benefit, be kind.

4 Tell the truth. Suspending judgment helps you tell the truth about yourself. "The truth will set you free" is a saying that endures for a reason. The closer you get to the truth, the more powerful your Discovery Statements will be. And if you notice that you are avoiding the truth, don't blame yourself. Just tell the truth about it.

Intention Statements

1 Make intentions positive. The purpose of writing intentions is to focus on what you want rather than what you don't want. Instead of writing "I will not fall asleep while studying accounting," write "I intend to stay awake when studying accounting."

Also avoid the word *try*. Trying is not doing. When we hedge our bets with *try*, we can always tell ourselves, "Well, I *tried* to stay awake." We end up fooling ourselves into thinking we succeeded.

2 Make intentions observable. Experiment with an idea from educational trainer Robert Mager, who suggests that goals be defined through behaviors that can be observed and measured.[2] Rather than writing "I intend to work harder on my history assignments," write "I intend to review my class notes, and I intend to make summary sheets of my reading." Then, when you review your progress, you can determine more precisely whether you have accomplished what you intended.

3 **Make intentions small and keepable.** Give yourself opportunities to succeed by setting goals you can meet. Break large goals into small, specific tasks that can be accomplished quickly. If you want to get an A in biology, ask yourself, "What can I do today?" You might choose to study biology for an extra hour. Make that your intention.

When setting your goals, anticipate self-sabotage. Be aware of what you might do, consciously or unconsciously, to undermine your best intentions. If you intend to study differential equations at 9 p.m., notice when you sit down to watch a two-hour movie that starts at 8 p.m.

Also, be careful of intentions that depend on others. If you write that you intend for your study group to complete an assignment by Monday, then your success depends on the other students in the group.

4 **Set timelines that include rewards.** Timelines can focus your attention. You already notice this when setting a goal to train for an athletic event. A novice pole-vaulter doesn't just grab a fiberglass pole and declare, "Today I will clear 16 feet!" He approaches the task incrementally by setting and reaching more reasonable goals over time. Your coaches recognize the need to acknowledge achievement. They cheer their athletes on when they see them perform at their best and achieve new personal records. They will also push you to be prepared in a timely manner, so when the big day comes you are ready for it.

Timelines are also powerful when applied to academics. For example, if you are assigned to write a paper, break the assignment into small tasks and set a precise due date for each one. You might write "I intend to select a topic for my paper by 9 a.m. Wednesday."

Timelines are especially useful when your intention is to experiment with a technique suggested in this book. The sooner you act on a new idea, the better. Consider practicing a new behavior within four hours after you first learn about it.

Remember that you create timelines for your own benefit, not to set yourself up to feel guilty. And you can always change the timeline.

When you meet your goal on time, reward yourself. Rewards that are an integral part of a goal are powerful. For example, your reward for earning a degree might be the career you've always dreamed of. External rewards,

journal entry 1

Discovery Statement

Welcome to the first Journal Entry in this book. You'll find Journal Entries in every chapter, all with a similar design that allows space for you to write.

In the space below, write a description of a time in your life when you learned or did something well. This experience does not need to be related to school. It could be a time when you did particularly well in an athletic competition. Describe the details of the situation, including the place, time, and people involved. Describe how you felt about it, how it looked to you, how it sounded. Describe the physical sensations you associate with the event. Also describe your emotions.

I discovered that . . .

_____

_____

_____

_____

_____

_____

_____

_____

_____

_____

_____

such as a movie or an afternoon in the park, are valuable, too. These rewards work best when you're willing to withhold them. If you plan to take a nap on Sunday afternoon whether or not you've finished your English assignment, the nap is not an effective reward.

Another way to reward yourself is to sit quietly after you have finished your task and savor the feeling. One reason why success breeds success is that it feels good. ⬧

Making the transition to higher education

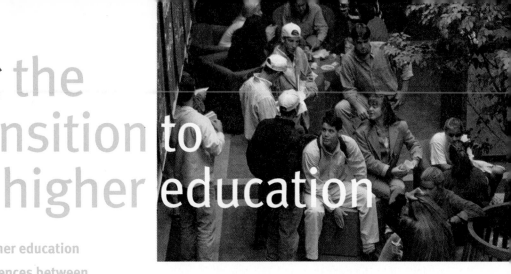

Students who are new to higher education immediately face many differences between secondary and post-secondary education.

Some examples include:

- *New academic standards.* Often there are fewer tests in higher education than in high school, and the grading might be tougher.

- *A larger playing field.* The institution you've just joined might seem immense, impersonal, and even frightening. The sheer size of the campus, the variety of courses offered, the large number of deparments— all of these factors can be overwhelming at times.

- *The presence of many outstanding athletes in your sport.* In high school, you might have been the star performer on your team. Now, in higher education, you might discover that everyone on your team is an outstanding athlete in her own right. The level of competition just to be able to play could be higher than you've ever experienced. If you develop to become one of the outstanding student athletes at your school, this visibility can bring added pressure and responsibility as well.

There's an opportunity that comes with all of these changes. You are now responsible for deciding what classes to take, how to structure your time, and with whom to associate. Perhaps more than ever before, you'll find that your education is your own creation. Perhaps more than ever before, you'll find that your education is your own creation. To make the most of your newfound freedom, keep the following in mind.

Admit your feelings—whatever they are. School can be an intimidating experience for new students. People of diverse cultures, adult learners, commuters, and people with disabilities can feel excluded. Anyone can feel anxious, isolated, homesick, or worried about doing well academically. Don't be afraid to tell your coach how you feel. Coaches know that emotions can have a significant impact on athletic performance. You can also share your feelings with family members, friends, advisors, and a counselor at your student health service.

Meet with your academic advisor. One person in particular can help you access resources and make the transition to higher education—your academic advisor in the college of your major field of study or one who focuses on the needs of student athletes. Academic-athletic advisors can tune in to the emotions and difficulties you are experiencing since many of them were student athletes themselves at some time. Meet with this person regularly. Advisors generally have a big picture of course requirements, options for declaring majors, and the resources available at your school. Peer advisory programs might also be available.

As a student athlete you will have academic demands that you must achieve to stay eligible for competition and to retain your athletic scholarship, if you have one. Be sure that you understand these requirements. Remember that these rules can go beyond semester-to-semester hours and can affect your entire college career from the beginning. Meet with your academic advisor early and often to make sure that you are on track academically and balancing your time between courses and athletics.

Attend class. The amount that you pay in tuition and fees—or the amount of your athletic scholarship—makes a powerful argument for going to classes regularly and getting your money's worth. In large part, the material that you're tested on comes from events that take place in class. As a student athlete you will already be missing a number of classes due to your competition schedule. Avoid missing any more of them. Know the excused absence policy at your college or university. Let your teachers know that you are traveling to compete. Also investigate all of your options for staying up-to-date in your course work. If your classes are taught in multiple sections throughout the week, for example, you might be able to sit in on another class.

Take the initiative in meeting new people. Promise yourself to meet one new person each week. Then write an Intention Statement describing specific ways to do this. Introduce yourself to student athletes from other universities before or after competitions. Also make an effort to meet nonathletes on your campus. They can give you a different perspective on the collegiate experience, and be helpful to you in your classes as well. Realize that most of the people in this new world of higher education are waiting to be welcomed. You can help them and help yourself at the same time. ⬧

→ Mastering transitions

During your lifetime, you'll get many chances to master the art of transition. The transition to higher education and collegiate sports is just one example. Use the following strategies to deal with any transition that comes your way.

Remember earlier transitions. Recall times in the past when you coped with a major change. Write about those experiences in detail. Describe how you felt and list any strategies you used to make those transitions effectively. You've weathered major change before. You can do it again.

Learn optimism. Martin Seligman, author of *Learned Optimism,* states that the key difference between optimists and pessimists is explanatory style—the way that they talk about events such as making transitions.[3] Pessimists might describe the transition to higher education in ways that are:

- *Permanent:* "I'll never be able to handle college-level classes."
- *Pervasive:* "Whenever I get involved in a new situation, I always make a lot of mistakes."
- *Personal:* "I'm just no good at making transitions."

In contrast, optimists tend to make statements that can be described as:

- *Temporary:* "I'm feeling anxious about starting school, and that's normal at first."
- *Specific:* "While this transition might be hard for me, on the whole I can learn to handle change well."
- *External:* "My circumstances have changed a lot, so it's natural to find that I have a lot of new feelings."

The key point is that *over time* you can learn to change your explanatory style. Doing so can make a difference in how you think and feel about any transition. Notice when you talk about difficult events in terms that are permanent, pervasive, or personal. Make a point to speak in ways that are temporary, specific, or external.

Seek stability zones. Any kind of transition can bring a kind of culture shock—and the thought "I don't know who I am anymore." This is particularly difficult for student athletes who become highly visible to the community and scrutinized by the media. To deal with this level of change, remember that not every part of your life has to change at the same time. Balance change in one area with stability in another. While in school, keep in contact with family members and old friends. Maintain long-term relationships, including relationships with key places, such as your childhood home. Postpone other major changes for now.

Balance work, athletic, and academic schedules. As you coordinate your work and study schedules, consider the limits on your energy and time. You may determine that you simply cannot work or participate in athletics if either threatens the quality of your academic performance. To create balance in your life, experiment with options such as these:

- Register for fewer classes during a term when you are in your season of competition or when you expect heavier demands at your job.
- Avoid loading your schedule with classes that require unusually heavy amounts of reading or writing during the same semester.
- Create "buffer zones" in your schedule—pockets of unplanned time that you can use for unforeseen events.

Stay in the present moment. Anxiety can arise when we allow our thoughts to dwell on how long it might take to adjust to new circumstances. Return to the present moment, and such worries start to fade. Accomplished athletes on the brink of a championship focus on the moment before them, not the past or future. This perspective is as useful in academics as in athletics. Ask what you can do right here, right now to ease your transition. Take it one day at a time, even one hour at a time. Handle each task as it arises, and the future will take care of itself.

Connect to resources

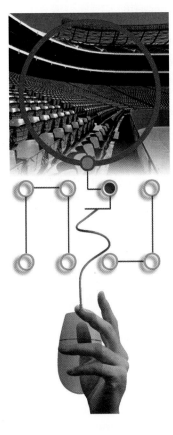

Athletic resources

When you entered higher education, you also signed up for a world of student services. Many of them are free. All of them can help you succeed. The resources listed below are geared specifically to student athletes.

Athletic centers and gymnasiums often open exercise classes, weight rooms, swimming pools, indoor tracks, basketball courts, and racket-sport courts to all students.

The **athletics director** aims to keep your school's teams competitive. This person wants you to have a satisfying experience in higher education.

The **head coach** is often more approachable than you might think. Take advantage of this person's knowledge and experience.

Your **assistant coach**, or the assistant coach who recruited you, may know more about you than anyone on the team's staff. Having spent the most time in your home or at your previous school, this person is uniquely qualified to guide you.

The **academic athletic advisor** for you and your team knows NCAA rules and university policies and procedures. This person may have been a student athlete herself. The programs this advisor offers may also address study skills, life skills, and career planning and development.

The **athletics compliance office** can provide financial assistance through the Student Athlete Assistance Fund or the Student Athlete Opportunities Fund. People at this office can help you maintain your athletic eligibility and deal with boosters and agents.

The **senior women's administrator** oversees the operation of women's sports and related student issues.

A **life skills counselor** can help you solve problems related to finances, health, personal conflicts with teammates and coaches, and alcohol and drug use. Also see this person for help with career planning and development and dealing with the media.

Athletic financial aid officers can make sure you understand your athletic grant-in-aid and take advantage of other loans, grants, or scholarships.

Team trainers assist you to take care of your body to avoid or repair injuries. Consult them before you take any medication so you can avoid testing positive for drug use.

Team doctors are trained specifically to care for athletes. Share your concerns with them openly, and follow their recommendations to the letter.

Team managers are ready with towels, warm-ups, and water to prevent dehydration. These people are usually the first to offer first aid for a minor injury.

Visit **athletic ticket managers** early in the week before a game to get tickets for your family. That way you can avoid last-minute stress about tickets when you have a project due or a big test to take.

School resources

As you take advantage of services for student athletes, remember the wider range of resources available to all students on your campus. Check your school catalog, newspaper, and Web site for more specifics. Your school fees pay for these resources. Now use them.

Academic advisors can help you with selecting courses, choosing majors, planning your career, and adjusting in general to the culture of higher education. As a student athlete, you might have access to two advisors: one who assists you with academics in general, and one who specializes in issues unique to student athletes. Let these advisors know about each other and determine what kinds of questions you can ask each one. For example, a general academic advisor might be able to tell you more about courses required for your major. An advisor from the athletics department might have the latest information about NCAA requirements.

Alumni organizations aren't just for graduates. Alumni publications and alumni themselves can be good sources of information about the benefits and potential pitfalls of being a student at your school. Remember that accepting gifts from alumni based on your athletic activities could violate NCAA rules. Ask your academic athletic advisor for more information.

→ **Get to know the organizations that govern college athletics**

If you want to master the transition to higher education, then learn about the organizations that govern collegiate sports in the United States. Their purpose is to help you succeed in the classroom, stay safe on the field, and stay eligible for athletics.

The dominant organization is the National Collegiate Athletic Association (NCAA). Its membership includes over 1,000 colleges and universities across the country. Originally formed in response to serious injuries and deaths in college football, the NCAA later expanded its role to establish guidelines for recruiting and financial aid.

Over its history, the NCAA has made sweeping changes in college athletics to promote high academic performance by student athletes. The goal is for colleges and universities to retain and graduate their student athletes at rates that rival those of their overall student body. If member schools fail to meet NCAA requirements, the consequences can include a warning, reductions in recruiting and scholarship opportunities, and even elimination from post-season competition.

The second major organization is the National Association of Intercollegiate Athletics (NAIA). Its 360-plus members are typically colleges with smaller athletic budgets than many of their NCAA counterparts.

Other governing organizations exist, each with a focus on different kinds of schools. All these organizations set and enforce rules for playing seasons, recruiting, scholarships, eligibility, and other key aspects of collegiate sports. Find out which organizations govern sports at your school. Their policies directly affect what you do as a student athlete.

To learn more about the organizations mentioned in this article and others, visit this book's Web site at

masterstudent.college.hmco.com

Arts resources can include museums, galleries, and concert halls.

Chapels are usually open to students of any religion.

Childcare is sometimes made available to students at a reasonable cost through the early childhood education department.

The *financial aid office* assists students with loans, scholarships, and grants.

Job placement offices can help you find part-time employment while you are in school and a job after you graduate.

The *registrar* handles information about transcripts, grades, changing majors, transferring credits, and dropping or adding classes.

School security agencies can provide information about parking, bicycle regulations, and traffic rules. Some offer safe escorts at night.

Student government can help you develop skills in leadership and

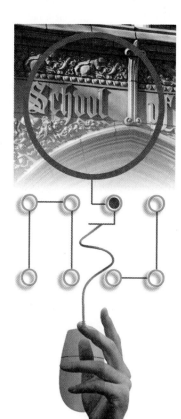

teamwork. If you have experience with student government, many employers will take notice.

Student health clinics often provide free or inexpensive treatment for minor problems.

Student organizations present an opportunity to explore fraternities, sororities, service clubs, veterans' organizations, religious groups, sports clubs, and political groups. Also look for programs for special populations. This includes women's centers, multicultural student centers, and organizations for international students, disabled students, and gay and lesbian students.

Student unions are hubs for social activities, special programs, and free entertainment.

Tutoring services can help, even if you think you are hopelessly stuck in a course. Such services are usually free and are available through individual academic departments, counseling centers, or your athletic advising center. ✖

journal entry 2

Discovery Statement

Success is a choice—your choice. To *get* what you want, it helps to *know* what you want. That is the purpose of this Journal Entry, which has two parts.

You can begin choosing success right now by setting a date, time, and place to complete this Journal Entry. Write your choices here, then block out the time on your calendar.

Date: _____

Time: _____

Place: _____

Part 1

Select a time and place when you know you will not be disturbed for at least 20 minutes. (The library is a good place to do this.) Relax for two or three minutes, clearing your mind. Next, complete the following sentences—and then keep writing.

When you run out of things to write, stick with it just a bit longer. Be willing to experience a little discomfort. Keep writing. What you discover might be well worth the extra effort.

What I want from my education is . . .

_____

_____

_____

When I complete my education, I want to be able to . . .

_____

_____

_____

I also want . . .

_____

_____

_____

Part 2

After completing Part 1, take a short break. Reward yourself by doing something that you enjoy. Then come back to this Journal Entry.

Now, review the list of things that you want from your education. See if you can summarize them in a one-sentence, polished statement. This will become a statement of your purpose for taking part in higher education.

Allow yourself to write many drafts of this mission statement, and review it periodically as you continue your education. With each draft, see if you can capture the essence of what you want from higher education and from your life. State it in a vivid way—a short sentence that you can easily memorize, one that sparks your enthusiasm and makes you want to get up in the morning.

You might find it difficult to express your purpose statement in one sentence. If so, write a paragraph or more. Then look for the sentence that seems most charged with energy for you.

Following are some sample purpose statements:

- My purpose for being in school is to gain skills that I can use to contribute to others.

- My purpose for being in school is to live an abundant life that is filled with happiness, health, love, and wealth.

- My purpose for being in school is to enjoy myself by making lasting friendships and following the lead of my interests.

Write at least one draft of your purpose statement below:

_____

_____

_____

_____

_____

_____

_____

Ways to change a habit

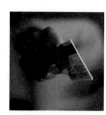

Consider a new way to think about the word *habit*. Imagine for a moment that many of our most troublesome problems and even our most basic traits are just habits.

That expanding waistline that someone blames on a spouse's cooking—maybe that's just a habit called overeating.

That fit of rage that a student blames on a teacher—maybe that's just the student's habit of closing the door to new ideas.

Procrastination, stress, and money shortages might just be names that we give to collections of habits—scores of simple, small, repeated behaviors that combine to create a huge result. The same goes for health, wealth, love, and many of the other things that we want from life.

One way of thinking about success is to focus on habits. When you discover a behavior that undermines your goals or creates a circumstance that you don't want, consider a new attitude: It's just a habit. And it can be changed.

After interviewing hundreds of people, psychologists James Prochaska, John Norcross, and Carlo DiClemente identified stages that people typically go through when adopting a new behavior.[4] These stages take people from *contemplating* a change and making a clear *determination* to change to taking *action* and *maintaining* the new behavior. Following are ways to help yourself move successfully through each stage.

Choose and commit to a new behavior. It often helps to choose a new habit to replace an old one. First, make a commitment to practice the new habit. Tell key people in your life about your decision to change. Set up a plan for when and how. Answer questions such as these: When will I apply the new habit? Where will I be? Who will be with me? What will I be seeing, hearing, touching, saying, or doing? Exactly how will I think, speak, or act differently?

Take the student who always snacks when he studies. Each time he sits down to read, he positions a bag of potato chips within easy reach. For him, opening a book is a cue to start chewing. Snacking is especially easy, given the place he chooses to study: the kitchen. He decides to change this habit by studying at a desk in his bedroom instead of at the kitchen table. And every time he feels the urge to bite into a potato chip, he drinks from a glass of water instead.

Rehearse your intention. Before you apply the new habit, rehearse it in your mind. Mentally picture what actions you will take and in what order.

When you discover a behavior that undermines your goals or creates a circumstance that you don't want, consider a new attitude: It's just a habit. And it can be changed.

Say that you plan to improve your handwriting when taking notes. Imagine yourself in class with a blank notebook poised before you. See yourself taking up a finely crafted pen. Notice how comfortable it feels in your hand. See yourself writing clearly and legibly. You can even picture how you will make individual letters—the *e*'s, *i*'s, and *r*'s. Then, when class is over, see yourself reviewing your notes and taking pleasure in how easy they are to read.

Act as if your intention is already a reality, as if the new habit is already a part of you. Be the change you want to see—today.

Get feedback and support. It's easy to practice your new behavior with great enthusiasm for a few days. After the initial rush of excitement, however, things can get a little tougher. We begin to find excuses for slipping back into old habits: "One more cigarette won't hurt." "I can get back to my diet tomorrow." "It's been a tough day. I deserve this beer."

One way to get feedback is to bring other people into the picture. Ask others to remind you that you are changing your habit. If you want to stop an old behavior, such as cramming for tests, then it often works to tell everyone you know that you intend to stop.

Design a system to monitor your behavior. You can create your own charts or diagrams to track your behavior or you can write about your progress in your journal. Figure out a way to track your progress.

Practice, practice, practice—without self-judgment. Psychologists such as B. F. Skinner define learning as a stable change in behavior that comes as a result of practice.[5] This idea is key to changing habits. Act on your intention. If you fail or forget, let go of any self-judgment. Just keep practicing the new habit and allow whatever time it takes to make a change.

Making mistakes as you practice doesn't mean that you've failed. Even when you don't get the results you want from a new behavior, you learn something valuable in the process. Once you understand ways to change one habit, you understand ways to change almost any habit.

→ Following instructions

Your experience in higher education hinges on your ability to follow instructions. And following instructions is often far more complicated than it appears. The next time you are at practice, notice how often you have to repeat a drill because someone didn't understand the instructions. The cost of misunderstanding instructions can range from missing points on a test to missing the team bus.

Distinguish between outcomes and tasks. At practice, your coach might ask you to increase your outside shooting accuracy by 20 percent. This is an instruction to produce a certain *outcome*. Or the coach might give you a list of spots on the court from which to take your shot. In this case, the instruction assigns you *tasks* to help produce that 20 percent increase. Instructions given in your classes can also distinguish between outcomes and tasks.

This distinction has important implications for you as an instruction follower. When your focus is on the outcome, you might have the freedom to choose from several different paths to achieve that result. If your instruction is to follow a sequence of tasks, you might have less flexibility. Skilled instruction followers look for this difference and clarify what's expected before they move into action.

Distinguish between sequential instructions and lists of options. In many cases, you'll benefit by seeing instructions as a series of steps to perform in a certain order. These are called sequential instructions. They often apply to tasks such as following a recipe, troubleshooting a computer problem, or running a play against a 1-3-1 zone defense.

In other cases, instructions consist of a list of options that you can apply in almost any order. *Becoming a Master Student Athlete* frequently gives this kind of instruction. When reading an article such as this one, you can choose one suggestion to apply now and come back for more later. The suggestion you start with does not have to appear first in the list.

Make sure that you understand all of the instructions. Take notes on the directions, or, if written, highlight key points. Reread for clarification. If the directions are numerous or complex, make a checklist to ensure that you don't miss a step. Ask questions when you are unsure about what to do. Anticipate possible problems and plan what you'll do to solve them.

On the other hand, don't make instructions any harder than they need to be. When following instructions, estimate the time you'll take to complete a task. If a one-hour project starts looking like a full day's enterprise, it's time to adjust your estimate—or review the instructions and weed out unnecessary steps.

power process

Discover what you want

Imagine a person who walks up to a counter at the airport to buy a plane ticket for his next vacation. "Just give me a ticket," he says to the reservation agent. "Anywhere will do."

The agent stares back at him in disbelief. "I'm sorry, sir," he replies. "I'll need some more details. Just minor things—such as the name of your destination city and your arrival and departure dates."

"Oh, I'm not fussy," says the would-be vacationer. "I just want to get away. You choose for me."

Compare this with another traveler who walks up to the counter and says, "I'd like a ticket to Ixtapa, Mexico, departing on Saturday, March 23, and returning Sunday, April 7. Please give me a window seat, first class, with vegetarian meals."

Now, ask yourself which traveler is more likely to end up with a vacation that he'll enjoy.

The same principle applies in any area of life. Knowing where we want to go increases the probability that we will arrive at our destination. Discovering what we want makes it more likely that we'll attain it. Once our goals are defined precisely, our brains reorient our thinking and behavior to align with those goals—and we're well on the way there.

Mastery lies in the details

The example about the traveler with no destination seems far-fetched. Before you dismiss it, do an informal experiment: Ask three other students what they want to get out of their education. Be prepared for hemming and hawing, vague generalities, and maybe even a helping of pie-in-the-sky à la mode.

That's amazing, considering the stakes involved. Our hypothetical vacationer is about to invest a couple weeks of his time and hundreds of dollars—all with no destination in mind. Students routinely invest years of their lives and thousands of dollars with an equally hazy idea of their destination in life.

Suppose that you ask someone what she wants from her education and you get this answer: "I plan to get a degree in journalism with double minors in earth science and Portuguese so that I can work as a reporter covering the environment in Brazil." Chances are you've found a master student. The details of a person's vision offer a clue to mastery.

Discover the benefits

Discovering what you want greatly enhances your odds of succeeding in higher education. Many students quit school simply because they are unsure of their goals. With well-defined objectives in mind, you can constantly look for connections between what you want and what you study. The more connections you discover, the more likely you'll stay in school—and the more likely you'll benefit from higher education.

Having a clear idea of your goals makes many decisions easier. Knowing what you want from your education helps you choose the school you'll attend, the courses you'll take, the major you'll declare, and the next career you'll pursue.

Discovering what you want also enhances your study skills. An example is memorizing. A skydiver will not become bored learning how to pack her parachute. Her reward for learning the skill is too important. Likewise, when information helps you get something you want, it becomes easier to remember.

You can have more energy when your daily activities lead to what you want. If you're bogged down in quadratic equations, stand back for a minute. Think about how that math course ties in with your goal of becoming an electrical engineer, how your philosophy course relates to your aim of becoming a minister, or how your English course can help you become a better teacher.

Succeeding in higher education takes effort. When you follow the path of getting what you truly want, you can enjoy yourself even if the path is uphill. You can expend great energy and still feel fresh and eager to learn. When you take on courses that you care about and prepare for a career that you look forward to, you can play full out. You can work even to the point of exhaustion at times, and do it happily.

That's one purpose of discovering what you want. Your vision is not meant to be followed blindly—it's meant to pull you forward.

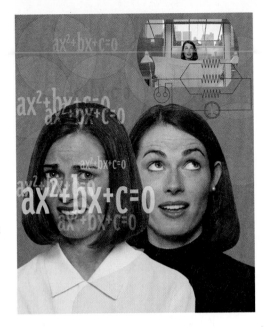

Put it in writing

For maximum clarity, write down what you want. Goals that reside strictly in your head can remain fuzzy. Writing them down brings them into sharper focus.

As you write about what you want, expand your imagination to many different time frames. Define what you want to be, do, and have next week, next month, and next year. Write about what you want five years from now—and five minutes from now.

Approach this process with a sense of adventure and play. As you write, be willing to put any option on the table. List the most outrageous goals—those that sound too wonderful to ever come true.

You might want to become an Olympic champion in your sport of choice, or a coach of a college team. Write those goals down.

You might want to travel to India, start a consulting business, or open a library in every disadvantaged neighborhood. Write those goals down.

You might want to own a ranch in a beautiful valley, become a painter, or visit all of the hot springs in the world. Write those down, too.

With well-defined objectives in mind, you can constantly look for connections between what you want and what you study.

Perhaps you want to restore the integrity of the ozone layer or eliminate racism through international law. Or perhaps you simply want to be more physically fit, more funny, or more loving. Whatever you want, write it down.

Later, if you want, you can let go of some goals. First, though, live with them for a while. Goals that sound outlandish right now might seem more realistic in a few weeks, months, or years. Time often brings a more balanced perspective, along with an expanded sense of possibility.

Move from discovery to action

Discovering what you want can be heady fun. And it can quickly become an interesting but irrelevant exercise unless you take action to get what you want. Most discoveries come bundled with hints to *do* something—perhaps to change a habit, contact someone, travel, get educated, or acquire a new skill. Dreams that are not followed with action tend to die on paper. On the other hand, dreams that lead to new behaviors can lead to new results in your life.

To move into action, use this book. It's filled with places to state what you want to accomplish and how you intend to go about it. Every Journal Entry and exercise exists for this purpose. Fill up those pages. Take action and watch your dreams evolve from fuzzy ideals into working principles.

With your dreams and new behaviors in hand, you might find that events fall into place almost magically. Start telling people about what you want, and you'll eventually find some who are willing to help. They might offer an idea or two or suggest a person to call or an organization to contact. They might even offer their time or money. The sooner you discover what you want, the sooner you can create the conditions that transform your life.[6]

1

First Steps

No one can make you feel inferior without your consent.

ELEANOR ROOSEVELT

The most challenging aspect of the decathlon is not the events themselves, but how you train to become the best 100-meter runner you are on the same day that you're the best 1,500-meter runner.

BRUCE JENNER

why
this chapter matters . . .

Visible measures of success—such as top grades and athletic awards—start with invisible assets called attitudes.

what
is included . . .

First Step: Truth is a key to mastery
If you skipped the introduction . . .
The Discovery Wheel
The Master Student
The value of higher education
Learning by seeing, hearing, and moving: The VAK system
Learning styles: Discovering how you learn
Learning Style Inventory
Using your learning style profile to succeed in school
The magic of metacognition
Claim your multiple intelligences
Attitudes, affirmations, and visualizations
Motivation
Power Process: "Ideas are tools"
Master Student Profile: Ken Procaccianti

how
you can use this chapter . . .

Experience the power of telling the truth about your current skills.
Discover your preferred learning styles and develop new ones.
Consciously choose attitudes that promote your success.

as you read, ask yourself
what if . . .

I could create attitudes that would help me achieve my goals?

First Step: Truth is a key to mastery

A prominent NCAA Division I football coach was taking heat from the media and his university's booster club for choosing to start a quarterback who was clearly not as gifted as another player competing for that spot. When asked why he chose the less gifted player to start an important bowl game, the coach said, "I trust him to tell me exactly what is going on out there [on the field]."

This coach used The First Step technique. This technique is simple: Tell the truth about who you are, what you are doing, and what you want. End of discussion. Now proceed to Chapter Two.

Well, it's not *quite* that simple.

The First Step is one of the most valuable tools in this book. It magnifies the power of all the other techniques. It is a key to becoming a master student. Unfortunately, a First Step is easier to explain than it is to use. Telling the truth sounds like pie-in-the-sky moralizing, but there is nothing pie-in-the-sky or moralizing about a First Step. It is a practical, down-to-earth way to change our behavior. No technique in this book has been field-tested more often or more successfully—or under tougher circumstances.

Success starts with telling the truth about what *is* working—and what *isn't*—in our lives right now. It is not about boasting, or about blaming someone else for our shortcomings. When we acknowledge our strengths, we gain an accurate picture of what we can accomplish. When we admit that we have a problem, we free up energy to find a solution. Ignoring the truth, on the other hand, can lead to problems that stick around.

The principle of telling the truth is applied universally by people who want to turn their lives around. For members of Alcoholics Anonymous, the First Step is acknowledging that they are powerless over alcohol. For people who join Weight Watchers, the First Step is admitting how much they weigh. For a student athlete, a First Step might include an admission that it's tough to keep up with courses while traveling with the team. This is an alternative to denying his need for help and telling his coach that everything is okay—and then getting caught when grades come out.

It's not easy to tell the truth about ourselves. And for some of us, it's even harder to recognize our strengths. Maybe we don't want to brag. Maybe we're attached to poor self-images. The reasons don't matter. The point is that using the First Step technique in *Becoming a Master Student Athlete* means telling the truth about our positive qualities, too. You can state your accomplishments without boasting.

journal entry 3

Discovery/Intention Statement

Take five minutes to skim the Discovery Wheel exercise starting on page 22. Find one statement that describes a skill you already possess—a personal strength that will promote your success at the collegiate level. Write that statement here:

_____

_____

_____

_____

The Discovery Wheel might also prompt some thoughts about skills you want to acquire. Describe one of those skills by completing the following sentence:

I discovered that . . .

_____

_____

_____

_____

Now, skim the appropriate chapter in this book for at least three articles that could help you develop this skill. For example, if you want to take more effective notes, turn to Chapter Five. List the names of your chosen articles here and a time when you will read them in more detail.

I intend to . . .

_____

_____

_____

_____

Today's world-class elite athletes undergo all sorts of high-tech performance evaluations. Their respiration is tested. Their blood is examined. Every movement of their body is scrutinized, and they are required to be candid so that researchers can pinpoint what they can do to be better. Many times "better" means a few thousandths of a second faster, a couple of yards longer, or a fraction of a centimeter higher. These outstanding athletes acknowledge the importance of candor and the value of truthful self-evaluation.

Success as a student athlete goes beyond your athletic performance. This kind of success starts with telling the truth about your academic preparation and the life skills you want to gain. Believe it or not, you can begin working with your list of weaknesses by admitting and even celebrating them.

Consider the most accomplished, "together" athletes you know. If they were totally candid with you, you'd soon hear about their mistakes and regrets. The more successful athletes are, the more willing they are to look at their flaws.

It might seem natural to judge our own shortcomings and feel bad about them. Some people believe that such feelings are necessary in order to bring about change. There is an alternative. We can discover a way to gain any type of skill without feeling rotten about the past. We can change the way things *are* without having to be upset about the way things *have been.*

It might also help to remember that weaknesses are often strengths taken to an extreme. The student who carefully studies the technique of her dives can make significant improvements. If she does this just before the dive has to be executed, though, her marks are likely to suffer. Any success strategy carried too far or employed too late can backfire.

Whether written or verbal, First Steps are more powerful when they are specific. For example, if you want to improve your note-taking skills, you might write "I am an awful note taker." It would be more effective to write "I can't read 80 percent of the notes I took in Introduction to Psychology last week, and I have no idea what was important in that class." Complete the exercises in this chapter, and your courage will be rewarded. The Discovery Wheel exercise and the rest of the activities in this book can help you tap resources you never knew you had. They're all First Steps—no kidding. It's just that simple. The truth has power. 🗙

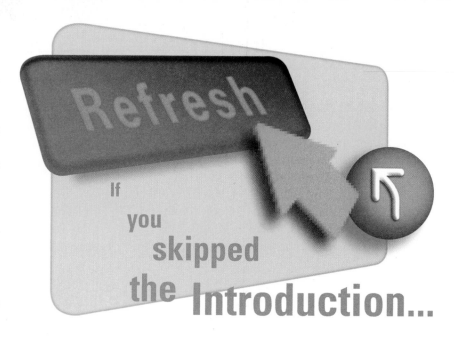

If you skipped the Introduction...

Some people think introductions have little to offer and are a waste of time. The Introduction to *Becoming a Master Student Athlete* is important. It suggests ways to get your money's worth out of this book—and out of your experience as a student athlete.

Here are some of the informative articles that await you:

- Get the most out of this book
- The Discovery and Intention Journal Entry system
- Making the transition to higher education
- Connect to resources
- Ways to change a habit
- Power Process: "Discover what you want"

Please go back and read the Introduction now. 🗙

TAKING THE FIRST STEP

The purpose of this exercise is to give you a chance to discover and acknowledge your own strengths, as well as areas for improvement. For many students, this is the most difficult exercise in the book. To make the exercise worthwhile, do it with courage.

Some people suggest that looking at areas for improvement means focusing on personal weaknesses. They view it as a negative approach that runs counter to positive thinking. Well, perhaps. Positive thinking is a great technique. So is telling the truth, especially when we see the whole picture—the negative aspects as well as the positive ones.

If you admit that you can't add or subtract and that's the truth, then you have taken a strong, positive First Step toward learning basic math. If you tell a coach that you don't understand the development of a particular play during practice, that is also a positive First Step. On the other hand, if you say that you are a terrible math student and that's not the truth, then you are programming yourself to accept unnecessary failure.

The point is to tell the truth. This exercise is similar to the Discovery Statements that appear in every chapter. The difference is that in this case, for reasons of confidentiality, you won't write down your discoveries in the book.

Be brave. If you approach this exercise with courage, you are likely to disclose some things about yourself that you wouldn't want others to read. You might even write down some truths that could get you into trouble. Do this exercise on separate sheets of paper; then hide or destroy them. Protect your privacy.

To make this exercise work, follow these suggestions:

Be specific. It is not effective to write "I can improve my communication skills." Of course you can. Instead, write down precisely what you can *do* to improve your communication skills, for example, "I can spend more time really listening while the coach is talking, instead of thinking about what I'm going to say next."

Look beyond the classroom. What goes on outside of school often has the greatest impact on your ability to be an effective student athlete.

Be courageous. This exercise is a waste of time if it is done half-heartedly. Be willing to take risks. You might open a door that reveals a part of yourself that you didn't want to admit was there, like a temper that causes you to lose focus on your game. The power of this technique is that once you know what is there, you can do something about it.

Part 1

Time yourself, and for 10 minutes write as fast as you can, completing each of the following sentences at least 10 times with anything that comes to mind. If you get stuck, don't stop. Just write something-even if it seems crazy.

I never succeed when I . . .

I'm not very good at . . .

Something I'd like to change about myself is . . .

Part 2

When you have completed the first part of the exercise, review what you have written, crossing off things that don't make any sense. The sentences that remain suggest possible goals for becoming a master student athlete.

Part 3

Here's the tough part. Time yourself, and for 10 minutes write as fast as you can, completing the following sentences with anything that comes to mind. As in Part 1, complete each sentence at least 10 times. Just keep writing, even if it sounds silly.

I always succeed when I . . .

I am very good at . . .

Something I like about myself is . . .

Part 4

Review what you have written and circle the things that you can fully celebrate. This is a good list to keep for those times when you question your own value and worth.

THE DISCOVERY WHEEL

The Discovery Wheel is another opportunity to tell the truth about the kind of student athlete you are and the kind of student athlete you want to become.

This is not a test. There are no trick questions, and the answers will have meaning only for yourself.

Here are two suggestions to make this exercise more effective. First, think of it as the beginning of an opportunity to change. There is another Discovery Wheel at the end of this book. You will have a chance to measure your progress, so be honest about where you are now. Second, lighten up. A little laughter can make self-evaluations a lot more effective.

Here's how the Discovery Wheel works. By the end of this exercise, you will have filled in a circle similar to the one on this page. The Discovery Wheel circle is a picture of how you see yourself. The closer the shading comes to the outer edge of the circle, the higher the evaluation of a specific skill. In the example to the right, the student has rated her reading skills low and her note-taking skills high.

The terms "high" and "low" are not meant to reflect a negative judgment. The Discovery Wheel is not a permanent picture of who you are. It is a picture of how you view your strengths and weaknesses today. To begin this exercise, read the following statements and award yourself points for each one, using the point system described below. Then add up your point total for each section and shade the Discovery Wheel on page 25 to the appropriate level.

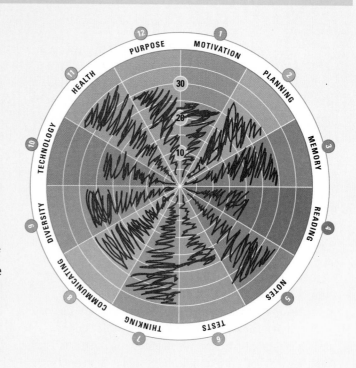

5 points
This statement is always or almost always true of me.

4 points
This statement is often true of me.

3 points
This statement is true of me about half the time.

2 points
This statement is seldom true of me.

1 point
This statement is never or almost never true of me.

Do this exercise online at `masterstudent.college.hmco.com`

1. _____ I enjoy learning.
2. _____ I understand and apply the concept of multiple intelligences.
3. _____ I connect my courses and athletic experiences to my purpose for being in school.
4. _____ I make a habit of assessing my personal strengths and areas for improvement.
5. _____ I am satisfied with how I am progressing toward achieving my academic and athletic goals.
6. _____ I use a knowledge of learning styles to support my success.
7. _____ I am willing to consider any idea that can help me succeed-even if I initially disagree with that idea.
8. _____ I take responsibility for my attitudes.

_____ ***Total score (1) Motivation***

1. _____ I set long-term goals and periodically review them.
2. _____ I set short-term goals to support my long-term goals.
3. _____ I write a plan for each day and each week.
4. _____ I assign priorities to what I choose to do each day.

5. _____ I work and socialize with others outside the athletic realm.

6. _____ I schedule my time to effectively balance my academic and athletic commitments.

7. _____ I have adequate time each day to accomplish what I plan.

8. _____ I am confident that I will find the resources to finance my education

_____ **Total score (2) Planning**

1. _____ I am confident of my ability to remember.

2. _____ I can remember people's names.

3. _____ At the end of a presentation, I can summarize the key points.

4. _____ I apply techniques that enhance my memory skills.

5. _____ I can recall information when I'm under pressure in the classroom or during competition.

6. _____ I remember important information clearly and easily.

7. _____ I can jog my memory when I have difficulty recalling.

8. _____ I can relate new information to what I've already learned.

_____ **Total score (3) Memory**

1. _____ I preview and review reading assignments.

2. _____ When reading, I ask myself questions about the material.

3. _____ I underline or highlight important passages when reading.

4. _____ When I read, I am alert and awake.

5. _____ I keep up with my reading assignments and other study tasks while I'm on the road.

6. _____ I select a reading strategy to fit the type of material I'm reading.

7. _____ I take effective notes when I read.

8. _____ When I don't understand what I'm reading, I note my questions and find answers.

_____ **Total score (4) Reading**

1. _____ I take notes during class and other key presentations.

2. _____ When I take notes, I focus my attention.

3. _____ I am aware of various methods for taking notes and choose those that work best for me.

4. _____ When listening, I distinguish important material and note key phrases.

5. _____ I copy down key material that an instructor, coach, or other presenter displays visually—via a chalkboard, overhead projector, or slide presentation.

6. _____ I can put important concepts into my own words.

7. _____ My notes are valuable for review.

8. _____ Before I miss classes due to my athletic schedule, I let instructors know and I take responsibility for keeping up with course work and getting notes from classmates.

_____ **Total score (5) Notes**

1. _____ I feel confident and calm during an exam.

2. _____ I manage my time during exams and am able to complete them.

3. _____ I am able to predict test questions.

4. _____ I adapt my test-taking strategy to the kind of test I'm taking.

5. _____ I understand what essay questions ask and can answer them completely and accurately.

6. _____ I start reviewing for tests at the beginning of the term.

7. _____ I continue reviewing for tests throughout the term.

8. _____ My sense of personal worth is independent of my test scores, athletic record, or other measures of performance.

_____ **Total score (6) Tests**

1. _____ I have flashes of insight and often think of solutions to problems at unusual times.

2. _____ I use brainstorming to generate solutions to a variety of problems.

3. _____ When I get stuck on a creative project, I use specific methods to get unstuck.

4. _____ I see problems and tough decisions as opportunities for learning and personal growth.

5. _____ I am willing to consider different points of view and alternative solutions.

6. _____ I can detect common errors in logic.

7. _____ I construct viewpoints by drawing on information and ideas from many sources.

8. _____ As I share my viewpoints with others, I am open to their feedback.

_____ **Total score (7) Thinking**

1. _____ I am candid with others about who I am, what I feel, and what I want.

2. _____ Other people tell me that I am a good listener.

3. _____ I can communicate my upset and anger without blaming others.

4. _____ I can make friends and create valuable relationships in a new setting.

5. _____ I communicate effectively in a variety of contexts—with classmates, other student athletes, coaches, alumni, and members of the media.

6. _____ I can effectively plan and research a large writing assignment.

7. _____ I create first drafts without criticizing my writing, then edit later for clarity, accuracy, and coherence.

8. _____ I know ways to prepare and deliver effective speeches.

_____ **Total score (8) Communicating**

1. _____ I am aware of my biases and am open to understanding people from other cultures, races, and ethnic groups.

2. _____ I build rewarding relationships with people from other backgrounds.

3. _____ I can point out examples of discrimination and sexual harassment and effectively respond to them.

4. _____ I am learning ways to thrive with diversity-attitudes and behaviors that will support my success in higher education and in my career.

5. _____ I can effectively resolve conflict with people from other cultures.

6. _____ My writing and speaking are free of sexist expressions.

7. _____ I can recognize bias and discrimination in the media.

8. _____ I am aware of the changing demographics in my country and community.

_____ **Total score (9) Diversity**

1. _____ I learn effectively from materials and activities that are posted online.

2. _____ I can efficiently find information on the Internet.

3. _____ I think critically about information and ideas that I access online.

4. _____ I write clear and concise e-mail messages that generate the results I want.

5. _____ My online communication is fair and respectful to other people.

6. _____ I monitor new technology that can support my success at the collegiate level.

7. _____ I monitor new technology that can support my success in my career.

8. _____ I effectively use libraries to find the resources and information I want.

_____ **Total score (10) Technology**

1. _____ I have enough energy to meet my academic and athletic commitments-while fully enjoying other areas of my life.

2. _____ If the situation calls for it, I have enough reserve energy to put in a long day.

3. _____ The way that I train for athletics supports my long-term health.

4. _____ The way I eat is independent of my feelings of self-worth.

5. _____ I engage in healthy relationships, always mindful of my health and well-being.

6. _____ My emotional health supports my ability to succeed as a student athlete.

7. _____ I notice changes in my physical condition and respond effectively.

8. _____ I am in control of any alcohol or other drugs I put into my body.

_____ **Total score (11) Health**

1. _____ I see learning as a lifelong process.

2. _____ I understand that while not every class I take will relate directly to my specific purpose in college, I can relate all of my experiences in higher education to the rest of my life.

3. _____ My life includes opportunities to contribute to others.

4. _____ I revise my plans as I learn, change, and grow.

5. _____ I am clear about my purpose in life.

6. _____ I know that I am responsible for my own education.

7. _____ I take responsibility for the quality of my life.

8. _____ I am willing to accept challenges even when I'm not sure how to meet them.

_____ **Total score (12) Purpose**

Filling in your Discovery Wheel

Using the total score from each category, shade in each section of the Discovery Wheel. Use different colors, if you want. For example, you could use green to denote areas you want to work on. When you have finished, complete the Journal Entry on the next page.

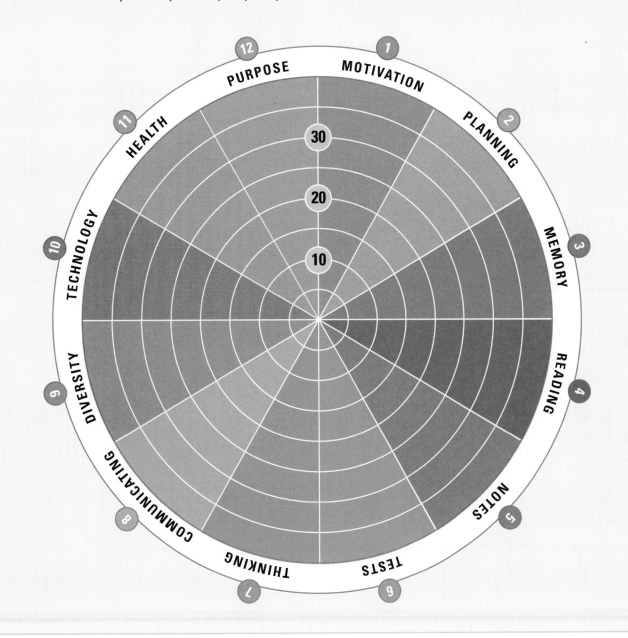

journal entry 4

Discovery/Intention Statement

Now that you have completed your Discovery Wheel, spend a few minutes with it. Get a sense of its weight, shape, and balance. Can you imagine running your hands around it? If you could lift it, would it feel light or heavy? How would it sound if it rolled down a hill? Would it roll very far? Would it wobble? Make your observations without judging the wheel as good or bad. Simply be with the picture you have created.

After you have spent a few minutes studying your Discovery Wheel, complete the following sentences in the space below. Don't worry if you can't think of something to write. Just put down whatever comes to mind. Remember, this is not a test.

This wheel is an accurate picture of my ability as a student because . . .

_____

_____

My self-evaluation surprises me because . . .

_____

_____

The two areas in which I am strongest are . . .

_____

_____

The areas in which I want to improve are . . .

_____

_____

I want to concentrate on improving these areas because . . .

_____

_____

_____

Now, select one of your discoveries and describe how you intend to benefit from it. Complete the statement below.

To gain some practical value from this discovery, I will . . .

_____

_____

_____

Textbook reconnaissance, take two

The first chapter of any textbook usually includes key material—ideas that the author wants you to have up front. Likewise, this book is packed with articles that could benefit you right now. There just wasn't enough room to put them all in the first chapter.

While skimming the book for Exercise #1: "Textbook reconnaissance," you might have spotted the following articles in later chapters. If not, consider sampling them right now.

The seven-day antiprocrastination plan, page 65

More ways to stop procrastination, page 66

25 ways to get the most out of now, page 68

20 memory techniques, page 92

Muscle Reading, page 109

Reading on the road, page 120

The note-taking process flows, page 130

Disarm tests, page 151

Gaining skill at decision making, page 185

Communicating with coaches and with instructors, page 206

Writing and delivering speeches, page 221

Communicating across cultures, page 234

Becoming an online learner, page 259

Take care of your machine, page 274

Career planning: Begin the process now, page 309

In 1482, **Leonardo da Vinci** wrote a letter to a wealthy baron, applying for work. In excerpted form, he wrote,

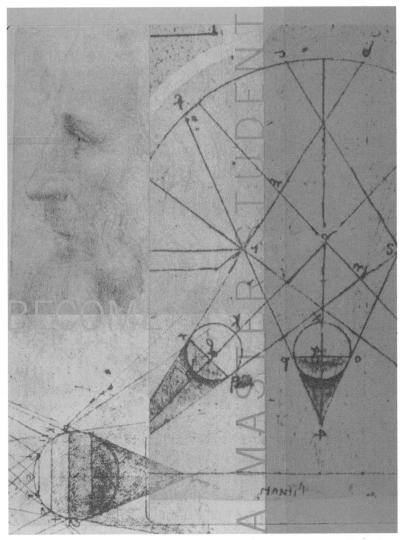

"I can contrive various and endless means of offense and defense. . . . I have all sorts of extremely light and strong bridges adapted to be most easily carried. . . . I have methods for destroying every turret or fortress. . . . I will make covered chariots, safe and unassailable. . . . In case of need I will make big guns, mortars, and light ordnance of fine and useful forms out of the common type." And then he added, almost as an afterthought, *"In times of peace I believe I can give perfect satisfaction and to the equal of any other in architecture . . . can carry out sculpture . . . and also I can do in painting whatever may be done."*

The **Mona Lisa,** for example.

Mastery can lead to flashy results—an incredible painting, for example, or an unforgettable game. In basketball, mastery might result in an unbelievable shot at the buzzer. For a musician, it might be the performance of a lifetime, the moment when everything comes together. Often the result of mastery is a sense of profound satisfaction, well-being, and timelessness. Athletes sometimes refer to these moments as being in a "zone". Work seems self-propelled. The master is *in* control by being *out* of control. He lets go and allows the creative process to take over. That's why after a spectacular performance, it is often said of an athlete or a performer, "He was playing out of his mind."

Likewise, the master student athlete is one who "learns out of her mind." Of course, that statement makes no sense. Mastery, in fact, doesn't make sense. It cannot be captured with words. It defies analysis. Mastery cannot be taught, only learned and experienced.

Examine the following list of characteristics of master students in light of your own experience. The list is not complete. It merely points in a direction. Look in that direction, and you'll begin to see the endless diversity of master students. These people are old and young, male

The Master Student

This book is about something that cannot be taught. It's about becoming a master student.

A master is a person who has attained a level of skill that goes beyond technique. For a master, methods and procedures are automatic responses to the needs of the task. Work is effortless. The master carpenter is so familiar with her tools, they are part of her. To a master chef, utensils are old friends. A master athlete skillfully executes her role, even as struggle evaporates. Because these masters don't have to think about the details of the process, they bring more of themselves to their work.

and female. They exist in every period of history. And they come from every culture, race, and ethnic group.

Also remember to look to yourself. No one can teach us to be master students; we already *are* master students. We are natural learners by design.

Inquisitive. The master student is curious about everything. By posing questions she can generate interest in the most mundane, humdrum situations. When she is bored during a biology lecture, she thinks to herself, "I always get bored when I listen to this instructor. Why is that? Maybe it's because he reminds me of my boring uncle Ralph, who always tells those endless fishing stories. He even looks like Uncle Ralph. Amazing! Boredom is certainly interesting." Then she asks herself, "What can I do to get value out of this lecture, even though it seems boring?" And she finds an answer. A baseball or softball player in the outfield should be posing questions about each batter's tendencies for various situations. Does he hit it deep? Does she pull the ball left? Does he bunt often? In life, in athletics, you have to be in the game to get in the game.

Able to focus attention. Watch a 2-year-old at play. Pay attention to his eyes. The wide-eyed look reveals an energy and a capacity for amazement that keep his attention absolutely focused in the here and now. The master student's focused attention has a childlike quality. The world, to a child, is always new. Because the master student can focus attention, to him the world is always new, too.

Likewise, the basketball player who is sitting on the bench during a game has to maintain her focus on the game. She must be alert for at any moment she could be called upon to step onto the court. If she doesn't train her mind to be actively involved in the game now, she will find it difficult to maintain the needed level of intensity and remain in control when she does play.

Willing to change. The unknown does not frighten the master student. In fact, she welcomes it—even the unknown in herself. We all have pictures of who we think we are, and these pictures can be useful. They also can prevent learning and growth.

The master student athlete is open to changes in her environment and in herself. As she faces her first tennis opponent on a clay court, she is uncertain about how well she will play. She could make excuses after slipping and sliding at the beginning of the match. Or she could make the necessary adjustments—shorten her steps, realize how the clay causes the ball to bounce, and play hard all throughout the contest.

Able to organize and sort. The master student can take a large body of information and sift through it to discover relationships. He can play with information, organizing data by size, color, function, timeliness, and hundreds of other categories. Weather is a constant variable that has to be analyzed. The place kicker, the golfer, the runner, the pole vaulter and many others in numerous sports have to account for wind, rain, heat, and cold. Each element can impact the distance a ball will travel and the accuracy of the flight of the ball.

Competent. Mastery of skills is important to the master student. When she learns mathematical formulas, she studies them until they become second nature. She practices until she knows them cold, then puts in a few extra minutes.

Joyful. More often than not, the master student is seen with a smile on his face—sometimes a smile at nothing in particular other than amazement at the world and his experience of it. Collegiate athletes who step out onto the field of a packed stadium feel a sense of elation that they find difficult to express. There is nervousness. There is excitement. And there is the joy of having "made it."

Able to suspend judgment. The master student has opinions and positions, and she is able to let go of them when appropriate. She realizes she is more than her thoughts. She is part of a program, a team. She can quiet her internal dialogue and listen to an opposing viewpoint. She doesn't let judgment get in the way of learning her course work or her sport. Rather than approaching discussions with a "Prove it to me and then I'll believe it" attitude, she asks herself, "What if this is true?" and explores possibilities.

Energetic. Notice the student athlete with a spring in his step, the one who is enthusiastic and involved in class, the one who comes to practice every day ready to give 100 percent. When he reads or practices or competes, he does so with a high level of intensity. He is a master student.

Well. Health is important to the master student, though not necessarily in the sense of being free of illness. Rather, she values her body and treats it with respect. She listens to her body and responds in a timely and realistic manner to its needs. She tends to her emotional and spiritual health, as well as her physical health. As an athlete, she immediately addresses her injuries and follows prescribed rehabilitation.

Self-aware. The master student is willing to evaluate himself and his behavior. He regularly tells the truth about his strengths and those aspects that could be improved. He steps aside when he knows that another teammate would have a greater likelihood of success and the team will benefit.

Responsible. There is a difference between responsibility and blame, and the master student knows it well. She is willing to take responsibility for everything in her life—even for events that most people would blame on others. She admits fault when she does not correctly execute a play.

For example, if a master student athlete is served cold eggs at the training table, she chooses to take responsibility for getting cold eggs. This is not the same as blaming herself for cold eggs. Rather, she looks for ways to change the situation and get what she wants. She could choose to eat breakfast earlier, or she might tell someone in the kitchen that the eggs are cold and request a change. Even if the cold eggs continue, the master student takes responsibility by choosing her response to the situation.

Willing to take risks. The master student often takes on projects with no guarantee of success. He participates in class dialogues at the risk of looking foolish. He accepts playing at a different position. He welcomes the risk of a challenging course.

Willing to participate. Don't look for the master student on the sidelines. She's in the game, even when she is sitting or standing on the sidelines. She is a player who can be counted on. She is willing to make a commitment and to follow through on it.

A generalist. The master student is interested in everything around him. He has a broad base of knowledge in many fields and can find value that is applicable to his specialties. As an athlete, he knows that poets write about sports, that scientists are responsible for the lush grass he plays on, and that sports themselves pale in importance to other issues in the world.

Willing to accept paradox. The word *paradox* comes from two Greek words, *para* (beyond) and *doxen* (opinion). A paradox is something that is beyond opinion or, more accurately, something that might seem contradictory or absurd yet might actually have meaning.

For example, the master student can be committed to managing money and reaching her financial goals. At the same time, she can be totally detached from money, knowing that participating in sport as an amateur for the love of the game is more valuable than any money she could earn. The master student recognizes the limitations of the mind and accepts ambiguity.

Courageous. The master student admits his fear and fully experiences it. For example, he approaches a tough exam as an opportunity to explore feelings of anxiety and tension related to the pressure to perform. He relishes the hype of a weeklong media frenzy leading to a game with an archrival. He does not deny fear. He embraces it as a personal test through which he can experience the joy of victory.

Self-directed. Rewards or punishments provided by others do not motivate the master student. Her motivation to learn comes from within. Losses, though hard to swallow at first, become learning moments from which she draws direction and purpose.

Spontaneous. The master student is truly in the here and now. He is able to respond to the moment in fresh, surprising, and unplanned ways.

Relaxed about grades. Grades make the master student neither depressed nor euphoric. She recognizes that sometimes grades are important, and grades are not the only reason she studies. She does not measure her worth as a human being by the grades she receives. Yet she is realistic about their importance in shaping her future and her continuation as an eligible athlete.

Intuitive. The master student has an inner sense that cannot be explained by logic. He has learned to trust his feelings, and he works to develop this intuitive sense.

Creative. Where others see dull details and trivia, the master student sees opportunities to create. She can gather pieces of knowledge from a wide range of subjects and put them together in new ways.

Willing to be uncomfortable. The master student does not place comfort first. When discomfort is necessary to reach a goal, he is willing to experience it. With his eye upon the athletic and academic prize, he can endure personal hardships and can look at unpleasant things with detachment.

Accepting. The master student athlete accepts herself, the people around her, and the challenges that life offers. She recognizes that no one teammate or classmate is perfect.

Willing to laugh. The master student might laugh at any moment, and his sense of humor includes the ability to laugh at himself and relieve moments of stress, such as during a competition.

Going to school is a big investment. The stakes are high. It's OK to be serious about that, but you don't have to go to school on the deferred-fun program. A master student celebrates learning, and one of the best ways to do that is to have a laugh now and then.

Hungry. Human beings begin life with a natural appetite for knowledge. In some people it soon gets dulled. The master student taps that hunger. She desires to learn for the sake of learning in an academic or athletic situation.

Willing to work. Once inspired, the master student is willing to follow through with sweat. He knows that genius and creativity are the result of persistence and work. When in high gear, the master student athlete works with the intensity of a child at play. He is willing to fail over and over again until he succeeds.

Caring. A master student cares about knowledge and has a passion for ideas. She also cares about people and appreciates learning from others. She values the teaching of her professors and coaches. She flourishes in a community that values "win-win" outcomes, cooperation, and love.

The master student in you. The master student is in all of us. By design, human beings are learning machines. We have an innate ability to learn in settings that are athletic and not athletic, and all of us have room to grow and improve.

It is important to understand the difference between learning and being taught. Human beings can resist being taught anything. Carl Rogers goes so far as to say that anything that can be taught to a human being is either inconsequential or just plain harmful.[1] What is important in education, Rogers asserts, is *learning*. And everyone has the ability to learn.

Unfortunately, people also learn to hide that ability. As they experience the pain that sometimes accompanies learning, they shut down. If a child experiences embarrassment in front of a group of people, he could learn to avoid similar situations. In doing so, he restricts his possibilities.

Some children "learn" that they are slow learners. If they learn it well enough, their behavior comes to match that label.

→ Master Student Profiles

IN EACH CHAPTER of this text there is an example of a person who embodies several qualities of a master student.

As you read about these people and others like them, ask yourself: "How can I apply this?" Look for the timeless qualities in the people you read about. Many of the strategies used by master students from another time or place are tools that you can use today.

The master students in this book were chosen because they demonstrate unusual and effective ways to learn. Remember that these are just 12 examples of master students (one for each chapter). You can read about more in the Master Student Hall of Fame at **masterstudent.college.hmco.com**. Also reflect on other master students you've read about or know personally. As you meet new people, look for those who excel at learning. The master student is not a vague or remote ideal. Rather, master students move freely among us.

In fact, there's one living inside your skin.

As people grow older, they sometimes accumulate a growing list of ideas to defend, a catalog of familiar experiences that discourages them from learning anything new.

Still, the master student within survives. To tap that resource, you don't need to acquire anything. You already have everything you need. Every day you can rediscover the natural learner within you. ✖

voices

student

A personal interest in pursuing the unknown, digging deeper, and taking that one extra step makes the difference between an ordinary student and a master student. A master student has a desire to learn and absorb, and to find the essence that exists in the world around her. Every master student also knows that time is not limitless and that the quest for knowledge is retained in a lifetime.

—JENNIFER FAY

Some of your peers might assume that they'll become professional athletes who make lots of money—and therefore don't need a college education. The odds are overwhelmingly against them.

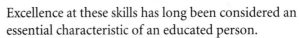

The value of higher education

Most student athletes never "go pro." Besides, a professional athletic career often lasts less than four years. That raises a question about what to do with the rest of your life.

Think of your life as developing in chapters, like a book. Some chapters are long. Others are short. Consider how the chapter about your college education will read. It could mark the point at which life begins a steep decline. Or it could continue your path toward an abundant future.

The most obvious benefits to earning a college degree are economic. Over their lifetimes, college graduates on average earn much more than high school graduates. That's just one potential payoff. Consider the others explained below.

Master the liberal arts. According to one traditional model of education, there are two essential tasks for people to master—the use of language and the use of numbers. To acquire these skills, students once immersed themselves in subjects such as grammar, logic, and geometry. These subjects were called the "liberal" arts. They complemented the fine arts, such as poetry, and the practical arts, such as farming.

This model of liberal arts education still has something to offer. Today we master the use of language through the basic processes of communication: reading, writing, speaking, and listening. In addition, courses in mathematics and science help us understand the world in quantitative terms. The abilities to communicate and calculate are essential to almost every profession.

Excellence at these skills has long been considered an essential characteristic of an educated person.

The word *liberal* comes from the Latin verb *libero*, which means "to free." Liberal arts are those that promote critical thinking. Studying them can free us from irrational ideas, half-truths, racism, and prejudice. The liberal arts grant us freedom to explore alternatives and create a system of personal values. These benefits are priceless, the very basis of personal fulfillment and political freedom.

Discover your values. We do not spend all of our waking hours at our jobs. That leaves us with a decision that affects the quality of our lives: how to spend leisure time. By cultivating our interest in the arts and community affairs, the liberal arts provide us with many options for activities outside of work. These studies add a dimension to life that goes beyond having a job and paying the bills.

Discover new interests. Taking a broad range of courses has the potential to change your direction in life. A student previously committed to a career in science might try out a drawing class and eventually switch to a degree in studio arts. Or a person who swears that she has no aptitude for technical subjects might change her major to computer science after taking an introductory computer course.

Learn skills that apply across careers. Jobs that involve responsibility, prestige, and higher incomes depend on self-management skills. These include knowing ways to manage time, resolve conflicts, set goals, learn new skills, and control stress. Higher education is a place to learn and practice such skills.

Hang out with the great. Today we enjoy a huge legacy from our ancestors. The creative minds of our species have given us great works of art, systems of science, and technological advances that defy the imagination. Through higher education we can gain firsthand knowledge of humanity's greatest creations. The poet Ezra Pound defined literature as "news that stays news."[2] Most of the writing in newspapers and magazines becomes dated quickly. In contrast, many of the books you read in higher education have passed the hardest test of all—time. Such works have created value for people for decades, sometimes for centuries. These creations are inexhaustible. We can return to them time after time and gain new insights. These are the works we can justifiably deem great. Hanging out with them transforms us. Getting to know them exercises our minds, just as running exercises our bodies. 🗶

PRACTICING CRITICAL THINKING

Review the article "The Master Student" in this chapter. Then skim the master student profiles throughout this book, near the end of each chapter. Finally, choose one of the people profiled and describe in the space below how this person embodies qualities of a master student.

_____

_____

_____

_____

_____

_____

_____

_____

_____

_____

_____

*The Practicing Critical Thinking exercises that appear throughout this book incorporate ideas from Peter Facione, Dean of the College of Arts and Sciences, Santa Clara University, and creator of the California Critical Thinking Disposition Inventory. Mr. Facione provided substantial suggestions for these exercises and edited them. He can be contacted through the California Academic Press on the World Wide Web at **http://www.insightassessment.com/about.html**.*

Adapted with permission from Critical Thinking: What It Is and Why It Counts *by Peter Facione (Millbrae, CA: The California Academic Press, 1996).*

Learning by seeing, hearing, and moving:

The VAK system

You can approach the topic of learning styles with a simple and powerful system—one that focuses on just three ways of perceiving through your senses:

- Seeing, or *visual* learning
- Hearing, or *auditory* learning
- Movement, or *kinesthetic* learning

To recall this system, remember the letters *VAK*, which stand for **v**isual, **a**uditory, and **k**inesthetic. The theory is that each of us prefers to learn through one of these sense channels. And we can enrich our learning with activities that draw on the other channels.

To reflect on your VAK preferences, answer the following questions. Each question has three possible answers. Circle the answer that best describes how you would respond in the stated situation. This is not a formal inventory—just a way to prompt some self-discovery.

When you have problems spelling a word, you prefer to:
1. *Look it up in the dictionary.*
2. *Say the word out loud several times before you write it down.*
3. *Write out the word with several different spellings and choose one.*

You enjoy courses the most when you get to:
1. *View slides, overhead transparencies, videos, and readings with plenty of charts, tables, and illustrations.*
2. *Ask questions, engage in small-group discussions, and listen to guest speakers.*
3. *Take field trips, participate in lab sessions, or apply the course content while working as a volunteer or intern.*

When learning a new set of plays or routines, you understand most clearly when:
1. *Watching someone else perform first, or viewing a video of the new material.*
2. *Listening to the coach's instruction.*
3. *Getting out there and practicing it yourself.*

When giving someone directions on how to drive to a destination, you prefer to:

1. *Pull out a piece of paper and sketch a map.*
2. *Give verbal instructions.*
3. *Say, "I'm driving to a place near there, so just follow me."*

When planning an extended vacation to a new destination, you prefer to:
1. *Read colorful, illustrated brochures or articles about that place.*
2. *Talk directly to someone who's been there.*
3. *Spend a day or two at that destination on a work-related trip before taking a vacation there.*

You've made a commitment to learn to play the guitar. The first thing you do is:
1. *Go to a library or music store and find an instruction book with plenty of diagrams and chord charts.*
2. *Pull out your favorite CDs, listen closely to the guitar solos, and see if you can sing along with them.*
3. *Buy or borrow a guitar, pluck the strings, and ask someone to show you how to play a few chords.*

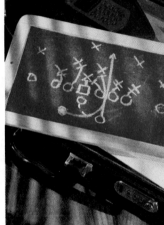

You've saved up enough money to lease a car. When choosing from among several new models, the most important factor in your decision is:
1. *The car's appearance.*
2. *The information you get by talking to people who own the cars you're considering.*
3. *The overall impression you get by taking each car on a test drive.*

You've just bought a new computer system—monitor, central processing unit, keyboard, CD burner, cable modem, and external speakers. When setting up the system, the first thing you do is:
1. *Skim through the printed instructions that come with the equipment.*
2. *Call up someone with a similar system and ask her for directions.*
3. *Assemble the components as best as you can, see if everything works, and consult the instructions only as a last resort.*

Now take a few minutes to reflect on the meaning of your responses. All of the answers numbered "1" are examples of visual learning. The "2's" refer to auditory learning, and the "3's" illustrate kinesthetic learning. Finding a consistent pattern in your answers indicates that you prefer learning through one sense channel more than the others. Or you might find that your preferences are fairly balanced.

Listed below are suggestions for learning through each sense channel. Experiment with these examples and create more techniques of your own. Use them to build on your current preferences and develop new options for learning.

To enhance *visual* learning:

- Preview reading assignments by looking for elements that are highlighted visually—bold headlines, charts, graphs, illustrations, and photographs.

- When taking notes in class, leave plenty of room to add your own charts, diagrams, tables, and other visuals later.

- Whenever an instructor writes information on a blackboard or overhead projector, copy it exactly in your notes.

- Transfer your handwritten notes to your computer. Use word processing software that allows you to format your notes in lists, add headings in different fonts, and create visuals in color.

- Before you begin an exam, quickly sketch a diagram on scratch paper. Use this diagram to summarize the key formulas or facts you want to remember.

- During tests, see if you can visualize pages from your handwritten notes or images from your computer-based notes.

To enhance *auditory* learning:

- Reinforce memory of your notes and readings by talking about them. When studying, stop often to recite key points and examples in your own words.

- After doing several verbal summaries, record your favorite version or write it out.

- Read difficult passages in your textbooks slowly and out loud.

- Join study groups and create short presentations about course topics.

- Visit your instructors during office hours to ask questions.

As an athlete, you may already have a highly developed kinesthetic intelligence. You can take advantage of this ability by using strategies such as these:

- Look for ways to translate course content into three-dimensional models that you can build. While studying biology, for example, create a model of a human cell using different colors of clay.

- Supplement lectures with trips to museums, field observations, lab sessions, tutorials, and other hands-on activities.

- Recite key concepts from your courses while you train.

- Intentionally set up situations in which you can learn by trial and error.

- Create a practice test and write out the answers in the room where you will actually take the exam.

To extend your range as a master student, also explore visual and auditory strategies for learning.

Note: This chapter introduces several approaches to learning styles: the Learning Style Inventory, multiple intelligences, and the VAK system. Remember that each approach presents an option, not the final word on learning styles. Look for ideas from any of these methods that you can put to immediate use. When you write Intention Statements, keep these questions in mind: How can I use this idea to *be* more successful in school? What will I *do* differently as a result of reading about learning styles? If I develop new learning styles, what skill will I *have* that I don't have now? ◼

learning styles

what if · why · how · what

Discovering
how you learn

When we learn, two things initially happen. First, we notice new information. We *perceive* and take in what's before us. Second, we make sense of the information. We *process* it in a way that helps us understand what's going on and makes the information our own.

Consider, for example, baseball players as they watch an opposing team's new pitcher for the first time. They *perceive* the pitcher's size and delivery of the ball, along with the speed and rhythm of the pitches. They also *process* this information in very personal ways to predict what kind of pitches will come their way and choose their strategies for hitting the ball. *Learning styles* is a term that takes into account differences in how people prefer to perceive and process information.

Knowing your preferred learning style helps you understand why some courses appeal to you while others seem dull or boring. Figuring out when to use your preferences—and when it might be helpful to include another style of learning—can help you function successfully as a student in many different settings.

Perceiving information

The ways that people perceive information typically range from a preference for concrete experience (CE) to a preference for abstract conceptualization (AC):

- People who favor perceiving by *concrete experience* like to absorb information through their five senses. They learn by getting directly involved in new experiences. When solving problems, they rely on their intuition as much as their intellect. These people typically function well in unstructured learning classes that allow them to take the initiative.

- People who favor perceiving by *abstract conceptualization* take in information best when they can think about it as a subject separate from themselves. They analyze, intellectualize, and create theories. Often these people take a scientific approach to problem solving and excel in traditional classrooms.

Processing information

The ways that people process information typically range from a preference for active experimentation (AE) to a preference for reflective observation (RO):

- People who favor processing information by *active experimentation* prefer to jump in and start doing things immediately. They do not mind taking risks as they attempt to make sense of things, because this helps them learn. They are results-oriented and look for practical ways to apply what they have learned.

- People who favor processing information by *reflective observation* prefer to stand back, watch what is going on, and think about it. Often they consider several points of view as they attempt to make sense of things and can generate many ideas about how something happens. They value patience, good judgment, and a thorough approach to understanding information.

Completing the cycle

According to David Kolb, a psychologist who developed the theory of experiential learning, learners have natural preferences for how they perceive and process information.[3] Yet they benefit most fully if they allow themselves to participate in all four points of the continuums described above. Successful learners:

1. involve themselves fully, openly, and without bias in new experiences (CE);

2. observe and reflect on these experiences from many points of view (RO);

3. integrate these observations into logically sound theories (AC) that include predictions about the consequences of new behaviors; and

4. use these theories to make decisions, solve problems, and take effective action (AE).

This view of learning is quite flexible. You can start learning at any one of the four points listed above and cycle through the rest. In any case, the power of your learning derives from testing theories in your daily life—and in changing those theories based on the feedback you get from concrete experiences.

You can use Kolb's ideas to increase your skills at learning anything—during practice, in the classroom, or in any other situation. First, start by understanding your natural preferences. Then balance them with activities that you consciously choose to support your learning.

Taking your Learning Style Inventory

To help you become more aware of what you currently do to support your learning, David Kolb has developed the Learning Style Inventory (LSI), which is included on the next few pages. Completing this inventory will help you discover more about how you learn.

Step 1 Keep in mind that this is not a test. There are no right or wrong answers. Your goal is to develop a profile of your learning. Take the inventory quickly. There's no need to agonize over your responses. Recalling a recent situation in which you learned something new at school, at work, or in your life might make it easier for you to focus and answer the questions.

Step 2 Remove the sheet of paper following page LSI-2. When you're ready to write on the inventory, press firmly so that your answers will show up on the page underneath the questions.

Step 3 Note that the LSI consists of 12 sentences, each with four different endings. You will read each sentence, then write a "4" next to the ending that best describes the way you currently learn. Then you will continue ranking the other endings with a "3," "2," or "1." This is a forced choice inventory, so you must rank each ending; no items can be left out. *Look at the example provided at the top of page LSI-1 before you begin.*

When you understand the example, you're ready to respond to the 12 sentences of the LSI:

- After you answer item #1, check to be sure that you wrote one "1," one "2," one "3," and one "4."

- Also check to make sure that your markings are showing through onto the scoring page (LSI-3).

- After you have responded to the 12 items, go to page LSI-3, which has instructions for computing your results. ◪

Learning Style Inventory

Remove the sheet of paper following this page. Press firmly while writing.

1. When I learn: __1__ I like to deal with my feelings.   __2__ I like to think about ideas.   __4__ I like to be doing things.   __3__ I like to watch and listen.

2. I learn best when: __1__ I listen and watch carefully.   __3__ I rely on logical thinking.   __2__ I trust my hunches and feelings.   __4__ I work hard to get things done.

3. When I am learning: __3__ I tend to reason things out.   __1__ I am responsible about things.   __4__ I am quiet and reserved.   __2__ I have strong feelings and reactions.

4. I learn by: __1__ feeling.   __4__ doing.   __3__ watching.   __2__ thinking.

5. When I learn: __3__ I am open to new experiences.   __2__ I look at all sides of issues.   __4__ I like to analyze things, break them down into their parts.   __1__ I like to try things out.

6. When I am learning: __4__ I am an observing person.   __3__ I am an active person.   __1__ I am an intuitive person.   __2__ I am a logical person.

7. I learn best from: __4__ observation.   __3__ personal relationships.   __2__ rational theories.   __1__ a chance to try out and practice.

8. When I learn: __4__ I like to see results from my work.   __3__ I like ideas and theories.   __2__ I take my time before acting.   __1__ I feel personally involved in things.

9. I learn best when: __4__ I rely on my observations.   __2__ I rely on my feelings.   __3__ I can try things out for myself.   __1__ I rely on my ideas.

10. When I am learning: __3__ I am a reserved person.   __4__ I am an accepting person.   __2__ I am a responsible person.   __1__ I am a rational person.

11. When I learn: __3__ I get involved.   __4__ I like to observe.   __1__ I evaluate things.   __2__ I like to be active.

12. I learn best when: __3__ I analyze ideas.   __2__ I am receptive and open-minded.   __1__ I am careful.   __4__ I am practical.

Interpreting Your Learning Style Graph

NOTE: **Before you read this page,** score your inventory by following the directions on page LSI-3. Then complete the Learning Style Graph on page LSI-5. The following information appears on this page so that you can more easily compare your completed graph to the samples below. You will make this comparison *after* you remove page LSI-3.

Four modes of learning

When we're learning well, we tend to search out the answers to four key questions: *Why? What? How?* and *What if?* Each of these questions represents a different *mode of learning.* The modes of learning are patterns of behavior— unique combinations of concrete experience, reflective observation, abstract conceptualization, and active experimentation. When you are in a learning situation, you might find that you continually ask yourself one of these key questions more than the others. Or you might routinely ask several of these questions. Read the descriptions below to get a better idea of how you approach learning.

Mode 1: Why? Some of us question why we are learning things. We seek a purpose for information and a personal connection with the content. We want to know a rationale for what we're learning—why the course content matters and how it challenges or fits in with what we already know.

Mode 2: What? Some of us crave information. When learning something, we want to know critical facts or steps in a procedure. We seek a theory or model to explain what's happening and follow up to see what experts have to say on the topic. We break course content or a complex play down into its key components or steps and master each one.

Mode 3: How? Some of us hunger for an opportunity to try out what we're studying. We ask ourselves: Does this idea make sense? Will it work, and, if so, *how* does it work? How can I make use of this information? We want to apply and test theories and models. We excel at taking the parts of a subject or key steps of a maneuver and assembling them into a meaningful sequence.

Mode 4: What if? Some of us get excited about going beyond classroom assignments or the immediate content of a coach's presentation. We aim to adapt what we're learning to another context—another course, competition, or sport, or a situation at work or at home. By applying our knowledge, we want to make a difference in some area that we care about. We ask ourselves: What if we tried . . . ? or What if we combined . . . ?

Your preferred learning mode

When you examine your completed Learning Style Graph on page LSI-5, you will notice that your learning style profile (the "kite" that you drew) might be located primarily in one part of the graph. This will give you an idea of your preferred mode of learning, that is, the kind of behaviors that feel most comfortable and familiar to you when you are learning something. Using the descriptions below and the sample graphs, identify your preferred learning mode.

Mode 1: Why? If the majority of your learning style profile is in the upper right-hand corner of the Learning Style Graph, you probably prefer Mode 1 learning. You like to consider a situation from many different points of view and determine why it is important to learn a new idea or technique.

Mode 2: What? If your learning style profile is mostly in the lower right-hand corner of the Learning Style Graph, you probably prefer Mode 2 learning. You are interested in knowing what ideas or techniques are important. You enjoy learning lots of facts and then arranging these facts in a logical and concise manner.

Mode 3: How? If most of your learning style profile is in the lower left-hand corner of the Learning Style Graph, you probably prefer Mode 3 learning. You get involved with new knowledge by testing it out. You investigate how ideas and techniques work, and you put into practice what you learn.

Mode 4: What if? If most of your learning style profile is in the upper left-hand corner of the Learning Style Graph, you probably prefer Mode 4 learning. You like to take what you have practiced and find other uses for it. You seek ways to apply this newly gained skill or information at your workplace or in your personal relationships.

Combinations. Some learning style profiles combine all four modes. The profile to the right reflects a learner who is focused primarily on gathering information—*lots* of information! People with this profile tend to ask for additional facts from an instructor, or they want to know where they can go to discover more about a subject.

The profile to the right applies to learners who focus more on understanding what they learn and less on gathering lots of information. People with this profile prefer smaller chunks of data with plenty of time to process it. Long lectures can be difficult for these learners.

The profile to the right indicates a learner whose preferences are fairly well balanced. People with this profile can be highly adaptable and tend to excel no matter what the instructor does in the classroom. These people enjoy learning in general and do well in school.

Scoring your Inventory

Now that you have taken the Learning Style Inventory, it's time to fill out the Learning Style Graph (page LSI-5) and interpret your results. To do this, please follow the next five steps.

1 First, add up all of the numbers you gave to the items marked with brown **F** letters. Then write down that total to the right in the blank next to "**Brown F.**" Next, add up all of the numbers for "**Teal W**," "**Purple T**," and "**Orange D**," and also write down those totals in the blanks to the right.

2 Add the four totals to arrive at a GRAND TOTAL and write down that figure in the blank to the right. (*Note:* The grand total should equal 120. If you have a different amount, go back and re-add the colored letters; it was probably just an addition error.) Now remove this page and continue with Step 3 on page LSI-5.

Brown **F** total	25
Teal **W** total	35
Purple **T** total	27
Orange **D** total	33
GRAND TOTAL	120

F	T	D	W
W	T	F	D
T	D	W	F
F	D	W	T
F	W	T	D
W	D	F	T
W	D	T	D
D	T	W	F
W	F	D	T
W	F	D	T
F	W	T	D
T	F	W	D

Remove this page after you have completed Steps 1 and 2 on page LSI-3. Then continue with Step 3 on page LSI-5.

Once you have completed Step 3, discard this page so that you can more easily compare your completed Learning Style Graph with the examples on page LSI-2.

Learning Style Graph

3 Remove the piece of paper that follows this page and then transfer your totals from Step 2 on page LSI-3 to the lines on the Learning Style Graph below. On the brown (F) line, find the number that corresponds to your "**Brown F**" total from page LSI-3. Then write an X on this number. Do the same for your "**Teal W**," "**Purple T**," and "**Orange D**" totals.

4 Now, pressing firmly, draw four straight lines to connect the four X's and shade in the area to form a "kite." This is your learning style profile. Each X that you placed on these lines indicates your preference for a different aspect of learning:

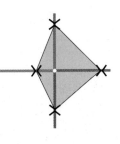

Concrete experience ("Feeling"). The number where you put your X on this line indicates your preference for learning things that have personal meaning. The higher your score on this line, the more you like to learn things that you feel are important and relevant to yourself.

Reflective observation ("Watching"). Your number on this line indicates how important it is for you to reflect on the things you are learning. If your score is high on this line, you probably find it important to watch others as they learn about an assignment and then report on it to the class. You probably like to plan things out and take the time to make sure that you fully understand a topic.

Abstract conceptualization ("Thinking"). Your number on this line indicates your preference for learning ideas, facts, and figures. If your score is high on this line, you probably like to absorb many concepts and gather lots of information on a new topic.

Active experimentation ("Doing"). Your number on this line indicates your preference for applying ideas, using trial and error, and practicing what you learn. If your score is high on this line, you probably enjoy hands-on activities that allow you to test out ideas to see what works.

5 Read page LSI-2 to understand further your preferences for learning.

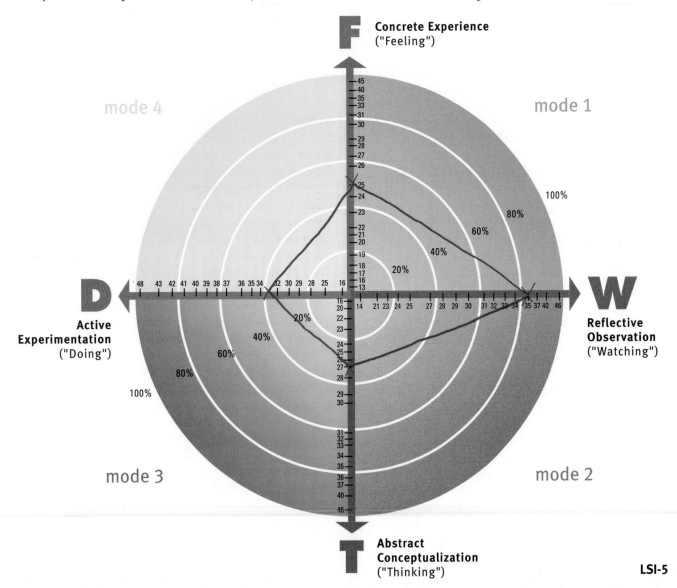

Cycle of learning

These examples show how the learning cycle works. You're interested in something (Mode 1), so you gather information about it (Mode 2). You try out what you're learning (Mode 3), then you integrate it into your day-to-day life (Mode 4). You go through this cycle many times as one learning experience generates another.

Example 1 Learning about a historical issue

You're required to take an elective in history, and you decide to take a course on the history of immigration in the United States. Your great-grandparents came to this country as immigrants, and immigration is still taking place today. You conclude that this topic is interesting—in part, because of your family background (Mode 1: *Why?*).

Soon you're in class, and you learn that from the early years of the country's history, many Americans have had misconceptions and fears about immigration that persist to the present day (Mode 2: *What?*).

You find yourself re-evaluating your own beliefs and assumptions. You decide to become more active in a community organization that deals firsthand with the impact of immigration policies (Mode 3: *How?*).

You also start to consider what it would be like to become an attorney and devote your career to creating a system that treats all immigrants with fairness and respect. You realize that you want to make a positive difference in the lives of people who are coming to live in the United States today (Mode 4: *What if?*).

Example 2 Learning to use a personal digital assistant (PDA)

Learning begins with developing an interest in this technology. Maybe you want to manage your to-do lists and appointments in a way that is more efficient than writing notes to yourself on random bits of paper. Or maybe you want to store your planning information digitally and exchange files with your personal computer. You conclude that this technology could help you finally get organized. (Mode 1: *Why?*). Next, you learn as much as you can about the different PDAs on the market. You visit Web sites, go to a computer store, and ask for a demonstration. You also talk to friends who swear by PDAs—and those who swear never to use them—and weigh their advice and differing opinions (Mode 2: *What?*).

After you gather this information, you decide to buy your own PDA. You take the handwritten information from your pocket calendar and to-do lists and enter it all into your new PDA. This takes several hours, including the time spent learning to write with a stylus (Mode 3: *How?*).

Once you've conquered the mechanics of using a PDA, you begin to use it on a daily basis—and encounter some unexpected hassles. Writing with the stylus requires you to form individual letters in a special way. Also, your

friends who stick with paper-based planning can simply open up their pocket calendars and quickly pencil in appointments. Meanwhile, you have to turn on your PDA and wait for it to boot up before you can use it. Instead of feeling more organized, you end up feeling behind. You wonder what it would be like to switch back to paper-based planning. After your experiences with a PDA, you decide to do just that. This time, however, you introduce a change in your behavior. Instead of recording your to-do items on any scrap of paper, you put a pen and some 3x5 index cards in your pocket and carry them with you at all times. Whenever you want to make a note to yourself, you simply pull out a card and jot down your thoughts. Cards are easy to store and sort. This new system, while it seems so simple and so "low-tech," finally helps you achieve that sense of organization you've been craving (Mode 4: *What if?*).

Example 3 Considering your career options

Your coach has talked to you about the benefits of career planning. He's mentioned that most student athletes don't make it to the professional level. Many of your peers in athletics dismiss this idea. However, you've heard about student athletes who graduated and drifted into unsatisfying jobs. You now have a reason to learn about career planning, especially as it applies to student athletes (Mode 1: *Why?*).

Your next step is to find out what career planning is all about. You skim several books on this subject and search the Internet for information. To round out your reading, you make an appointment to see a counselor at the career planning and job placement office on your campus. You want to gather as much information as possible (Mode 2: *What?*).

After taking these actions, you learn about several models of career planning. Now your aim is to move from theory to practice. Your learning styles profile reveals that you thrive on concrete experiences and active experimentation. So you pick your favorite book about career planning and start doing the recommended exercises. You schedule regular appointments with a career counselor to discuss what you learn from this activity. You're anxious to find out how career planning will actually work for *you* (Mode 3: *How?*).

Over time, you start to experience the benefits of career planning. You gain clarity about your interests, pairing them with specific career options. You also find that your course work and athletic experience take on a new meaning. You now see them as opportunities to develop marketable skills that can lead to an exciting and satisfying job immediately after graduation. Having experienced the power of career planning firsthand, you desire to share the process with other student athletes and consider ways to do that (Mode 4: *What if?*).

Name _____ Date _____/_____/_____

Note: After completing your Learning Style Inventory (page LSI-1) and filling in the Learning Style Graph (page LSI-5), be sure to read the sections titled "Interpreting your Learning Style Graph" (page LSI-2) and "Cycle of learning" (page LSI-6). Then complete the following Journal Entry.

journal entry 5

Discovery/Intention Statement

To make this concept of the learning cycle more useful, start applying it right away. You can begin with the content of this book. For example, as you read the Master Student Profiles, ask questions based on each mode of learning: *Why* is this person considered a master student? *What* attitudes or behaviors helped to create her mastery? *How* can I develop those qualities? *What if* I could use her example to create significant new results in my own life? (Or, *What if* I ignore the lessons to be learned from this Master Student Profile and experience significant costs as a result?) Also see the Master Student Map at the beginning of each chapter for sample answers to *Why? What? How?* and *What if?* questions.

Regarding my preferences for learning, I discovered that . . .

_____

_____

Given my preferences for learning, I intend to . . .

_____

_____

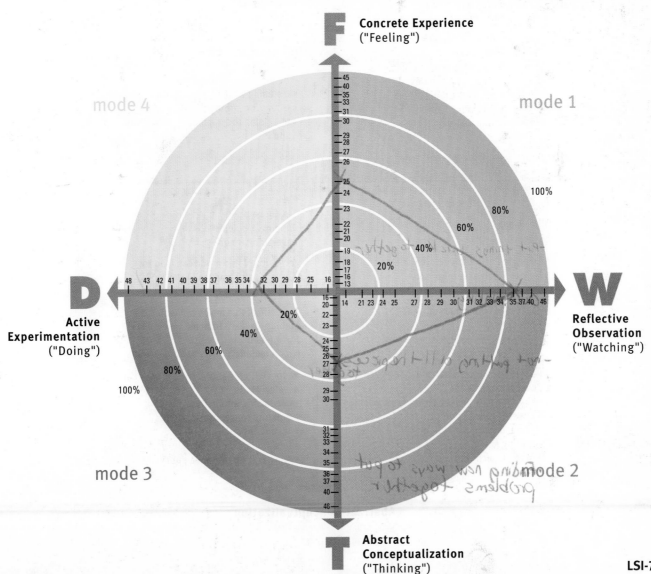

F Concrete Experience ("Feeling")

mode 4

mode 1

100%
80%
60%
40%
20%

D Active Experimentation ("Doing")

48 43 42 41 40 39 38 37 36 35 34 32 30 29 28 25 16
14 21 23 24 25 27 28 29 30 31 32 33 34 35 37 40 46

W Reflective Observation ("Watching")

20%
40%
60%
80%
100%

mode 3

mode 2

T Abstract Conceptualization ("Thinking")

Balancing your preferences

The chart below identifies some of the natural talents as well as challenges for people who have a strong preference for any one mode of learning. For example, if most of your "kite" is in Mode 2 of the Learning Style Graph, then look at the lower right-hand corner of the following chart to see if this is an accurate description of yourself.

After reviewing the description of your preferred learning mode, read all of the sections that start with the words "People with other preferred modes." These sections explain what actions you can take to become a more balanced learner.

Concrete Experience

mode 4

Strengths:
Getting things done
Leadership
Risk taking

Too much of this mode can lead to:
Trivial improvements
Meaningless activity

Too little of this mode can lead to:
Work not completed on time
Impractical plans
Lack of motivation to achieve goals

People with other preferred modes can develop Mode 4 by:
• Making a commitment to objectives
• Seeking new opportunities
• Influencing and leading others
• Being personally involved
• Dealing with people

mode 1

Strengths:
Imaginative ability
Understanding people
Recognizing problems
Brainstorming

Too much of this mode can lead to:
Feeling paralyzed by alternatives
Inability to make decisions

Too little of this mode can lead to:
Lack of ideas
Not recognizing problems and opportunities

People with other preferred modes can develop Mode 1 by:
• Being aware of other people's feelings
• Being sensitive to values
• Listening with an open mind
• Gathering information
• Imagining the implications of ambiguous situations

Active Experimentation ←———————————————→ **Reflective Observation**

Strengths:
Problem solving
Decision making
Deductive reasoning
Defining problems
—Put things back together

Too much of this mode can lead to:
Solving the wrong problem
Hasty decision making
—Overthinking

Too little of this mode can lead to:
Lack of focus
Reluctance to consider alternatives
Scattered thoughts
—not putting all the pieces together

People with other preferred modes can develop Mode 3 by:
• Creating new ways of thinking and doing
• Experimenting with fresh ideas
• Choosing the best solution
• Setting goals
• Making decisions
• Finding new ways to put problems together

mode 3

Strengths:
Planning
Creating models
Defining problems
Developing theories

Too much of this mode can lead to:
Vague ideals ("castles in the air")
Lack of practical application

Too little of this mode can lead to:
Inability to learn from mistakes
No sound basis for work
No systematic approach

People with other preferred modes can develop Mode 2 by:
• Organizing information
• Building conceptual models
• Testing theories and ideas
• Designing experiments
• Analyzing quantitative data

mode 2

Abstract Conceptualization

Using your learning style profile
to succeed in school

what if · why · how · what

Tolerate discomfort. Discomfort is a natural part of the learning process. Resist the temptation to skip a mode of learning or move too quickly through it. By tolerating discomfort and using all of the modes, you increase your chances for success in academic and athletic situations.

Ask for what you want. You might find that the way an instructor teaches is not the way you prefer to learn, or that coaches don't always promote all four modes of learning. Once you know your learning preferences, you can take a more active role in ensuring that your learning needs are met.

■ *If you have a strong preference for Mode 1,* you are likely to spend time observing others and planning out your course of action. To assist yourself in school, ask questions that help you understand why it is important for you to learn about a specific topic or aspect of a sport. You might also want to form a study group or plan a time for you and your teammates to walk through the plays you are preparing to use.

■ *If you have a strong preference for Mode 2,* you are skilled in understanding theories and concepts. When in learning situations, you are likely to enjoy lectures and individual class assignments. Chances are that you also enjoy solitary time and are not fond of working in groups. This is a common learning style for runners, golfers, divers, and other athletes who compete on their own. To assist yourself in school, ask questions that help you gather enough information to understand what you are learning. Emphasize that you are not questioning the authority of a teacher or coach, but that you want to increase your understanding.

■ *If you have a strong preference for Mode 3,* you probably excel at working with your hands and at laboratory stations. Athletes who play baseball, basketball, softball, and other sports that require fine-motor skills are likely to exhibit this learning style. When in a learning situation, you are interested in knowing how things work. In addition, you

probably enjoy working alone or with a small group. To assist yourself in school, ask questions that help you understand how something works and how you can experiment with these new ideas. Also allow time to practice and apply what you learn through hands-on practice.

■ *If you have a strong preference for Mode 4,* you are skilled at teaching others what you have learned and helping them see the importance of these concepts. You probably enjoy carrying out game plans and responding to new and unexpected challenges. You also prefer working with others and are likely to have a large social circle. To assist yourself, ask questions that help you determine where else in your life you can apply what you have just learned.

Associate with students who have different learning style profiles. If your instructor asks your class to form groups to complete an assignment, avoid joining a group in which everyone shares your preferred modes of learning. In particular, associate with students who are not athletes. You may find that they demonstrate study skills or learning styles that differ from those of your teammates. Get together with people who both complement and challenge you. This is one way you can develop skills in all four learning modes and become a more well-rounded student.

When learning styles conflict, remember that you have options. When they experience difficulty in school, some students make excuses that the work is too hard or the class doesn't fit their learning style. To stay in charge of your learning, say to yourself: "I will discover the value in learning this information," or "I will study this information with modes of learning that are not my preferred style." Note that you can base your behaviors on such statements even if you don't fully agree with them. One way to change your attitudes is to adopt new behaviors and watch for new results in your life.

The magic of metacognition

It's pronounced "metta-cog-ni-shun." *Meta* means *beyond* or *above*, and *cognition* refers to everything that goes on inside your brain—thinking, perceiving, and learning. *Metacognition* is thinking about thinking, learning about learning. It's your ability to stand "above" your mental processes—to observe them and to take conscious control of them.

Metacognition is one of the main benefits of higher education. Mastering this skill allows you to learn anything you want, any time. Among other things, metacognition includes:

- *Planning*—the ability to determine your purpose, choose from alternative behaviors, predict their consequences, and monitor your progress in meeting goals

- *Analysis*—the ability to separate a whole subject into its parts

- *Synthesis*—the ability to combine parts to form a meaningful whole

- *Application*—the ability to transfer new concepts and skills from one life situation to another

Each aspect of metacognition dovetails nicely with a mode of learning. Mode 1 involves planning—connecting the content of a course to your personal interests and goals. In Mode 2, you analyze by taking key ideas apart, separating skills into their component steps, and learning each step in turn. In Mode 3, you synthesize—that is, combine all of the separate ideas, facts, and skills you learned to see how they work in a real-life situation. And in Mode 4, you take what you have learned in one course and apply it in other courses and outside the classroom.

Students who master metacognition can do things such as:

- state the ways that they'll benefit from learning a subject;

- describe their preferred learning styles and develop new ones;

- make accurate statements about their current abilities;

- monitor their behavior and change their habits;

- choose and apply various strategies for reading, writing, speaking, listening, managing time, practicing, and competing; and

- modify strategies so that they work in several contexts.

That last point is especially important for you as a student athlete. Metacognition allows you to master a core set of success strategies and apply them in academic and athletic settings, as the following chart illustrates:

The strategies you learn to...	Can also help you...
Manage time (see Chapter Two)	Set aside time for practice (and rehabilitation, if necessary)
Communicate across cultures (see Chapter Eight)	Adapt to coaches and players from many backgrounds
Learn cooperatively (see Chapter Six)	Work with team members to learn plays
Think critically (see Chapter Seven)	Analyze what your coach says
Write and speak effectively (see Chapter Eight)	Deal accurately and effectively with the media
Take tests effectively (see Chapter Six)	Prepare mentally and physically for competition
Take classroom notes and review them effectively (see Chapter Five)	Monitor your athletic records to uncover ways to compete more effectively

These are just a few examples. The point is that your academic skills can give you an athletic advantage. Sometimes student athletes are stunned when a coach chooses to give a scholarship to an athlete who seems to be a bit less skilled—and better academically prepared. With new rules that challenge student athletes to maintain their eligibility for competition, coaches are less willing to take a chance on someone who is an academic risk. Coaches are learning that someone who demonstrates strong academic skills is likely to be an effective student of his or her sport.

You can translate your athletic skills into success in the classroom. All it takes is asking the four learning styles questions: *Why? What? How?* and *What if?* Asking and answering these questions can transform your life as a student athlete.

Remember that the teachers and coaches in your life will come and go. Some are more skilled than others. None of them are perfect. With metacognition, you can view any course or athletic event as one step along the path to learning what you want to learn—in the way that *you* prefer to learn it. The magic of metacognition is that you become your own best coach. ◪

Academic skill vs. athletic skill

Look at these academic skills and consider how they apply to you as a student athlete:

Academic skill	Athletic skill
Managing time to read and study	Setting time to practice (and rehabilitation, if necessary)
Avoiding distractions	Focusing on what the coach is telling you to do
Being persistent	Repeating an athletic activity over and over until it is right
Determination	Pushing yourself to be better in each competition and to win
Conflict management	Adapting to deal with coaches or players from backgrounds that you have never experienced before
Cooperative learning	Working together to learn plays or to scout the opposition
Critical thinking during lectures	Intently listening and analyzing what a coach is explaining
Uncovering assumptions	Being prepared to change your game plan to be able to win
Maintaining accurate records	Monitoring and reading your athletic records to determine how to be a better competitor
Writing and speaking with correct grammar	Dealing accurately and effectively with the media
Note taking	Being introspective so you focus on how to be a better athlete
Test taking	Being mentally and physically prepared to compete
Editing	Putting the playbook and other instructions into your words to fit your learning style

When well developed, each of these academic skills gives you an advantage in your athletic endeavors. There are more than are listed here that you will find in other chapters in this text. Similarly, if you are able to exhibit the listed athletic skills, look at the corresponding academic skill that you are able to perform in that setting. Your life as a student athlete benefits you once you realize that there is an interrelationship between these corresponding skills in the academic and athletic areas.

Claim your multiple intelligences

People often think that being smart means the same thing as having a high IQ, and that having a high IQ automatically leads to success. However, psychologists are finding that IQ scores do not always foretell which students will do well in academic settings—or after they graduate.

Howard Gardner of Harvard University believes that no single measure of intelligence can tell us how smart we are. Instead, Gardner identifies many types of intelligence, as described below.[4] Gardner's theory of several types of intelligence complements the discussion in this chapter on different learning styles—both recognize that there are alternative ways for people to learn and assimilate knowledge. You can use Gardner's concepts to explore additional methods for achieving success in school, work, and relationships. People using **verbal/linguistic intelligence** are adept at language skills and learn best by speaking, writing, reading, and listening. They are likely to enjoy activities such as telling stories and doing crossword puzzles.

Those using **mathematical/logical intelligence** are good with numbers, logic, problem solving, patterns, relationships, and categories. They are generally precise and methodical, and are likely to enjoy science. A sports statistician could use this type of intelligence to succeed.

When people learn visually and by organizing things spatially, they display **visual/spatial intelligence.** They think in images and pictures, and understand best by seeing the subject. They enjoy charts, graphs, maps, mazes, tables, illustrations, art, models, puzzles, and costumes. The athlete who pictures a competitive moment in her mind and visualizes how she will respond uses this intelligence.

People using **bodily/kinesthetic intelligence** prefer physical action. They enjoy activities such as building things, woodworking, dancing, skiing, sewing, and crafts. They would rather participate in games than just watch. Student athletes often develop this intelligence to a high degree.

Gymnasts and figure skaters are among those using **musical/rhythmic intelligence**. They enjoy musical expression through songs, rhythms, and musical instruments. They are responsive to various kinds of sounds, remember melodies easily, and might enjoy drumming, humming, and whistling. People using **intrapersonal intelligence** are exceptionally aware of their own feelings and values. They are generally reserved, self-motivated, and intuitive.

Evidence of **interpersonal intelligence** is seen in outgoing people. They do well with cooperative learning and are sensitive to the feelings, intentions, and motivations of others. They often make good team captains and coaches.

Those using **naturalist intelligence** love the outdoors and recognize details in plants, animals, rocks, clouds, and other natural formations. These people excel in observing fine distinctions among similar items. For example, a skilled golfer notices the way that the grass is cut on a green and then determines the effect it will have on the roll of his ball.

Each of us has all of these intelligences to some degree. And each of us can learn to enhance them. Experiment with learning in ways that draw on a variety of intelligences—including those that might be less familiar. When we acknowledge all of our intelligences, we can constantly explore new ways of being smart. ⌧

Attitudes, affirmations, and visualizations

Some of us see our attitudes the way we see our height or build: "I might not like it, but I might as well accept it."

Perhaps you've seen a student athlete with negative attitudes get kicked out of athletics or excluded from social circles due to behavior that, in effect, says: "It's the way I am. Get used to it.".

Acceptance is certainly a worthwhile approach to things we cannot change. When it comes to attitudes, acceptance is not necessary. Attitudes can change.

Attitudes are powerful. They create behaviors that teammates, peers, coaches, teachers, and employers can see. Success in school starts with attitudes. Some attitudes will help you benefit from all the money and time you invest in higher education. Other attitudes will render your investment worthless.

You can change your attitudes through regular practice with affirmations and visualizations.

Affirm it. An affirmation is a statement describing what you want. The most effective affirmations are personal, positive, and written in the present tense.

Affirmations have an almost magical power. They are used successfully by athletes and actors, executives and ballerinas, and thousands of people who have succeeded in their lives. Affirmations can change your attitudes and behaviors.

To use affirmations, first determine what you want, then describe yourself as if you already have it. To get what you want from your education, you could write "I, (insert your name here), am a master student. I take full responsibility for my education. I learn with enthusiasm, and I use my experiences in each course to create the life that I want."

What makes the affirmation work is detail. Use brand names, people's names, and your own name. Involve all of your senses—sight, sound, smell, taste, touch. Take a positive approach. Instead of saying, "I am not fat," say, "I am slender."

Once you have written the affirmation, repeat it. Practice saying it out loud several times a day. Sit in a chair in a relaxed position. Take a few deep and relaxing breaths, and then repeat your affirmation with emotion. Say it like you mean it. It's also effective to look in a mirror while saying the affirmation. Keep looking and repeating until you are saying your affirmation with conviction.

Visualize it. Athletes know the power of regular practice. The problem is that most of us limit what we consider to be practice. Effective practice can occur even when we are not moving a muscle.

You can improve your golf swing, tennis serve, or batting average while lying in bed. You can become a better driver, speaker, or cook while sitting silently in a chair. This is all possible through visualization—the technique of seeing yourself be successful.

Here's one way to begin. Decide what you want to improve, and write down what it would look like, sound like, and feel like to have that improvement in your life. If you are learning to play the piano, for example, then write down briefly what you would see, hear, and feel if you were playing skillfully.

Once you have a sketch of what it would be like to be successful, practice it in your imagination—successfully. As you play out the scenario, include as many details as you can. Always have your practices be successes.

You can also use visualizations to replay errors. When you make a mistake, replay it in your imagination. After a bad golf shot, stop and imagine yourself making that same shot again, this time successfully.

Visualizations and affirmations can restructure your attitudes and behaviors. Be clear about what you want—and then practice it. ⊠

As an athlete, you already know a lot about motivation. You can transfer that knowledge to success in the classroom, on the job, or in any other context. And a First Step in making that transfer is getting some definitions straight.

Motivat

The terms *self-discipline, willpower,* and *motivation* are often used to describe something missing in ourselves. Time after time we invoke these words to explain another person's success—or our own shortcomings: "If I were more motivated, I'd get more involved in school." "Of course she got an A. She has self-discipline." "If I had more willpower, I'd lose weight." It seems that certain people are born with lots of motivation, while others miss out on it.

An alternative is to stop assuming that motivation is mysterious, determined at birth, or hard to come by. Perhaps what we call *motivation* is something that you already possess—simply a habit that you can develop with practice. The following suggestions offer ways to do that.

Promise it. Motivation can come simply from being clear about your goals and acting on them. Say that you want to start a voluntary practice during the off-season. You can commit yourself by inviting teammates and setting a time and place to meet. Promise your teammates that you'll do this, and ask them to hold you accountable. Questions about motivation don't have to get in your way. Just make a promise and keep your word.

Befriend your discomfort. Sometimes keeping your word means doing a task you'd rather put off. The mere thought of doing laundry, reading a chapter in a statistics book, or lifting weights can lead to discomfort. In the face of such discomfort, we can procrastinate. Or we can use this barrier as a means to get the job done.

Begin by investigating the discomfort. Notice the thoughts running through your head and speak them out loud: "I'd rather walk on a bed of coals than do this." "This is the last thing I want to do right now."

Motivation can come simply from being clear about your goals and acting on them.

Also observe what's happening with your body. For example, are you breathing faster or slower than usual? Is your breathing shallow or deep? Are your shoulders tight? Do you feel any tension in your stomach?

Once you're in contact with your mind and body, stay with the discomfort a few minutes longer. Don't judge it as good or bad. Accepting the thoughts and body sensations robs them of power. They might still be there, but in time they can stop being a barrier for you.

Discomfort can be a gift—an opportunity to do valuable work on yourself. On the other side of discomfort lies mastery.

Change your mind—and your body. You can also get past discomfort by planting new thoughts in your mind or changing your physical stance. For example, instead of slumping in a chair, sit up straight or stand up. You can also get physically active by taking a short walk. Notice what happens to the discomfort.

Work with thoughts, also. Replace "I can't stand this exercise" with "I'll be in better shape when this is done" or "Doing this will help me get better before the next competition."

Sweeten the task. Sometimes it's just one aspect of a task that holds us back. We can stop procrastinating merely by changing that aspect. If distaste for our physical environment keeps us from studying, we can change that environment. Reading about social psychology might seem like a yawner when we're alone in a dark corner of the house. Moving to a cheery, well-lit library can sweeten the task.

Turn up the pressure. Sometimes motivation is a luxury. Pretend that the first competition of the season has been moved up one month, one week, or one day.

"I'm just not in the MOOD"

Raising the stress level slightly can spur you into action. Then the issue of motivation seems beside the point, and meeting the due date moves to the forefront.

Turn down the pressure. The mere thought of starting a huge task can induce anxiety. To get past this feeling, turn down the pressure by taking "baby steps." On each day, focus on one aspect of your opponent's playing scheme rather than trying to cover everything in a single practice. Divide a large class assignment into small tasks. In 30 minutes or less, you could preview a book, create a rough outline for a paper, or solve a few math problems. Careful planning can help you discover many such steps to make a big job doable.

Ask for support. Other people can become your allies in overcoming procrastination. For example, form a study group for your toughest course and declare what you intend to accomplish at each meeting Then contribute as much as you can to the group. Ask members for the kind of help you need to succeed in the course. None of this is an admission of weakness or failure. Rather, seeking support means taking charge of the quality of your education—and your life.

Adopt a model. One strategy for succeeding at any task is to hang around the masters. Check out the students who balance their athletic, academic, and personal lives. Find someone you consider successful and spend time with her. You can "try on" this person's actions and attitudes. Look for tools that feel right for you.

Compare the payoffs to the costs. Behaviors such as cramming for exams or neglecting to study your playbook have payoffs. Cramming might give you more time that's free of commitments. Neglecting your playbook can give you more time to sleep.

One way to let go of such unwanted behaviors is first to openly acknowledge the payoffs. This can be especially powerful when we follow it up with the next step—determining the costs. For example, skipping a reading assignment can give you time to go to the movies. However, you might be unprepared for class and have twice as much to read the following week.

Maybe there is another way to get the payoff (going to the movies) without paying the cost (skipping the reading assignment). With some thoughtful weekly planning, you might choose to give up a few hours of television and end up with enough time to read the assignment *and* go to the movies.

Comparing the costs and benefits of any behavior can fuel our motivation. We can choose new behaviors because they align with what we want most.

Do it later. At times, it's effective to save a task for later. For example, writing a résumé can wait until you've taken the time to analyze your job skills and map out your career goals. This is not a lack of motivation—it's planning.

When you do choose to do a task later, turn this decision into a promise. Estimate how long the task will take and schedule a specific date and time for it on your calendar.

Heed the message. Sometimes lack of motivation carries a message that's worth heeding. An example is the student who majors in accounting but seizes every chance to be with children. His chronic reluctance to read accounting textbooks might not be a problem. Instead, it might reveal his desire to major in elementary education. His original career choice might have come from the belief that "real men don't teach kindergarten." In such cases, an apparent lack of motivation signals a deeper wisdom trying to get through. ⊠

power process

Ideas are tools

There are many ideas in this book. When you first encounter them, don't believe any of them. Instead, think of them as tools.

For example, you use a hammer for a purpose—to drive a nail. When you use a new hammer, you might notice its shape, its weight, and its balance. You don't try to figure out whether the hammer is "right." You just use it. If it works, you use it again. If it doesn't work, you get a different hammer.

This is not the attitude most people adopt when they encounter new ideas. The first thing most people do with new ideas is to measure them against old ones. If a new idea conflicts with an old one, the new one is likely to be rejected.

People have plenty of room in their lives for different kinds of hammers, but they tend to limit their capacity for different kinds of ideas. A new idea, at some level, is a threat to their very being—unlike a new hammer, which is simply a new hammer.

Most of us have a built-in desire to be right. Our ideas, we often think, represent ourselves. And when we identify with our ideas, they assume new importance in our lives. We put them on our mantels. We hang them on our walls. We wear them on our T-shirts and display them on our bumpers. We join associations of people who share our most beloved ideas. We make up rituals about them, compose songs about them, and write stories about them. We declare ourselves dedicated to these ideas. If we as athletes define ourselves as players of a particular sport, we limit our identity even more.

Some ideas are worth dying for. But please note: This book does not contain any of those ideas. The ideas on these pages are strictly "hammers."

Imagine someone defending a hammer. Picture this person holding up a hammer and declaring, "I hold this hammer to be self-evident. Give me this hammer or give me death. Those other hammers are flawed. There are only two kinds of people in this world: people who believe in this hammer and people who don't."

That ridiculous picture makes a point. This book is not a manifesto. It's a toolbox, and tools are meant to be used. This viewpoint is much like one advocated by psychologist and philosopher William James. His approach to philosophy, which he called "pragmatism," emphasized the usefulness of ideas as a criterion of truth.[5] James liked to talk about the "cash value" of an idea—whether it leads to new actions and new results.

If you read about a tool in this book that doesn't sound "right" or one that sounds a little goofy, remember that the ideas here are for using, not necessarily for believing. Suspend your judgment. Test the idea for yourself.

If it works, use it. If it doesn't, don't.

Ask: What if it's true?

When presented with a new idea, some of us take pride in being critical thinkers. We look for problems. We probe for weaknesses. We continue to doubt the idea until there's clear proof. Our main question seems to be "What's wrong with this idea?"

This approach can be useful when it is vital to expose flaws in ideas or reasoning. On the other hand, when we constantly look for what's wrong with new ideas, we might not recognize their value. A different and potentially more powerful approach is to ask yourself: "What if that idea is true?" This opens up all sorts of new possibilities and variations. Rather than looking for what's wrong, we can look for what's potentially valuable. Faced with a new idea, we can stay in the inquiry, look deeper, and go further.

Keep looking for answers

The light bulb, the airplane, the computer chip, the notion of the unconscious—these and many other tools became possible when their inventors practiced the art of continually looking for additional answers. In athletics, world records appear to indicate the farthest or fastest a human could possibly run, jump, or throw. Yet, over time, someone does improve on that mark. The "impossible" becomes real.

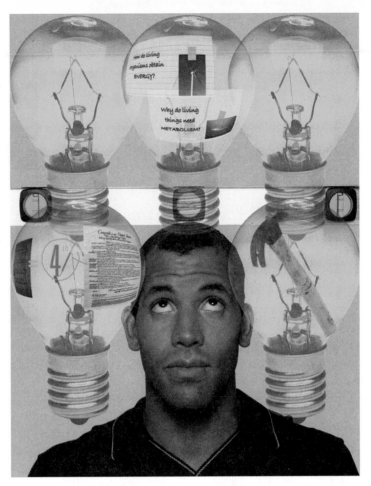

Another way to expand your toolbox is to keep on looking for answers. Much of your education will be about finding answers to questions. Every subject you study—from algebra to history to philosophy—poses a unique set of questions. Some of the most interesting questions are those that admit many answers: How can we create a just society? How can we transmit our values to the next generation? What are the purposes of higher education? How can we prevent an environmental crisis?

Other questions are more personal: What career shall I choose? Shall I get married? Where shall I live and how shall I spend my leisure time? What shall I have, do, and be during my time on earth?

Perhaps you already have answers to these questions. Answers are wonderful, especially when they relate to our most persistent and deeply felt questions. Answers can

This book is not a manifesto. It's a toolbox, and tools are meant to be used.

also get in the way. Once we're convinced that we have the "right" answer, it's easy to stop looking for more answers. We then stop learning. Our range of possible actions becomes limited.

Instead of latching on to one answer, we can look for more. Instead of being content with the first or easiest options that come to mind, we can keep searching. Even when we're convinced that we've finally handled a problem, we can brainstorm until we find five more solutions.

When we keep looking for answers, we uncover fresh possibilities for thinking, feeling, and behaving. Like children learning to walk, we experience the joy of discovery.

A caution

A word of caution: Any tool—whether it's a hammer, a computer program, or a study technique—is designed to do a specific job. A master mechanic carries a variety of tools because no single tool works for all jobs. If you throw a tool away because it doesn't work in one situation, you won't be able to pull it out later when it's just what you need. So if an idea doesn't work for you and you are satisfied that you gave it a fair chance, don't throw it away. File it away instead. The idea might come in handy sooner than you think.

And remember, this book is not about figuring out the "right" way. Even the "ideas are tools" approach is not "right."

It's a hammer . . . (or maybe a saw). ⬧

put it to work

The skills you develop as a student athlete can assist you long after graduation. You can take almost any strategy from Becoming a Master Student Athlete *and transfer it to the workplace. Look for examples in the* Put It to Work *feature that appears in each chapter of this book. Here the focus is on the job rather than the classroom or athletic competition. Come back to these suggestions as you enter the workforce and advance through the career of your choice.*

At work, you can benefit by remembering the concept of learning styles. In the workplace, people act in a variety of ways that express their preferences for perceiving information, processing ideas, and acting on what they learn.

Discover learning styles in your workplace. You can learn a lot about your coworkers' learning styles simply by observing them during the workday. Just look for clues.

One clue is how they *approach a learning task*. Some people process new information or ideas by sitting quietly and reading or writing. When learning to use a piece of equipment, such as a new computer, they'll read the instruction manual first. Those who use a trial-and-error approach will skip the manual, unpack all the boxes, and start setting up equipment. Other coworkers might ask a more experienced colleague to guide them in person, step by step.

Another clue is *word choice*. Some people like to process information visually. You might hear them say, "I'll look into that" or "Give me the big picture first." Those who like to solve problems verbally might say, "Let's talk though this problem" or "I hear you!" In contrast, some of your coworkers express themselves using body sensations ("This product feels great") or action ("Let's run with this idea and see what happens").

In addition, notice *process preferences*—patterns in the way that your coworkers meet goals. When attending meetings, for example, some might stick closely to the agenda and keep an eye on the clock. Others might prefer to "go with the flow," even if it means working an extra hour or scrapping the agenda.

Once you've discovered such differences among your coworkers, look for ways to accommodate their learning styles.

Gear presentations to different learning styles. When you want coworkers to agree to a new procedure or promote a new product, you'll probably make a speech or give a presentation. To persuade more people, gear your presentation to several learning styles.

Some people want to see the overall picture first. You can start by saying, "This product has four major features." Then explain the benefits of each feature in order.

Also allow time for verbally oriented people to ask questions and make comments. For those who prefer a hands-on approach, offer a chance to try out the new product for themselves—to literally "get the feel of it."

Finish with a handout that includes plenty of illustrations, charts, and step-by-step instructions. Visual learners and people who like to think abstractly will appreciate it.

Gear projects to different learning styles. When working on project teams, look for ways to combine complementary skills. If you're adept at planning, find someone who excels at active experimentation. Also seek people who can reflect on and interpret the team members' experiences. Pooling different learning styles allows you to draw on everyone's strengths.

Remember that a person's learning style is both stable and dynamic. People gravitate toward the kinds of tasks they've succeeded at in the past. They can also broaden their learning styles by taking on new tasks to reinforce different aspects of learning.

Name _____ Date _____/_____/_____

1. Explain three ways that you can use knowledge of your learning styles to succeed in school.

2. Define the term *mastery* as it is used in this chapter.

3. The First Step technique refers only to telling the truth about your areas for improvement. True or False? Explain your answer.

4. The four modes of learning are associated with certain questions. List the appropriate question for each mode.

5. According to the text, motivation is mysterious and hard to develop. True or False? Explain your answer.

6. Give three examples of how your academic skills can relate to your athletic skills.

7. Briefly describe how being aware of your own multiple intelligences can help you thrive in higher education.

8. According to the Power Process: "Ideas are tools," if you want the ideas in this book to work, you must believe in them. True or False? Explain your answer.

9. Students who are skilled in metacognition can do which of the following:
   (A) Choose and apply various strategies for reading, writing, speaking, listening, managing time, and related tasks.
   (B) Modify strategies so that they work in several contexts.
   (C) Monitor their behavior and change habits.
   (D) State the ways that they'll benefit from learning a subject.
   (E) All of the above.

10. 10. List two strategies that you can use to enhance kinesthetic learning.

learning styles application

Even though you have preferred ways to learn new ideas or skills, you can benefit from using several learning styles. The questions below will "cycle" you through four styles, or modes, of learning as explained in the article "Learning styles: Discovering how you learn" earlier in this chapter. Each question will help you explore a different mode.

Remember that you do not have to start with *Why?* of Mode 1. Any of the four questions can serve as your point of entry into the cycle of learning.

Look for a similar Learning Styles Application at the end of every chapter in this book. Also notice that the first page of each chapter includes a preview based on the four questions that represent the four modes of learning: *Why? What? How?* and *What if?*

what if
Review this chapter and the Introduction, looking for ideas that could help you make the transition from being in school to working in your next career. List two or three suggestions, stating each one in a short sentence.

why
Think about why the subject of transitions matters to you. Describe a major transition that you have experienced in the past. Examples might include adjusting from high school to college athletics, adjusting to a new team, considering your major, moving to a new city, starting a job, or going to college. In a sentence or two, describe what you did to cope with this change in your life.

how
In a short paragraph, explain how you can use one suggestion from this book to master a future transition that you will experience in education. Examples include declaring a major, changing majors, or transferring to a new school.

what
Review this chapter and the Introduction, looking for ideas that could help you make a major transition in your life. List two or three suggestions, stating each one in a short sentence.

master student
profile

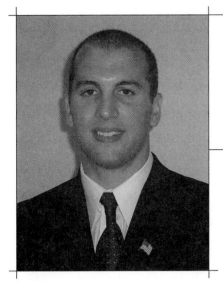

KEN PROCACCIANTI

(1982–   ) Founded Hammered, an organization that provides drinking alternatives for college students, as an undergraduate at Northeastern University, MA after a serious injury ended his college soccer career.

From the time they set foot on campus, most students are inundated with messages warning about the dangers of drug and alcohol use. As a recruited member of the men's soccer team at Northeastern University, Ken Procaccianti witnessed his friends' seeming dependence on alcohol and drugs to have a good time. He began to see how "pop culture bombards us with images that embrace alcohol and drugs."

The dependence on substances by many students did not allow much room for more productive pursuits, academic or otherwise: "There needs to be a balance." Ken, he did not know what to do, and with his hectic schedule of being a collegiate student-athlete he did not think he had the time to do anything that would be meaningful. Playing soccer 24/7, he was having trouble establishing his own balance between athletics and anything else.

A career-ending injury forced Ken to come to grips with the loss of competitive participation in the sport that had been the focal point of his life. "I was left with a huge void

when I got injured," he says. But Ken was able to turn this devastating event into something productive: "It afforded me the opportunity to look around at the college culture and frankly, I didn't like what I saw." He set out to find a way to achieve that balance and satisfy the need of those students who were looking for something to do in their free time besides drinking and using drugs.

As part of Northeastern's cooperative education program, Ken applied his efforts to finding a different approach. His research showed him that admonishing, preaching, citing statistics, and viewing gory videos were not getting the message across in a way that resulted in more positive behavior. He drafted a mission statement, created a Web site, and began promoting his concept on campus. The result was "Hammered," a nonprofit, student-run organization that is not "in your face" about drinking issues, but is there to show students that there are other options to alcohol consumption—particularly binge drinking. Hammered uses the activities that are appealing to college-age students to encourage questioning of the social and cultural role of drugs and alcohol. The message is that you can live your life, or one night of your weekend for that matter, without drugs and alcohol.

At none of its meetings or events will there be any beer games or keg

parties. Hammered members will not be there criticizing those who do drink or use drugs. They also will not be citing the harm that these elements can do. Instead they present alternative activities on campus and identify activities that occur within the community. The best part for Ken and his Hammered cohorts is that everyone has a great time without any reliance on alcohol or drugs.

The success of the original chapter has served as the catalyst for establishing a national office. Ken graduated in May 2004 and now leads Hammered National, Inc. Chapters will be created at colleges and universities throughout the United States based on the model at Northeastern. Hammered National, Inc. has the potential to make a significant impact on an issue that has been plaguing the higher education community for decades. ▨

Written from interviews conducted by Dr. Karl P. Mooney.

For more biographical information about Ken Procaccianti, visit the Master Student Hall of Fame on the *Becoming a Master Student Athlete* Web site at

masterstudent.college.hmco.com

2

Planning

Even if you are on the right track,
you'll get run over if you just sit there.

WILL ROGERS

Time should be used as a tool, not as a crutch.

JOHN F. KENNEDY

why

this chapter matters . . .

Your ability to manage time and money
  is a major predictor of your success in
  academic and athletic life.

what

is included . . .

You've got the time
Developing your game plan: Setting
  and achieving goals
The ABC daily to-do list
Planning sets you free
Strategies for scheduling
The seven-day antiprocrastination
  plan
More ways to stop procrastination
25 ways to get the most out of now
Time management for right-brained
  people
Gearing up: Using a long-term planner
Financial planning: Meeting your
  money goals
Take charge of your credit card
Power Process: "Be here now"
Master Student Profile: Greg Louganis

how

you can use this chapter . . .

Know exactly what you want to
  accomplish today, this month, this
  year—and beyond.
Eliminate stress due to poor planning
  and procrastination.
Gain freedom from money worries.

as you read, ask yourself
what if . . .

I could have more than enough time
  and money to accomplish whatever I
  choose?

You've got the time

The words *time management* can call forth images of restriction and control. You might envision a prune-faced coach, stopwatch in hand, hunched over you as you loosen up, scrutinizing every move you make.

Bad news.

Good news: You do have enough time for the things you want to do. All it takes is planning.

Planning is about time, and time is an equal opportunity resource. All of us, regardless of gender, race, creed, or national origin, have exactly the same number of hours in a week. True, some of us have enough money to delegate tasks or hire others to do them for us. Yet no matter how newsworthy we are, no matter how rich or poor, we get 168 hours to spend each week—no more, no less.

Time is also an unusual commodity. It cannot be saved. You can't stockpile time like wood for the stove or food for the winter. It can't be seen, felt, touched, tasted, or smelled. You can't sense time directly. Even scientists and philosophers find it hard to describe. Because time is so elusive, it is easy to ignore. That doesn't bother time at all. Time is perfectly content to remain hidden until you are nearly out of it. And when you are out of it, you are out of it.

Time is a nonrenewable resource. If you're out of wood, you can chop some more. If you're out of money, you can earn a little extra. If you're out of love, there is still hope. If you're out of health, it can often be restored. But when you're out of time, that's it. When this minute is gone, it's gone.

Time seems to pass at varying speeds. Sometimes it crawls and sometimes it's faster than a speeding bullet. The minutes before a competition starts can seem like hours. A year in school can stretch out to an eternity. At the other end of the spectrum, time flies. There are moments when you are so absorbed in what you're doing that hours disappear like magic.

You can manage this commodity so you won't waste it or feel regretful about how you spent it. Approach time as if you are in control. Sometimes it seems that your friends, teammates, teachers, and coaches control your time. Maybe that is not true. When you say you don't have enough time, you might really be saying that you are not spending the time you *do* have in the way that you want.

Planning involves determining what you want to achieve and how you intend to go about it. You can state your wants as written goals. Then use your time-management skills to schedule activities that will help you meet those goals. As you plan, be willing to include all areas of your life. In addition to setting academic goals, write down goals relating to your career, athletics, family life, social life, or anything else that matters to you. Since money is a concern for many students, this chapter includes specific suggestions for financial planning.

Planning gives you a chance to spend your most valuable resource in the way you choose. Start by observing how you use time. The next exercise gives you this opportunity. ⊠

journal entry 6

Discovery/Intention Statement

Think back to a time during the past year when you rushed to finish a project or when you did not find time to adequately prepare for an athletic event that was important to you. List one thing you might have done to create this outcome.

I discovered that I . . .

_____

_____

_____

Take a few minutes to skim this chapter. Find three to five articles that might help you avoid such outcomes in the future and list them below.

Title	Page number
_____	_____
_____	_____
_____	_____

If you don't have time to read these articles in depth right now, schedule a time to do so.

I intend to . . .

_____

_____

_____

THE TIME MONITOR/TIME PLAN PROCESS

The purpose of this exercise is to transform time into a knowable and predictable resource. You can do this by repeating a two-phase cycle of monitoring and planning.

This exercise takes place over two weeks. During the first week, you can monitor your activities to get a detailed picture of how you spend your time. Then you can plan the second week thoughtfully. Monitor your time during the second week, compare it to your plan, and discover what changes you want to make in the following week's plan.

Monitor your time in 15-minute intervals, 24 hours a day, for seven days. Record how much time you spend sleeping, eating, studying, attending lectures, traveling to and from class, weightlifting, practicing, competing, working, watching television, listening to music, getting together with family, running errands—everything.

If the idea of keeping track of your time in 15-minute intervals sounds crazy, hang on for a minute. You don't have to do this for the rest of your life—just for a few days. This is an opportunity to become conscious of how you spend your time, your life. Use the Time Monitor/Time Plan process only for as long as it is helpful to do so.

When you know how your time is spent, you can find ways to adjust and manage it so that you spend your life doing the things that are most important to you. Monitoring your time is a critical first step toward putting you in control of your life.

Some students choose to keep track of their time on 3x5 cards, calendars, campus planners, or software designed for this purpose. You might even develop your own form for monitoring your time.

1. Get to know the Time Monitor/Time Plan. Look at the Time Monitor/Time Plan on page 53. Note that each day has two columns, one labeled "monitor" and the other labeled "plan." During the first week, use only the "monitor" column. After that, use both columns simultaneously to continue the monitor-plan process.

To become familiar with the form, look at the example on page 53. When you begin an activity, write it down next to the time you begin and put a line just above that spot. Round off to the nearest 15 minutes. If, for example, you begin eating at 8:06, enter your starting time as 8:00. Over time, it will probably even out. In any case, you will be close enough to realize the benefits of this exercise. (Note that you can use the blank spaces in the

Do this exercise online at

masterstudent.college.hmco.com

"monitor" and "plan" columns to cover most of the day.)

On Monday, the student in this example got up at 7:00 a.m., showered, and had breakfast at 7:15. He put this new activity in at the time he began. He ate from 7:15 to 7:30. It took him 15 minutes to walk to campus (7:30 to 7:45), and he went to the weight room from 8:00 to 9:00.

Note: During some 15-minute periods, you could be engaged in activities that fall into more than one category. For instance, you might read a textbook on a bus while traveling to and from competition.

Keep your Time Monitor/Time Plan with you every minute you are awake for one week. Take a few moments every two or three hours to record what you've done. Or enter a note each time you change activities.

Here's an eye opener for many students. If you think you already have a good idea of how you manage time, predict how many hours you will spend in a week on each category of activity listed in the form on page 54. (Some categories are already provided; you can add more at any time.) Do this before your first week of monitoring. Write your predictions in the margin to the left of each category. After monitoring your time for one week, see how accurate your predictions were.

2. Remember to use your Time Monitor/Time Plan. It might be easy to forget to fill out your Time Monitor/Time Plan. One way to remember is to create a visual reminder for yourself. You can use this technique for any activity you want to remember.

Relax for a moment, close your eyes, and imagine that you see your Time Monitor/Time Plan. Imagine that it has arms and legs and is as big as a person. Picture the form sitting at your desk at home, in your car, in one of your classrooms, or in your favorite chair. Visualize it sitting wherever you're likely to sit. When you sit down, the Time Monitor/Time Plan will get squashed.

You can make this image more effective by adding sound effects. The Time Monitor/Time Plan might scream, "Get off me!" Or since time can be related to money, you might associate the Time Monitor/Time Plan with the sound of an old-fashioned cash register. Imagine that every time you sit down, a cash register rings.

3. Evaluate the Time Monitor/Time Plan. After you've monitored your time for one week, group your activities together by categories. The form on page 54 lists categories, including "sleep," "class," "study," "exercise," "practice," and "meals." Think of other categories you could add.

Discovery Statement

After one week of monitoring my time, I discovered that . . .

_____

_____

_____

_____

I want to spend more time on . . .

_____

_____

_____

I want to spend less time on . . .

_____

_____

_____

_____

_____

I was surprised that I spent so much time on . . .

_____

_____

_____

_____

_____

I was surprised that I spent so little time on . . .

_____

_____

_____

I had strong feelings about my use of time when (describe the feeling and the situation) . . .

_____

_____

_____

_____

Developing your game plan: setting and achieving goals

Many of us have vague, idealized notions of what we want out of different areas of our lives. They are wonderful, fuzzy thoughts such as "I want to be a good athlete," "I want to be financially secure," or, "I want to be happy."

Such outcomes are great possible goals. Left in a generalized form, however, these goals can leave us confused about ways to actually achieve them.

If you really want to meet a goal, then translate it into specific, concrete behaviors. Find out what that goal looks like. Listen to what it sounds like. Pick it up and feel how heavy that goal is. Inspect the switches, valves, joints, cogs, and fastenings of the goal. Make your goal as real as a chain saw.

As a student athlete, you know that competition calls for a detailed game plan. Think of goal setting as a game plan for your life.

If you really want to meet a goal, then translate it into specific, concrete behaviors.

Goals describe changes you want to make in your behavior, your values, your circumstances—or all of these. To keep track of your goals, write each one on a separate 3x5 card or other piece of paper. Post them in a visible place such as on the wall above the desk where you study, in your locker, or on your computer desktop. You can also write your goals in a calendar that you carry around and check daily.

There are many useful methods for setting goals. Following is one of them. This method is based on several key words: _specific, time, areas,_ and _reflect._ Combine the first letter of each word and you get the acronym *STAR*. Use this acronym to remember the suggestions that follow.

Write specific goals. In writing, state your goals as observable actions or measurable results. Think in detail about how things will be different once your goals are attained. List the changes in what you'd see, feel, touch, taste, hear, be, do, or have.

Suppose that one of your goals is to become a better athlete by practicing more. You're headed in a powerful direction; now go for the specifics. Translate that goal into a concrete action, such as: "I will practice skill development on my own for two hours on my off days." Specific goals help define what actions are needed or what results are expected. Consider these examples:

Vague goal	Specific goal
Get a good education.	Graduate with a B.S. degree in engineering, with honors, by 2009.
Enhance my spiritual life.	Meditate for 15 minutes daily.
Become a better swimmer.	Reduce my personal best by 1.5 seconds.

When stated specifically, a goal might look different to you. The more specific a goal is, the better you will know what to do to meet it. If you examine it closely, a goal you once thought you wanted might not be something you want after all. Or you might discover a new path to achieve a goal.

Write goals in several time frames. To get a comprehensive vision of your future, write down:

- *Long-term goals.* Long-term goals represent major targets in your life. These goals can take 5 to 20 years to achieve. In some cases, they will take a lifetime. They can include goals in your sport (to play professionally), education (to complete a graduate degree by age 30), careers (to become a teacher), personal relationships (to have a family), travel (to visit Europe at least once), financial security (to be able to retire at 55).

- *Mid-term goals.* Mid-term goals are objectives you can accomplish in one to five years. They include goals such as completing an undergraduate degree or paying off a car loan. These goals usually support your long-term goals.

- *Short-term goals.* Short-term goals are those you can accomplish in a year or less. Examples might include becoming a starter on your college soccer team or organizing a family reunion. A financial goal would probably include an exact dollar amount. Whatever your short-term goals are, they call for action now or in the near future.

Write goals in several areas of life. People who set goals in only one area of life—such as their sport—can find that their personal growth becomes one-sided. They could experience success on the field or court while neglecting their health, academics, or relationships. To avoid this outcome, set goals in a variety of areas, such as education, career, finances, family life, and spiritual life.

Reflect on your goals. Each week, take a few minutes to think about your goals. You can perform the following "spot checks":

- *Check in with your feelings.* Think about how the process of setting your goals felt. Consider the satisfaction you'll gain in getting what you want. If you don't feel a significant emotional connection with a goal, consider revising it, letting it go, or filing it away to review later.

- *Check for alignment.* Look for connections between your goals. Do your short-term goals align with your mid-term goals? Will your mid-term goals help you achieve your long-term goals? Also look for a "fit" between all of your goals and your purpose for taking part in higher education, as well as your overall purpose in life. Make sure that achieving one goal doesn't get in the way of achieving others. For example, staying late after practice every night to work on your technique may help you to reach your goal to become a starter on the team. Ask yourself whether doing so could reduce your study time and undercut your goal to achieve a higher grade point average.

- *Check for obstacles.* Many things can come between you and your goals. Anticipate obstacles and start looking for workable solutions. For example, although you cannot always avoid injuries, you can take specific steps to lower the risk of injury.

- *Check for immediate steps.* Create a list of small, achievable steps you can take right away to accomplish each of your short-term goals. Write these small steps down on a daily to-do list. Or if you want to accomplish some steps by a certain date, enter them in a calendar that you consult daily. Over the coming weeks, review your to-do list and calendar. Take note of your progress and celebrate your successes. ▩

→ Balancing athletics and academics

Every time you practice and every time you compete, you focus on something other than your reason for going to college—to earn a degree. Students who forget this fact can quickly find themselves lagging in both academics and athletics.

One student athlete at a major university was a record-breaker in high school and widely considered a "shoe-in" for a professional team. Shortly after arriving on campus, he decided to skip the first week of his American history class so that he could arrive at practices early and impress his coach. As a result, he missed the first class assignment and a pop quiz.

When the coach heard about this, he called the student into his office. "If I can't count on you to do what you know is needed to stay academically eligible, I can't count on you to be able to compete," said the coach. "You're staying home from competition this weekend to get caught up on your studies."

Succeeding in your courses can keep you eligible, give you a mental break from competition, help you keep scholarships, promote your overall confidence—and even improve your athletic performance. Go to almost any campus and you'll find students who excel in both athletics and academics. Following are some of the strategies that they use to achieve balance.

Balance from a big picture. You can begin by achieving balance on paper—that is, by planning. One fundamental strategy is planning from a big picture of your life. Start with a long-term planner (see page 76) or master monthly calendar (page 74). List major commitments such as due dates for assignments and tests, competition dates, and travel days. When you look ahead at least a month, you can often spot schedule conflicts soon enough to fix them.

Fine-tune your schedule. Next, use a daily or weekly calendar to create a detailed schedule. Keep this calendar with you in a backpack, briefcase, or gym bag. Check it at least once a day to jog your memory. Also enter changes in your schedule as soon as you know about them.

Record class times, practices, games, work hours, study times, and social events. Whenever possible, schedule course work first. Fill in other events around academic commitments.

Choose courses with care. Another path to balance lies in your course load. With the help of an advisor, list the courses you plan to take each term that you're in college. Include all required courses and possible electives. Fine-tune this list after you declare a major, and update it every term.

Be careful about taking several time-intensive classes at once, especially when you're in season. If you're unsure about the workload for a course, meet with the instructor. Look for possible conflicts between competitions, travel days, and class meetings. Then brainstorm solutions.

Get academic support. Asking for help in tough subjects such as math or writing is not a sign of weakness. Rather, it's gaining a competitive edge before your next class in that subject begins. Meeting with a tutor now can save you needless hours of struggle later on.

Be ready to study anytime, anywhere. Successful student athletes learn to use odd moments to academic advantage. Keep class notes, textbooks, flash cards, and other review tools on hand, organized and ready for immediate use. You can develop the ability to quickly enter "the zone" mentally and get some studying done—even on the team bus.

Persevere. You wouldn't give up athletics after one poor performance. Likewise, an occasional scheduling failure is no reason to give up on planning for balance. Just look for ways to avoid the mistake in the future.

Choices that promote your academic success have a great impact on your options for the future. Even professional athletes need to prepare for a post-athletic career. The time to strike the balance between athletics and academics is now.

GET REAL WITH YOUR GOALS

One way to make goals effective is to examine them up close. That's what this exercise is about. Using a process of brainstorming and evaluation, you can break a long-term goal into smaller segments until you have taken it completely apart. When you analyze a goal to this level of detail, you're well on the way to meeting it.

For this exercise, you will use a pen, extra paper, and a watch with a second hand. (A digital watch with a built-in stopwatch is even better.) Timing is an important part of the brainstorming process, so follow the stated time limits. This entire exercise takes about an hour.

Part one: Long-term goals

Brainstorm. Begin with a brainstorm. For eight minutes write down everything you think you want in your life. Write as fast as you can and write whatever comes into your head. Leave no thought out. Don't worry about accuracy. The object of a brainstorm is to generate as many ideas as possible. Use a separate sheet of paper for this part of the exercise.

Evaluate. After you have finished brainstorming, spend the next six minutes looking over your list. Analyze what you wrote. Read the list out loud. If something is missing, add it. Look for common themes or relationships between goals. Then select three long-term goals from different areas of your life that are important to you (academic, athletic, or personal goals, for example)—goals that will take many years to achieve. Write these goals below in the space provided.

_____

_____

_____

Part two: Mid-term goals

Brainstorm. Read out loud the three long-term goals you selected in Part One. Choose one of them. Then brainstorm a list of goals you might achieve in the next one to five years that would lead to the accomplishment of that

Do this exercise online at

masterstudent.college.hmco.com

one long-term goal. These are mid-term goals. Spend eight minutes on this brainstorm. Remember, neatness doesn't count. Go for quantity.

Evaluate. Analyze your brainstorm of mid-term goals. Remember to keep these goals as specific and measurable as possible. Then select three that you determine to be important in meeting the long-term goal you picked. Allow yourself six minutes for this part of the exercise. Write your selections below in the space provided.

_____

_____

_____

Part three: Short-term goals

Brainstorm. Review your list of mid-term goals and select one. In another eight-minute brainstorm, generate a list of short-term goals—those you can accomplish in a year or less that will lead to achieving that mid-term goal. Write down everything that comes to mind. Do not evaluate or judge these ideas yet. For now, the more ideas you write down, the better.

Evaluate. Analyze your list of short-term goals. The most effective brainstorms are conducted by suspending judgment, so you might find some bizarre ideas on your list. That's fine. Now is the time to cross them out. Next, evaluate your remaining short-term goals and select three that you are willing and able to accomplish over the next year. Allow yourself six minutes for this part of the exercise, and then write your selections below in the space provided.

_____

_____

_____

You can repeat this exercise, employing the other long-term goals you generated or creating new ones. In any case, use this brainstorm and evaluation process to make goals come to life in the here and now.

The ABC daily to-do list

A typical day in the life of a student athlete is full of separate, often unrelated tasks—reading, attending lectures, reviewing notes, practicing, competing, attending team meetings, working at a job, writing papers, running errands. It's easy to forget an important task on a busy day. When that task is written down on a daily to-do list, you don't have to rely on your memory.

The following steps present one method for to-do lists. Experiment with these steps and invent other techniques that work for you.

1 Brainstorm tasks. To get started, list all of the tasks you want to get done tomorrow. Each task will become an item on a to-do list. Don't worry about putting the entries in order or scheduling them yet. Just list everything you want to accomplish on a sheet of paper, a planning calendar, or in a special notebook or computer file. You can also use 3x5 cards, writing one task on each card. Cards work well because you can slip them into your pocket and rearrange them. Also, you never have to copy to-do items from one list to another.

2 Estimate time. For each task you wrote down in step 1, estimate how long it will take you to complete it. This can be tricky. If you allow too little time, you end up feeling rushed. If you allow too much time, you become less productive. For now, give it your best guess. Your estimates will improve with practice.

Add up the time needed to complete *all* your to-do items. Also add up the number of unscheduled hours in your day. Then compare the two totals. The power of this step is that you can spot overload in advance. If you have eight hours' worth of to-do items but only four unscheduled hours, that's a problem. To solve it, proceed to step 3.

3 Rate each task by priority. To prevent overscheduling, decide which to-do items are the most important given the time you have available. One suggestion for doing this comes from the book *Take Control of Your Time and Life* by Alan Lakein: Simply label each task A, B, or C.[1]

The A's on your list are the most critical. These are assignments that are coming due or jobs that need to be done immediately. Also included are activities that lead directly to your short-term goals.

The B's on your list are important, but less so than the A's. B's might someday become A's. For the present, these tasks are not as urgent as A's. They can be postponed, if necessary, for another day.

The C's do not require immediate attention. C priorities include activities such as "shop for a new blender" and "research genealogy on the Internet." C's are often small, easy jobs with no set timeline. These, too, can be postponed.

Once you've labeled the items on your to-do list, schedule time for all of the A's. The B's and C's can be done randomly during the day when you are in between tasks and are not yet ready to start the next A.

4 Cross off tasks. Keep your to-do list with you at all times, crossing off activities when you finish them and adding new ones when you think of them. If you're using 3x5 cards, you can throw away or recycle the cards with completed items. Crossing off tasks and tossing cards can be fun—a visible reward for your diligence.

When using the ABC priority method, you might experience an ailment common to students: C fever. This is the uncontrollable urge to drop that A task and begin crossing C's off your to-do list. If your history paper is due tomorrow, you might feel compelled to vacuum the rug, call your third cousin in Tulsa, or go see the team equipment manager about new track shoes.

Use your to-do list to keep yourself on task, working on your A's. Don't panic or berate yourself when you realize that in the last six hours, you have completed 11 C's and not a single A. Calmly return to the A's.

5 Evaluate. At the end of the day, evaluate your performance. Look for A priorities you didn't complete. Look for items that repeatedly turn up as B's or C's on your list and never seem to get done. Consider changing these to A's or dropping them altogether. Similarly, you might consider changing an A that didn't get done to a B or C priority.

In any case, make starting your own to-do list an A priority. ◪

Final draft of history paper
vacuum room
~~*Call cousin*~~
~~*See equip. manager*~~

Planning
sets you free

Rather than being a restraint, planning is a way of living life to the fullest. One path to feeling calm, competent, fun-loving, and free is to have a plan. When we are uptight, worried, and hassled—when we're not feeling free—we often have no plan.

You set the plan

One freedom in planning stems from the simple fact that you set the plan. The course and direction are yours.

Often, particularly at work or in school, people do not feel this way. They feel that the plan is coming from someone else—an employer, a coach, a supervisor, or a teacher.

Consider that this view is inaccurate. If you look far enough into the future, you can choose to see almost any activity as supporting a long-term goal that you desire to achieve. You might not like aspects of off-season practice, for example. Yet this activity can help you develop athletic skills that you want. It might even help you achieve your goal to start next season.

You can change the plan

Another freedom in planning is the freedom to make changes. An effective plan is flexible, not carved in stone. In reality, we can change our plans frequently and still preserve the advantages of long-range planning. Those advantages come from choosing our overall direction and taking charge of our lives.

You choose how to achieve the plan

Suppose that you suddenly get a new coach and she outlines a detailed agenda of goals to achieve in one year. You might say, "I didn't choose these goals. I guess I'll just have to put up with them."

There is another point of view you can take in this situation: Even when others select the goals, you can choose whether to accept them. And, within reason, you can also choose your own way to achieve any goal. The outcome might be determined for you. The way you train to *produce* that outcome can be up to you.

When there's a plan, there's a chance

Planning to meet a goal doesn't ensure accomplishment, but it does boost the odds of success. Clearly defined goals and carefully chosen plans increase the probability that you'll achieve what you want. You have a goal. You lay out the necessary actions in logical sequence. You set a due date to perform each action. Now the goal seems possible, whereas before it might have seemed impossible.

Much of what people undertake at school, in athletics, at work, in relationships, and at home is simply "digging in"—frantic action with no plan. "We might never reach our goal," they say, "but at least we're out there trying." In this statement we hear a loss of hope. Planning can replace despair with a purpose and a timeline.

Planning makes adjustments easier

Suppose you just got back from a competition that caused you to be away from campus for several days. You thought that you were scheduled to give a talk in your speech class next week. Suddenly you find out there was a misprint in the course schedule. You're supposed to speak two days from now, not seven. Without a plan, you might panic: "When will I have time to get that speech done?"

Planning can produce a different outcome. You might say, "I don't have to worry about this. I've scheduled my week, and I know I have free time tomorrow night between 7 and 10 p.m. I can finish the speech then."

Planning enables you to respond to crises and handle unexpected change. With a plan, you can take initiative rather than merely react. When you plan, you *give* your time to things instead of allowing things to *take* your time.

Planning and action create your life

Of course, planning by itself is ineffective. Nothing in our lives will change until we take action. The value of planning is that it promotes consciously chosen action.

Planning is about creating your own experience. When you plan, your life does not just "happen." When you plan, you are the equal of the greatest sculptor, painter, or playwright. More than creating a work of art, you are designing a life. ◪

Strategies for scheduling

Schedule fixed blocks of time first. Start with class time, practice time, and competition, for instance. Also block out time for your travel schedule. These events are usually determined in advance. Schedule other activities around them. Then schedule essential daily activities such as sleeping and eating. No matter what else you do, you will sleep and eat. Be realistic about how much time you need for these functions.

Include time for errands. The time we spend buying toothpaste, paying bills, and doing laundry is easy to overlook. These little errands can destroy a tight schedule. Plan for them and remember to allow for travel time between locations.

Schedule time for fun. Fun is important. Brains that are constantly stimulated by new ideas and new challenges need time off to digest them. Recreation deserves a place in your priorities. It's important to "chill" once in a while.

Set realistic goals. Don't set yourself up for failure by telling yourself you can do a four-hour assignment in two hours. There are only 168 hours in a week. If you schedule 169 hours, you've already lost before you begin.

Allow flexibility in your schedule. Recognize that unexpected things will happen and plan for the unexpected. Leave some holes in your schedule—blocks of unplanned time. Consider setting aside time each week marked "flex time" or "open time." Use these hours for emergencies, spontaneous activities, catching up, or seizing new opportunities.

Study two hours for every hour in class. It's standard advice for students in higher education to allow two hours of study time for every hour spent in class. If you are taking 15 credit hours, plan to spend 30 hours a week studying. The benefits of following this advice will be apparent at exam time.

This guideline is just that—a guideline, not an absolute rule. Discover what works best for you. Also keep in mind that the "two hours for one" rule doesn't distinguish between focused time and unfocused time. In one four-hour block of study time, it's possible to use up two of those hours with phone calls, daydreaming, and doodling. When it comes to scheduling time, quality counts as much as quantity.

Note: If you are required to study a playbook or watch videotapes of upcoming opponents, then add another five to eight hours to your weekly study time.

Avoid scheduling marathon study sessions. When possible, study in shorter sessions. Three three-hour sessions are usually far more productive than one nine-hour session. When you do study in long sessions, stop and rest for a few minutes every hour. Give your brain a chance to take a break.

If you do study in a marathon block of time, work on several subjects and avoid studying similar topics one after the other.

Set clear starting and stopping times. Tasks often expand to fill the time we allot for them. "It always takes me an hour just to settle into a reading assignment" might become a self-fulfilling prophecy. Try scheduling a certain amount of time for an assignment. Set a timer, and stick to it. The same principle can apply to other tasks. For example, some people find they can get up 15 minutes earlier in the morning and still feel alert throughout the day. Over the course of a year, those extra minutes can add up to hours.

Feeling rushed or sacrificing quality is not the goal here. The point is to push ourselves a little and discover what our time requirements really are.

Plan for the unexpected. The best-laid plans can be foiled by the unexpected. Children and day care providers get sick. Cars break down. The team plane or bus may be delayed by bad weather. The electric power shuts off, silencing alarm clocks.

That's when it pays to have a backup plan. You can find someone to care for your children when the babysitter gets the flu. You can plan an alternative way to get to campus. You can set the alarm on your watch as well as the one on your bedside clock. Giving such items five minutes of careful thought today can save you hours in the future.

Use your injury time. During your athletic career you are likely to suffer at least one injury that keeps you away from practice and competition for some time. Rather than viewing this as a loss, see it as extra time to complete other tasks. Catch up on your assignments or work on some nonathletic projects—writing letters to friends or family, doing a community or campus service project, visiting the career planning office, or practicing the piano.

Involve others when appropriate. Sometimes the activities we schedule depend on gaining information, assistance, or direct participation from other people. If we neglect to inform them of our plans or forget to ask for their cooperation at the outset—surprise! Our schedules can crash.

Statements such as these often follow the breakdown: "I just assumed you were going to pick up the kids from school on Tuesday." "I'm working overtime this week and hoped that you'd take over the cooking for a while."

When you schedule a task that depends on another person's involvement, let that person know—the sooner, the better.

Back up to a bigger picture. When scheduling activities for the day or week, take some time to lift your eyes to the horizon. Step back for a few minutes and consider your longer-range goals—what you want to accomplish in the next six months, the next year, the next five years, and beyond. Ask whether the activities you've scheduled actually contribute to those goals. If they do, great. If not, ask whether you can delete some items from your calendar to make room for goal-related activities.

Aim to free up at least one hour each day for doing something you love instead of putting it off to a more "reasonable" or "convenient" time. Don't include "voluntary" workouts that your coach recommends in this hour. Do something different.

"Filter" tasks before scheduling them. To trim the "fat" from your schedule, ask some questions before you add an activi   your calendar or to-do list. For example: What do I need to accomplish before I can schedule this item? If I choose never to take this action, could I live with the consequences? What would be the outcome if I put this task off for a month? Six months? One year?

If you gain recognition as a student athlete, people may come to you with requests for your time. Coaches could want help with recruiting. Alumni groups may invite you to speak. Community groups might ask for your support. Balance these requests with the time needed to meet your academic goals.

Consider technology carefully. Today you can choose from a constantly expanding line of devices to assist with scheduling. These range from time-management software for your desktop computer to personal digital assistants. Many colleges now give student athletes laptop computers with Internet access to use during travel time. Consider maintaining your schedule with online software that you can access in any location via wireless connection to the Internet. You might enjoy experimenting with this technology.

If your budget is tight, remember that you can always rely on some old-fashioned technology—pencil and paper. ✖

For updates on useful technology for scheduling, visit this book's Web site at

masterstudent.college.hmco.com

MONDAY	TUESDAY	WEDNESDAY	THURSDAY	FRIDAY	SATURDAY	SUNDAY
Make it meaningful.	Take it apart.	Write an intention statement.	Tell everyone.	Find a reward.	Settle it now.	Say no.

The seven-day antiprocrastination plan

Listed here are seven strategies you can use to reduce or eliminate many sources of procrastination. The suggestions are tied to the days of the week to help you remember them. Use this list to remind yourself that each day of your life presents an opportunity to stop the cycle of procrastination.

MONDAY **Make it meaningful.** What is important about the task you've been putting off? List all the benefits of completing it. Look at it in relation to your short-, mid-, or long-term goals. Are you going to be an Academic All-Conference Athlete? Will you be able to claim a personal record? Be specific about the rewards for getting it done, including how you will feel when the task is completed. To remember this strategy, keep in mind that it starts with the letter *M*, like the word *Monday*.

TUESDAY **Take it apart.** Break big jobs into a series of small ones you can do in 15 minutes or less. If a long reading assignment intimidates you, then divide it into two-page or three-page sections. Make a list of the sections and cross them off as you complete them so you can see your progress. Don't try to swim too many laps at once. Set your goal to be achieved in increments. Even the biggest projects can

be broken down into a series of small tasks. This strategy starts with the letter *T*, so mentally tie it to *Tuesday*.

WEDNESDAY **Write an Intention Statement.** For example, if you can't get started on a term paper, you might write, "I intend to write a list of at least 10 possible topics by 9 p.m. I will reward myself with an hour of guilt-free recreational reading." Write your intention on a 3x5 card and carry it with you, or post it in your study area where you can see it often. In your memory, file the first word in this strategy—*write*—with *Wednesday*.

THURSDAY **Tell everyone.** Publicly announce your intention to get a task done. Tell a friend that you intend to learn

voices

student

Making lists has been one of my favorite tools to stay on track and prioritize. Not much gives me more pleasure than to cross off duties one by one and to see the number of items left to do shrink to nothing, or what can be put off until another time.

— LAURIE MURRAY

10 irregular French verbs by Saturday. Tell your spouse, roommate, teammate, coaches, parents, and children. Include anyone who will ask whether you've completed the assignment or who will suggest ways to get it done. Make the world your support group. Associate *tell* with *Thursday*.

FRIDAY **Find a reward.** Construct rewards to yourself carefully. Be willing to withhold them if you do not complete the task. Don't pick a movie as a reward for studying biology if you plan to go to the movie anyway. And when you legitimately reap your reward, notice how it feels. Remember that *Friday* is a fine day to *find* a reward. (Of course, you can find a reward on any day of the week. Rhyming *Friday* with *fine day* is just a memory trick.)

SATURDAY **Settle it now.** Do it now. The minute you notice yourself procrastinating, plunge into the task. Imagine yourself at a cold mountain lake, poised to dive. Gradual immersion would be slow torture. It's often less painful to leap. Then be sure to savor the feeling of having the task behind you. Link *settle* with *Saturday*.

SUNDAY **Say no.** When you keep pushing a task into a low-priority category, re-examine your purpose for doing it at all. If you realize that you really don't intend to do something, quit telling yourself that you will. That's procrastinating. Just say no. Then you're not procrastinating. You don't have to carry around the baggage of an undone task. If you find that you don't want to do an athletic or an academic task, ask yourself why. Are you in a major you just don't like but declared only to stay eligible? Do you want to skip practice because you no longer have the desire to compete? This is a good time to be honest with yourself. *Sunday*—the last day of this seven-day plan—is a great day to finally let go and just *say* no. ▣

More ways to stop procrastination

P erhaps you didn't get around to using the seven-day antiprocrastination plan. Well, there's plenty more where that plan came from. Consider seven more suggestions.

Observe your procrastination. Instead of rushing to fix your procrastination problem, take your time. Get to know your problem well. Avoid judgments. Just be a scientist and record the facts. Write Discovery Statements about the specific ways you procrastinate and the direct results. Find out if procrastination keeps you from getting what you want. Clearly seeing the costs of procrastination can help you kick the habit.

Discover your procrastination style. Psychologist Linda Sapadin identifies different styles of procrastination.[2] For example, *dreamers* have big goals that they seldom translate into specific plans. *Worriers* focus on the "worst case" scenario and are likely to talk more about problems than about solutions. *Defiers* resist new tasks or promise to do them and then don't follow through. *Overdoers* create extra work for themselves by refusing to delegate tasks and neglecting to set priorities.

Awareness of procrastination styles is a key to changing your behavior. For example, if you exhibit the characteristics of an overdoer, then say no to new projects. Also ask for help in completing your current projects.

Trick yourself into getting started. Practice being a con artist—and your own unwitting target. If you have a 50-page chapter to read, grab the book and say to yourself, "I'm not really going to read this chapter right now. I'm just going to flip through the pages and scan the headings for ten minutes." If you have a paper due next week, say, "I'm not really going to outline this paper today. I'll just spend five minutes writing anything that comes into my head about the assigned topic."

Tricks like these can get you started on a task you've been dreading. Once you get started, you might find it easy to keep going.

Let feelings follow action. If you put off exercising until you feel energetic, you might wait for months. Instead, get moving now and watch your feelings change. After five minutes of brisk walking, you might be in the mood for a 20-minute run. This principle—action generates motivation—can apply to any task that's been delegated to the back burner.

Choose to work under pressure. Sometimes people thrive under pressure. As one writer put it, "I don't do my *best* work because of a tight timeline. I do my *only* work with a tight timeline." Used selectively, this strategy might also work for you.

Put yourself in control. You might consciously choose to work with a timeline staring you in the face. If you do, then schedule a big block of time right before your project is due. Until then, enjoy!

Step back to the big picture. If you plan just a day or two ahead, you might lose sight of what's coming up over the next few weeks or months. That period of time can look different from one week to the next as your sport goes from being in season to out of season (or vice versa). Discover the benefits of backing up to a bigger picture of your life. For example, use the monthly calendar or the long-term planner at the back of this book to list due dates for assignments in all your courses. Using these tools, you can anticipate heavy demands on your time and take action to prevent last-minute crunches. Turn the pages of this book into your "home base"—the first place to turn in taking control of your schedule.

Take it easy. You can find shelves full of books with techniques for overcoming procrastination. Resist the temptation to use all of these techniques at once. You could feel overwhelmed, give up, and sink back into the cycle of procrastination.

Instead, make one small, simple change in behavior—today. Tomorrow, make the change again. Take it day by day until the new behavior becomes a habit. One day you might wake up and discover that procrastination is part of your past.

PRACTICING CRITICAL THINKING 2

Some thoughts fuel procrastination and keep you from experiencing the rewards in life that you deserve. Psychologists Jane Burka and Lenora Yuen list these examples:[3]

I must be perfect.
Everything I do should go easily and without effort.
It's safer to do nothing than to take a risk and fail.
If it's not done right, it's not worth doing at all.
If I do well this time, I must always do well.
If I succeed, someone will get hurt.

Choose one of these statements—or think of a similar one—and write a sentence or two about how it could promote procrastination.

_____

_____

In the space below, create an alternative to the statement you just wrote about. Write a sentence that puts you back in charge of your time and no longer offers an excuse for procrastination. For example: "Even if I don't complete a task perfectly, I can give it my best shot and learn from my mistakes."

_____
_____
_____
_____
_____
_____
_____
_____
_____

2.5

ways to
get the most out of now

As you read about the following techniques, pick one to use now. When it becomes a habit, come back to this article and select another one. Repeat this cycle and enjoy the results as they unfold in your life.

When to study

1 Study difficult (or "boring") subjects first. If your chemistry problems put you to sleep, get to them first, while you are fresh. We tend to give top priority to what we enjoy studying, yet the courses we find most difficult often require the most creative energy.

2 Be aware of your best time of day. Many people learn best in daylight hours. Others flourish after midnight. When you're in a time crunch, experiment. Get up earlier or stay up later. See what works for you. Remember that practice and competition can affect your energy for studying, and plan accordingly.

3 Use waiting time. Five minutes waiting for a subway, 20 minutes waiting for the dentist, 10 minutes in between classes—waiting time adds up fast. Have short study tasks ready to do during these periods. For example, you can carry 3x5 cards with facts, formulas, or definitions and pull them out anywhere.

Where to study

4 Use a regular study area. Using the same place to study, day after day, helps train your body and mind. When you arrive at that particular place, you can focus your attention more quickly.

5 Study where you'll be alert. In bed, your body gets a signal. For most students, that signal is more likely to be "Time to sleep!" than "Time to study!" Easy chairs and sofas are also dangerous places to study.

Remember that practice and competition can affect your energy for studying, and plan accordingly.

Learning requires energy. Give your body a message that energy is needed. Put yourself in a situation that supports this message.

6 Use a library. Libraries are designed for learning. You might get more done in a shorter time frame at the library than anywhere else.

Ways to handle the rest of the world

7 Pay attention to your attention. Breaks in concentration are often caused by internal interruptions. Your own thoughts jump in to divert you from your studies. When this happens, notice these thoughts and let them go.

Perhaps the thought of getting something else done is distracting you. One option is to handle that other task now and study later. Or you can write yourself a note about it and schedule a specific time to do it.

8 Agree with living mates about study time. This includes roommates and teammates. Make the rules clear, and be sure to follow them yourself. Explicit agreements—even written contracts—work well.

9 Get off the phone. If a simple "I can't talk, I'm studying" doesn't work, use dead silence. It's a conversation killer. Or short-circuit the whole problem: Unplug or turn off the phone.

10 Learn to say no. This can be done effectively and courteously. Others want you to succeed as a student. When you tell them that you can't do what they ask because you are busy educating yourself, most people will understand.

11 Hang a "do not disturb" sign on your door. Many hotels will give you a free sign for the advertising. Or you can create a sign yourself.

12 Get ready the night before. Just before you go to bed, check your schedule to make sure that you have what you need for tomorrow.

13 Call ahead. Used wisely, the telephone can actually help manage time. Before you go shopping, call the store to see if it carries the items you want. If you're driving, call for directions to your destination. A few seconds on the phone can save hours in wasted trips and wrong turns.

14 Avoid noise distractions. To promote concentration, turn off the television. Many students insist that they study better with some background noise or carefully selected and controlled music. This might be true for you as well. Or after experimenting, you might find that silence is best.

Schedule study sessions during periods when your living environment is usually quiet. If you live in a residence hall, ask if study rooms are available. Or go somewhere else where it's quiet, such as the library. Some students have even found refuge in quiet cafés, self-service laundries, and places of worship.

15 Notice how others misuse your time. Ask yourself if there are certain people who consistently interrupt your study time. Sometimes they don't realize that they are breaking your concentration. You can give them a gentle yet firm reminder.

Things to ask yourself if you get stuck

16 Ask: What is one task I can accomplish toward achieving my goal? This is a helpful technique to use when faced with a big, imposing job. Pick out one small task, preferably one you can complete in a short period of time. Then do it. The satisfaction of getting one thing done can spur you on to get one more thing done. As in sports, success breeds success.

⤷ Keep on going?

Some people keep on going, even when they get stuck or fail again and again. To such people belongs the world. Consider the athlete who compiled this record:

- Was cut from his high school team
- Missed more than 9,000 shots in his NBA career
- Lost nearly 300 NBA games
- Missed the potential winning shot 26 times
- Quit participating in AA minor league baseball

Who was the fool who kept on going despite so many failures?

Answer: Michael Jordan, the five-time MVP and NBA Hall of Fame inductee.

17 **Ask: Am I being too hard on myself?** If your attention wanders repeatedly, or if you've fallen behind on an assignment, take a time-out. Listen to the messages you are giving yourself. You might be scolding yourself for wasting time. Lighten up, let go of your self-critic, and return to the task at hand.

Worrying about the future is another way people beat themselves up: *How will I ever get all this done?* Such questions fuel anxiety and defeat. Let them go and focus on what you can do right now.

Labeling and generalizing weaknesses are other ways people are hard on themselves. Being objective and specific will help eliminate this form of self-punishment and will likely generate new possibilities. An alternative to saying "I'm terrible in algebra" is to say "I don't understand factoring equations." This rewording suggests a plan to improve.

18 **Ask: Is this a piano?** Carpenters who construct rough frames for buildings have a saying they use when they bend a nail or accidentally hack a chunk out of a two-by-four: "Well, this ain't no piano." It means that perfection is not necessary. Ask yourself if what you are doing needs to be perfect. Perhaps you don't have to apply the same standards of grammar to lecture notes that you would apply to a term paper. If you can complete a job 95 percent perfectly in two hours and 100 percent perfectly in four hours, ask yourself whether the additional 5 percent improvement is worth doubling the amount of time you spend.

Sometimes it *is* a piano. A tiny miscalculation can ruin an entire lab experiment. A misstep in solving a complex math problem can negate hours of work. Computers are notorious for turning little errors into nightmares. Accept lower standards only when appropriate.

A related suggestion is to weed out low-priority tasks. The to-do list for a large project can include dozens of items, not all of which are equally important. Some can be done later, while others could be skipped altogether, if time is short.

19 **Ask: Would I pay myself for what I'm doing right now?** If you were employed as a student, would you be earning your wages? Ask yourself this question when you notice that you've taken your third snack break in 30 minutes. Most students are, in fact, employed as students. It's their job. (Student athletes have at least two jobs: student and athlete.) They are investing in their own productivity and paying a big price for the privilege of being a student. Sometimes they don't realize that doing a mediocre job now might result in fewer opportunities for the future. Time management is critical for success and a skill that you can transfer to any career.

20 **Ask: Can I do just one more thing?** Ask yourself this question at the end of a long day. Almost always you will have enough energy to do just one more short task. The overall increase in your productivity might surprise you.

21 **Ask: Am I making time for things that are important but not urgent?** If we spend most of our time putting out fires, we can feel drained and frustrated.

The satisfaction of getting one thing done can spur you on to get one more thing done.

According to Stephen R. Covey,[4] this happens when we forget to take time for things that are not urgent but are truly important. Examples include exercising regularly, reading, praying or meditating, spending quality time alone or with family members and friends. Each of these can contribute directly to a long-term goal or life mission. Yet when schedules get tight, we often forgo these things, waiting for that elusive day when we'll "finally have more time."

That day won't come until we choose to make time for what's truly important. Knowing this, we can use some of the suggestions in this chapter to free up more time.

22 **Ask: Can I delegate this?** Instead of slogging through complicated tasks alone, you can draw on the talents and energy of other people. Busy executives know the value of delegating tasks to coworkers. Without delegation, many projects would flounder or die.

voices

student

I am a person who can be easily distracted, and the library has the fewest distractions for me. My home has the most distractions, with TV, food, people coming over, and my cat begging for attention. I know that if I really want to learn, I need to make a trip to the library.

— JAMES HEAD

→ Remember cultural differences

It is likely that you will meet student athletes from cultures that are new to you. Your reaction to them can shape team chemistry—and perhaps make the difference between a losing or winning season.

Remember that there are as many different styles of managing time as there are people. These styles vary across cultures. In the United States and England, for example, business meetings typically start on time. That's also true in Scandinavian countries such as Norway and Sweden. However, travelers to Panama might find that meetings start about a half-hour late. And people who complain about late meetings while doing business in Mexico might be considered rude.

When you study, compete, or work with people of different races and ethnic backgrounds, look for differences in their approach to time. A behavior that you might view as rude or careless—such as showing up late for practice—could simply result from seeing the world in a different way.

You can also prevent misunderstanding based on cultural differences in time management. Find out exactly what your teachers and coaches expect when they tell you to be "on time." Share your understanding with a teammate or classmate whose "time style" differs from your own.

Find additional articles about cultural differences online at | masterstudent.college.hmco.com

---

You can apply the same principle. Rather than making a trip to the library to look up a simple fact, for example, you can call and ask a library assistant to research it for you.

It's not practical to delegate certain study tasks, such as writing term papers or completing reading assignments. However, you can still draw on the ideas of others in completing such tasks. For instance, form a writing group to edit and critique papers, brainstorm topics or titles, and develop lists of sources.

If you're absent from a class, find a classmate to summarize the lecture, discussion, and any upcoming assignments. Presidents depend on briefings. You can use this technique, too.

One way to accomplish big things in life is to make big promises.

23 Ask: How did I just waste time? Notice when time passes and you haven't accomplished what you had planned to do. Take a minute to review your actions and note the specific ways you wasted time. We tend to operate by habit, wasting time in the same ways over and over again. When you are aware of things you do that drain your time, you are more likely to catch yourself in the act next time. Remember that this suggestion is not intended to make you feel guilty. The point is to get specific information about how you use time.

24 Ask: Could I find the time if I really wanted to? The way people speak often rules out the option of finding more time. An alternative is to speak about time with more possibility.

The next time you're tempted to say "I just don't have time," pause for a minute. Question the truth of this statement. Could you find four more hours this week for studying? Suppose that someone offered to pay you $10,000 to find those four hours. Suppose, too, that you will get paid only if you don't lose sleep, skip a class, or sacrifice anything important to you. Could you find the time if vast sums of money were involved? Remember that when it comes to school, vast sums of money *are* involved.

25 Ask: Am I willing to promise it? If you want to find time for a task, promise yourself—and others—that you'll get it done. To make this technique work, do more than say that you'll try or that you'll give it your best shot. Take an oath, as you would in court. Give it your word.

One way to accomplish big things in life is to make big promises. There's little reward in promising what's safe or predictable. No athlete promises to place last in the Olympic games.

The point of making a promise is not to chain ourselves to a rigid schedule or to impossible expectations. We can also promise to reach goals without unbearable stress.

At times we can go too far. Some promises are truly beyond us, and we might break them. However, a broken promise is seldom the end of the world.

Promises can work magic. When our word is on the line, it's possible to discover reserves of time and energy we didn't know existed. ⌧

Time management for right-brained people (...or what to do if **to-do lists** are not your style)

Ask some people
about managing
time, and a
dreaded image
appears in
their minds.

They see a person with a 50-item to-do list clutching a calendar loaded with appointments. They imagine a robot who values cold efficiency, compulsively accounts for every minute, and is too rushed to develop personal relationships or do anything that is just plain fun.

These stereotypes about time management hold a kernel of truth. Sometimes people who pride themselves on efficiency are merely keeping busy. In their rush to check items off their to-do lists, they might be fussing over things that don't need doing—insignificant tasks that create little or no value in the first place.

If this is one of your fears, relax. The point of managing time is not to overload your schedule with extra obligations. Instead, the aim is to get the important things done and still have time to be human. An effective time manager is productive and relaxed at the same time.

Personal style enters the picture, too. Many of the suggestions in this chapter appeal to "left-brained" people—those who thrive on making lists, scheduling events, and handling details. These suggestions might not work for those people who like to see wholes and think visually.

Remember that the strategies discussed in this chapter represent just one set of options for managing time. The trick is to discover what works for you. A few basic principles can do that as well as a truckload of cold-blooded techniques.

Know your values. Begin by managing time from a bigger picture. Instead of thinking in terms of minutes or hours, view your life as a whole. Consider what that expanse of time is all about.

As a thought-provoking exercise, write your own obituary. Describe the way you want to be remembered.

List the contributions you intend to make during your lifetime. If this is too spooky, then just write a short mission statement for your life—a paragraph that describes your values and the kind of life you want to lead. Periodically during the day, stop to ask if what you're doing contributes to those values.

Do less. Managing time is as much about dropping worthless activities as about adding new and useful ones. Eliminate activities with a low payoff. When you add a new item to your schedule, consider dropping a current one.

Slow down. Sometimes it's useful to hurry, such as when you're late for a team meeting or about to miss a ride to campus. At other times, haste is a choice that serves no real purpose. If you're speeding through the day like a launched missile, consider what would happen if you got to your next destination a little bit later than planned. Rushing to stay a step ahead might not be worth the added strain.

Remember people. Few people on their deathbed ever say, "I wish I'd spent more time at the office." They're more likely to say, "I wish I'd spent more time with my family and friends." We can often benefit by allowing extra time for the people we cherish.

Focus on outcomes. You might feel guilty when you occasionally stray from your schedule and spend two hours napping or watching soap operas. But if you're regularly meeting your goals and leading a fulfilling life, there's probably no harm done. As a student athlete, you'll find that the overall goal of personal effectiveness counts more than the means used to achieve it.

Likewise, there are many methods for planning your time. Some people prefer a written action plan that carefully details each step leading to a long-range goal. Others just note the due date for accomplishing a goal and periodically assess their progress. Either strategy can work.

Visualizing the desired outcome can be as important as having a detailed action plan. Here's an experiment: Write a list of goals you plan to accomplish over the next six months. Include both academic and athletic goals. Then create vivid mental pictures of yourself attaining them and enjoying the resulting benefits. Visualize these images several times in the next few weeks. Then file your list of goals away, making a note on your calendar to review it in six months. When six months have passed, look over the list and note how many of your goals you have actually accomplished.

Handle it now. A backlog of unfinished tasks can result from postponing decisions or procrastinating. An alternative is to handle the task or decision immediately. Answer that letter now. Make that phone call as soon as it occurs to you. You can also save time by graciously saying no immediately to projects that you don't want to take on.

Buy less. Before you purchase an item, estimate how much time it will take to locate, assemble, use, repair, and maintain it. You might be able to free up hours by doing without. If the product comes with a 400-page manual or 20 hours of training, beware.

Before rushing to the store to add another possession to your life, see if you can reuse or adapt something you already own. Consider the full impact of purchases before you buy. An impulsive purchase could make major demands on your time.

Forget about time. Schedule "downtime"—a period when you're accountable to no one else and have nothing to accomplish—into every day. This is time to do nothing, free of guilt. Even a few minutes spent in this way can yield a sense of renewal.

Also experiment with decreasing your awareness of time. Leave your watch off for a few hours each day. Spend time in an area that's free of clocks. Notice how often you glance at your watch, and make a conscious effort to do so less often.

If you still want some sense of time, then use alternatives to the almighty, unforgiving clock. Measure your day with a sundial, hourglass, or egg timer. Or synchronize your activities with the rhythms of nature, for example, by rising at dawn. You can also plan activities to harmonize with the rhythms of your body. Schedule your most demanding tasks for times when you're normally most alert. Eat when you're hungry, not according to the clock. Toss out schedules when it's appropriate. Sometimes the best-laid plans are best laid to rest.

Take time to retreat from time. Create a haven, a safe place where you can take frequent breaks from schedules, to-do lists, and needs for accomplishment. This might be an actual place—anything from a picnic table in the backyard to a resort in the mountains. (Share the location of this place with someone who won't disturb you but will contact you in case of emergency.) The key thing is to find a timeless space. One of the most effective ways to manage time is periodically to forget about it. ▨

voices

student

My first educational goal is to get my associate degree in Early Childhood Education at College of Menominee Nation. My second goal is to get my bachelor's degree in education. My third goal is to get a teaching job with my four-year degree. That would be a dream come true.

—ANGEL M. FOWLER

MASTER MONTHLY CALENDAR

This exercise will give you an opportunity to step back from the details of your daily schedule and get a bigger picture of your life. The more difficult it is for you to plan beyond the current day or week, the greater the benefit of this exercise.

Your basic tool is a one-month calendar. Use it to block out specific times for upcoming events, such as study group meetings, review periods before tests, practice, competitions, travel related to competitions, and other time-sensitive tasks.

To get started, you might want to copy the blank monthly calendar at the back of this book onto both sides of a sheet of paper. Or make several copies of those pages and tape them together so that you can see several months at a glance.

Also be creative. Experiment with a variety of uses for your monthly calendar. For instance, you can note day-to-day changes in your health or moods. If you know that practice is going to be hard on a particular day, you may want to schedule more rest on the next day or adjust your study time. List the places you visit while you are on vacation, or circle each day that you practice a new habit. For examples of filled-in monthly calendars, see below.

Gearing up:
Using a long-term planner

With a long-term planner, you can eliminate a lot of unpleasant surprises. Long-term planning allows you to avoid scheduling conflicts—the kind that obligate you to be in two places at the same time three weeks from now. You can also anticipate busy periods, such as finals week, and start preparing for them now. Good-bye, all-night cram sessions. Hello, serenity.

As a student athlete, you may find a long-term planner to be especially useful. Long-term planning can help you anticipate and prevent conflicts between academics and athletics—especially when your sport is in season and you are likely to be more tired, miss more classes due to travel, and even have greater mood swings.

Find a long-term planner, or make your own. Many office supply stores carry academic planners in paper form that cover an entire school year. Computer software for time management offers the same feature. You can also be creative and make your own long-term planner. A big roll of newsprint pinned to a bulletin board or taped to a wall will do nicely.

Enter scheduled dates that extend into the future. Use your long-term planner to list commitments that extend beyond the current month. Enter test dates, lab sessions, days that classes will be cancelled, and other events that will take place over this term and next term.

Create a master assignment list. Find the syllabus for each course you're currently taking. Then, in your long-term planner, enter the due dates for all of the assignments in all of your courses. This can be a powerful reality check. Do this early in the semester. Notice possible conflicts between due dates for assignments and athletic events,

including travel time to competitions. Talk to your teachers about conflicts as soon as possible. Also ask your academic athletic advisor about your school's policy on missed classes due to student participation in off-campus events.

The purpose of this master assignment list is not to make you feel overwhelmed with all the things you have to do. Rather, its aim is to help you take a First Step toward recognizing the demands on your time. Armed with the truth about how you use your time, you can make more accurate plans.

Include nonacademic events. In addition to tracking academic commitments, you can use your long-term planner to mark significant events in your life outside of school. Include birthdays, doctor's appointments, concert dates, credit card payment due dates, and car maintenance schedules.

Use your long-term planner to divide and conquer. Big assignments such as term papers or major presentations pose a special risk. Competitions also require adequate preparation time. When you have three months to do a project or get ready to compete, you might say to yourself, "That looks like a lot of work, but I've got plenty of time. No problem." Two months, three weeks, and six days from now, it could suddenly be a problem.

For some students, an academic-athletic life is a series of last-minute crises punctuated by periods of exhaustion. You can avoid that fate. The trick is to set due dates *before* the final due date.

When planning to write a term paper, for instance, enter the final due date in your long-term planner. Then set individual due dates for each milestone in the writing process—creating an outline, completing your research, finishing a first draft, editing the draft, and preparing the final copy. By meeting these interim due dates, you make steady progress on the assignment throughout the term. That sure beats trying to crank out all those pages at the last minute. ⊠

Week of	Monday	Tuesday	Wednesday	Thursday	Friday	Saturday	Sunday
9 / 5						Swim meet (home)	
9 / 12		English quiz					
9 / 19			English paper due		Speech #1	Swim meet (away)	
9 / 26	Chemistry test						
10 / 3		English quiz			Speech #2	Swim meet (home)	
10 / 10				Geography project due			
10 / 17				--- No classes ---		Swim meet (away)	

LONG-TERM PLANNER ___ / ___ / ___ to ___ / ___ / ___

Week of	Monday	Tuesday	Wednesday	Thursday	Friday	Saturday	Sunday
___ / ___							
___ / ___							
___ / ___							
___ / ___							
___ / ___							
___ / ___							
___ / ___							
___ / ___							
___ / ___							
___ / ___							
___ / ___							
___ / ___							
___ / ___							
___ / ___							
___ / ___							
___ / ___							
___ / ___							

exercise 8

CREATE A LIFELINE

On a large sheet of paper, draw a horizontal line. This line will represent your lifetime. Now add key events in your life to this line in chronological order. Examples are your birth, first day at school, first athletic competition, first ribbon or trophy, and graduation from high school. You can also include the times you won a championship, broke a record, and enrolled in higher education. Note each individual event as a dot on the line, and add the year the event took place.

Now extend the lifeline into the future. Write down key events you would like to see occur in 1 year, 5 years, and 10 or more years from now. Choose events that align with your core values. (Don't be surprised to see your number of athletic goals gradually get smaller as the years add up.) Work quickly in the spirit of a brainstorm, bearing in mind that this is not a final plan.

Afterward, take a few minutes to review your lifeline. Select two key events for the future—one athletic and one academic—and list any actions you could take in the next month to bring yourself closer to those goals. Do the same with the other key events on your lifeline. You now have the rudiments of a comprehensive plan for your life.

Finally, extend your lifeline another 50 years beyond the year when you would reach age 100. Describe in detail what changes in the world you'd like to see as a result of the goals you attained in your lifetime.

Do this exercise online at

masterstudent.college.hmco.com

Meeting your money goals

Financial planning

Many of the skills that help you plan—such as monitoring your behavior and setting priorities—can also help you manage money. An important part of planning is setting and meeting financial goals.

Some people shy away from setting financial goals. They think that money is a complicated subject. Yet most money problems result from spending more than is available. It's that simple, even though often we do everything we can to make the problem much more complicated.

The solution also is simple: *Don't spend more than you have.* If you are spending more money than you have, increase your income, decrease your spending, or do both. This idea has never won a Nobel Prize in economics, but you won't go broke applying it.

Starting today, you can take three simple steps to financial independence: Tell the truth about how much money you have and how much you spend; make a commitment to spend no more than you have; and begin saving money.

If you do these three things consistently, you could meet your monetary goals and even experience financial independence. This does not necessarily mean having all of the money you could ever desire. Rather, you can be free from money worries by living within your means. Soon you will control money instead of letting money control you.

Increase money in

For many of us, making more money is the most appealing way to fix a broken budget. This approach is reasonable—and it has a potential problem: When our income increases, most of us continue to spend more than we make. Our money problems persist, even at higher incomes. You can avoid this dilemma by managing your expenses no matter how much money you make.

There are several ways to increase your income while you go to school. One of the most obvious ways is to get a job. You could also apply for scholarships and grants. You might borrow money, inherit it, or receive it as a gift. You could sell property, collect income from investments, or use your savings. Other options—such as lotteries and gambling casinos—pose obvious risks. Stick to making money the old-fashioned way: Earn it.

Work while you're in school. If you work while you go to school, you can earn more than money. Working helps you gain experience, establish references, and expand your contacts in the community. Doing well at a work-study position or an internship while you're in school can also help you land a good job after you graduate.

Regular income, even at a lower wage scale, can make a big difference. Look at your monthly budget to see how it would be affected if you worked just 15 hours a week (times 4 weeks a month) for $8 an hour.

Remember that there are restrictions on how student athletes can earn money, and on the amount they can earn. Ask your coach, your academic athletic advisor, and your school's athletics compliance office about these restrictions. Be wary of accepting a work situation that offers payment that is too good to be true.

Find a job. Make a list of several places that you would like to work. Include places that have advertised job openings and those that haven't. Then go to each place on your list and tell someone that you would like a job. This will yield more results than depending on the want ads alone. The people you speak to might say that there isn't a job available, or that the job is filled. That's OK. Ask to see the person in charge of hiring and tell him that you want to be considered for future job openings. Then ask when you can check back.

Be sure that any prospective employer is willing to report what you do on the job and how much you get paid to the athletics compliance office on your campus. Failure to provide this information could make you ineligible for athletic competition.

Keep your job in perspective. If your job is in your career field, great. If it is meaningful and contributes to society, great. If it involves working with people you love and respect, fantastic. If not—well, remember that almost any job can help you reach your educational goals.

It's also easy to let a job eat up time and energy that you need for your education. Be careful about accepting overtime. Balance the extra money against the risk of inferior academic or athletic performance.

You can avoid this risk by managing your time effectively. Use suggestions from this chapter to balance commitments to work, academics, and athletics. In particular, set a limit to the number of hours you will work each week. That leaves the remaining hours to focus on your top-priority goal—becoming a master student athlete.

Decrease money out

You do not have to live like a miser, pinching pennies and saving used dental floss. There are many ways to decrease the amount of money you spend and still enjoy life. Consider the ideas that follow.

Look to the big-ticket items. Your choices about which school to attend, what car to buy, and where to live can save you tens of thousands of dollars. When you look for places to cut expenses, start with the items that cost the most.

For example, there are several ways to keep your housing costs reasonable. Sometimes a place a little farther from your school or a smaller house will be much less expensive. You can cut your housing costs in half by finding a roommate. Find someone who will be at your apartment or house when you are traveling. In addition, look for opportunities to house-sit rather than paying rent. Some homeowners will even pay a responsible person to live in their house when they are away.

Look to the small-ticket items. Decreasing the money you spend on small purchases can also help you balance your budget. A three-dollar cappuccino is tasty, but the amount that some students spend on such treats over the course of a year could give anyone the jitters.

Monitor money out. Each month, review your checkbook, receipts, and other financial records. Sort your expenditures into major categories such as school expenses, housing, personal debt, groceries, eating out, and entertainment. At the end of the month, total up how much you spend in each category. You might be surprised. Once you discover the truth, it might be easier to decrease unnecessary spending.

Create a budget. When you have a budget and stick to it, you don't have to worry about whether you can pay your bills on time. The basic idea is to project how much money is coming in and how much is going out. Then, make sure that those two amounts balance.

Creating two kinds of budgets is even more useful. A *monthly budget* includes regularly recurring income and expense items such as paychecks, food costs, and housing.

A *long-range budget* includes unusual monetary transactions such as annual dividends, grants, and tuition payments that occur only a few times a year. With an eye to the future, you can make realistic choices about money today.

Do comparison shopping. Prices vary dramatically on just about anything you want to buy. You can clip coupons and wait for sales or shop around at secondhand stores, mill outlets, or garage sales. When you first go shopping, leave your checkbook and credit cards at home, a sure way to control impulse buying. Look at all of the possibilities, then make your decision later when you don't feel pressured. To save time, money, and gas, you can also search the Internet for sites that compare prices on items.

Use public transportation or car pools. Aside from tuition, a car can be the biggest financial burden in a student's budget. The purchase price is often only the tip of the iceberg. Be sure to consider the cost of parking, insurance, repairs, gas, maintenance, and tires. When you add up all of those items, you might find it makes more sense to car-pool or to take the bus or a cab instead.

Notice what you spend on "fun." Blowing your money on fun is fun. It is also a quick way to ruin your budget. When you spend money on entertainment, ask yourself what the benefits will be and whether you could get the same benefits for less money.

For example, you can read or borrow magazines for free at the library. Most libraries also loan CDs, DVDs, and videotapes at no cost. Student councils often sponsor activities, such as dances and music performances, for which there is no fee. Student athletes at many schools get into intercollegiate sporting events for free. On-campus recreation centers typically set aside times when students can use them at no charge. Meeting your friends for a pick-up basketball game at the gym can be more fun than meeting at a bar, where there is a cover charge.

Free entertainment is everywhere, both on- and off-campus. However, it may not be advertised, so search it out. Start with your school bulletin boards and local newspapers.

Redefine money. Reinforce all of the above ideas by understanding money in a new way. According to authors Joe Dominguez and Vicki Robin, money is what we accept in exchange for the time, passion, and effort that we put into our work.[5] When you take this view of money, you might naturally find yourself being more selective about how often you spend it and what you spend it on. It's not just cash you're putting on the line—it's your life energy.

Remember that education is worth it . . .

A college degree is one of the safest and most worthwhile investments you can make. Money invested in land, gold, oil, or stocks can be lost. Your trophies, medals, and newspaper clippings can rust, corrode, or be lost. In contrast, your education will last a lifetime.

Think about all of the services and resources that are available to you as a student athlete: academic advising, the student health center and counseling services, career planning and job placement offices, sports medicine, tutors, arts and entertainment events, and a student center where you can meet people and socialize. If you live on campus, you also get a place to stay with meals provided. And, by the way, you also get to attend classes.

In the long run, education usually pays off in increased income, job promotions, career satisfaction, and more creative use of your leisure time. These are benefits that you can sustain for decades by dedicating yourself to academics and athletics for only a few years.

. . . and you can pay for it

Create a master plan—a long-term budget listing how much you need to complete your education and where you plan to get the money. Having a plan for paying for your entire education makes completing your degree work a more realistic possibility.

Most students can afford higher education. If you demonstrate financial need, you can usually get financial aid. In general, financial need equals the cost of your schooling minus the amount that you can reasonably be expected to pay. Receiving financial assistance has little to do with "being poor." Your prospects for aid depend greatly on the costs of the school you attend.

Financial aid includes money you don't pay back (grants and scholarships), money you do pay back (low-interest loans), and work-study programs that land you a job while you're in school. Most students receive aid awards that include several of these elements. Visit the financial aid office on campus to discover the many sources of help that are available.

In applying for financial aid, you'll need to fill out a form called the Free Application for Federal Student Aid (FAFSA). You can access it on the World Wide Web at **http://www.fafsa.ed.gov.** There is no charge to file the FAFSA. For links to a wealth of information about financial aid in general, access **http://www.students.gov.**

Once you've lined up financial aid, keep it flowing. Most financial aid requires minimum hours of enrollment and dates to complete a degree. Some scholarships and grants require that you earn a particular grade point average. Athletic scholarships can also be based on academic achievement. Find out the requirements for renewing your loans, grants, and scholarships by visiting the financial aid officer at your school. Also check with your athletics compliance official for specific rules.

Sometimes there are limits on the number of scholarships each team can provide. You might find that one of your scholarships is discontinued and offered to another student athlete who is new to your school. This makes it doubly important to stay on top of your financial aid renewals.

Remember that most athletically related financial aid will not come directly to you. Rather, it will be paid directly to the school that you attend. (There may be exceptions if you live off-campus and get a scholarship that covers part of your room and board.) Also keep in mind that many schools automatically reduce financial aid to pay library fines and parking tickets. When ignored, these charges can add up and lead to unpleasant surprises.

If you do get a financial aid check, stick to your budget. Avoid large purchases that will drain your funds for later in the school year.

Create money for the future

You don't have to wait until you finish school to begin saving and investing. You can start now, even if you are in debt and living on a diet of macaroni.

One key goal is to have savings equal to at least six months of living expenses. Build this nest egg first as a cushion for financial emergencies. Then save for major, long-term expenses such as a car, house, or graduate school.

Put your money into insured savings accounts, money market funds, savings bonds, or certificates of deposit. These are low-risk options that you can immediately turn into cash. Even a small amount of money set aside each month can grow rapidly. The sooner you begin to save, the more opportunity your money has to grow. Time allows you to take advantage of the power of compound interest. ✖

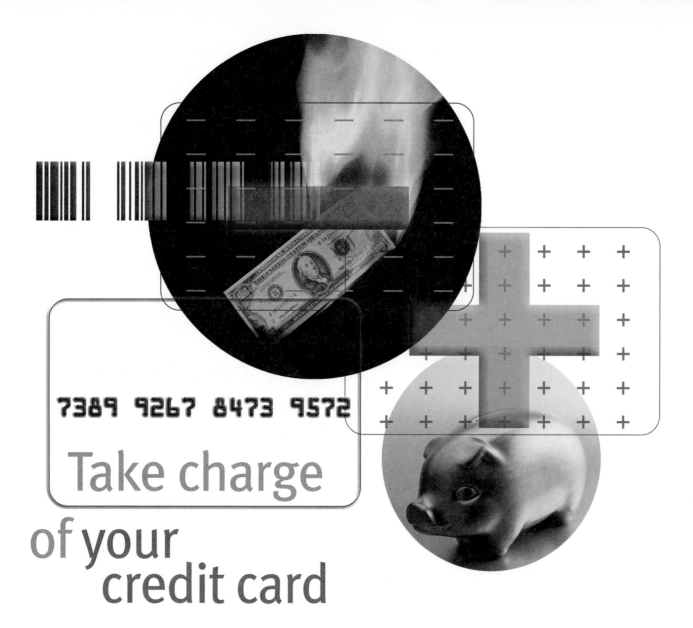

7389 9267 8473 9572

Take charge of your credit card

A credit card is compact and convenient. That piece of plastic seems to promise peace of mind. Low on cash this month? Just whip out your card, slide it across the counter, and relax. Your worries are over—that is, until you get the bill.

Credit cards often come with a hefty interest rate, sometimes as high as 27 percent. That can be over one-fifth of your credit card bill. Imagine working five days a week and getting paid for only four: You'd lose one-fifth of your income. Likewise, when people rely on high-interest credit cards to get by from month to month, they lose one-fifth of their monthly payments to interest charges. In a 2000 survey by Nellie Mae, a student loan corporation, 78 percent of undergraduate students had credit cards. Their average credit card debt was $2,748. Suppose that a student with this debt used a card with an annual percentage rate of 18 percent. Also suppose that he pays only the minimum balance due

each month. He'll be making payments for 15 years and will pay an additional $2,748 in interest fees.

Credit cards do offer potential benefits. Getting a card is one way to establish a credit record. Many cards offer rewards, such as frequent flier miles and car rental discounts. Your monthly statement also offers a way to keep track of your expenses.

Used wisely, credit cards can help us become conscious of what we spend. Used unwisely, they can leave us with a load of debt that takes decades to repay. That load can seriously delay other goals—paying off student loans, financing a new car, buying a home, or saving for retirement.

Use the following three steps to take control of your credit cards before they take control of you. Write these steps on a 3x5 card and don't leave home without it.

Do a First Step about money. See your credit card usage as an opportunity to take a financial First Step. If you rely on credit cards to make ends meet every month, tell the truth about that. If you typically charge up to the maximum limit and pay just the minimum balance due each month, tell the truth about that, too.

Write Discovery Statements focusing on what doesn't work—and what does work—about the way you use credit cards. Follow up with Intention Statements regarding steps you can take to use your cards differently. Then take action. Your bank account will directly benefit.

Scrutinize credit card offers. Beware of cards offering low interest rates. These rates are often only temporary. After a few months, they could double or triple. If you are late with a payment or fail to make one, the percentage rate can skyrocket. Also look for annual fees and other charges buried in the fine print.

To simplify your financial life and take charge of your credit, consider using only one card. Choose one with no annual fee and the lowest interest rate. Don't be swayed by offers of free T-shirts or coffee mugs. Credit card companies with special offers are usually hoping you will ignore their high interest rate when you sign up. Consider the bottom line and be selective.

Pay off the balance each month. Keep track of how much you spend with credit cards each month. Then save an equal amount in cash. That way, you can pay off the card balance each month and avoid interest charges. Following this suggestion alone might transform your financial life.

If you do accumulate a large credit card balance, ask your bank about a "bill-payer" loan with a lower interest rate. You can use this loan to pay off your credit cards. Then promise yourself never to accumulate credit card debt again. ▨

voices

student

The "Education by the hour" exercise made me realize that school is costing me a lot and everything counts when I don't attend class or do an assignment. I couldn't believe how much of my money I was wasting for not attending only one of my classes.

— LUZ LOPEZ

EDUCATION BY THE HOUR

Determine exactly what it costs you to go to school. Fill in the blanks below using totals for a semester, quarter, or whatever term system your school uses. (An asterisk has been placed after items that may be covered by an athletics scholarship.)

Note: Include only the costs that relate directly to going to school. For example, under "Transportation" list only the amount that you pay for gas to drive back and forth to school—not the total amount you spend on gas for a semester.

Tuition*	$_____
Books*	$_____
Fees*	$_____
Transportation	$_____
Clothing	$_____
Food*	$_____
Housing*	$_____
Entertainment	$_____
Other (such as insurance, medical, childcare)	$_____
Subtotal	$_____
Salary you could earn per term if you weren't in school	$_____
Total (A)	$_____

Now figure out how many classes you attend in one term. This is the number of your scheduled class periods per week multiplied by the number of weeks in your school term. Put that figure below:

Total (B) _____

Divide the **Total (B)** into the **Total (A)** and put that amount here:

$_____

This is what it costs you to go to one class one time. On a separate sheet of paper, describe your responses to discovering this figure. Also list anything you will do differently as a result of knowing the hourly cost of your education.

power process

Be here now

Being right here, right now is such a simple idea. It seems obvious. Where else can you be but where you are? When else can you be there but when you are there?

The answer is that you can be somewhere else at any time—in your head. It's common for our thoughts to distract us from where we've chosen to be. When we let this happen, we lose the benefits of focusing our attention on what's important to us in the present moment.

To "be here now" means to do what you're doing when you're doing it and to be where you are when you're there. Students consistently report that focusing attention on the here and now is one of the most powerful tools in this book.

Leaving the here and now

We all have a voice in our head that hardly ever shuts up. If you don't believe it, conduct this experiment: Close your eyes for 10 seconds and pay attention to what is going on in your head. Please do this right now.

Notice something? Perhaps your voice was saying, "Forget it. I'm in a hurry." Another might have said, "I wonder when 10 seconds is up." Another could have been saying, "What little voice? I don't hear any little voice." That's the voice.

This voice can take you anywhere at any time—when you are studying and when you are competing. When the voice takes you away, you might appear to be studying or trying to make the final turn and get a good push for the last lap. Your brain, however, is at the beach.

All of us have experienced this voice, as well as the absence of it. When our inner voices are silent, time no longer seems to exist. We forget worries, aches, pains, reasons, excuses, and justifications. We fully experience the here and now. Life is magic.

There are many benefits of such a state of consciousness. It is easier to discover or deal with the world around us when we are not chattering away to ourselves about how we think it ought to be, has been, or will be. Letting go of inner voices and pictures—being totally in the moment—is a powerful tool.

Do not expect to be rid of inner voices entirely. That is neither possible nor desirable. Your stream of consciousness serves a purpose. When you are working on a term paper, your inner voices might suggest ideas. When you are listening to your sociology instructor, your inner voices can alert you to possible test questions. When you're about to leap from a diving platform, they could remind you to keep your legs perpendicular to the water for a clean entry. The trick is to consciously choose when to be with your inner voices—and when to let them go.

Returning to the here and now

A powerful step toward returning to the here and now is to notice when we leave it. Our mind has a mind of its own, and it seems to fight back when we try to control it too much. If you doubt this, for the next 10 seconds do not, under any circumstances, think of a pink elephant. Please begin not thinking about one now.

Persistent image, isn't it? Most ideas are this insistent when we try to deny them or force them out of our consciousness.

For example, during class you might notice yourself thinking about a test you took the previous day, or a party planned for the weekend, or the throw back jersey you'd like to have. Student athletes can lose focus, especially on days when they are scheduled to compete. They find it easy to slip into their "game face" attitude.

Instead of trying to force a stray thought out of your head—a futile enterprise—simply notice it. Accept it. Tell yourself, "There's that thought again." Then gently return your attention to the task at hand. Do this each time that your mind drifts, bringing yourself back to the here and now.

Another way to return to the here and now is to notice your physical sensations. Notice the way the room looks or smells. Notice the temperature and how the chair feels. You can regain control of your attention by becoming aware of your physical surroundings.

We can often immediately improve our effectiveness—and our enjoyment—by fully entering into each of our activities, doing one thing at a time. For example, take something as simple as peeling and eating an orange. Carefully notice the color, shape, and texture of the orange. Hold it close to your nose and savor the pungent, sweet smell. Then chew each piece slowly, letting the delicious juice bathe your taste buds. Note the sensations of pleasure that ripple through your body as you sample this delicious treat.

"Be here now" can turn the act of eating an orange or participating in an athletic contest into a rich experience. Imagine what can happen when you bring this quality of attention to almost everything that you do.

Choose when to be here now

Remember that no suggestion is absolute—including the suggestion to do one thing at a time with full, focused attention. Sometimes choosing to do two or more things at once is useful, even necessary. For example, you might study while doing laundry. You might ask your roommate to quiz you with flash cards while you fix dinner.

The key to this Power Process is to *choose*. When you choose, you stay in charge of your attention.

The here and now in your future

You can use this Power Process to keep yourself pointed toward your goals. In fact, one of the best ways to get

To "be here now" means to do what you're doing when you're doing it and to be where you are when you're there.

what you want in the future is to realize that you do not have a future. The only time you have is right now.

The problem with this idea is that some people think: "No future, huh? Terrific! Party time!" Being in the here and now, however, is not the same as living for today and forgetting about tomorrow.

Nor is the "be here now" idea a call to abandon goals. Goals are actually tools we create to direct our actions right now. They are useful only in the present.

The power of this idea lies in a simple but frequently overlooked fact: The only time to do anything is now. You can think about doing something next Wednesday. You can write about doing something next Wednesday. You can daydream, discuss, ruminate, speculate, and fantasize about what you will do next Wednesday.

But you can't do anything on Wednesday until it is Wednesday.

Sometimes student athletes think of goals as things that exist in the misty future. And it's easy to postpone action on things in the misty future, especially when everyone else is going to a not-so-misty party.

However, the word *goal* comes from the Anglo-Saxon *gaelan,* which means "to hinder or impede," as in the case of a boundary. That's what a goal does. It restricts, in a positive way, our activity in the here and now. It channels our energy into actions, such as consistent athletic practice, that are more likely to get us what we really want. Goals direct action in the here and now.

The idea behind this Power Process is simple. When you plan for the future, plan for the future. When you listen to a lecture, listen to a lecture. When you read this book, read this book. And when you choose to daydream, daydream. Do what you're doing when you're doing it.

Be where you are when you're there. Be here now . . . and now . . . and now. ⬧

put it to work

Being skilled at managing time and money will serve you in any career you choose. Following are ways that you can transfer techniques from this chapter to the workplace.

Monitor work time. Use the Time Monitor/Time Plan process to analyze the way you currently use your time at work. With this awareness, you can minimize downtime and boost your productivity. Look for low-value activities to eliminate. Also note your peak periods of energy during the workday and schedule your most challenging tasks for these times.

Use a long-term planner to manage major projects at work. Besides scheduling a due date for the final product, set interim due dates—what you'll produce at key points leading up to that final date. For example, you're planning to launch a new in-house training program in one year. Set individual due dates for finishing each major component of the program, such as manuals, Web sites, and videotapes.

Avoid the perils of multi-tasking. Our effectiveness often decreases when we try to do several things at once, such as talking on a cell phone while driving. When you get busy at work, you might feel tempted to multi-task.

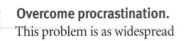

Yet studies indicate that multi-tasking reduces metabolic activity in the brain, lowers ability to complete tasks efficiently, and increases the number of errors made in following a procedure.[6] Turn to the Power Process: "Be here now" to find a solution. Plan your workday as a succession of tasks, then do each task with full attention. Use the ABC priority system to weed out tasks of lower importance. This can give you more time to focus on the A's.

Overcome procrastination. This problem is as widespread in the workplace as it is on any campus. Apply the suggestions from "The seven-day antiprocrastination plan" and "More ways to stop procrastination" to work tasks.

Calculate the cost of attending meetings. Meetings are a way of life for countless people in the workplace. In fact, if you're in a management or supervisory position, meetings can take up most of your workday. See if you can modify the "Education by the hour" exercise to calculate what it costs you to attend a one-hour business meeting. With this data in hand, write an Intention Statement about how you plan to get the most value out of the meetings you will attend in the future.

Use a lifeline to chart your career path. Your career plan can extend decades into the future. Below are some possible lifeline entries for a person focusing on a career in education.

May 2009	Graduate with a teaching degree
August 2010	Begin teaching high school physics
September 2017	Begin saving 5 percent of income to fund a personal sabbatical
September 2021	Return to school for a graduate degree in school administration
September 2023	Begin career as a high school principal
September 2027	Take a one-year sabbatical to live and work part-time in New Zealand
September 2028	Return to job as a high school principal
January 2031	Begin a home-based consulting business, advising teachers and principals about ways to avoid job burnout

Do long-term planning for your organization. The strategies for long-term planning in this chapter can help you set goals for your company that extend well into the future. For example, create a lifeline for your organization, listing specific outcomes to achieve during each of the next five years. ⊠

Name _____ Date _____/_____/_____

quiz

1. List three techniques that you can use to balance the demands of academics and athletics.

2. It is effective to leave holes in your schedule to allow for the unexpected. True or False? Explain your answer.

3. Examples of the suggestion to write specific goals include:
   (A) Spend at least four hours in the batting cages during the off-season.
   (B) Enhance my spiritual life.
   (C) Increase my playing time by two minutes each game.
   (D) Graduate with a B.S. degree in engineering, with honors, by 2009.
   (E) Get a good education.

4. What are at least 5 of the 25 ways to get the most out of now?

5. In time-management terms, what is meant by "This ain't no piano"?

6. Define "C fever" as it applies to the ABC priority method.

7. Scheduling marathon study sessions once in a while is generally an effective strategy. True or False? Explain your answer.

8. Describe at least three strategies for overcoming procrastination.

9. According to this chapter, most money problems have a simple source. What is it?

10. List the three steps toward financial independence explained in the text.

learning styles application

The questions below will "cycle" you through four styles, or modes, of learning as explained in the article "Learning styles: Discovering how you learn" in Chapter One. Each question will help you explore a different mode. You can answer the questions in any order.

what if *After implementing a method of improving your planning skills from this chapter, consider how well this new method has worked for you. Which actions do you intend to continue on a regular basis? Are there any new actions you intend to take?*

why *Suppose that you could use the techniques in this chapter to free up four additional hours each week to do whatever you please. Describe the things you would do with this extra time and why these activities matter to you.*

how *Choose one technique from this chapter and create a plan for how you will implement this strategy in your life. Then put this experiment into action.*

what *Choose three techniques from this chapter that you could use to free up four additional hours in the next week. Summarize those techniques in a single phrase or sentence and list them here.*

master student profile

GREG LOUGANIS

(1960–   ) Four-time Olympic Gold Medal diving champion, published his autobiography in 1995 to tell his story of facing challenges of fear and discrimination regarding his Samoan heritage, dyslexia, substance abuse, sexual orientation, domestic violence, and living with AIDS.

Going into 1980, Ron and I talked about what we thought was possible for me at the upcoming Olympics in Moscow.

Ron wasn't someone who talked about expectations, but based on how well I'd been doing at competitions, he thought it was possible for me to win both 3-meter springboard and 10-meter platform at the Olympic trials and at the Moscow Games. Ron [Louganis' coach] didn't expect me to do it, but he thought it was possible, and we both thought it was something we could work toward. It was a goal to reach for . . .

It didn't matter how much effort I made in preparing for the Olympics, because history intervened and there was no 1980 Olympics for the U. S. Olympic team. The Soviet Union invaded Afghanistan in December 1979, and President Carter demonstrated the U.S. government's displeasure by deciding to boycott the Moscow Olympics.

Despite the boycott, we still had the Olympic trials. At first it was like we were just going through the motions. The trials were held at the end of June, in Austin, Texas, at the Texas Swimming Center at the University of Texas. Fifty-three of the top men and women divers from around the country came to compete.

Success in diving is never guaranteed. All it takes is one mistake, and you can blow your entire lead. I had to concentrate from my first dive to my last.

In the springboard competition, I was happiest with my seventh dive of the final round, a reverse two-and-a-half pike, which is a difficult dive. I got six 10's and a 9.5, an almost-perfect score. My total score at the end of the final round was 940 points, 28 points ahead of the second-place finisher. Then on platform I finished 65 points ahead of the next diver. I scored several 10's in that round despite the fact that I cut my palm on a pipe at the bottom of the 18-foot pool on my first dive.

When you dive off the 10-meter platform, you're going at 32 miles per hour when you hit the water, and your hands hit the water first. So with a cut palm, it really hurt. But by that point in my career, I didn't let a minor injury get in the way of a good dive.

Ron once told me that I dove with more pain and suffering and sickness than any diver he had ever had. A lot of my injuries were just routine, sprains and stomach viruses, but sometimes I did klutzy things. One time I sat down on a glass when I was in a boat and cut my butt. That doesn't sound like anything big, but when you're in the middle of a dive and you're pulling your legs up to your chest, the stitches hurt like crazy.

A week later, I was diving on springboard and I slipped going up the ladder and gashed and bruised my leg right on the spot where I had to grab my leg and squeeze hard during the dive. Each time I dove I wanted to scream.

One time I almost didn't get through it. At the national championships in Indianapolis in 1986, I caught a stomach virus. I was very sick, but I did a few dives, went into the bathroom, threw up, and came back out and did a few more dives. I don't know how, but I won.

I may cry easily, but I never give up. ✖

From *Breaking the Surface* by Greg Louganis with Eric Marcus. Copyright © 1995 by Greg Louganis. Reprinted by permission of Random House, Inc.

For more biographical information about Greg Louganis, visit the Master Student Hall of Fame on the *Becoming a Master Student Athlete* Web site at

masterstudent.college.hmco.com

3

Memory

Memory is a way of holding on to the things you love, the things you are, the things you never want to lose.

KEVIN ARNOLD

Memory is the mother of imagination, reason and skill. . . . This is the companion, this is the tutor, the poet, the library with which you travel.

MARK VAN DOREN

why

this chapter matters . . .

Learning memory techniques can boost your skills at test taking, reading, note taking, and many other academic tasks.

what

is included . . .

Take your memory out of the closet
The memory jungle
20 memory techniques
Remembering names
Mnemonic devices
Power Process: "Love your problems (and experience your barriers)"
Master Student Profile: Dot Richardson

how

you can use this chapter . . .

Focus your attention.
Make conscious choices about what to remember.
Recall facts and ideas with more ease.

as you read, ask yourself

what if . . .

I could use my memory to its full potential?

Take your memory out of the closet

Once upon a time, people talked about human memory as if it were a limited space, like a closet. You stored individual memories there like old shirts and stray socks. Remembering something was a matter of rummaging through all that stuff. If you were lucky, you found what you wanted.

Brain researchers have shattered this image to bits. Memory is not an area of limited space. It's not a place or a thing. Instead, memory is a *process*.

On a conscious level, memories appear as distinct and unconnected mental events: words, sensations, images. They can include details from the distant past—the smell of cookies baking in your grandmother's kitchen or the feel of sunlight warming your face through the window of your first-grade classroom. On a biological level, each of those memories involves millions of nerve cells, or neurons, firing chemical messages to each other. If you could observe these exchanges in real time, you'd see regions of cells all over the brain glowing with electrical charges at speeds that would put a computer to shame.

When a series of cells connects several times in a similar pattern, the result is a memory. Psychologist Donald Hebb uses the aphorism "Neurons which fire together, wire together" to describe this principle.[1]

This means that memories are not really "stored." Instead, remembering is a process in which you *encode* information as links between active neurons that fire together and *decode*, or reactivate, neurons that wired together in the past. Memory is the probability that certain patterns of brain activity will occur again in the future. In effect, you re-create a memory each time you recall it.

Whenever you learn something new, your brain changes physically by growing more connections between neurons. The more you learn, the greater the number of connections.

You can enhance these connections through various techniques. One is visualization, where you create multisensory images of yourself performing well. According to David Yukelson, a sports psychologist at Penn State University, your neurons fire in the same patterns during a visualization as they do when you actually train or compete.[2] Visualization can also help you remember plays, recall information about competitors, and summon up the ideas you need to answer an essay question.

There's a lot you can do to wire those neural networks into place. That's where the memory techniques described in this chapter come into play. Step out of your crowded mental closet into a world of infinite possibilities. ▨

journal entry 8

Discovery/Intention Statement

Write a sentence or two describing the way you feel when you want to remember something but have trouble doing so. Think of a specific incident in which you experienced this problem, such as trying to remember someone's name or a fact you needed during a test.

I discovered that I . . .

_____

_____

_____

Now spend five minutes skimming this chapter and find three to five memory strategies you think could be helpful. List the strategies below and note the page numbers where they are explained. Then write an Intention Statement scheduling a time to study them in more detail.

Strategy   *Page number*

_____

_____

_____

_____

_____

I intend to . . .

_____

_____

_____

_____

The memory
jungle

Think of your memory as a vast, overgrown jungle. This memory jungle is thick with wild plants, exotic shrubs, twisted trees, and creeping vines. It spreads over thousands of square miles— dense, tangled, forbidding.

The more often you recall information, and the more often you put the same information into your memory, the easier it is to find.

Imagine that the jungle is encompassed on all sides by towering mountains. There is only one entrance to the jungle, a small meadow that is reached by a narrow pass through the mountains.

In the jungle there are animals, millions of them. The animals represent all of the information in your memory. Imagine that every thought, mental picture, or perception you ever had is represented by an animal in this jungle. Every single event ever perceived by any of your five senses— sight, touch, hearing, smell, or taste— has also passed through the meadow and entered the jungle. Some of the thought animals, such as the color of your seventh-grade teacher's favorite sweater, are well hidden. Other thoughts, such as your cell phone number or the position of the reverse gear in your car, are easier to find.

There are two rules of the memory jungle. Each thought animal must pass through the meadow at the entrance to the jungle. And once an animal enters the jungle, it never leaves.

The meadow represents short-term memory. You use this kind of memory when you look up a telephone number and hold it in your memory long enough to make a call. Short-term memory appears to have a limited capacity (the meadow is small) and disappears fast (animals pass through the meadow quickly).

The jungle itself represents long-term memory. This is the kind of memory that allows you to recall information from day to day, week to week, and year to year. Remember that thought animals never leave the long-term memory jungle. The following visualizations can help you recall useful concepts about memory.

Visualization #1: A well-worn path

Imagine what happens as a thought, in this case we'll call it an elephant, bounds across short-term memory and into the jungle. The elephant  leaves a trail of broken twigs and footprints that you can follow. Brain research suggests that thoughts can wear paths in the memory.[3] These paths are called *neural traces*. The more well-worn the neural trace, the easier it is to retrieve (find) the thought. In other words, the more often the elephant retraces the path, the clearer the path becomes. The more often you recall information, and the more often you put the same information into your memory, the easier it is to find.

When you buy a new car, for example, the first few times you try to find reverse, you have to think for a moment. After you have found reverse gear every day for a week, the path is worn into your memory. After a year, the path is so well-worn that when you dream about driving your car backward, you even dream the correct motion for putting the gear in reverse.

Visualization #2: A herd of thoughts

The second picture you can use to your advantage is the picture of many animals gathering at a clearing—like thoughts gathering at a central location in the memory. It is easier to retrieve thoughts that are grouped together, just as it is easier to find a herd of animals than it is to find a single elephant.

Pieces of information are easier to recall if you can associate them with similar information. For example, you can more readily remember a particular player's  batting average if you can associate it with other baseball statistics.

Visualization #3: Turning your back

Imagine releasing the elephant into the jungle, turning your back, and counting to 10. When you turn around, the elephant is gone. This is exactly what happens to most of the information you receive.

Generally, we can recall only 50 percent of the material we have just read. Within 24 hours, most of us can recall only about 20 percent. This means that 80 percent of the material has not been encoded and is wandering around, lost in the memory jungle.

The remedy is simple: Review quickly. Do not take your eyes off the thought animal as it crosses the short-  term memory meadow, and review it soon after it enters the long-term memory jungle. Wear a path in your memory immediately.

Visualization #4: You are directing the animal traffic

The fourth picture is one with you in it. You are standing at the entrance to the short-term memory meadow, directing herds of thought animals as they file through the pass, across the meadow, and into your long-term memory. You  are taking an active role in the learning process. You are paying attention. You are doing more than sitting on a rock and watching the animals file past into your brain. You have become part of the process, and in doing so, you have taken control of your memory. ✖

Experience these visualizations online at masterstudent.college.hmco.com

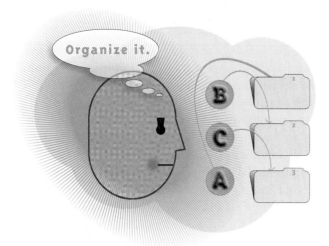

Organize it.

20 memory techniques

Experiment with these techniques to develop a flexible, custom-made memory system that fits your style of learning the content of your courses and the skills of your sport. The 20 techniques are divided into four categories, each of which represents a general principle for improving memory.

To get the most out of this article, first survey the following techniques by reading each heading. Then read the techniques. Next, skim them again, looking for the ones you like best. Mark those and use them.

Organize it

1 Be selective. To a large degree, the art of memory is the art of selecting what to remember in the first place. As you dig into your textbooks, playbooks, and notes, make choices about what is most important to learn. Imagine that you are going to create a test on the material and consider the questions you would ask.

When reading, look for chapter previews, summaries, and review questions. Pay attention to anything printed in bold type. Also notice visual elements—tables, charts, graphs, and illustrations. All of these are clues pointing to what's important. During lectures, notice what the instructor emphasizes. During practice, focus on what your coach requires you to repeat. Anything that's presented visually—on the board, on overheads, or with slides—is also key.

2 Make it meaningful. One way to create meaning is to learn from the general to the specific. Before tackling the details, get the big picture.

Before you begin your next reading assignment, for example, skim it to locate the main idea. If you're ever lost, step back and recall that idea. The details might make more sense.

You can also organize any list of items—even random ones—in a meaningful way to make them easier to remember. In his book *Information Anxiety*, Richard Saul Wurman proposes five principles for organizing any body of ideas, facts, or objects:[4]

Principle	Example
Organize by **time**	Events in history or in a novel flow in chronological order.
Organize by **location**	Addresses for a large company's regional offices are grouped by state and city.
Organize by **category**	Nonfiction library materials are organized by subject categories.
Organize by **continuum**	Products rated in *Consumers Guide* are grouped from highest in price to lowest in price, or highest in quality to lowest in quality.
Organize by **alphabet**	Entries in a book index are listed in ABC order.

3 Create associations. The data already encoded in your neural networks is arranged according to a scheme that makes sense to you. When you introduce new data, you can remember it more effectively if you associate it with similar or related data. Think, for example, about your favorite courses. They probably relate to subjects that you already know something about.

Preview reading assignments, and complete those readings before you attend lectures. Before taking upper-level courses, master the prerequisites. Even when you're tackling a new subject, you can build a mental store of basic background information—the raw material for creating associations.

The bottom line: To remember more, associate new facts and ideas with something that you already know.

Use your body

4 Learn it once, actively. To remember an idea, go beyond thinking about it. *Do* something with it. Action is a great memory enhancer. Study your assignments with the same energy that you bring to the dance floor or the basketball court.

You can create your own opportunities for action. For example, your sociology class might include a discussion about how groups of people resolve conflict. See if you can apply any of these ideas to resolving conflict in your own family.

Use other simple and direct methods to infuse your learning with action. When you sit at your desk, sit up straight. Sit on the edge of your chair, as if you were about to spring out of it and sprint across the room.

Also experiment with standing up when you study. It's harder to fall asleep in this position. Some people insist that their brains work better when they stand.

Pace back and forth and gesture as you recite material out loud. Use your hands. Get your whole body involved in studying.

Learning can be deceptive. Most learning, especially in higher education, takes place in a passive setting. Students are seated, quiet, and subdued.

Don't be fooled. Learning takes energy. When you learn effectively, you are burning calories, even if you are sitting at a desk reading a textbook.

5 Relax. When you're relaxed, you absorb new information quickly and recall it with greater ease and accuracy. Students who can't recall information under the stress of a final exam can often recite the same facts later when they are relaxed.

Relaxing might seem to contradict the idea of active learning as explained in technique #4, but it doesn't. Being relaxed is not the same as being drowsy, zoned out, or asleep. Relaxation is a state of alertness, free of tension, during which your mind can play with new information and apply memory techniques.

"Mellowing out" might do more than lower your blood pressure. It might help you succeed in school.

6 Create pictures. Draw diagrams. Make cartoons. Use these images to connect facts and illustrate relationships. Associations within and among abstract concepts can be "seen" and recalled more easily when they are visualized. The key is to use your imagination.

For example, Boyle's law states that at a constant temperature, the volume of a confined ideal gas varies inversely with its pressure. Simply put, cutting the volume in half doubles the pressure. To remember this concept, you might picture someone "doubled over" using a bicycle pump. As she increases the pressure in the pump by decreasing the volume in the pump cylinder, she seems to be getting angrier. By the time she has doubled the pressure (and halved the volume) she is boiling ("Boyle-ing") mad.

To visualize abstract relationships effectively, create an action-oriented image, such as the person using the pump. Make the picture vivid, too. The person's face could be bright red. And involve all of your senses. Imagine how the cold metal of the pump would feel and how the person would grunt as she struggled with it. (Most of us would have to struggle. It would take incredible strength to double the pressure in a bicycle pump, not to mention a darn sturdy pump.)

7 Recite and repeat. When you repeat something out loud, you anchor the concept in two different senses. First, you get the physical sensation in your throat, tongue, and lips when voicing the concept. Second, you hear it. The combined result is synergistic, just as it is when you create pictures. That is, the effect of using two different senses is greater than the sum of their individual effects.

The repetition part is important, too. Repetition is a common memory device because it works. Repetition blazes a trail through the pathways of your brain, making the information easier to find. Repeat a concept out loud until you know it, then say it five more times.

Recitation works best when you recite concepts in your own words. For example, if you want to remember that the acceleration of a falling body due to gravity at sea level equals 32 feet per second per second, you might say, "Gravity makes an object accelerate 32 feet per second faster for each second that it's in the air at sea level." Putting it in your own words forces you to think about it.

Have some fun with this technique. Recite by writing a song about what you're learning. Sing it in the shower.

Or imitate someone. Imagine your textbook being read by Bill Cosby, Madonna, or Clint Eastwood ("Go ahead, punk. Make my density equal mass over volume").

8 Write it down. This technique is obvious, yet easy to forget. Writing a note to yourself helps you remember an idea, even if you never look at the note again.

Writing engages a different kind of memory than speaking. Writing prompts us to be more logical, coherent, and complete. Written reviews reveal gaps in knowledge that oral reviews miss, just as oral reviews

To remember an idea, go beyond thinking about it. Do something with it.

reveal gaps that written reviews miss.

In addition, writing is physical. Your arm, your hand, and your fingers join in. Remember, learning is an active process—you remember what you *do*.

Use your brain

9 Engage your emotions. One powerful way to enhance your memory is to make friends with your amygdala. This is an area of your brain that lights up with extra neural activity each time you feel a strong emotion. When a topic excites love, laughter, or fear, the amygdala sends a flurry of chemical messages that say, in effect: *This information is important and useful. Don't forget it.*

You're more likely to remember course material when you relate it to a goal—whether academic, personal, or career—that you feel strongly about. This is one reason why it pays to be specific about what you want. The more goals you have and the more clearly they are defined, the more channels you create for incoming information.

You can use this strategy even when a subject seems boring at first. If you're not naturally interested in a topic, then create interest. Find a study partner in the class—if possible, someone you know and like—or form a study group. Also consider getting to know the instructor personally. When a course creates a bridge to human relationships, you engage the content in a more emotional way.

You're more likely to remember course material when you relate it to a goal— whether academic, personal, or career— that you feel strongly about.

10 Overlearn. One way to fight mental fuzziness is to learn more than you need to know about a subject simply to pass a test. You can pick a subject apart, examine it, add to it, and go over it until it becomes second nature.

This technique is especially effective for problem solving. Do the assigned problems, and then do more problems. Find another textbook and work similar problems. Then make up your own problems and solve them.

11 Escape the short-term memory trap. Short-term memory is different from the kind of memory you'll need during exam week. For example, most of us can look at an unfamiliar seven-digit phone number once and remember it long enough to dial it. See if you can recall that number the next day.

Short-term memory can fade after a few minutes, and it rarely lasts more than several hours. A short review within minutes or hours of a study session can move material from short-term memory into long-term memory.

12 Use your times of peak energy. Study your most difficult subjects during the times when your energy peaks. Many people can concentrate more

effectively during daylight hours. The early morning hours can be especially productive, even for those who hate to get up with the sun. Observe the peaks and valleys in your energy flow during the day and adjust study times accordingly.

13 Distribute learning. As an alternative to marathon study sessions, experiment with shorter, spaced-out sessions. These are particularly helpful when your sport is in its competitive season. You might find that you can get far more done in three two-hour sessions than in one six-hour session.

For example, when you are studying for your American history exam, study for an hour or two and then wash the dishes. While you are washing the dishes, part of your mind will be reviewing what you studied. Return to American history for a while, then call a friend. Even when you are deep in conversation, part of your mind will be reviewing history.

You can get more done if you take regular breaks. You can even use the breaks as mini-rewards. After a productive study session, give yourself permission to log on and check your e-mail, listen to a song, or play 10 minutes of hide-and-seek with your kids.

By taking periodic breaks while studying, you allow information to sink in. During these breaks, your brain is taking the time to literally rewire itself by growing new connections between cells. Psychologists call this process *consolidation*.[5]

There is an exception to this idea of allowing time for consolidation. When you are so engrossed in a textbook that you cannot put it down, when you are consumed by an idea for a term paper and cannot think of anything else—keep going. The master student athlete within you has taken over. Enjoy the ride.

14 Be aware of attitudes. If you think a subject is boring, remind yourself that everything is related to everything else. Look for connections that relate to your own interests.

For example, consider a person who is fanatical about cars. She can rebuild a motor in a weekend and has a good time doing so. From this apparently specialized interest, she can explore a wide realm of knowledge. She can relate the workings of an engine to principles of physics, math, and chemistry. Computerized parts in newer cars can lead her to the study of data processing. She can research how the automobile industry has changed our cities and helped create suburbs, a topic that includes urban planning, sociology, business, economics, psychology, and history.

15 Give your "secret brain" a chance. Sometimes the way you combine studying with other activities can affect how well you remember information. The trick is to avoid what psychologists call *retroactive inhibition*, something that happens when a new or unrelated activity interferes with previous learning.

Say that you've just left your evening psychology class, which included a fascinating lecture on Sigmund Freud's theory of dreams. You then check your team schedule and realize that you have a competition coming up in two days. You begin to analyze your opponent and soon find that you can think about little else. In this scenario, the key concepts of the psychology lecture are pushed aside by your gripping concern about the competition.

Consider another scenario instead. You arrange to car-pool with a teammate who is in the same class. On the way home, you talk about the lecture. The discussion ignites into a debate as you and your friend take opposite stands on a principle of Freud's theory. Later, just before going to sleep, you mull over the conversation. While you sleep, your brain can now process the key points of the lecture—something that will come in handy for the mid-term exam. The beauty of this scenario is that you keep your head in your course work rather than worrying about the competition. In the process, your memory benefits.

16 Combine techniques. All of these memory techniques can work even better in combination. Choose two or three techniques to use on a particular assignment and experiment for yourself. For example, after you take a few minutes to get an overview of a reading assignment, you could draw a quick picture or diagram to represent the main point. Or you could overlearn a chemistry equation by singing a jingle about it all the way to work.

Recall it

17 Remember something else. When you are stuck and can't remember something that you're sure you know, remember something else that is related to it.

During an economics exam, if you can't remember anything about the aggregate demand curve, recall what you do know about the aggregate supply curve. If you cannot recall specific facts, remember the example that

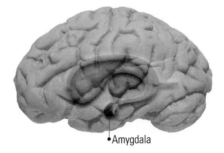

•Amygdala

The amygdala, highlighted in this illustration, is an area of your brain that sends neural messages associated with strong emotions. When you link new material to something that you feel strongly about, you activate this part of your brain. In turn, you're more likely to remember that material.

the instructor used during her lecture. Information is encoded in the same area of the brain as similar information. You can unblock your recall by stimulating that area of your memory.

Brainstorming is another memory jog. If you are stumped when taking a test, start writing down lots of answers to related questions, and—pop!—the answer you want may appear.

You can take this technique one step further with a process that psychologists call *elaboration*.[6] The key is to ask questions that prompt you to create more associations. For example, when you meet someone new, ask yourself: "What are the distinctive features of this person's face? Does she remind me of someone else?"

18 Notice when you do remember. To develop your memory, notice when you recall information easily and ask yourself what memory techniques you're using naturally. Also notice when it's difficult to recall information and adjust your learning techniques. And remember to congratulate yourself when you remember.

19 Use it before you lose it. To remember something, access it a lot. Read it, write it, speak it, listen to it, apply it—find some way to make contact with the material regularly. Each time you do so, you widen the neural pathway to the material and make it easier to recall the next time.

Another way to make contact with the material is to teach it. Teaching demands mastery. When you explain the function of the pancreas to a fellow student, you discover quickly whether you really understand it yourself.

Study groups are especially effective because they put you on-stage: The friendly pressure of knowing that you'll teach the group helps focus your attention.

20 Adopt the attitude that you never forget. You might not believe that an idea or a thought never leaves your memory. That's OK. In fact, it doesn't matter whether you agree with the idea or not. It can work for you anyway.

Test the concept. Instead of saying, "I don't remember," you can say, "It will come to me."

Or even "I never forget!" ⊠

USE Q-CARDS TO REINFORCE MEMORY

One memory strategy you might find useful involves a special kind of flash card. It's called a *Question Card*, or *Q-Card* for short.

To create a standard flash card, you write a question on one side of a 3x5 card and its answer on the other side. Q-Cards have a question on *both* sides. Here's the trick: The question on each side of the card contains the answer to the question on the other side.

The questions you write on Q-Cards can draw on both lower- and higher-order thinking skills. Writing these questions forces you to encode material in different ways. You activate more areas of your brain and burn the concepts even deeper into your memory.

For example, say that you want to remember the subject of the 18th Amendment to the United States Constitution, the one that prohibited the sale of alcohol. On one side of a 3x5 card, write *What amendment prohibited the sale of alcohol?* Turn the card over and write *What did the 18th Amendment do?*

To get the most from Q-Cards:

- Add a picture to each side of the card. This helps you learn concepts faster and develop a more visual learning style.

- Read the questions and recite the answers out loud. Two keys to memory are repetition and novelty, so use a different voice whenever you read and recite. Whisper the first time you go through your cards, then shout or sing the next time. Doing this develops an auditory learning style.

- Carry Q-Cards with you and pull them out during waiting times, or when you're in the bus on a road trip. To develop a kinesthetic learning style, handle your cards often.

- Create a Q-Card for each new and important concept within 24 hours after attending a class or completing an assignment. This is your *active stack* of cards. Keep answering the questions on these cards until you learn each new concept.

- Review all of the cards from the term for a certain subject on one day each week. For example, on Monday, review all cards from biology; on Tuesday, review all cards from history. These cards make up your *review stacks*.

How do living organisms obtain ENERGY?

Why do living things need METABOLISM?

What is the formula for factoring the difference of squares?

$$a^2 - b^2 = (a+b)(a-b)$$

voices

student

An example of how valuable these memory techniques are occurred when I had to study for my psychology test. The class covers many different names and terminology. The tools Create associations, Recite and repeat, Write it down, *and* Use your times of peak energy *are what I applied to my study routine. The tools were so useful that I was the first one to complete the exam, and I received a 92.*

—SUZANA KOTSONAS

Notable failures

You might feel discouraged about your failure to remember information at critical moments, such as during a test. Before you despair over your test scores or grade point average, remember that history is filled with examples of people who struggled academically and then went on to achieve great things. These notable failures, some of whom are listed below, are emblazoned in our collective memory, while their detractors are long forgotten.

Bruce Jenner earned an Olympic gold medal in the decathlon. He was diagnosed as dyslexic and barely graduated from high school.

Albert Einstein's parents thought he was retarded. He spoke haltingly until age nine, and after that he answered questions only after laboring in thought about them. He was advised by a teacher to drop out of high school: "You'll never amount to anything, Einstein."

Charles Darwin's father said to his son, "You will be a disgrace to yourself and all your family." (Darwin did poorly in school.)

Henry Ford barely made it through high school.

Sir Isaac Newton did poorly in school and was allowed to continue only because he failed at running the family farm.

Pablo Picasso was pulled out of school at age 10 because he was doing so poorly. A tutor hired by Pablo's father gave up on Pablo.

Giacomo Puccini's first music teacher said that Puccini had no talent for music. Later Puccini composed some of the world's greatest operas.

The machines of the world's greatest inventor, **Leonardo da Vinci**, were never built, and many wouldn't have worked anyway.

Clarence Darrow became a legend in the courtroom as he lost case after case.

Edwin Land's attempts at instant movies (Polarvision) failed completely. He described his efforts as trying to use an impossible chemistry and a nonexistent technology to make an unmanufacturable product for which there was no discernible demand.

After the success of the show *South Pacific*, composer **Oscar Hammerstein** put an ad in *Variety* that listed over a dozen of his failures. At the bottom of the ad, he repeated the credo of show business, "I did it before, and I can do it again."

Asked about how he felt when his team lost a game, **Joe Paterno**, coach of the Penn State University football team, once replied that losing was probably good for them since that was how the players learned what they were doing wrong.

The game Monopoly was developed by **Charles Darrow**, an unemployed heating engineer. Darrow presented his first version of the game to a toy company in 1935. That company originally rejected the game for containing 52 "fundamental errors." Today the game is so successful that its publisher, Parker Brothers, prints more than $40 billion of Monopoly money each year. That's twice the amount of real money printed annually by the United States Mint.

Robert Pirsig's best-selling book, *Zen and the Art of Motorcycle Maintenance*, was rejected by 121 publishers.

Spike Lee applied for graduate study at the top film schools in the country, including the University of Southern California and the University of California at Los Angeles. Due to his scores on the Graduate Record Exam, both schools turned Lee down.

Jaime Escalante is a nationally known educator and the subject of the film *Stand and Deliver*. When he first tried to get a teaching job in California, the state refused to accept his teaching credentials from Bolivia.

Before **Alan Page** became the first African American to sit on the Minnesota Supreme Court, he played in the American Football League. Seeking a career change, he entered law school. After three weeks he dropped out and did not enroll again for another eight years.

After being rejected as a ball boy for a Davis Cup tennis match because he was "too awkward and clumsy," **Stan Smith** went on to win Wimbledon, the U. S. Open, and eight Davis Cups.

Carl Lewis, who won the gold medal for the long jump in the 1996 Olympic games, was asked for the secret of his success. His answer: "Remembering that you have both wins and losses along the way. I don't take either one too seriously."

Someone once said of **Vince Lombardi**: "He possesses minimal football knowledge and lacks motivation."

Before the career-planning book *What Color Is Your Parachute?* became a perennial best-seller, author **Richard Nelson Bolles** got laid off from a job and ended up broke. One Friday in 1971, his cash reserves included only the $5.18 in his pocket. Bolles sold two copies of his book that day and was able to survive through the weekend. Today, *What Color Is Your Parachute?* sells nearly 20,000 copies every month.

Portions of this text reprinted with permission by Stillpoint Publishing, Walpole, NH (USA) 03608 from the book *Diet for a New America* by John Robbins. Copyright © 1987. From *Information Anxiety* by Richard Saul Wurman, copyright © 1989 by Richard Saul Wurman. Used by permission of Doubleday, a division of Bantam Doubleday Dell Publishing Group, Inc.

More examples of notable failures are available online at *But They Did Not Give Up*, http://www.emory.edu/EDUCATION/mfp/OnFailing.html.

exercise 11

REMEMBERING YOUR CAR KEYS— OR ANYTHING ELSE

Pick something you frequently forget. Some people chronically lose their car keys or forget to write down checks in their check register. Others let anniversaries and birthdays slip by.

Pick an item or a task you're prone to forget. Then design a strategy for remembering it. Use any of the techniques from this chapter, research others, or make up your own from scratch. Describe your technique and the results in the space below.

_____

_____

_____

_____

In this exercise, as in most of the exercises in this book, a failure is also a success. Don't be concerned with whether your technique will work. Design it, and then find out. If it doesn't work for you this time, use another method.

journal entry 9

Discovery Statement

Take a minute to reflect on the memory techniques in this chapter. You probably use some of them already without being aware of it. In the space below, list at least three techniques you have used in the past and describe how you used them.

_____

_____

_____

_____

_____

_____

_____

_____

_____

_____

Keep your brain fit for life

Your brain is an organ that needs regular care and exercise. Higher education gives you plenty of chances to exercise that organ. Don't let those benefits fade after you leave school. Starting now, adopt habits to keep your brain lean and fit for life.

Seek out new experiences. If you sit at a desk most of the workday, take a dance class. If you seldom travel, start reading maps of new locations and plan a cross-country trip. Seek out museums, theaters, concerts, and other cultural events. Even after you graduate, consider learning another language or taking up a musical instrument. Your brain thrives on novelty. Build it into your life. Shaking up your routines might involve some initial discomfort. Hang in there. Remind yourself that new experiences give your brain a workout just like sit-ups condition your abs.

Take care of your health. Exercising regularly, staying tobacco-free, and getting plenty of sleep can reduce your risk of cancer, heart disease, stroke, and other conditions that interfere with memory. Eating well also helps. A diet rich in fruits and vegetables boosts your supply of antioxidants—natural chemicals that nourish your brain.

Drink alcohol moderately, if at all. A common definition of moderate consumption for people of legal drinking age is no more than one drink per day for women and no more than two drinks per day for men. Heavier drinking can affect memory. In fact, long-term alcoholics tend to develop conditions that impair memory. One is Wernicke-Korsakoff syndrome, a disorder that causes people to forget the incidents of daily life immediately after they happen.

For more suggestions on maintaining health, see Chapter Eleven.

Engage life fully. Research sponsored by the MacArthur Foundation indicates that engagement with life acts as a strong predictor of successful aging.[7] Researchers define *engagement* as maintaining close relationships with friends and family, and staying productive in paid or volunteer work. Both loving and working help keep your brain fit to handle a lifetime of memories.

Remembering names

One way to immediately practice memory techniques is to use them to remember names. As a student athlete, you will meet many coaches, boosters, and other athletes. The booster whose name you recall today could become your future employer.

Recite and repeat in conversation. When you hear a person's name, repeat it. Immediately say it to yourself several times without moving your lips. You could also repeat the name out loud in a way that does not sound forced or artificial: "I'm pleased to meet you, Coach Martin."

Ask the other person to recite and repeat. Let other people help you remember their names. After you've been introduced to someone, ask that person to spell the name and pronounce it correctly for you. Most people will be flattered by the effort you're making to learn their names.

Visualize. After the conversation, construct a brief visual image of the person. For a memorable image, make it unusual. Imagine the name painted in your school colors on the person's forehead.

Admit you don't know. Most people will sympathize if you say, "I'm working to remember names better. Yours is right on the tip of my tongue. What is it again?" (By the way, that's exactly what psychologists call that feeling—the "tip of the tongue" phenomenon.)

Introduce yourself again. Most of the time we assume introductions are one-shot affairs. If we miss a name the first time around, our hopes for remembering it are dashed. Instead of giving up, reintroduce yourself: "Hello, again. We met earlier. I'm Jesse, and please tell me your name again."

Use associations. Link each person you meet with one characteristic that you find interesting or unusual. For example, you could make a mental note: "James Washington—coach of Central College swim team, wears thick glasses." To reinforce your associations, write them down as soon as you can.

Limit the number of new names you learn at one time. Occasionally, we find ourselves in situations where we're introduced to many people at the same time: "Dad, these are all the members of my wrestling team." "Let's take a tour so you can meet everyone in this department." When meeting a group of people, concentrate on remembering just a few names. Or avoid memory overload by limiting yourself to learning just first names. Last names can come later.

Ask for photos. In some cases, you might be able to get photos of all the people you meet. For example, a small business where you apply for a job might have a brochure with pictures of all the employees. Ask for individual or group photos and write in the names if they're not included. You can use these photos as "flash cards" as you drill yourself on names. Team media guides also offer a list of names.

Go early. Consider going early to conventions, parties, and classes. Sometimes just a few people show up on time at these occasions. That's fewer names for you to remember. And as more people arrive, you can overhear them being introduced to others—an automatic review for you.

Make it a game. In situations where many people are new to one another, consider pairing up with another person and staging a contest. Challenge each other to remember as many new names as possible. Then choose an "award"—such as a movie ticket or free meal—for the person who wins.

Intend to remember. The simple act of focusing your attention at key moments—such as when you are introduced to a coach or booster—can do wonders for your memory. Test this idea for yourself. The next time you're introduced to someone, direct 100 percent of your attention to hearing that person's name. Do this consistently and see what happens to your ability to remember names.

The intention to remember can be more powerful than any single memory technique. ⊠

Mnemonic devices

It's pronounced *ne-mon´-ik*. The word refers to tricks that can increase your ability to recall everything from grocery lists to speeches.

Mnemonic devices have three serious limitations. First, they don't always help you understand or digest material. Mnemonics rely only on rote memorization. Second, the mnemonic device itself is sometimes complicated to learn and time-consuming to develop. Third, mnemonic devices can be forgotten.

Even so, mnemonic devices can be useful. Following are examples.

New words. Acronyms are words created from the initial letters of a series of words. An example is NASA, which stands for **N**ational **A**eronautics and **S**pace **A**dministration. You can make up your own acronyms to recall series of facts. A common mnemonic acronym is Roy G. Biv, which has helped thousands of students remember the colors of the visible spectrum (**r**ed, **o**range, **y**ellow, **g**reen, **b**lue, **i**ndigo, and **v**iolet).

Creative sentences. Acrostics are sentences that help you remember a series of letters that stand for something. Here's an example from music notation: The first letters of the words in the sentence "Every good boy does fine" are E, G, B, D, and F. These are also the names of notes that fall on the lines of the treble clef staff.

Rhymes. Rhymes have been used for centuries to teach children basic facts: "In fourteen hundred and ninety-two, Columbus sailed the ocean blue" or "Thirty days hath September."

The loci system. The word *loci* is the plural of *locus*, a synonym for *place* or *location*. Use this system to create visual associations with familiar locations. Unusual associations are the easiest to remember.

The loci system is an old one. Ancient Greek orators used it to remember long speeches. For example, if an orator's position was that road taxes must be raised to pay for school equipment, his loci visualizations might have looked like the following.

First, as he walks in the door of his house, he imagines a large *porpoise* jumping through a hoop. This reminds him to begin by telling the audience the *purpose* of his speech.

Next, he visualizes his living room floor covered with paving stones, forming a road leading into the kitchen. In the kitchen, he pictures dozens of schoolchildren sitting on the floor because they have no desks.

Now it's the day of the big speech. The Greek politician is nervous. He is perspiring, and his toga sticks to his body. He stands up to give his speech, and his mind goes blank. Then he starts thinking to himself:

> *I am so nervous that I can hardly remember my name. But no problem—I can remember the rooms in my house. Let's see, I'm walking in the front door and—wow! I see the porpoise. That reminds me to talk about the purpose of my speech. And then there's that road leading to the kitchen. Say, what are all those kids doing there on the floor? Oh, yeah, now I remember—they have no desks! We need to raise taxes on roads to pay for their desks and the other stuff they need in classrooms.*

The peg system. This technique employs key words that are paired with numbers. Each word forms a "peg" on which you can "hang" mental associations. To use this system effectively, learn the following peg words and their associated numbers well:

bun goes with 1	*sticks* goes with 6
shoe goes with 2	*heaven* goes with 7
tree goes with 3	*gate* goes with 8
door goes with 4	*wine* goes with 9
hive goes with 5	*hen* goes with 10

Believe it or not, you can use the peg system to remember the Bill of Rights (the first 10 amendments to the United States Constitution). For example, amendment number *four* is about protection from unlawful search and seizure. Imagine people knocking at your *door* who are demanding to search your home. This amendment means that you do not have to open your door unless those people display a proper search warrant. ⬛

PRACTICING CRITICAL THINKING

3

Take five minutes to remember a time when you enjoyed learning something. In the space below, describe that experience in a sentence or two. Then make a brief list of the things you found enjoyable about that experience.

_____

_____

_____

_____

_____

_____

_____

_____

_____

_____

Within the next 24 hours, compare your list with those of other classmates. Look for similarities and differences in the descriptions of your learning experiences.

Based on your comparison, form a tentative explanation about what makes learning enjoyable for people. Summarize your explanation here:

_____

_____

_____

_____

_____

_____

_____

_____

_____

_____

_____

_____

exercise 12

BE A POET

Construct your own mnemonic device for remembering some of the memory techniques in this chapter. Make up a poem, jingle, acronym, or acrostic, or use another mnemonic system. Describe your mnemonic device in the space below.

_____

_____

_____

_____

_____

_____

_____

_____

_____

| Power Process | Put It to Work | Quiz | Learning Styles Application | Master Student Profile |

power process

Love your problems

(and experience your barriers)

We all have problems and barriers that block our progress or prevent us from moving into new areas. Often, the way we respond to our problems puts boundaries on our experiences. We place limitations on what we allow ourselves to be, do, and have.

Our problems might include fear of speaking in front of a group, anxiety about math problems, or reluctance to sound ridiculous when learning a foreign language. We might have a barrier about looking silly when trying something new. Some of us even have anxiety about being successful.

Problems often work like barriers. When we bump up against one of our problems, we usually turn away and start walking along a different path. And all of a sudden—bump!—we've struck another barrier. And we turn away again. As we continue to bump into problems and turn away from them, our lives stay inside the same old boundaries. Inside these boundaries, we are unlikely to have new adventures. We are unlikely to improve or to make much progress.

The word *problem* is a wonderful word coming from the ancient Greek word *proballein,* which means "to throw forward." In other words, problems are there to provide an opportunity for us to gain new skills. If we respond to problems by loving them instead of resisting them, we can expand the boundaries in which we live our lives. When approached with acceptance, and even love, problems can "throw" us forward.

Three ways to handle a barrier

It's natural to have barriers, but sometimes they limit our experience so much that we get bored, angry, or frustrated with life. When this happens, consider the following three ways of dealing with a barrier. One way is to pretend it doesn't exist. Avoid it, deny it, lie about it. It's like turning your head the other way, putting on a fake grin, and saying, "See, there's really no problem at all. Everything is fine. Oh, that problem. That's not a problem—it's not really there."

In addition to making us look foolish, this approach leaves the barrier intact, and we keep bumping into it. We deny the barrier and might not even be aware that we're bumping into it. For example, a student who has a barrier about math might subconsciously avoid enriching experiences that include math.

A second approach is to fight the barrier, to struggle against it. This usually makes the barrier grow. It increases the barrier's magnitude. A person who is obsessed with weight might constantly worry about being fat. She might struggle with it every day, trying diet after diet. And the more she struggles, the bigger the problem gets.

The third alternative is to love the barrier. Accept it. Totally experience it. Tell the truth about it. Describe it in detail. When you do this, the barrier loses its power. You can literally love it to death.

The word *love* might sound like an overstatement. In this Power Process, the word means to accept your problems, to allow and permit them. When we fight a problem, it grows bigger. The more we struggle against it, the stronger it seems to become. When we accept the fact that we have a problem, we are more likely to find effective ways to deal with it.

Suppose one of your barriers is being afraid of speaking in front of a group. You can use any of these three approaches.

First, you can get up in front of the group and pretend that you're not afraid. You can fake a smile, not admitting to yourself or the group that you have any concerns about speaking—even though your legs have turned to rubber bands and your mind to jelly. The problem is that everyone in the room, including you, will know you're scared when your hands start shaking, your voice cracks, and you forget what you were going to say.

The second way to approach this barrier is to fight it. You can tell yourself, "I'm not going to be scared," and then try to keep your knees from knocking. Generally, this doesn't work. In fact, your knee-knocking might get worse.

The third approach is to go to the front of the room, look out into the audience, and say to yourself, "I am scared. I notice that my knees are shaking and my mouth feels dry, and I'm having a rush of thoughts about what might happen if I say the wrong thing. Yup, I'm scared, and that's OK. As a matter of fact, it's just part of me, so I accept it and I'm not going to try to fight it. I'm going to give this speech even though I'm scared." You might not actually eliminate the fear; however, your barrier about the fear— which is what inhibits you—might disappear. And you might discover that if you examine the fear, love it, accept it, and totally experience it, the fear itself also disappears.

Applying this process

Applying this process is easier if you remember three ideas. First, loving a problem is not necessarily the same as enjoying it. Love in this sense means total and unconditional acceptance.

This can work even with problems as thorny as physical pain. When we totally experience pain, it often diminishes and sometimes it disappears. This strategy can work with emotions as well as with physical pain. Make it your aim to love the pain, that is, to fully accept the pain and know all the details about it. Most pain has a wavelike quality. It rises, reaches a peak of intensity, and then subsides for a while. See if you can watch the waves as they come and go.

Second, unconditional acceptance is not the same as unconditional surrender. Accepting a problem does not mean escaping from it or giving up on finding a solution. Rather, this process involves freeing ourselves from the grip of the problem by diving *into* the problem head first and getting to know it in detail.

When we accept the fact that we have a problem, we are more likely to find effective ways to deal with it.

Third, love and laughter are allies. It's hard to resist a problem while you are laughing at it. Sure, that incident when you noticed the spinach in your teeth only *after* you got home from a first date was a bummer. But with the passage of time, you can admit that it was kind of funny. You don't have to wait weeks to gain that perspective. As long as you're going to laugh anyway, why wait? The sooner you can see the humor in your problems, the sooner you can face them.

When people first hear about loving their problems, they sometimes think it means being resigned to problems. Actually, loving a problem does not need to stop us from solving it. In fact, fully accepting and admitting the problem usually helps us take effective action—which can free us of the problem once and for all. ▧

put it to work

Meeting your professional goals might call for continual training to update your skills—perhaps even an advanced degree. The memory techniques in this chapter can serve you at every stage of your career. Following are examples of ways to transfer those techniques to the workplace.

Focus on solving problems.
When applying for jobs, review the Power Process: "Love your problems." Present yourself as someone who can spot an organization's areas for improvement and take appropriate action. During the hiring process, transform yourself from a faceless job applicant to a potent problem solver. For example, you might say, "I've found it difficult to order products from your Web site. Five people have told me the same thing. I have a list of ideas that could solve this problem." Then explain one item from your list. You'll get an employer's attention.

If some of your solutions fail, return to the "Notable failures" sidebar in this chapter to renew your inspiration. Many of the people featured in the sidebar experienced career-related snafus.

Organize your workspace to promote memory.
When personal computers first became standard fixtures in office cubicles, some futurists predicted the imminent arrival of the "paperless office." It didn't happen. Data might be stored digitally, but workers in the twenty-first century still handle reams of paper—letters, memos, manuals, meeting minutes, training materials, newsletters, magazines, technical journals, and books. That's all in addition to e-mail, Web pages, and other Internet-based documents.

Faced with such an information glut, you might find it challenging to remember where you *put* a particular document, let alone remember what's *in* it. Memory techniques from this chapter can help:

- **Be selective.** Instead of letting paper-based and digital documents pile up and telling yourself you'll get to them later, make quick decisions about which documents to keep. You might know right away that you'll never refer to some of them again. Be bold and trash them immediately. If only one article out of a magazine interests you, tear it out and toss the rest. Out of the millions of words and images that filter into your life at work, extract the gems and commit those to memory. A recycling bin that's full of paper is one sign of a healthy brain at work.

- **Create a meaningful organization for your files.** Take the documents you decide to keep and consider your options for filing them. You can group them alphabetically by subject, chronologically by date, or on a continuum from high to low priority. Documents that call for immediate action can go in a file that you check daily. Put lower-priority items in other files to review weekly, monthly, or quarterly. You don't have to memorize everything that's in these documents—even the most urgent ones. Just know where to find them on a moment's notice.

- **Create a personal system of cues and reminders.** In 1999, the winner of the U.S. National Memory Championship was a 27-year-old woman, Tatiana Cooley. To gain her title, she memorized lists of hundreds of randomly organized numbers and words. Yet Cooley confessed to a CNN reporter that she is absent-minded at work and plasters her office with handwritten Post-it Notes to aid her memory. The same approach can work for you.[8] This is a highly kinesthetic memory system. You might prefer instead to write notes on 3x5 cards or key to-do items into a computer file.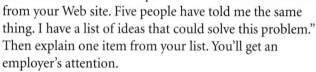

Name _____ Date _____/_____/_____

1. Explain how the "recite and repeat" memory technique leads to synergy.

2. Define the term *elaboration* as used in this chapter and give an example.

3. Describe a visualization that can help you remember Boyle's law.

4. Define *acronym* and give an example.

5. Memorization on a deep level can take place if you:
   (A) Repeat the idea.
   (B) Repeat the idea.
   (C) Repeat the idea.
   (D) All of the above.

6. Mnemonic devices are tricks that can increase your ability to:
   (A) Manage your time.
   (B) Understand or digest material.
   (C) Recall information that you already understand.

7. Briefly describe at least three memory techniques.

8. There are several categories of mnemonic devices given in the text. Explain two of them.

9. Briefly describe two ideas that can help you unconditionally accept a problem you're having right now.

10. Explain a strategy that can help transfer information from your short-term memory into your long-term memory.

learning styles application

The questions below will "cycle" you through four styles, or modes, of learning as explained in the article "Learning styles: Discovering how you learn" in Chapter One. Each question will help you explore a different mode. You can answer the questions in any order.

what if *Describe how you intend to use a technique from this chapter in a situation outside school where memory skills are important.*

why *List some important situations in which you could be more effective by improving your memory skills.*

how *Describe how you intend to use a technique from this chapter in a class where memory skills are important.*

what *List the three most useful memory techniques you learned from this chapter.*

master student profile

DOT RICHARDSON

(1961–   ) Highly decorated in college and professional sports, she helped win Olympic gold for the U.S. softball team in 1996.

Having an education opens doors of opportunity, as well as stimulating dreams. It is through schooling that we discover ourselves and the world around us. And in finding ourselves we creatively find ways our abilities can be used to make a contribution to society.

It is truly a blessing to have learned lessons and developed skills on the athletic field that helped me become a better surgeon. Mostly, athletics taught me how to work well with other people, and to appreciate their individual talents.

A surgeon has to know how to work together with others as a team in order to perform a successful surgery. A surgeon does not work alone. From the moment you walk into the operating room, there is an anesthesiologist, a scrub tech, a scrub nurse, and a number of other supportive personnel. They're all there to help make the surgery go smoothly. It is the team's effort that makes a difference in the outcome.

Combining softball with medicine has certainly been a challenge. I plan my athletics around my hospital responsibilities, because in order to play, I need to make sure my doctor's schedule is clear.

My two careers have often conflicted and battled for my attention, causing a lot of tough times and a lot of heartaches. There have been many victories, but also some serious sacrifices as I worked to find the right balance between medical school and softball.

My first major defeat came when I was in my second year of medical school in 1990. At the year's end, I took the boards that would allow me to go on to the next year of school. Throughout that year, I had done what was required at school but in the upcoming months before the exam my focus was on the excitement of making the USA World Championship team. I had thought it would be my third and last World Championship. I would go to the batting cage and fine tune my swing, work on ground balls, and tirelessly strengthen my throwing arm.

The board exam was scheduled a couple of weeks after our academic year was completed. I crammed for the exam, but made sure my softball practice time didn't suffer. I left for the Olympic Training Center after I finished taking the two-day examination. At the end of the tryout, I was named to the USA World Championship team! It worked out perfectly because the World Championships were the last week of my vacation month. I took the examination seriously—with two years of medical school behind me I

thought I had prepared enough. But I was wrong.

A classmate and my best friend at medical school, Walter Montgomery, drove up to see me play at the World Championships held in Normal, Illinois—only a five hour drive from Louisville. He brought with him the results of my exam. I struggled to accept what he was telling me. "You've got to be kidding me, I failed the test?" I didn't comprehend failure, especially in academics. Over and over again, I came up with the conclusion that I needed to put more effort into my studies. I needed to develop a stronger commitment than the one I was giving.

I felt I needed to devote myself more to my commitment of becoming a great doctor . . . My commitment and my understanding that my medical degree was going to get me a top-flight position as a resident had made me a success in the classroom. There was a real satisfaction in knowing that I was more than a successful athlete; I was also a successful student. ⊠

For more biographical information about Dot Richardson, visit the Master Student Hall of Fame on the *Becoming a Master Student Athlete* Web site at

masterstudent.college.hmco.com

4

Reading

Reading furnishes our mind only with materials of knowledge; it is thinking that makes what we read ours.

JOHN LOCKE

There would seem to be almost no limit to what people can and will misunderstand when they are not doing their utmost to get at a writer's meaning.

EZRA POUND

why
this chapter matters . . .

Higher education requires extensive reading that results in comprehension of facts, figures, and concepts.

what
is included . . .

Muscle Reading
How Muscle Reading works
Phase one: Before you read
Phase two: While you read
Phase three: After you read
Reading fast
When reading is tough
English as a second language
Reading on the road
Power Process: "Notice your pictures and let them go"
Master Student Profile: Jim Abbott

how
you can use this chapter . . .

Analyze what effective readers do and experiment with new techniques.
Increase your vocabulary and adjust your reading speed for different types of material.
Comprehend difficult texts with more ease.

as you read, ask yourself
what if . . .

I could finish my reading with time to spare and easily recall the key points?

Muscle Reading

Picture yourself sitting at a desk, a book in your hands. Your eyes are open, and it looks as if you're reading. You've just crossed two time zones while flying back to campus from a national competition. You're tired, still feeling out of synch with local time. Suddenly your head jerks up. You blink. You realize your eyes have been scanning the page for 10 minutes. You can't remember a single thing you've read.

Or picture this: You've had a hard day. You were up at 6 a.m. for practice. After a full day of classes, you finally get to your books at 8 p.m. You begin a reading assignment on something called "the equity method of accounting for common stock investments." "I am preparing for the future," you tell yourself as you plod through two paragraphs and begin the third.

Suddenly, everything in the room looks different. Your head is resting on your elbow, which is resting on the equity method of accounting. The clock reads 11:00 p.m. Say good-bye to three hours.

Sometimes the only difference between a sleeping pill and a textbook is that the textbook doesn't have a warning on the label about operating heavy machinery.

It's easy to fool yourself about reading. Just having an open book in your hand and moving your eyes across a page doesn't mean you are reading effectively.

Muscle Reading is a technique you can use to avoid mental minivacations and reduce the number of unscheduled naps during study time, even after a hard day. More than that, Muscle Reading is a way to decrease effort and struggle by increasing energy and skill.

This is not to say that Muscle Reading will make your education a breeze. Muscle Reading might even look like more work at first. Give it time. Once you learn this technique, you can actually spend less time on your reading and get more out of it.

There's a saying about corporation presidents—that they wear out the front of their chairs first. Approach your reading assignments like a chief executive. Get off the couch. Sit up straight at a desk or table, on the edge of your chair, with your feet flat on the floor. Effective reading is an active, energy-consuming, sit-on-the-edge-of-your-seat business. That's why this strategy is called Muscle Reading. ⬧

journal entry 10

Discovery/Intention Statement

Recall a time when you encountered problems with reading, such as words you didn't understand or paragraphs you paused to reread more than once. Sum up the experience and how you felt about it by completing the following statement.

I discovered that I . . .

_____

_____

_____

_____

_____

Now list three to five specific reading skills you want to gain from this chapter.

_____

_____

_____

_____

_____

_____

_____

_____

_____

_____

_____

How Muscle Reading works

Muscle Reading is a three-phase technique you can use to extract the ideas and information you want.

Phase one includes steps to take *before* you read. Phase two includes steps to take *while* you read. Phase three includes steps to take *after* you read. Each phase has three steps.

Phase one: Before you read
Step 1: Preview
Step 2: Outline
Step 3: Question

Phase two: While you read
Step 4: Read
Step 5: Underline
Step 6: Answer

Phase three: After you read
Step 7: Recite
Step 8: Review
Step 9: Review again

A nine-step reading strategy might seem cumbersome and unnecessary for a two-page reading assignment. It is. Use the steps appropriately. Choose which ones to apply as you read.

To assist your recall of Muscle Reading strategies, memorize three short sentences:

Pry Out Questions.
Root Up Answers.
Recite, Review, and Review again.

These three sentences correspond to the three phases of the Muscle Reading technique. Each sentence is an acrostic. The first letter of each word stands for one of the nine steps listed above.

Take a moment to invent images for each of those sentences. For *phase one*, visualize yourself prying out questions that you want answered based on a brief survey of the assignment. Make a mental picture of yourself scanning the material, spotting a question, and reaching into the text to pry it out. Hear yourself saying, "I've got it. Here's my question."

Then for *phase two*, get your muscles involved. Feel the tips of your fingers digging into the text as you root up the answers to your questions.

Finally, you enter *phase three*. Hear your voice reciting what you have learned. Listen to yourself making a speech or singing a song about the material as you review it.

To jog your memory, write the first letters of the Muscle Reading acrostic in a margin or at the top of your notes. Then check off the steps you intend to follow. Or write the Muscle Reading steps on 3x5 cards and then use them for bookmarks.

Muscle Reading could take a little time to learn. At first you might feel it's slowing you down. That's natural when you're gaining a new skill. Mastery comes with time and practice.

PHASE ONE
Before you read

Step 1 — Preview

Before you start reading, preview the entire assignment. Previewing sets the stage for incoming information by warming up a space in your mental storage area.

If you are starting a new book, look over the table of contents and flip through the text page by page. If you're going to read one chapter, flip through the pages of that chapter. Even if your assignment is merely a few pages in a book, you can benefit from a brief preview of the table of contents.

Keep the preview short. If the entire reading assignment will take less than an hour, your preview might take five minutes. Previewing is also a way to get yourself started when an assignment looks too big to handle. It is an easy way to step into the material.

Keep an eye out for summary statements. If the assignment is long or complex, read the summary first.

Read all chapter headings and subheadings. Like the headlines in a newspaper, these are usually printed in large, bold type. Often headings are brief summaries in themselves.

When previewing, seek out familiar concepts, facts, or ideas. These items can help increase comprehension by linking new information to previously learned material.

Look for ideas that spark your imagination or curiosity. Inspect drawings, diagrams, charts, tables, graphs, and photographs. Imagine what kinds of questions will show up on a test.

Previewing helps to clarify your purpose for reading. Ask yourself what you will do with this material and how it can relate to your goals.

Step 2 — Outline

Outlining helps you understand the structure of what you are about to read. If your textbook provides chapter outlines, spend some time studying them. When an outline is not provided, sketch a brief one in the margin of your book or at the beginning of your notes on a separate sheet of paper. Later, as you read and take notes, you can add to your outline.

Headings in the text can serve as major and minor entries in your outline. For example, the heading for this article is "Phase one: Before you read," and the subheadings list the three steps in this phase.

When you outline, feel free to rewrite headings so that they are more meaningful to you.

The amount of time you spend on this step will vary. For some assignments, a 10-second mental outline is all you might need. For other assignments (fiction and poetry, for example), you can skip this step altogether.

Step 3 — Question

Before you begin a careful reading, write down a list of questions, including any that resulted from your preview of the materials.

One useful technique is to turn chapter headings and subheadings into questions. For example, if a heading is "Transference and suggestion," you can ask yourself, "What are *transference* and *suggestion*? How does *transference* relate to *suggestion*?" Make up a quiz as if you were teaching this subject to your classmates.

If there are no headings, look for key sentences and turn these into questions. These sentences usually show up at the beginnings or ends of paragraphs and sections.

Have fun with this technique. Make the questions playful or creative. You don't need to answer every question that you ask. The purpose of making up questions is to get your brain involved in the assignment. Take your unanswered questions to class, where they can be springboards for class discussion.

READ

Demand your money's worth from your textbook. If you do not understand a concept, write specific questions about it. The more detailed your questions, the more powerful this technique becomes.

PHASE TWO

While you read

Step 4 Reflect
At last! You have previewed the assignment and formulated questions. Now you are ready to begin reading.

Before you dive into the first paragraph, take a few moments to reflect on what you already know about this subject. Do this even if you think you know nothing. This technique prepares your brain to accept the information that follows.

As you read, be conscious of where you are and what you are doing. Use the Power Process: "Be here now." When you notice your attention wandering, gently bring it back to the present moment.

One way to stay focused is to avoid marathon reading sessions. Most students find that shorter periods of reading distributed throughout the day and week can be more effective than long sessions.

You can also use the following three techniques to stay focused as you read.

First, form mental pictures. If you read that a voucher system can help control cash disbursements, picture a voucher handing out dollar bills.

Second, get a "feel" for the subject. For example, let's say you are reading about a microorganism, a paramecium, in your biology text. Imagine what it would feel like to run your finger around the long, cigar-shaped body of the organism. Imagine feeling the large fold of its gullet on one side and the tickle of the hairy little cilia as they wiggle in your hand.

Third, remember that a goal of your reading is to answer the questions you listed during phase one. After you've identified the key questions, predict how the author will answer them. Then read to find out if your predictions were accurate.

A final note: Reading takes energy, even if you do it sitting down. Sit up. Keep your spine straight. Avoid reading in bed, except for fun.

Step 5 Underline
The purpose of making marks in a text is to call out important concepts or information that you will need to review later. Underlining can save lots of time when you study for tests.

When you read with a pen or pencil in your hand, you also involve your kinesthetic senses of touch and motion. Being physical with your books can help build strong neural pathways in your memory.

Avoid underlining too soon. Wait until you read a chapter or section to make sure you know the key points. Then mark up the text. Sometimes, underlining after you read each paragraph works well.

Underline sparingly, usually less than 10 percent of the text. If you mark up too much on a page, you defeat the purpose—to flag the most important material for review.

UNDERLINE   **ANSWER**

In addition to underlining, you can mark up a text in the following ways:

- Write a "Q" in the margin to highlight possible test questions, passages you don't understand, and questions to ask in class.

- Write personal comments in the margin—points of agreement or disagreement with the author.

- Write mini-indexes in the margin—numbers of other pages in the book where the same topic is discussed.

- Write summaries by listing the main points or key events covered in a chapter.

- Draw diagrams, pictures, tables, or maps that translate text into visual terms.

- Number each step in a list or series of related points.

for every clue, sitting erect in your straight-back chair, demanding that your textbook give you what you want—the answers.

PHASE THREE
After you read

Step 7 **Recite** Talk about what you've read. When you recite, you practice an important aspect of metacognition—synthesis, or combining individual ideas and facts into a meaningful whole.

Step 6 **Answer** As you read, seek out the answers to your questions and write them down. Fill in your outline. Jot down new questions and note when you don't find the answers you are looking for. Use these notes to ask questions in class, or see your instructor personally.

When you read, create an image of yourself as a person in search of the answers. You are a detective, watching

RECITE

REVIEW

NOT ONCE

REVIEW

One way to get yourself to recite is to look at each underlined point. Note what you marked, then put the book down and start talking out loud. Explain as much as you can about that particular point.

To make this technique more effective, do it in front of a mirror. It might seem silly, but the benefits can be enormous. Reap them at exam time.

Classmates are even better than mirrors. Form a group and practice teaching each other what you have read. One of the best ways to learn anything is to teach it to someone else.

Talking about your reading reinforces a valuable skill—the ability to summarize. To practice this skill, pick one chapter (or one section of one chapter) from any of your textbooks. State the main topic covered in this chapter. Then state the main points that the author makes about this topic.

For example, the main topic up to this point in this chapter is Muscle Reading. The main point about this topic is that Muscle Reading includes three phases—steps to take before you read, while you read, and after you read. For a more detailed summary, you could name each of the nine steps.

Note: This "topic-point" method does not work so well when you want to summarize short stories, novels, plays, and other works of fiction. Instead, focus on action. In most stories, the main character confronts a major problem and takes a series of actions to solve it. Describe that problem and talk about the character's key actions—the turning points in the story.

Step 8 **Review** Plan to do your first complete review within 24 hours of reading the material. This moves information from your short-term memory to your long-term memory. If you read it on Wednesday, review it on Thursday. During this review, look over your notes and clear up anything you don't understand. Recite some of the main points again.

This review can be short. You might spend as little as 15 minutes reviewing a difficult two-hour reading assignment. Investing that time now can save you hours later when studying for exams.

Step 9 **Review again** The final step in Muscle Reading is the weekly or monthly review. This step can be very short—perhaps only four or five minutes per assignment. Simply go over your notes. Read the highlighted parts of your text. Recite one or two of the more complicated points.

You can accomplish these short reviews anytime, anywhere, if you are prepared. Conduct a five-minute review while you are waiting for a bus, for your socks to dry, or for the water to boil. Three-by-five cards are a handy review tool. Write ideas, formulas, concepts, and facts on cards and carry them with you.

Sometimes longer review periods are appropriate. For example, if you found an assignment difficult, consider rereading it. Start over, as if you had never seen the material before. Sometimes a second reading will provide you with surprising insights. ✖

voices

student

I always pictured the master student with Scotch-taped glasses, an array of pens in the shirt pocket, and with a copy of the latest Popular Mechanics *or the* Wall Street Journal *under his arm. Equipped with a sky-high IQ and supportive parents, he would be bound to find his way into the NASA space program or the Supreme Court . . .. Where do we find this inspired, determined, and persistent student? We do not have to look too far. Every single student has the potential to become a master in his or her quest. Feel free to join us on a trip worthwhile. You don't even have to wear Scotch-taped glasses.*

—MALTE STRAUSS

One way to read faster is to read faster. This might sound like double talk, but it is a serious suggestion. The fact is, you can probably read faster—without any loss in comprehension—simply by making a conscious effort to do so. Your comprehension might even improve.

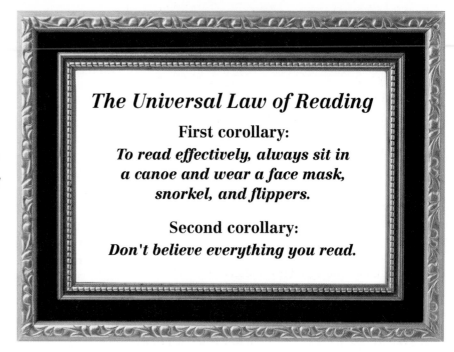

The Universal Law of Reading

First corollary:
To read effectively, always sit in a canoe and wear a face mask, snorkel, and flippers.

Second corollary:
Don't believe everything you read.

Reading fast

Experiment with the "just do it" method right now. Read the rest of this article as fast as you can. After you finish, come back and reread the same paragraphs at your usual rate. Note how much you remember from your first sprint through the text. You might be surprised to find out how well you comprehend material even at dramatically increased speeds. Build on that success by experimenting with the following guidelines.

Set a time limit. When you read, use a clock or a digital watch with a built-in stopwatch to time yourself. You are not aiming to set speed records, so be realistic. For example, set a goal to read two or three sections of a chapter in an hour, using all of the Muscle Reading steps. If that works, set a goal of 50 minutes for reading the same number of sections. Test your limits. The idea is to give yourself a gentle push, increasing your reading speed without sacrificing comprehension.

Relax. It's not only possible to read fast when you're relaxed, it's easier. Relaxation promotes concentration.

The idea is to give yourself a gentle push, increasing your reading speed without sacrificing comprehension.

And remember, relaxation is not the same as sleep. You can be relaxed *and* alert at the same time.

Move your eyes faster. When we read, our eyes leap across the page in short bursts called *saccades* (pronounced *saˇ- käds´*). A saccade is also a sharp jerk on the reins of a horse—a violent pull to stop the animal quickly. Our eyes stop like that, too, in pauses called *fixations.*

Although we experience the illusion of continuously scanning each line, our eyes actually take in groups of words, usually about three at a time. For more than 90 percent of reading time, our eyes are at a dead stop, in those fixations.

One way to decrease saccades is to follow your finger as you read. The faster your finger moves, the faster your eyes move. You can also use a pen, pencil, or 3x5 card as a guide.

Your eyes can move faster if they take in more words with each burst—for example, six instead of three. To practice taking in more words between fixations, find a newspaper with narrow columns. Then read down one column at a time and fixate only once per line.

In addition to using the above techniques, simply make a conscious effort to fixate less. You might feel a little uncomfortable at first. That's normal. Just practice often, for short periods of time.

Notice and release ineffective habits. Our eyes make regressions; that is, they back up and reread words. You can reduce regressions by paying attention to them. Use the handy 3x5 card to cover words and lines that you have just read. You can then note how often you stop and move the card back to reread the text. Don't be discouraged if you stop often at first. Being aware of it helps you regress less frequently.

Also notice vocalizing. You are more likely to read faster if you don't read out loud or move your lips. You can also increase your speed if you don't subvocalize— that is, if you don't mentally "hear" the words as you read them. To stop doing it, just be aware of it.

Another habit to release is reading letter by letter. When we first learn to read, we do it one letter at a time. By now you have memorized many words by their shape, so you don't have to focus on the letters at all. Read this example: "Rasrhcers at Cbmrigae Uivnretisy funod taht eprxert raeedrs dno't eevn look at the lteters." You get the point. Skilled readers recognize many words and phrases in this way, taking them in at a single glance.

When you first attempt to release these habits, choose simpler books and articles. Gradually work your way up to more complex material.

If you're pressed for time, skim. When you're in a hurry, experiment by skimming the assignment instead of reading the whole thing. Read the headings, subheadings, lists, charts, graphs, and summary paragraphs.

Stay flexible. Remember that speed isn't everything. Skillful readers vary their reading rate according to their purpose and the nature of the material. An advanced text in analytic geometry usually calls for a different reading rate than the Sunday comics.

You also can use different reading rates on the same material. For example, you might first sprint through an assignment for the key words and ideas, then return to the difficult parts for a slower and more thorough reading.

Explore more resources. You can find many books about speed-reading. For more possibilities, including courses and workshops, go to your favorite search engine on the Internet and key in the term *speed-reading*.

In your research, you might discover people who offer to take you beyond speed-reading. According to some teachers, you can learn to flip through a book and "mentally photograph" each page—hundreds or even thousands of words at once.

You might find these ideas controversial. Approach them in the spirit of the Power Process: "Ideas are tools." Before you lay out any money, check the instructor's credentials and talk to people who've taken the course. Also find out whether the instructor offers free "sampler sessions" and whether you can cancel at some point in the course for a full refund.

Finally, remember the first rule of reading fast: Just do it! ◪

exercise 13

RELAX

Eye strain can be a result of continuous stress. Take a break from your reading and use this exercise to release tension.

1. Sit on a chair or lie down and take a few moments to breathe deeply.

2. Close your eyes, place your palms over your eyes, and visualize a perfect field of black.

3. Continue to be aware of the blackness for two or three minutes while you breathe deeply.

4. Now remove your hands from your eyes and open your eyes slowly.

5. Relax for a minute more, then continue reading.

When reading is tough

Sometimes ordinary reading methods are not enough. Many students get bogged down in a murky reading assignment. If you are ever up to your neck in textbook alligators, you can use the following techniques to drain the swamp.

Read it again. Difficult material—such as the technical writing in science texts—is often easier the second time around. If you read an assignment and are completely lost, do not despair. Admit your confusion. Sleep on it. When you return to the assignment, regard it with fresh eyes.

Look for essential words. If you are stuck on a paragraph, mentally cross out all of the adjectives and adverbs and read the sentence without them. Find the important words. These will usually be verbs and nouns.

Read with a dictionary in your lap. Students regularly use two kinds of dictionaries: a desk dictionary and an unabridged dictionary. A desk dictionary is an easy-to-handle abridged dictionary. Keep this book within easy reach (maybe in your lap). Look up unfamiliar words while reading. You can find a large, unabridged dictionary in a library or bookstore. It provides more complete information about words and definitions not included in your desk dictionary, as well as synonyms, usage notes, and word histories. Both kinds of dictionaries are available for personal computers.

When you come across an unfamiliar word, write it down on a 3x5 card. Look up each word immediately, or accumulate a stack of these cards and look up the words later. Write the definition of each word on the back of the 3x5 card. You can also create a file of new words and definitions on a computer.

Read it out loud. Make noise. Read a passage out loud several times, each time using a different inflection and emphasizing a different part of the sentence. Be creative. Imagine that you are the author talking.

Talk to your instructor. Admit when you are stuck and make an appointment with your instructor. Most teachers welcome the opportunity to work individually with students. Be specific about your confusion. Point out the paragraph that you found toughest to understand.

Stand up. Changing positions periodically can combat fatigue. Experiment with standing as you read, especially if you get stuck on a tough passage and decide to read it out loud.

Skip around. Jump immediately to the end of the article or chapter. You might have lost the big picture, and sometimes simply seeing the conclusion or summary is all you need to put the details in context. Retrace the steps in a chain of ideas and look for examples. Absorb facts and ideas in whatever order works for you—which may be different from the author's presentation.

Find a tutor. Many schools provide free tutoring services. If tutoring services are not provided by your school, other students who have completed the course can assist you.

Use another text. Find a similar text in the library. Sometimes a concept is easier to understand if it is expressed another way. Children's books, especially children's encyclopedias, can provide useful overviews of baffling subjects.

Pretend you understand, then explain it. We often understand more than we think we do. Pretend that the material is clear as a bell and explain it to another person, or even yourself. Write down your explanation. You might be amazed by what you know.

Ask: "What's going on here?" When you feel stuck, stop reading for a moment and diagnose what's happening. At these stop points, mark your place in the margin of the page with a penciled "S" for "Stuck." A pattern to your marks over several pages might indicate a question you want to answer before going further. Or you might discover a reading habit you'd like to change.

Stop reading. When none of the above suggestions work, do not despair. Admit your confusion and then take a break. Catch a movie, go for a walk, study another subject, or sleep on it. The concepts you've already absorbed might come together at a subconscious level as you move on to other activities. Allow some time for that process. When you return to the reading material, see it with fresh eyes. ▨

voices

journal entry 11

Discovery Statement

Now that you've read about Muscle Reading, review your assessment of your reading skills in the Discovery Wheel on page 22. Do you still think your evaluation was accurate? What new insights do you have about the way you read? Are you a more effective reader than you thought you were? Less effective? Record your observations below.

_____

_____

_____

_____

_____

_____

_____

_____

_____

_____

_____

_____

_____

_____

_____

_____

_____

_____

_____

_____

_____

_____

_____

_____

_____

English as a second language

If you grew up speaking a language other than English, you're probably called a student of English as a Second Language (ESL). This term might not do full justice to your experience. Your cultural background as a whole might differ greatly from many of your fellow students. You might also speak *several* languages in addition to English.

Knowing a language other than English offers advantages. You can think thoughts that are not possible in English and see the world in ways that are unique to people who speak your native language.

If you are having difficulties mastering English, experiment with the following suggestions to learn with more success.

Celebrate mistakes

English is a complex language. Whenever you extend your vocabulary and range of expression, the likelihood of making mistakes increases. The person who wants to master English yet seldom makes mistakes is probably being too careful. Do not look upon mistakes as a sign of weakness. Mistakes can be your best teachers—if you are willing to learn from them.

Analyze mistakes

To learn from your mistakes, first make a list of them. Ask an instructor or an English-speaking friend to help you.

Analyze the list and note your most common errors in English vocabulary, grammar, and usage. Write down several examples of these mistakes. For each example, write a corresponding sentence in your native language. Then write the examples correctly in English. Comparing the sets of examples will help you understand how the languages differ and can help you discover the source of your errors.

Learn by speaking and listening

You probably started your English studies by using textbooks. Writing and reading in English are important. To gain greater fluency, also make it your goal to hear and speak English.

For example, listen to radio talk shows. Imitate the speaker's pronunciation by repeating phrases and sentences that you hear. During conversations, also notice the facial expressions and gestures that accompany certain English words and phrases.

If you speak English with an accent, do not be concerned. Many people speak clear, accented English. Work on your accent only if you can't be easily understood.

When in doubt, use expressions you understand

Native speakers of English use many informal expressions that are called *slang*. You are more likely to find slang in conversations than in written English.

Native speakers also use *idioms*—colorful expressions with meanings that are not always obvious. Idioms can often be misunderstood. For instance, a "fork in the road" does not refer to an eating utensil discarded on a street.

Learning how to use slang and idioms is part of gaining fluency in English. However, these elements of the language are tricky. If you mispronounce a key word or leave one out, you can create a misunderstanding. In important situations—such as applying for a job or meeting with a teacher—use expressions you fully understand.

Create a community of English learners

Learning as part of a community can increase your mastery. For example, when completing a writing assignment in English, get together with other people who are learning the language. Read each other's papers and suggest revisions. Plan on revising your paper a number of times based on feedback from your peers.

You might feel awkward about sharing your writing with other people. Accept that feeling—and then remind yourself of everything you have to gain by learning from a group. In addition to learning English more quickly, you can raise your grades and make new friends.

Native speakers of English might be willing to assist your group. Ask your instructors to suggest someone. This person can benefit from the exchange of ideas and the chance to learn about other cultures.

Celebrate your gains

Every time you analyze and correct an error in English, you make a small gain. Celebrate those gains. Taken together over time, they add up to major progress in mastering English as a second language. ⧖

Reading
on the road

Student athletes at the college level can spend a lot of time traveling to and from competitions. Use this time to get some reading done. You might even find that staying on top of your assignments while you're on the road reduces your precompetition stress. Remember that your classmates are not on break while you're on the road. Neither are you.

Estimate reading time

To begin, estimate the hours you will have available for reading on the road. Take into account the number of days you will travel. Also determine when you can study between meals, sleep, practices, and competitions. Your coach might schedule quiet time for study while you are at a hotel.

Also consider how you will travel. A coach bus or airplane with air conditioning, overhead lighting, and comfortable seats lends itself to quality reading time. If you're squeezing into a 15-passenger van or small commuter plane instead, then reduce your reading estimate accordingly.

Weather changes and equipment breakdowns can significantly increase your time on the road. In turn, this can decrease the time you have to complete assignments once you return to campus.

On the other hand, you can take advantage of delays or sudden cancellations. They offer opportunities to make extra progress on a reading assignment.

When estimating your reading time for road trips, be fair to yourself. It's easy to overestimate. At the same time, don't underestimate what you can accomplish. Budgeting your reading time is a skill that improves with practice.

Plan your reading

Once you estimate *how much* time you have, you can efficiently choose *what* to read while you're on the road.

Start with a current and complete list of your assignments. Be specific, for instance: "Pages 23–67 of *Business Ethics*," "Section 16 of *Keys for Writers*." If you're assigned exercises or review questions related to your reading, then list those items also.

Before you pack, rank the items on your reading list by ABC priority.

On your A list, include assignments that you're confident you can complete on the road. Examples might include shorter pieces—articles, handouts, and printouts of PowerPoint presentations. Other possible A's are textbooks divided into short sections with bold headings and summaries. Also consider bringing along copies of class notes that you can summarize and review.

B-priority items call for longer sessions of focused attention. Short stories from an English class and longer, denser textbooks could fall on this list. Consider taking one of these assignments along to tackle if you finish your A's.

The items on your C-priority list will probably be most challenging and least useful on the road. Examples might be long, complex novels and technical texts in science and math.

Keep in mind that the word *reading* can include a variety of tasks—any of the nine steps of Muscle Reading, in fact. While sitting in a bus, plane, train, or van, you can: preview a long assignment and list questions to answer later after a more detailed reading; outline or underline a chapter you've already read; create flash cards or Q-Cards (see page 96) and quiz yourself with them; or talk to teammates about what you're reading or form a study group.

Some reading assignments may be so challenging that you simply choose not to take them on the road. That's fine. Just schedule time for this reading when your trip is done.

Also be aware of the times when you can be most effective by focusing on the upcoming competition—not macroeconomic theory or math problems.

Seize the moment

Pack reading assignments that you can pick up during spare minutes. Sandwich these tasks into your travel schedule as study time becomes available. Whenever possible, tote along an extra small textbook or paperback novel. Be prepared to shift gears and grab these materials whenever unexpected reading opportunities come your way. ◪

PRACTICING CRITICAL THINKING

4

Read an editorial in a newspaper or magazine. Analyze this editorial by taking notes in the three-column format below. Use the first column for listing major points, the second for supporting points, and the third for key facts or statistics that support the major or minor points. For example:

Major point

The "female condom" has not yet been proved effective as a method of birth control.

Supporting point

Few studies exist on this method.

Key fact

One of the few studies showed a 26 percent failure rate for the female condom.

Major point	Supporting point	Key fact

Ask another student to do this exercise with you. Then compare and discuss your notes. See if you identified the same main points.

power process

Notice your pictures
and let them go

One of the brain's primary jobs is to manufacture images. We use mental pictures to make predictions about the world, and we base much of our behavior on those predictions.

When a cook adds chopped onions, mushrooms, and garlic to a spaghetti sauce, he has a picture of how the sauce will taste and measures each ingredient according to that picture. When an artist is creating a painting or sculpture, he has a mental picture of the finished piece. Novelists often have mental images of the characters that they're about to bring to life. Many parents have a picture about what they want their children to become.

These kinds of pictures and many more have a profound influence on us. Our pictures direct our thinking, our conversations, and our actions—all of which help create our immediate circumstances. That's amazing, considering that we often operate with little, if any, conscious knowledge of our pictures.

Just about any time we feel a need, we conjure up a picture of what will satisfy that need. A baby feels hunger pangs and starts to cry. Within seconds, his mother appears and he is satisfied. The baby stores a mental picture of his mother feeding him. He connects that picture with stopping the hunger pangs. Voilà! Now he knows how to solve the hunger problem. The picture goes on file.

According to psychologist William Glasser, our minds function like a huge photo album.[1] Its pages include pictures of all the ways we've satisfied needs in the past. Whenever we feel dissatisfied, we mentally search the album for a picture of how to make the dissatisfaction

go away. With that picture firmly in mind, we act in ways to make the world outside our heads match the pictures inside.

Remember that pictures are not strictly visual images. They can involve any of the senses. When you buy a CD, you have a picture of how it will sound. When you buy a sweater, you have a picture of how it will feel.

A problem with pictures

The pictures we make in our heads are survival mechanisms. Without them, we couldn't get from one end of town to the other. We couldn't feed or clothe ourselves. Without a picture of a socket, we couldn't screw in a light bulb.

Pictures can also get in our way. Take the case of a student who plans to attend a school he hasn't visited. He chose this school for its strong curriculum and good academic standing, but his brain didn't stop there. In his mind, the campus has historic buildings with ivy-covered walls and tree-lined avenues. The professors, he imagines, will be as articulate as Bill Moyers and as entertaining as Oprah Winfrey. His roommate will be his best friend. The cafeteria will be a cozy nook serving delicate quiche and fragrant teas. He will gather there with fellow students for hours of stimulating, intellectual conversation. The library will have every book, while the computer lab will boast the newest technology.

The school turns out to be four gray buildings downtown, next to the bus station. The first class he attends is taught by an overweight, balding professor, who is wearing a purple-and-orange bird of paradise tie and has a bad case of the sniffles. The cafeteria is a nondescript hall with machine-dispensed food, and the student's apartment is barely large enough to accommodate his roommate's tuba. This hypothetical student gets depressed. He begins to think about dropping out of school.

The problem with pictures is that they can prevent us from seeing what is really there. That happened to the student in this story. His pictures prevented him from noticing that his school is in the heart of a culturally vital city—close to theaters, museums, government offices, clubs, and all kinds of stores. The professor with the weird tie is not only an expert in his field but is also a superior teacher. The school cafeteria is skimpy because it can't compete with the variety of inexpensive restaurants in the area. There might even be hope for a tuba-playing roommate.

Anger and disappointment are often the results of our pictures. We set up expectations of events before they occur, which can lead to disappointment. Sometimes we don't even realize that we have these expectations. The next time you discover you are angry, disappointed, or frustrated, look to see which of your pictures aren't being fulfilled.

Take charge of your pictures

Having pictures is unavoidable. Letting these pictures control our lives *is* avoidable. Some techniques for dealing with pictures are so simple and effortless, they might seem silly.

One way to deal with pictures is to be aware of them. Open up your mental photo album and notice how the pictures there influence your thoughts, feelings, and actions. Just becoming aware of your pictures—and how they affect you—can help you take a huge step toward dealing with them effectively.

When you notice that pictures are getting in your way, then, in the most gentle manner possible, let your pictures go. Let them drift away like wisps of smoke

Our pictures direct our thinking, our conversations, and our actions—all of which help create our immediate circumstances.

picked up by a gentle wind.

Pictures are persistent. They come back over and over. Notice them again and let them go again. At first, a picture might return repeatedly and insistently. Pictures are like independent beings. They want to live. If you can see the picture as a thought independent from you, you will likely find it easier to let it go.

You are more than your pictures. Many images and words will pop into your head in the course of a lifetime. You do not have to identify with these pictures. You can let pictures go without giving up yourself.

If your pictures are interfering with your education, visualize them scurrying around inside your head. See yourself tying them to a brightly colored helium balloon and letting them go. Let them float away again and again.

Sometimes we can let go of old pictures and replace them with new ones. We stored all of those pictures in the first place. We can replace them. Our student's new picture of a great education can include the skimpy cafeteria, the professor with the weird tie, and the roommate with the tuba.

We can take charge of the images that float through our minds. We don't have to be ruled by an album of outdated pictures. We can stay aware of our pictures and keep looking for new ones. And when *those* new pictures no longer serve us, we can also let them go. ◪

put it to work

In the year 2000, researchers from the University of California, Berkeley, estimated that the world produces between one and two exabytes of information each year.[2] To put this figure in perspective, consider that one exabyte equals 250 megabytes for each individual on earth. (The complete works of Shakespeare would take up only five megabytes of space on your computer's hard drive.)

Much of your personal 250 megabytes might come in the form of work-related reading: technical manuals, sales manuals, policies and procedures, memos, e-mail, Web pages, newsletters, invoices, application forms, meeting minutes, brochures, annual reports, job descriptions, and more.

The techniques of Muscle Reading will help you plow through all that material and extract what you want to know. Also keep the following suggestions in mind.

Read with a purpose. At work, you're probably reading in order to produce an outcome. Determine your purpose in reading each document and extract only what you need to effect that outcome.

Print out online documents to read later. Research indicates that people can read faster on paper than on the computer screen.[3] Be kind to your eyes. Print out long attachments and e-mails and read them afterwards.

Make several passes through reading material. You don't have to "get it all" the first time you read a document. Make your first pass a quick preview. Then go for a second pass, reading the first sentence of each paragraph or the first and last paragraphs in each section. If you want more detail, then make a third pass, reading the material paragraph by paragraph, sentence by sentence.

Read only the relevant sections of documents. Don't feel obligated to read every document completely. Many business documents include executive summaries. Look for them. Everything you want to know might be there, all in a page or two.

Schedule regular reading time at work. Read during times of the day when your energy peaks.

Discuss what you read with coworkers. Make time for one-on-one, face-to-face conversations. Talking about what you read is a powerful way to transform data into insight.

Create "read anytime" files. Much of the papers and online documents that cross your desk will probably consist of basic background material—items that are important to read but not urgent. Place these documents in a folder and save them for a Friday afternoon or a plane trip. ⊠

Name _____ Date _____/_____/_____

quiz

1. Name the acrostic that can help you remember the steps of Muscle Reading.

2. You must complete all nine steps of Muscle Reading to get the most out of any reading assignment. True or False? Explain your answer.

3. Describe at least three strategies you can use to preview a reading assignment.

4. What is one benefit of outlining a reading assignment?

5. Describe a strategy for learning new words.

6. To get the most benefit from marking a book, underline at least 25 percent of the text. True or False? Explain your answer.

7. Explain at least three techniques you can use when reading is tough.

8. According to the Power Process in this chapter, mental pictures are strictly visual images. True or False? Explain your answer.

9. Define the "topic-point" method of summarizing.

10. List at least three techniques for increasing your reading speed.

learning styles application

The questions below will "cycle" you through four styles, or modes, of learning as explained in the article "Learning styles: Discovering how you learn" in Chapter One. Each question will help you explore a different mode. You can answer the questions in any order.

what if *Consider how you might adapt or modify Muscle Reading to make it more useful. List any steps that you would add, subtract, or change.*

why *List current reading assignments that you could use to practice Muscle Reading.*

how *Briefly describe how you will approach reading assignments differently after studying this chapter.*

what *List the three most useful suggestions for reading that you gained from this chapter.*

master student profile

JIM ABBOTT

(1967–   ) After winning numerous awards as an athlete in high school and college, pitched the gold-medal victory game in the 1988 Seoul Olympics as a member of the U.S. National Team. In spite of being being born without a right hand, enjoyed a 10-year professional career, which included a no-hitter in 1993.

One looks for turning points. How is it that he has come this far, this way? Maybe it was the time when Jim Abbott was five years old and came home from school, angry and tearful, and held up the steel hook a doctor had recommended he use for a right hand. "I don't want to wear this anymore," he told his parents. Other children were afraid to play with him and, in the way that small children can be cruel, called him names like "Mr. Hook." Even then he struggled not to appear different. He never wore the hook again.

Or maybe it was when his father, in a park in Flint, Michigan, taught him to throw a baseball and then remove the glove ever so smoothly and swiftly from his right wrist and place it on his left throwing hand in order to catch his dad's quick throw back, and then switch the glove back again in order to throw. He developed the technique so skillfully that when he was pitching in high school, the story goes, the first nine batters on an opposing team tried to bunt for hits. He threw the runners out each time.

Maybe it was simply the concept that his parents, Mike and Kathy Abbott, had come to live by, that Jim, except for the strange fate of having been born with one hand—there is a stub with one small, fingerlike protrusion where the right hand would be—was as normal as any other kid, and should think of himself that way.

"I just don't think that all of this about me playing with one hand is as big an issue as everyone wants to make it," said Abbott. "I don't try to run from the attention about it, I just accept it."

"I don't really believe in this stuff about ballplayers as role models. But if I can be of help to anyone, if anyone can take something from the fact that I'm a baseball pitcher, then fine. But when I'm out on the mound pitching, I'm pitching because I love it, because I like the challenge of trying to get people out. I'm not pitching because I want to prove anything to anyone."

"There was this one boy, about seven years old, who came into the clubhouse with his parents," Abbott recalled. "He had only parts of two fingers on one hand. He asked me if kids were mean when I was growing up. He said they called him 'crab' at camp. I said, 'Yeah, they used to say that my hand looks like a foot.' I said to him, 'Do you think that teasing is a problem?' He said, 'No.' I said to him, 'Is there anything you can't do?' And he said, 'No.' And I said, 'Well, I don't think so either.'

"Then I looked around the room and said to him, 'Look, I'm playing with guys like Dave Winfield and Wally Joyner and Dave Parker. I'm playing with them and I'm just like you.' I'd never said that before, that I was thrilled to be here and it didn't matter if I had two good hands. But I put myself into his shoes and remembered what I was like at his age. And I'm sure that kids need someone to relate to. But so do their parents. Most of the time I think it's my parents these people should be talking to, not me."

From *The Minority Quarterback and Other Lives in Sports* by Ira Berkow; Ivan R. Dee ©2002. Reprinted by permission of Ivan R. Dee, publisher.

For more biographical information about Jim Abbott, visit the Master Student Hall of Fame on the *Becoming a Master Student Athlete* Web site at

masterstudent.college.hmco.com

5

Notes

Rather than try to gauge your note-taking skill by quantity, think in this way: am I simply doing clerk's work or am I assimilating new knowledge and putting down my own thoughts? To put down your own thoughts you must put down your own words . . . . If the note taken shows signs of having passed through a mind, it is a good test of its relevance and adequacy.

JACQUES BARZUN AND HENRY GRAFF

why
this chapter matters . . .

Effective note taking helps you remember information, acquire new skills, and perform better on tests.

what
is included . . .

The note-taking process flows
Observe
Record
Review
The instructor gameplan
Taking notes while reading
Power Process: "I create it all"
Master Student Profile: Billie Jean King

how
you can use this chapter . . .

Experiment with several formats for note taking.
Create a note-taking format that works especially well for you.
Take effective notes in special situations—while reading, in meetings, and when instructors talk fast.

as you read, ask yourself
what if . . .

I could take notes that remain informative and useful for weeks, months, or even years to come?

The note-taking process flows

One way to understand note taking is to realize that taking notes is just one part of the process. Effective note taking consists of three parts: observing, recording, and reviewing. First, you observe an "event"—a statement by an instructor, a lab experiment, a slide show of an artist's works, or a chapter of required reading. Then you record your observations of that event—that is, you "take notes." Finally, you review what you have recorded.

Each part of the process is essential, and each depends on the others. Your observations determine what you record. What you record determines what you review. And the quality of your review determines how effective your next observations will be.

For example, consider how you learn during practice. You observe a model—someone who demonstrates a strategy that you can use to succeed in competition. You record your observations, mentally or in writing. And you review by acting on your observations—applying the strategy yourself and reflecting further on how to use it more effectively. Each step relies on the previous one, and the observe-record-review cycle repeats continuously.

Legible and speedy handwriting is useful in taking notes. A knowledge of outlining is handy, too. A nifty pen, a new notebook, and a laptop computer are all great note-taking devices. And they're all worthless—unless you participate as an energetic observer *in* class and regularly review your notes *after* class. If you take those steps, you can turn even the most disorganized chicken scratches into a powerful tool.

Sometimes note taking looks like a passive affair, especially in large lecture classes. One person at the front of the room does most of the talking. Everyone else is seated and silent, taking notes. The lecturer seems to be doing all of the work.

Don't be deceived. Observe more closely, and you'll see some students taking notes in a way that radiates energy. They're awake and alert, poised on the edge of their seats. They're writing, a physical activity that expresses mental engagement. These students listen for levels of ideas and information, make choices about what to record, and compile materials to review.

In higher education, you might spend hundreds of hours taking notes. Making them more effective is a direct investment in your success. Think of your notes as a textbook that *you* create—one that's more current and more in tune with your learning preferences than any textbook you could buy. ▨

journal entry 12

Discovery/Intention Statement

Think about the possible benefits of improving your skills at note taking. Recall a recent incident in which you had difficulty taking notes. Perhaps you were listening to an instructor who talked fast, or you got confused and stopped taking notes altogether. Describe the incident in the space below.

_____

_____

_____

_____

_____

Now preview this chapter to find at least five strategies that you can use right away to help you take better notes. Sum up each of those strategies in a few words and note page numbers where you can find out more about each suggestion.

Strategy   *Page number*

_____

_____

_____

_____

_____

Reflect on your intention to experiment actively with this chapter. Describe a specific situation in which you might apply the strategies you listed above. If possible, choose a situation that will occur within the next 24 hours.

I intend to . . .

_____

_____

_____

_____

OBSERVE

The note-taking process flows

Sherlock Holmes, a fictional master detective and student of the obvious, could track down a villain by observing the fold of his scarf and the mud on his shoes. In real life, a doctor can save a life by observing a mole—one a patient has always had—that undergoes a rapid change.

An accountant can save a client thousands of dollars by observing the details of a spreadsheet. A student can save hours of study time by observing that she gets twice as much done at a particular time of day. And a good coach observes video clips of an upcoming opponent over and over, taking notes in preparation for competition.

Keen observers see facts and relationships. They know ways to focus their attention on the details, then tap their creative energy to discover patterns. To sharpen your classroom observation skills, experiment with the following techniques and continue to use those that you find most valuable.

Set the stage

Complete outside assignments. Nothing is more discouraging (or boring) than sitting through a lecture about the relationship of Le Chatelier's principle to the principle of kinetics if you've never heard of Henri Louis Le Chatelier or kinetics. Instructors usually assume that students complete assignments, and they construct their lectures accordingly. The more familiar you are with a subject, the more easily you can absorb important information during class lectures.

Bring the right materials. A good pen does not make you a good observer, but the lack of a pen or a notebook can be distracting enough to take the fine edge off your concentration. Make sure you have a pen, pencil, notebook, and any other materials you will need. Bring your textbook to class, especially if the lectures relate closely to the text.

If you are consistently unprepared for a class, that might be a message about your intentions concerning the course. Find out if it is. The next time you're in a frantic scramble to borrow pen and paper 37 seconds before the class begins, notice the cost. Use the borrowed pen and paper to write a Discovery Statement about your lack of preparation. Consider whether you intend to be successful in the course.

Sit front and center. Students who get as close as possible to the front and center of the classroom often do better on tests for several reasons. The closer you sit to the lecturer, the harder it is to fall asleep. The closer you sit to the front, the fewer interesting, or distracting, classmates are situated between you and the instructor. Material on the board is easier to read from up front. Also, the instructor can see you more easily when you have a question.

Instructors are usually not trained to perform. While some can project their energy to a large audience, others cannot. A professor who sounds boring from the back of the room might sound more interesting up close.

In addition, sound waves from the human voice begin to degrade at a distance of 8 to 12 feet. If you sit more than 15 feet from the speaker, your ability to hear and take effective notes might be compromised. Get close to the source of the sound. Get close to the energy.

Sitting close also helps you stay alert. After a night of post-competition travel you may want an incentive to give full attention during a lecture. Sitting in front is one solution.

Sitting close to the front is a way to commit yourself to getting what you want out of school. One reason students gravitate to the back of the classroom is that they think the instructor is less likely to call on them. Sitting in back can signal a lack of commitment. When you sit up front, you are declaring your willingness to take a risk and participate.

Conduct a short preclass review. Arrive early, then put your brain in gear by reviewing your notes from the previous class. Scan your reading assignment. Look at the sections you have underlined. Review assigned problems and exercises. Note questions you intend to ask.

Clarify your intentions. Take a 3x5 card to class with you. On that card, write a short Intention Statement about what you plan to get from the class. Describe your intended level of participation or the quality of attention you will bring to the subject. Be specific. If you found your previous class notes to be inadequate, write down what you intend to do to make your notes from this class session more useful.

"Be here now" in class

Accept your wandering mind. The techniques in the Power Process: "Be here now" can be especially useful when your head soars into the clouds. Don't fight day-dreaming. When you notice your mind wandering during class, look at this as an opportunity to refocus your attention. If thermodynamics is losing out to beach parties, let go of the beach.

Notice your writing. When you discover yourself slipping into a fantasyland, feel the weight of your pen in your hand. Notice how your notes look. Paying attention to the act of writing can bring you back to the here and now.

You also can use writing in a more direct way to clear your mind of distracting thoughts. Pause for a few seconds and write those thoughts down. If you're distracted by thoughts of errands you need to run after class, list them on a 3x5 card and stick it in your pocket. Or simply put a symbol, such as an arrow or asterisk, in your notes to mark the places where your mind started to wander. Once your distractions are out of your mind and safely stored on paper, you can gently return your attention to taking notes.

Be with the instructor. In your mind, put yourself right up front with the instructor. Imagine that you and the instructor are the only ones in the room and that the lecture is a personal conversation between the two of you. Pay attention to the instructor's body language and facial expressions. Look the instructor in the eye.

Notice your environment. When you become aware of yourself daydreaming, bring yourself back to class by paying attention to the temperature in the room, the feel of your chair, or the quality of light coming through the window. Run your hand along the surface of your desk. Listen to the chalk on the blackboard or the sound of the teacher's voice. Be in that environment. Once your attention is back in the room, you can focus on what's happening in class.

Postpone debate. When you hear something you disagree with, note your disagreement and let it go. Don't allow your internal dialogue to drown out subsequent material. If your disagreement is persistent and strong, make note of this and then move on. Internal debate can prevent you from absorbing new information. It is OK to absorb information you don't agree with. Just absorb it with the mental tag "My instructor says . . ., and I don't agree with this."

Let go of judgments about lecture styles. Don't let your attitude about an instructor's lecture style, habits, or appearance get in the way of your education. You can decrease the power of your judgments if you pay attention to them and let them go.

You can even let go of judgments about rambling, unorganized lectures. Turn them to your advantage. Take the initiative and organize the material yourself. While taking notes, separate the key points from the examples and supporting evidence. Note the places where you got confused and make a list of questions to ask.

Participate in class activities. Ask questions. Volunteer for demonstrations. Join in class discussions. Be willing to take a risk or look foolish, if that's what it takes for you to learn. Chances are, the question you think is "dumb" is also on the minds of several of your classmates. This is a another technique that can help you stay alert and focused, especially after hard practicing or late-night traveling.

Relate the class to your goals. If you have trouble staying awake in a particular class, write at the top of your notes how that class relates to a specific goal. Identify the reward or payoff for reaching that goal.

Think critically about what you hear. This might seem contrary to the previously mentioned technique "Postpone debate." It's not. It's fine not to think critically about the instructor's ideas during the lecture. You can do it later, as you review and edit your notes. This is a time to list questions or write down your agreements and disagreements.

Watch for clues

Be alert to repetition. When an instructor repeats a phrase or an idea, make a note of it. Repetition is a signal that the instructor thinks the information is important.

Listen for introductory, concluding, and transition words and phrases. These include phrases such as "the following three factors," "in conclusion," "the most important consideration," "in addition to," and "on the other hand." These phrases and others signal relationships, definitions, new subjects, conclusions, cause and effect, and examples. They reveal the structure of the lecture. You can use these phrases to organize your notes.

Watch the board or overhead projector. If an instructor takes the time to write something down, consider the material to be important. Copy all diagrams and drawings, equations, names, places, dates, statistics, and definitions.

Watch the instructor's eyes. If an instructor glances at her notes and then makes a point, it is probably a signal that the information is especially important. Anything she reads from her notes is a potential test question.

Highlight the obvious clues. Instructors will often tell students point-blank that certain information is likely to appear on an exam. Make stars or other special marks in your notes next to this information. Instructors are not trying to hide what's important.

Notice the instructor's interest level. If the instructor is excited about a topic, it is more likely to appear on an exam. Pay attention when she seems more animated than usual.

Get further help with note taking. After entering college, many students discover that they lack note-taking skills. Schools offer seminars on these skills, some geared to student athletes. Don't wait until you are behind in any class to get help with notes. You wouldn't wait until the second half of a tough competition to ask for coaching. It's the same with taking notes. Go on the offensive. Get the skills now. ⊠

journal entry 13

Discovery/Intention Statement

Think back on the last few lectures you have attended. How do you currently observe (listen to) lectures? How many of the suggestions from the article "Observe" do you already apply. Briefly describe specific behaviors in the space below.

I discovered that I . . .

_____

_____

_____

Now write an Intention Statement about any changes you want to make in the way you respond to lectures.

I intend to . . .

_____

_____

_____

What to do when you miss a class

For most courses, you'll benefit by attending every class session. If you miss a class, try to catch up as quickly as possible.

Clarify policies on missed classes. On the first day of classes, find out about your instructors' policies on absences. See if you can make up assignments, quizzes, and tests. Also inquire about doing extra-credit assignments.

Contact a classmate. Early in the semester, identify a student in each class who seems responsible and dependable. Exchange e-mail addresses and phone numbers. If you know you won't be in class, contact this student ahead of time. When you notice that your classmate is absent, pick up extra copies of handouts, make assignments lists, and offer copies of your notes.

Contact your instructor. If you miss a class, e-mail, phone, or fax your instructor, or put a note in her mailbox. Ask if she has another section of the same course that you could attend so you won't miss the lecture information. Also ask about getting handouts you might need before the next class meeting.

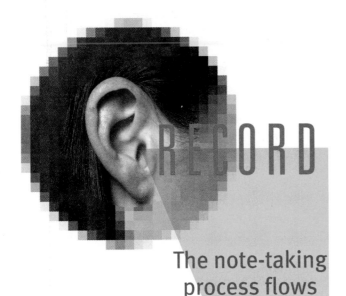

The note-taking process flows

The following techniques can improve the effectiveness of your notes. These techniques are based on a key idea: The format and structure of your notes are more important than the speed or elegance of your handwriting.

General techniques for note taking

Use key words. An easy way to sort the extraneous material from the important points is to take notes using key words. Key words or phrases contain the essence of communication. They include technical terms, names, numbers, equations, and words of degree: *most, least, faster,* etc. Key words evoke images and associations with other words and ideas. They trigger your memory. That makes them powerful review tools.

One key word can initiate the recall of a whole cluster of ideas. A few key words can form a chain from which you can reconstruct an entire lecture.

To see how key words work, take yourself to an imaginary classroom. You are now in the middle of an anatomy lecture. Picture what the room looks like, what it feels like, how it smells. You hear the instructor say:

OK, what happens when we look directly over our heads and see a piano falling out of the sky? How do we take that signal and translate it into the action of getting out of the way? The first thing that happens is that a stimulus is generated in the neurons— receptor neurons—of the eye. Light reflected from the piano reaches our eyes. In other words, we see the piano. The receptor neurons in the eye transmit

that sensory signal, the sight of the piano, to the body's nervous system. That's all they can do, pass on information. So we've got a sensory signal coming into the nervous system. But the neurons that initiate movement in our legs are effector neurons. The information from the sensory neurons must be transmitted to effector neurons or we will get squashed by the piano. There must be some kind of interconnection between receptor and effector neurons. What happens between the two? What is the connection?

Key words you might note in this example include *stimulus, generated, receptor neurons, transmit, sensory signals, nervous system, effector neurons,* and *connection.* You could reduce the instructor's 163 words to these 12 key words. With a few transitional words, your notes might look like this:

> Stimulus (piano) generated in receptor neurons (eye).
> Sensory signals transmitted by nervous system to effector neurons (legs).
> What connects receptor to effector?

Use pictures and diagrams. Make relationships visual. Copy all diagrams from the board and invent your own. A drawing of a piano falling on someone who is looking up, for example, might be used to demonstrate the relationship of receptor neurons to effector neurons. Label the eyes "receptor" and the feet "effector." This picture implies that the sight of the piano must be translated into a motor response.

Write notes in paragraphs. When it is difficult to follow the organization of a lecture or to put information into outline form, create a series of informal paragraphs. These paragraphs will contain few complete sentences. Reserve complete sentences for precise definitions, direct quotations, and important points that the instructor emphasizes by repetition or other signals— such as the phrase "This is an important point."

Copy material from the board. Record all formulas, diagrams, and problems that the teacher writes down. Copy dates, numbers, names, places, and other facts. If it's on the board, put it in your notes. You can even use your own signal or code to flag that material. If it appears on the board, it can appear on a test.

Use a three-ring binder. Three-ring binders have several advantages over other kinds of notebooks. First, pages can be removed and spread out when you review. This way, you can get the whole picture of a lecture. Second, the three-ring binder format allows you to insert handouts right into your notes. Third, you can insert your own out-of-class notes in the correct order. Fourth, you can easily make additions, corrections, and revisions.

Use only one side of a piece of paper. When you use one side of a page, you can review and organize all your notes by spreading them out side by side. Most students find the benefit well worth the cost of the paper.

Use 3x5 cards. As an alternative to using notebook paper, use 3x5 cards to take lecture notes. Copy each new concept onto a separate 3x5 card. Later, you can organize these cards in an outline form and use them as pocket flash cards.

Keep your own thoughts separate. For the most part, avoid making editorial comments in your lecture notes. The danger is that when you return to your notes, you might mistake your own idea for that of the instructor. If you want to make a comment—either a question to ask later or a strong disagreement—clearly label it as your own. Pick a symbol or code and use it in every class.

Use an "I'm lost" signal. No matter how attentive and alert you are, you might get lost and confused in a lecture. If it is inappropriate to ask a question, record in your notes that you were lost. Invent your own signal—for example, a circled question mark. When you write down your code for "I'm lost," leave space for the explanation or clarification that you will get later. The space will also be a signal that you missed something. Later, you can speak to your instructor or ask to see a fellow student's notes. As long as you are honest with yourself when you don't understand, you can stay on top of the course.

Label, number, and date all notes. Develop the habit of labeling and dating your notes at the beginning of each class. Number the page, too. Sometimes the sequence of material in a lecture is important. Write your name and phone number in each notebook in case you lose it. Class notes become more and more valuable as a term or semester progresses.

Use standard abbreviations. Be consistent with your abbreviations. If you make up your own abbreviations or symbols, write a key explaining them in your notes. Avoid vague abbreviations. When you use an abbreviation such as *comm.* for *committee*, you run the risk of not being able to remember whether you meant *committee, commission, common, commit, community, communicate,* or *communist.*

One way to abbreviate is to leave out vowels. For example, *talk* becomes *tlk, said* becomes *sd, American* becomes *Amrcn.*

If you use instant messaging with your friends, you might also use some of the same shortened words and phrases in your notes.

Leave blank space. Notes tightly crammed into every corner of the page are hard to read and difficult to use for review. Give your eyes a break by leaving plenty of space. Later, when you review, you can use the blank spaces in your notes to clarify points, write questions, or add other material.

Take notes in different colors. You can use colors as highly visible organizers. For example, you can signal important points with red. Or use one color of ink for notes about the text and another color for lecture notes. Notes that are visually pleasing can be easier to review. If you are using a laptop computer to take notes, you can create text with different colors and fonts.

Use graphic signals. Add a visual dimension to your notes. For example:

- Use brackets, parentheses, circles, and squares to group information that belongs together.

- Use stars, arrows, and underlining to indicate important points. Flag the most important points with double stars, double arrows, or double underlines.

- Use arrows and connecting lines to link related groups and to replace words such as *leads to, becomes,* and *produces.*

- Use equal signs and greater- and less-than signs to indicate compared quantities.

- Use question marks for their obvious purpose. Double question marks can signal tough questions or especially confusing points.

To avoid creating confusion with graphic symbols, use them carefully and consistently. Write a "dictionary" of your symbols in the front of your notebooks, such as the one shown here.

[ ], ( ), ◯, ☐ = info that belongs together

*, ↘, — = important

**, ↘↘, ≡, !!! = extra important

> = greater than   < = less than

= = equal to

⟶ = leads to, becomes
Ex: school → job → money

? = huh?, lost

?? = big trouble, clear up immediately

The Cornell format

A note-taking system that has worked for students around the world is the *Cornell format*.[1] Originally developed by Walter Pauk at Cornell University during the 1950s, this approach continues to be taught across the United States and in other countries as well.

The cornerstone of this system is what Pauk calls the *cue column*—a wide margin on the left-hand side of the paper. The cue column is the key to the Cornell format's many benefits. Here's how to use the Cornell format.

Format your paper. On each sheet of your note paper, draw a vertical line, top to bottom, about two inches from the left edge of the paper. This line creates the cue column—the space to the left of the line.

Take notes, leaving the cue column blank. As you read an assignment or listen to a lecture, take notes on the right-hand side of the paper. Fill up this column with sentences, paragraphs, outlines, charts, or drawings. Do not write in the cue column. You'll use this space later, as you do the next steps.

Condense your notes in the cue column. Think of the notes you took on the right-hand side of the paper as a set of answers. In the cue column, list potential test questions that correspond to your notes. Write one question for each major term or point.

As an alternative to questions, you can list key words from your notes. Yet another option is to pretend that your notes are a series of articles on different topics. In the cue column, write a newspaper-style headline for each "article."

In any case, be brief. If you cram the cue column full of words, you defeat its purpose—to reduce the number and length of your notes.

Write a summary. Pauk recommends that you reduce your notes even more by writing a brief summary at the bottom of each page. This step offers you another way to engage actively with the material. It can also make your notes easier to review for tests.

Cue column	Notes
What are some key changes in U.S. health over the last 50 years?	Over the past 50 years in the U.S.: — The number of smokers decreased. — Infant mortality dropped to a record low. — Life expectancy hit a record high—about 77 years.
Who announced these changes?	Source: *Health, United States 2002*, Centers for Disease Control. Health and Human Services Secretary Tommy Thompson announced this report.
Summary	
Changes in American health over the last 50 years include fewer smokers, lower infant mortality, and record life expectancy.	

Use the cue column to recite. Cover the right-hand side of your notes with a blank sheet of paper. Leave only the cue column showing. Then look at each item you wrote in the cue column and talk about it. If you wrote questions, answer each question. If you wrote key words, define each word and talk about why it's important. If you wrote headlines in the cue column, explain what each one means and offer supporting details. After reciting, uncover your notes and look for any important points you missed. Repeat this cycle of reciting and checking until you've mastered the material.

Mind mapping

This system, developed by Tony Buzan,[2] can be used in conjunction with the Cornell format. In some circumstances, you might want to use mind maps exclusively.

One benefit of mind maps is that they quickly, vividly, and accurately show the relationships between ideas. Also, mind mapping helps you think from general to specific. By choosing a main topic, you focus first on the big picture, then zero in on subordinate details. And by using only key words, you can condense a large subject into a small area on a mind map. You can review more quickly by looking at the key words on a mind map than by reading notes word for word.

Give yourself plenty of room. Use blank paper that measures at least 11 by 17 inches. If that's not available, turn regular notebook paper on its side so that you can

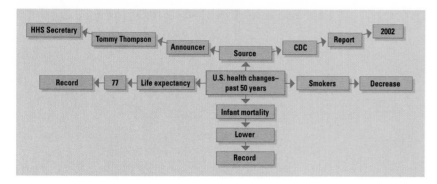

take notes in a horizontal (instead of vertical) format. Another option is to find computer software that allows you to draw flow charts or diagrams.

Determine the main concept of the lecture. Write that concept in the center of the paper and circle it, underline it, or highlight it with color. You can also write the concept in large letters. Record concepts related to the main concept on lines that radiate outward from the center. An alternative is to circle these concepts.

Use key words only. Whenever possible, reduce each concept to a single word per line or circle in your mind map. Using shorthand symbols and abbreviations can help.

Jazz it up. Use color to organize your mind map. If there are three main subjects covered in the lecture, you can record each subject in a different color. Add symbols and other images as well.

Create links. One mind map doesn't have to include all of the ideas in a book or an article. Instead, you can link mind maps. For example, draw a mind map that sums up the five key points in a chapter, and then make a separate, more detailed mind map for each of those key points. Within each mind map, include references to the other mind maps.

Outlining

Perhaps you've had negative experiences with outlining in the past. Teachers might have required you to use complex, rigid outlining formats based exclusively on Roman numerals or on some unfamiliar system. By playing with variations, you can discover the power of outlining to reveal relationships between ideas.

Technically, each word, phrase, or sentence that appears in an outline is called a *heading*. These are arranged in different levels:

- In the first or "top" level of headings, note the major topics that are presented in a lecture or reading assignment.

- In the second level of headings, record the key points that relate to each topic in the first-level headings.

- In the third level of headings, record specific facts and details that support or explain each of your second-level headings.

Each additional level of subordinate heading supports the ideas in the previous level of heading.

Roman numerals offer one way to illustrate the difference between levels of headings. See the following example.

> First-level heading
>
> I. Health and Human Services Secretary Tommy G. Thompson reports that Americans' health changed over the past 50 years.
>
> Second-level heading
>
> A. Thompson: "When you take the long view, you see clearly how far we've come in combating diseases, making workplaces safer, and avoiding risks such as smoking."
> B. Thompson referred to *Health, United States, 2002*, a report from the Centers for Disease Control and Prevention (CDC).
>
> II. By 2000, infant morality dropped to a record low and life expectancy hit a record high.
>
> A. Death rates among children up to age 24 were cut in half.
> B. Americans enjoyed the longest life expectancy in U.S. history.
>
> III. Among working-age adults, fewer are dying from unintentional injuries, heart disease, stroke, and AIDS.
>
> Third-level heading
>
> A. After 1995, deaths from AIDS dropped.
>   1. Powerful new drugs contributed to this result.
>   2. Other drugs are now in development.
> B. A decline in smoking contributed to the decline in heart disease.
>   1. More than 40 percent of adults were smokers in 1965.
>   2. In 2000, just 23 percent smoked.

You can also use other heading styles, as illustrated to the right.

Distinguish levels with indentations only:

First-level heading
  Second-level heading
    Third-level heading
      Fourth-level heading

Distinguish levels with bullets and dashes:

FIRST–LEVEL HEADING
- Second-level heading
  – Third-level heading

Distinguish headings by size:

FIRST–LEVEL HEADING
Second-level heading
Third-level heading

Combining formats

Feel free to use different note-taking systems for different subjects and to combine formats.

For example, combine mind maps along with the Cornell format. You can divide your note paper in half, reserving one half for mind maps and the other for linear information, such as lists, graphs, and outlines, as well as equations, long explanations, and word-for-word definitions. Do what works for you. ▨

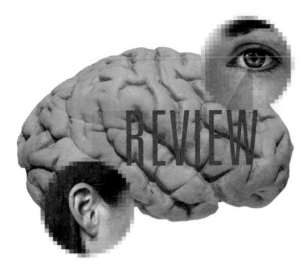

The note-taking process flows

Think of reviewing as an integral part of note taking rather than as an added task. To make new information useful, encode it in a way that connects to your long-term memory. The key is reviewing.

Review within 24 hours. Sound the trumpets! This point is critical. It might be the most powerful note-taking technique you can use—one that can save you hours of review time later in the term.

Many students are surprised that they can remember the content of a lecture in the minutes and hours immediately after class. They are even more surprised by how well they can read the sloppiest of notes. These are examples of short-term memory. Unfortunately, it deteriorates quickly.

The good news is that if you review your notes soon enough, you can move that information from short-term to long-term memory. And you can do this in just a few minutes—often 10 minutes or less.

The sooner you review your notes, the better, especially if the class was difficult. In fact, you can start reviewing during class. When your instructor pauses to set up the overhead projector or erase the board, scan your notes. Dot the i's, cross the t's, and write out unclear abbreviations.

Another way to use this technique is to get to your next class as quickly as you can. Then use the four or five minutes before the lecture begins to review the notes you just took in the previous class. If you do not get to your notes immediately after class, you can still benefit by reviewing later in the day. A review right before you go to sleep can also be valuable.

Think of the day's unreviewed notes as leaky faucets, constantly dripping, losing precious information until you shut them off with a quick review. Remember, it's possible to forget up to 80 percent of the material within 24 hours—unless you review.

Edit notes. During your first review, fix words that are illegible. Write out abbreviated words that might be unclear to you later. Make sure you can read everything. If you can't read something or don't understand something you *can* read, mark it, and make a note to ask your instructor or another student. Check to see that your notes are labeled with the date and class and that the pages are numbered. You can edit with a different colored pen or pencil if you want to distinguish between what you wrote in class and what you filled in later.

Fill in key words in the left-hand column. This task is important if you are to get the full benefit of using the Cornell format. Using the key word principles described earlier in this chapter, go through your notes and write key words or phrases in the left-hand column.

These key words will speed up the review process later. As you read your notes and focus on extracting important concepts, your understanding of the lecture is further reinforced.

Use your key words as cues to recite. With a blank sheet of paper, cover your notes, leaving only the key words in the left-hand margin showing. Take each key word in order and recite as much as you can about the point. Then uncover your notes and look for any important points you missed.

Conduct short weekly review periods. Once a week, review all of your notes again. The review sessions don't need to take a lot of time. Even a 20-minute weekly

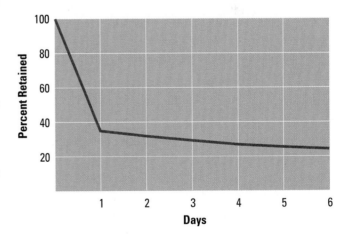

To study the process of memory and forgetting, Hermann Ebbinghaus devised a method for testing memory. The results, shown here in what has come to be known as the Ebbinghaus forgetting curve, demonstrate that forgetting occurs most rapidly shortly after learning and then gradually declines over time.

review period is valuable. Some students find that a weekend review, say, on Sunday afternoon, helps them stay in continuous touch with the material. Scheduling regular review sessions on your calendar helps develop the habit.

As you review, step back to see the larger picture. In addition to reciting or repeating the material to yourself, ask questions about it: "Does this relate to my goals? How does this compare to information I already know, in this field or another? Will I be tested on this material? What will I do with this material? How can I associate it with something that deeply interests me? Am I unclear on any points? If so, what exactly is the question I want to ask?"

Consider typing up your notes. Some students type up their handwritten notes using a desktop computer. The argument for doing so is threefold. First, typed notes are easier to read. Second, they take up less space. Third, the process of typing them forces you to review the material.

Another alternative is to bypass handwriting altogether and take notes in class on a laptop computer or handheld device such as a PDA (personal digital assistant). This solution has potential drawbacks: laptops are more expensive than desktop computers. And data loss can wipe out your notes, leaving you with no handwritten backup.

Experiment with typing notes and see what works for you. For example, you might type up only key portions of notes, such as summaries or outlines. Be sure to make backup copies of your note files.

Create mind map summaries. Mind mapping is an excellent way to make summary sheets for review. After drawing your map, look at your original notes and fill in anything you missed. This system is fun to use. It's quick, and it gives your brain a visual hook on which to fasten the material. ◪

journal entry 14

Discovery Statement

Think about the way you have conducted reviews of your notes in the past. Respond to the following statements by checking "Always," "Often," "Sometimes," "Seldom," or "Never" after each.

I review my notes immediately after class.
___Always ___Often ___Sometimes
___Seldom ___Never

I conduct weekly reviews of my notes.
___Always ___Often ___Sometimes
___Seldom ___Never

I make summary sheets of my notes.
___Always ___Often ___Sometimes
___Seldom ___Never

I edit my notes within 24 hours.
___Always ___Often ___Sometimes
___Seldom ___Never

Before class, I conduct a brief review of the notes I took in the previous class.
___Always ___Often ___Sometimes
___Seldom ___Never

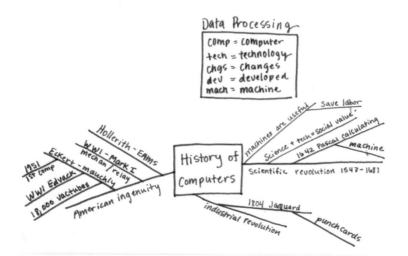

The Instructor Gameplan

When faced with an instructor you dislike, you can shut down and stop learning. Or you can keep taking responsibility for your education. Think of the following techniques as a gameplan for managing the way you experience instructors—and learning from all of them.

Research instructors. Before registering for courses, talk with other students about the best instructors they've had. Also introduce yourself to potential instructors. Set up a visit during office hours and ask about their courses.

Show up for class. Students who attend classes earn better grades than those who do not attend. Keep in mind the amount of money that you're investing in higher education. Showing up for class is one way to get your money's worth.

Show interest in class. Many students are passive observers. Passive athletes will not find themselves in competition for long. Passive freshmen may not be around to become sophomores.

As an alternative to passivity, show interest. Even if you find a class boring, create a massive display of attention. Ask lots of questions. Sit up straight, make eye contact, and take detailed notes. Your enthusiasm might enliven your instructor. If not, you are still creating a more enjoyable class for yourself.

Also arrive early for class and sit up front. You can visit with instructors and review notes.

Some instructors have preconceived notions about student athletes. With these instructors, it is particularly important that you show interest in class. Teachers are more likely to excuse your absences for competition if they know that you're committed to academic achievement.

Take responsibility for your learning. Maybe your instructor reminds you of someone you don't like— an annoying relative or a coach who yelled at you. Your attitudes are in your own head and beyond the instructor's control. Also, an instructor's views on politics or religion are not related to teaching ability.

If you don't like an instructor, acknowledge that fact. Then return to your purpose for being in school. Don't let your feelings about an instructor keep you from getting what you want out of higher education.

Get to know the instructor better. Meet with your instructor during office hours. Ask questions that weren't answered in class. Teachers who seem boring in class can be fascinating in person.

Avoid excuses. Instructors know them all. Most teachers can see a snow job coming before the first flake hits the ground. Accept responsibility for your own mistakes, and avoid thinking that you can fool the teacher. When you treat instructors honestly, you are more likely to be treated as a responsible adult in return.

Submit professional work. Prepare papers and projects as if you were competing. In your sport, you constantly strive for excellence. Apply the same standards to your course work.

Accept criticism. Learn from your teachers' comments about your work—just as you do from your coaches' comments about your athletic performance.

Plan for missed classes. If you miss practice, you won't be able to compete effectively. Similarly, missing class can hurt your ability to compete academically. Plan to catch up as quickly as possible:

- Inform your instructors when you will miss class for training or competition.

- Learn the instructor's specific policies for class absences.

- See if you can make up assignments, quizzes, and tests.

- Ask about doing extra-credit assignments.
- Request copies of handouts you missed.
- Find out if the instructor offers another section of the same course that you could attend.
- Look for another student athlete who is in the class but on another team (meaning that one of you is likely to be in class at all times).
- Ask classmates who take organized, neat, comprehensive notes to share them with you.
- See if your athletic or academic counselor can arrange to fax class notes to the location of your competition.
- Access class notes and other course materials online—remembering that they are no substitute for attending class.
- Join a study group and find out what was covered in each class you missed.

Use conference time effectively. Instead of trying to answer a complex question in a few minutes before or after class, set up a separate conference time. Bring your notes, text, and any other materials you might need. During this meeting you can also address more difficult subjects, such as grades, attendance policies, lecture styles, term papers, or personality conflicts.

Your instructor's office hours might conflict with your practice time. Schedule another time or ask to meet with the teaching assistant instead.

Use course evaluations. When you have an opportunity to evaluate instructors, be honest. Your instructors will not see your comments until after grades are submitted. And many of them will act on feedback.

Take further steps when appropriate. Sometimes severe conflict develops between students and instructors. In such cases, you might decide to file a complaint or ask for help from an administrator. Discuss the situation with your academic or athletic advisor.

Being a student athlete does not mean that you are an exception to course policies. However, if you feel that an instructor is discriminating against you because you are a student athlete, take action.

Be prepared to document your case in writing. Offer details. Describe specific actions that created problems for the class. Stick to the facts—events that other class members can verify. Use the established grievance procedures at your campus.

You are a consumer of education. You have a right to complain if you think you have been treated unfairly. ⊠

When your instructor talks fast

Take more time to prepare for class. Conduct a thorough preview of the material to be covered.

Become an active listener. When an instructor talks fast, focus your attention on key points. Instead of trying to write everything down, choose what you think is important. Occasionally, you will make a wrong choice and neglect an important point. Worse things could happen. Stay with the lecture and revise your notes immediately after class.

Exchange photocopies of notes with classmates. Your fellow students might write down something you missed. Study groups are useful here. As you share notes with your group, you can discuss what you don't understand.

Leave large empty spaces in your notes. Leave plenty of room for filling in information you missed.

See the instructor after class. Take your class notes with you and show the instructor what you missed.

Before class, take notes on your reading assignment. Your syllabus should identify the chapters or sections corresponding to each lecture. Leave plenty of blank space. Take these notes with you to class and simply add your lecture notes to them.

Go to the lecture again. Many classes are taught in multiple sections. That gives you the chance to hear a lecture at least twice—once in your regular class and again in another section of the class.

Learn shorthand. Some note-taking systems, known as shorthand, are specifically designed for getting ideas down fast. You can also devise your own shorthand method by inventing codes for common words and phrases. To avoid confusion, make a complete list of your codes.

Ask questions—even if you're totally lost. Many instructors allow a question session. This is the time to ask about the points you missed.

Remember the obvious. Politely ask the instructor to slow down.

Taking notes while reading

Taking notes while reading requires the same skills that apply to class notes: observing, recording, and reviewing. Just remember that there are two kinds of notes that apply to reading: review notes and research notes.

Review notes. These will look like the notes you take in class. Sometimes you will want more extensive notes than writing in the margin of your text allows. You can't underline or make notes in library books, so these sources will require separate notes, too.

Mind map summaries of textbook materials are particularly useful for review. You can also use outlining or take notes in paragraph form. Single out a particularly difficult section of a text and make separate notes. Or make mind map summaries of overlapping lecture and textbook materials. Use the left-hand column for key words and questions, just as you do in your class notes.

When you read scientific or other technical materials, copy important formulas or equations and write down data that might appear on an exam. Re-create important diagrams and draw your own visual representations of concepts.

Research notes. Writing essays and speeches is a special challenge, and the way you take notes can help you face that challenge.

Use the mighty 3x5 card. There are two kinds of research cards: source cards and information cards. Source cards identify where you found the information contained in your paper or speech. For example, a source card for a book will show the author, title, date and place of publication, and publisher. Source cards are also written for magazine articles, interviews, dissertations, tapes, or any other research materials.

When you write source cards, give each source a code—the initials of the author, a number, or a combination of numbers and letters. A key advantage of using source cards is that you are creating your bibliography as you do the research. When you are done, simply alphabetize the cards by author and—voilà!—instant bibliography.

Write the actual research notes on information cards. At the top of each information card, write the code for the source from which you got the information. Also include the page numbers your notes are based on.

Most important, write only one piece of information on each information card. You can then sort the cards and use them to construct an outline of your paper or speech.

Another option is to take notes using a computer. This offers the same advantage as 3x5 cards—ease of rearranging text and pictures—while enabling you to print out copies to exchange with other students.

Online material. You can print out anything that appears on a computer screen. This includes online course materials, articles, books, manuscripts, e-mail messages, chat room sessions, and more.

One potential problem: Students might skip taking notes on this material altogether. ("I can just print out everything!") These students miss the chance to internalize a new idea by restating it in their own words—a principal benefit of note taking. Result: Material passes from computer to printer without ever intersecting a student's brain.

To prevent this problem, find ways to engage actively with online materials. Take review notes in Cornell, mind map, concept map, or outline format. Write Discovery and Intention Statements to capture key insights from the materials and to state ways you intend to apply them. Also talk about what you're learning. Recite key points out loud and discuss what you read online with other students.

Of course, it's fine to print out online material. If you do, treat your printouts like a textbook and apply the steps of Muscle Reading explained in Chapter Four.

Thinking about notes. Whenever you take notes, use your own words as much as possible. When you do so, you are thinking about what you are reading. If you do quote your source word for word, put that material within quotation marks.

Close the book after reading an assignment and quickly jot down a summary of the material. This writing can be loose, without any structure or format. The important thing is to do it right away, while the material is still fresh in your mind. Restating concepts in this way helps you remember them.

Special cases. The style of your notes can vary according to the nature of the material. If you are assigned a short story or poem, read the entire work once without taking any notes. On your first reading, simply enjoy the piece. When you finish, write down your immediate impressions. Then go over the piece and make brief notes on characters, images, symbols, settings, plot, point of view, or other aspects of the work.

Normally, you would ask yourself questions *before* you read an assignment. When you read fiction or poetry, however, ask yourself questions *after* you have read the piece. Then reread it (or skim it, if it's long) to get answers. Your notes can reflect this question-and-answer process. ▨

REVISIT YOUR GOALS

 One powerful way to achieve any goal is to assess periodically your progress in meeting it. This is especially important with long-term goals—those that can take years to achieve.

When you did Exercise #6 "Get real with your goals" on page 60, you focused on one long-term goal and planned a detailed way to achieve it. This involved setting mid-term and short-term goals that will lead to achieving your long-term goal. Take a minute to review that exercise and revisit the goals you set. Then complete the following steps.

1. Take your long-term goal from Exercise #6 and rewrite it in the space below. If you can think of a more precise way to state it, feel free to change the wording.

_____

_____

_____

_____

2. Next, check in with yourself. How do you feel about this goal? Does it still excite your interest and enthusiasm? On a scale of 1 to 10, how committed are you to achieving this goal? Write down your level of commitment in the space below.

_____

_____

_____

_____

3. If your level of commitment is 5 or less, you might want to drop the goal and replace it with a new one. To set a new goal, just turn back to Exercise #6 and do it again. And release any self-judgment about dropping your original long-term goal. Letting go of one goal creates space in your life to set and achieve a new one.

4. If you're still committed to the goal you listed in step 1 of this exercise, consider whether you're still on track to achieve it. Have you met any of the short-term goals related to this long-term goal? If so, list your completed goals in the space below.

_____

_____

_____

Before going on to the next step, take a minute to congratulate yourself and celebrate your success.

5. Finally, consider any adjustments you'd like to make to your plan. For example, write additional short-term or mid-term goals that will take you closer to your long-term goal. Or cross out any goals that you no longer deem necessary. Make a copy of your current plan in the space below.

Long-term goal (to achieve within your lifetime):

_____

_____

_____

_____

Supporting mid-term goals (to achieve in one to five years):

_____

_____

_____

_____

_____

Supporting short-term goals (to achieve within the coming year):

_____

_____

_____

_____

_____

→ Get to the bones of your book with concept maps

Concept mapping, pioneered by Joseph Novak and D. Bob Gowin, is a tool to make the main ideas in a book leap off the page.[3] In creating a concept map, you reduce an author's message to its essence—its bare bones. Concept maps can also be used to display the organization underlying lectures, discussions, and other reading materials.

To develop the technique of concept mapping, Novak and Gowin drew on ideas from David Ausubel, an educational psychologist.[4] Ausubel stated that human knowledge consists of a series of propositions. A proposition states a relationship between two or more concepts. A subject that you study in school might include dozens or even hundreds of concepts and propositions. However, learning the subject relies on a simple, underlying process: You take one new concept at a time and link it to a concept that you already understand, creating a new proposition.

Concept maps take this process out of your head and put in on paper in a visual format. You list concepts and arrange them in a meaningful order. Then you explicitly state the relationships between concepts, forming meaningful propositions.

Concept maps also promote critical thinking. Creating a concept map can alert you to gaps in your understanding—missing concepts or concepts with illogical links.

To create a concept map, use the following four steps:

1. List the key concepts in the text. Aim to express each concept in three words or less. Most concept words are nouns, including terms and proper names. At this point, you can list the concepts in any order. For ease in ranking the concepts later, write each one on a single 3x5 card.

2. Rank the concepts so that they flow from general to specific. On a large sheet of paper, write the main concept at the top of the

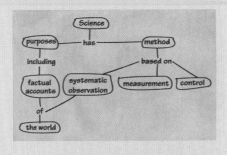

page. Place the most specific concepts near the bottom. Arrange the rest of the concepts in appropriate positions throughout the middle of the page. Circle each concept.

3. Draw lines that connect the concepts. On these connecting lines, add words that describe the relationship between the concepts. Again, limit yourself to the fewest words needed to make an accurate link—three words or less. Linking words are often verbs, verb phrases, or prepositions.

4. Finally, review your map. Look for any concepts that are repeated in several places on the map. You can avoid these repetitions by adding more links between concepts. Also look for accurate linking words and missing concepts.

As you gain facility with concept maps, you might wish to create them on a computer. Use any software with drawing capabilities. For example, the software program Inspiration, a visual thinking and learning tool, is specifically designed to create concept maps.

Sample concept maps based on selected articles in this book are available online at masterstudent.college.hmco.com

PRACTICING CRITICAL THINKING

5

Use a concept map as a tool to interpret and evaluate a piece of writing. First, list the key concepts from a chapter (or section of a chapter) in a textbook you're reading. Then connect these concepts with linking words, using the format described in the sidebar "Get to the bones of your book with concept maps." Create your concept map on a separate sheet of paper. Then take a few minutes to assess the author's presentation as reflected in your concept map. Pay special attention to the links between concepts. Are they accurate? Do they reveal false assumptions or lack of evidence? Write your evaluation of your concept map on a separate sheet of paper.

power process

I create it all

This is a powerful tool in times of trouble. In a crisis, "I create it all" can lead the way to solutions. "I create it all" means treating experiences, events, and circumstances in your life as if you created them.

When your dog tracks fresh tar on the white carpet, when your political science teacher is a crushing bore, when your spouse dents the car, when your test on Latin American literature focuses on an author you've never read—it's time for a Power Process. Tell yourself, "I created it all."

"Baloney!" you shout. "I didn't let the dog in, that teacher really is a bore, I wasn't even in the car, and nobody told me to read Gabriel García Márquez. I didn't create these disasters."

Good points. Obviously, "I create it all" is one of the most unusual and bizarre suggestions in this book. It certainly is not an idea that is easily believed. In fact, believing it can get you into trouble. "I create it all" is strictly a practical idea. Use it when it works. Don't when it doesn't.

Also consider how powerful this Power Process can be. It is really about the difference between two distinct positions in life: being a victim or being self-responsible.

A victim of circumstances is controlled by outside forces. We've all felt like victims at one time or another. When tar-footed dogs tromped on the white carpets of our lives, we felt helpless.

In contrast, we can take responsibility. *Responsibility* is the key word. It does not mean "blame." Far from it. Responsibility is "response-ability"—the ability to choose a response.

Practicing resignation

By not taking responsibility, we are acknowledging that the power to determine what happens in our lives is beyond our grasp. When we feel as if we don't have control over our lives, we feel resigned. The opposite of practicing "I create it all" is practicing resignation.

There is a phenomenon called *learned resignation*. An interesting experiment with dogs demonstrates how learned resignation works. A dog is put in a caged pen with a metal floor that can be electrified. When the cage door is left open and the dog is given a mild shock, she runs out of the cage to escape the discomfort. Then the dog is put back into the cage, the door is shut and locked, and a mild shock is given again. The dog runs around, looking for an escape. When she doesn't find one, she just lies down, sits, or stands there, and quits trying to find a way out. She has no control over her circumstances and is learning to be resigned.

Now, here comes the interesting part. After the dog has consistently stopped trying to escape the shock, the door is opened and the dog is led in and out several times. Then the dog is left in the cage, the door is left open, and the shock is administered once again. Amazingly, the dog doesn't even try to escape, even though the open door is right there in front of her. Instead, the dog continues to endure the shock. She has learned to be resigned.

A variety of this phenomenon can occur in human beings as well. When we consistently give control of our lives over to other people and to circumstances, we run the risk of learning to give up. We might develop the habit of being resigned, even though there is abundant opportunity all around us.

Applying this process

Many students approach grades from the position of being victims. When the student who sees the world this way gets an F, she reacts something like this:

"Oh, no!" (Slaps forehead)

"Rats!" (Slaps forehead again) (Students who get lots of F's often have flat foreheads.)

"Another F! That teacher couldn't teach her way out of a wet paper bag. She can't teach English for anything. And that textbook—what a bore! How could I read it with a houseful of kids making noise all the time? And then friends came over and wanted to party, and . . . ."

The problem with this viewpoint is that in looking for excuses, the student is robbing herself of the power to get any grade other than an F. She's giving all of her power to a bad teacher, a boring textbook, noisy children, and friends.

There is another way, called *taking responsibility*. You can recognize that you choose your grades by choosing your actions. Then you are the source, rather than the result, of the grades you get. The student who got an F could react like this:

"Another F! Oh, shoot! Well, hmmm . . . . How did I choose this F? What did I do to create it?"

Now, that's power. By asking, "How did I contribute to this outcome?" you give yourself a measure of control. You are no longer the victim. This student might continue by saying, "Well, let's see. I didn't review my notes after class. That might have done it." Or "I studied in the same room with my children while they watched TV. Then I went out with my friends the night before the test. Well, that probably helped me fulfill some of the requirements for getting an F."

The point is this: When the F is the result of your kids, your friends, the book, or the teacher, you probably can't do anything about it. However, if you *chose* the F, you can choose a different grade next time. You are in charge.

Choosing our responses

There are times when we don't create it all. We do not create earthquakes, floods, avalanches, or monsoons. Yet if we look closely, we discover that we *can* choose our responses to events.

To begin, we can choose our thoughts. In the above example, the student who got the F learned to think about that event in a new way. This student can also choose new behaviors in the future, such as staying home to study on the night before a test.

In large part, our moment-by-moment choices of thoughts and behaviors create our current circumstances—even circumstances that are not "our fault." After a car accident, we tell ourselves, "It just happened. That car came out of nowhere and hit me." We forget that driving five miles per hour slower and paying closer attention might have allowed us to miss the driver who was "to blame."

Some cautions

The presence of blame is a warning that this Power Process is being misused. "I create it all" is not about blaming yourself or others.

Feeling guilty is another warning signal. Guilt actually involves the same dynamic as blame. If you are feeling guilty, you have just shifted the blame from another person to yourself. Especially in team sports, recognize that wins and losses are usually the result of a team effort, not just yours.

Another caution is that this Power Process is not a religion. Saying that you "create it all" does not mean that you have divine powers. It is simply a way to expand the choices you already have.

This Power Process is easy to deny. Tell your friends about it, and they're likely to say, "What about world hunger? I didn't cause that. What about people who get cancer? Did they create that?"

These are good arguments—and they miss the point. Victims of rape, abuse, incest, and other forms of violence can still use "I create it all" to choose their response to the people and events that violated them.

Some people approach world hunger, imprisonment, and even cancer with this attitude: "Pretend for a moment that I am responsible for this. What will I do about it?" These people see problems in a new way, and they discover choices that other people miss.

"I create it all" is not always about disaster. It also works when life is going great. We often give credit to others for our good fortune when it's actually time to pat ourselves on the back.

By choosing our behavior and thoughts, we can create A's, interesting classes, enjoyable relationships, material wealth, and ways to contribute to a better world. ◪

put it to work

You can adapt any of the suggestions in this chapter for use in the workplace. For example:

- Before meetings, complete background reading on the topics to be discussed. You'll be better prepared to take notes.

- During meetings, experiment with taking notes in several formats: Cornell, mind mapping, outlining, concept mapping, or some combination.

- After meetings, review the notes you took. Edit or rewrite your notes for clarity. If you took handwritten notes, you might want to key the important points into a computer file.

- No matter what format you choose for note taking, include key items of information about any meeting: the time and place, the people present, a list of agreements reached, and any items that require follow-up action.

- During a presentation or training session, let go of any judgments about the presenter's speaking style or appearance. Focus on the content of this person's message and look for ideas to remember and use. Capture those ideas fully and accurately in your notes.

- When taking notes during fast-paced meetings and conference calls, use suggestions from the article "When your instructor talks fast." Immediately after the call or meeting, review and edit your notes. Flag items that require follow-up action.

- In your personal journal, write about ways to be more effective at work. State a work-related problem and brainstorm to come up with possible solutions. List career goals and write Intention Statements about how you plan to achieve them.

- Apply the Power Process: "I create it all" to people and situations at work. If you feel tempted to blame a problem on a coworker, look for any ways that you might have contributed to the problem. Consider what you will think, say, and do differently to create a better work environment. ✖

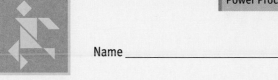

Power Process | Put It to Work | Quiz | Learning Styles Application | Master Student Profile

Name _____ Date _____/_____/_____

quiz

1. What are the three major steps of effective note taking as explained in this chapter? Summarize each step in one sentence.

2. Techniques you can use to "set the stage" for note taking do *not* include:
   (A) Complete outside assignments.
   (B) Bring the right materials.
   (C) Set aside questions in order to concentrate.
   (D) Conduct a short preclass review.
   (E) Sit front and center.

3. What is an advantage of sitting in the front and center of the classroom?

4. By the way they behave, instructors sometimes give clues that the material they are presenting is important. Describe at least three of these behaviors.

5. An effective method to postpone debate during a lecture is to ignore your own opinions and passively record the instructor's words. True or False? Explain your answer.

6. When using the Cornell system of note taking:
   (A) Write the main point on a line or in a box, circle, or any other shape.
   (B) Use only Roman numerals in an outline form.
   (C) Copy each new concept on a separate 3x5 card.
   (D) Remember never to combine it with mind mapping.
   (E) Draw a vertical line about two inches from the left edge of the paper.

7. Explain how key words can be used when taking notes. Then select and write down at least five key words from this chapter.

8. Reviewing within 24 hours assists short-term memory only. True or False? Explain your answer.

9. Compare and contrast source cards and information cards. How are they alike? How are they different?

10. Briefly explain one of the cautions given regarding the use of the Power Process: "I create it all."

learning styles application

The questions below will "cycle" you through four styles, or modes, of learning as explained in the article "Learning styles: Discovering how you learn" in Chapter One. Each question will help you explore a different mode. You can answer the questions in any order.

what if
Create an original format for taking notes. Think about how you could modify or combine the note-taking systems discussed in this chapter. Describe your format here.

why
Describe a situation in school or at work in which you could benefit by taking more effective notes.

how
Of the note-taking techniques in this chapter that you like and intend to apply, choose one and describe when and where you will use it.

what
Think back to the major note-taking systems discussed in this chapter: the Cornell format, mind mapping, outlining, concept mapping, or some combination. Choose one system that you intend to apply and briefly summarize its key features.

master student profile

BILLIE JEAN KING

(1943–   ) One of the most successful sports figures of her time and instrumental in the success of the first professional women's tennis tour, she broke gender barriers after defeating tennis star Bobby Riggs in the famous "Battle of the Sexes" tennis match in 1973.

All her life, King had been battling for equal rights for women, not only in tennis and in sports, but in society, and it is a cause she continues to champion in her post-tennis life.

But all of her hard work and dedication were dwarfed by what she accomplished in the two hours and four minutes it took to dismantle [Bobby] Riggs. In front of the largest crowd ever to watch a tennis match (30,472), in front of a television audience estimated at 40 million with viewers tuned in via satellite in 36 foreign countries, King proved that female athletes could indeed excel in pressure-filled situations, contrary to Riggs' belief.

She disproved Riggs' chauvinistic philosophies that females could not match a man's competitive fire and athletic skill, that the women's game was far inferior to the men's, and therefore women didn't deserve the same amount of prize money the men were receiving on their respective tours and at the major tournaments.

Perhaps best of all, she beat Riggs and did what no one thought was possible—she shut his bombastic mouth with a brilliant display of tennis, which he was ill-equipped to handle.

It was the tennis that mattered to King, not all the hyperbole that surrounded the match. While Riggs was making radio and TV appearances, doing hundreds of interviews, and trying everything in his power to mentally frazzle King, she kept to herself, practiced dutifully, and avoided the circus that Riggs was creating. "I tried to stay somewhat away from the show biz atmosphere," she said. "I realized the one thing Bobby wanted me to do was get caught up in everything. He's a hustler, but in order to hustle you, he's got to see you, know where you are, keep tabs on you. I felt if I hid from him, if I wasn't around physically, it would drive him nuts."

What drove Riggs nuts more than anything, though, was his inability to put up a fight.

"I couldn't believe how slow he was," King said. "I thought he was faking it. He had to be."

He wasn't.

During a long rally, he unleashed nearly his entire arsenal of shots, and King returned every one of them until finally missing a backhand wide. Riggs won that point, but he celebrated by bending over and trying desperately to catch his breath.

"I concentrated hard on winning that first set and when I did, I knew he was in trouble," said King. "That meant he'd have to play at least four tough sets to win the match, probably more hard competitive tennis than he'd played in years."

During her career, King won 20 titles at Wimbledon, including the singles crown six times. She won the U.S. Open four times. It is probably shameful that when her name is mentioned, that impressive résumé takes second billing to her victory over Riggs.

But this victory meant so much, not only to her, but to female athletes everywhere.

"This is the culmination of 19 years of work," she said. "Since the time they wouldn't let me be in a picture because I didn't have on a tennis skirt, I've wanted to change the game around."

She did.

As appeared on CBSSportsline.com.
Reprinted with permission.

For more biographical information about Billie Jean King, visit the Master Student Hall of Fame on the *Becoming a Master Student Athlete* Web site at

masterstudent.college.hmco.com

6

Tests

To give yourself the best possible chance of playing to your potential, you must prepare for every eventuality. That means practice.

STEVE BALLESTEROS

Keep in mind that neither success nor failure is ever final.

ROGER BABSON

why
this chapter matters . . .

Adopting a few simple techniques can make a major difference in how you feel about tests—and how you perform on them.

what
is included . . .

Disarm tests
What to do before the test
Cooperative learning: Studying with people
What to do during the test
The test isn't over until . . .
Integrity in test taking: The costs of cheating
Let go of test anxiety
Overcoming math and science anxiety
8 reasons to celebrate mistakes
Power Process: "Detach"
Master Student Profile: Mia Hamm

how
you can use this chapter . . .

Predict test questions and use your study time more effectively.
Harness the power of cooperative learning by studying with other people.
Perform more effectively under any type of pressure.

as you read, ask yourself
what if . . .

I could let go of anxiety about tests and athletic competitions—or anything else?

Disarm tests

On the surface, tests don't look dangerous. Yet sometimes we treat them as if they are land mines. Suppose a stranger walks up to you on the street and asks, "Does a finite abelian P-group have a basis?" Will you break out in a cold sweat? Will your muscles tense up? Will your breathing become shallow?

Probably not. Even if you have never heard of a finite abelian P-group, you are likely to remain coolly detached. However, if you find the same question on a test and if you have never heard of a finite abelian P-group, your hands might get clammy.

Grades (A to F) are what we use to give power to tests. And there are lots of misconceptions about what grades are. Grades are not a measure of intelligence or creativity. They are not an indication of our ability to contribute to society. Grades are simply a measure of how well we do on tests.

Some people think that a test score measures what a student has accomplished in a course. This is false. A test score is a measure of what a student scored on a test. If you are anxious about a test and blank out, the grade cannot measure what you've learned. The reverse is also true: If you are good at taking tests and a lucky guesser, the score won't be an accurate reflection of what you know.

Grades are not a measure of self-worth. Yet we tend to give test scores the power to determine how we feel about ourselves. Common thoughts include "If I fail a test, I am a failure" or "If I do badly on a test, I am a bad person." The truth is that if you do badly on a test, you are a person who did badly on a test. That's all.

Carrying around misconceptions about tests and grades can put undue pressure on your performance. It's like balancing on a railroad track. Many people can walk along the rail and stay balanced for long periods. Yet the task seems entirely different if the rail is placed between two buildings, 52 stories up.

It is easier to do well if you don't put too much pressure on yourself. Don't give the test some magical power over your own worth as a human being. Academic tests are not a matter of life and death. Scoring low on important tests—entrance tests for college or medical school, bar exams, CPA exams—usually means only a delay.

One way to deal with tests is to keep them in perspective. Keep the railroad track on the ground.

What to do before the test

One way to save hours of wasted study time is to look on each test as a performance. From this point of view, preparing for a test means *rehearsing*. Study for a test in the way that a successful athlete prepares for competition or an actor prepares for opening night: Simulate the physical and psychological conditions you'll encounter when you actually enter the exam room.

Rehearsing means doing the kind of tasks that you'll perform during a test—answering questions, solving problems, composing essays. Start this process with regular reviews of course content.

Manage review time

A big benefit of early reviewing is that facts have time to roam around in your head. A lot of learning takes place when you are not consciously studying. Your brain has time to create relationships that can show up when you need them—like during a test.

Use short daily review sessions to prepare the way for major review sessions. Reviewing with a group often generates new insights and questions.

Daily reviews. Concentrate daily reviews on two kinds of material: material you have just learned, either in class or in your reading, and material that involves simple memorization (equations, formulas, dates, definitions).

Daily reviews include short pre- and post-class reviews of lecture notes. Also conduct brief daily reviews when you read. Before reading a new assignment, for example, scan your notes and the sections you underlined in the previous assignment.

Conduct short daily reviews several times throughout the day. Use the time you spend waiting for the bus or doing the laundry for this purpose. Include reviews on your daily to-do list. Write down reminders, such as "5 min. review of biology," and give yourself the satisfaction of crossing them off your list.

Begin to review on the first day of class. Most instructors outline the whole course at that time. In fact, you can start reviewing within seconds after learning. During a lull in class, go over the notes you just took. Then immediately after class, review your notes again.

Weekly reviews. Weekly reviews are longer—about an hour per subject. They are also more structured than

short daily reviews. When a subject is complex, the brain requires time to dig into the material. Avoid skipping from subject to subject too quickly.

Review each subject at least once a week. Weekly sessions include reviews of assigned reading and lecture notes. Look over any mind map summaries or flash cards you have created. You can also practice working on sample problems.

Major reviews. Major reviews are usually conducted the week before finals or other critical exams. They help integrate concepts and deepen understanding of the material presented throughout the term.

These are longer review periods—two to five hours at a stretch, punctuated by sufficient breaks. Remember that the effectiveness of your review begins to drop after an hour or so unless you give yourself a short rest.

After a certain point, short breaks every hour might not be enough to refresh you. That's when it's time to quit. Learn your limits by being conscious of the quality of your concentration. During long sessions, study the most difficult subjects when you are the most alert—at the beginning of the session.

Your commitment to review is your most powerful ally. Create a system of rewards for time spent reviewing. Use the Intention Statements in this chapter or invent your own to draw detailed plans for review time.

Scheduling reviews. If you have a monthly or weekly planner, use it to schedule specific review periods. Plan on at least two major review sessions, lasting two to five hours each, for every course. If you think you'll need extra time for review, consider rearranging tasks or changing their priority in order to free up more study time. Being a student athlete can make this a challenge, particularly when key competitions coincide with important tests. Anticipating such conflicts will be beneficial.

Start reviewing key topics at least five days before you'll be tested on them. This allows plenty of time to find the answers to questions and close any gaps in your understanding.

Create review tools

One way to make the most of your time before a test is to condense and clarify your class notes for effective review.

Consider the following kinds of review tools. They're especially useful to have on hand when you travel.

Study checklists. A study checklist is not a review sheet; it is a to-do list. Checklists contain the briefest possible description of each item to study.

Study checklists are used the way a pilot uses a pre-flight checklist. Pilots go through a standard routine before they take off. They use a written list to be absolutely certain they don't miss anything. Once they are in the air, it's too late, and the consequences of failing to check the fuel tanks could be drastic.

Make a list for each subject. List reading assignments by chapters or page numbers. List dates of lecture notes. Write down various types of problems you will need to solve. Write down other skills you must master. Include major ideas, definitions, theories, formulas, and equations. For math and science tests, choose some problems and do them over again as a way to review for the test.

Mind map summary sheets. There are several ways to make a mind map as you study for tests. Start by creating a map totally from memory. You might be surprised by how much you already know. Mind maps release floods of information from the brain because the mind works by association. Each idea is linked to many other ideas. You think of one and other associations come to mind.

Let the associations flow. If one seems to go someplace else, simply start another branch on your map. After you have gone as far as you can using recall alone, go over your notes and text and fill in the rest of the map.

Another way to create a mind map summary is to go through your notes and pick out key words. Then, without looking at your notes, create a mind map of everything you can recall about each key word. Finally, go back to your notes and fill in material you left out. You can also start a mind map with underlined sections from your text.

Flash cards. Three-by-five flash cards are like portable test questions. Take them with you everywhere and use them anytime. On one side of the cards, write the questions. On the other, write the answers. It's that simple.

Use flash cards for formulas, definitions, theories, key words from your notes, axioms, dates, foreign language phrases, hypotheses, and sample problems. Create flash  cards regularly as the term progresses. Buy an inexpensive card file to keep your flash cards arranged by subject.

Always carry a pack of flash cards with you, and review them whenever you have a minute to spare.

Monitoring your reviews. Each day that you prepare for a test, assess what you have learned and what you still need to learn. See how many items you've covered from your study checklist. Look at the tables of contents in your textbooks and write an X next to the sections that you've summarized. Do the same for class notes. Using a monitoring system can help you gauge the thoroughness of your reviews and alert you to areas that still need attention.

Plan a test-taking strategy

Knowing what is going to be on a test doesn't require highly sophisticated technology or code breaking. With some practice, you can learn to predict the types of questions and their level of difficulty.

Do a dry run. Write up your own questions and take this "test" several times before the actual exam. Say that the exam will include mainly true/false or short-answer questions. Brainstorm a list of such questions—a mock test—and do a dry run. You might type up this "test" so that it looks like the real thing.

Meet with your professor, tutor, or academic advisor to go over your mock test. Ask whether your questions focus on appropriate topics and represent the kind of items you can expect to see on the actual test.

Ask the instructor what to expect. One great source of information about the test is your instructor. Ask him what to expect. What topics will be emphasized? What kinds of questions will be included? How can you best allocate your review time? The instructor might decline to give you any of this information. More often, instructors will answer some or all of your questions about the test.

Get copies of old exams. Copies of previous exams for the class might be available from the instructor, the instructor's department, the library, or an academic assistance office. Old tests can help you plan a review strategy.

One caution: If you rely on old tests exclusively, you might gloss over material the instructor has added since the last test. Don't look for past tests to simply serve as answer sheets. Master the current course content.

Also check your school's policy about making past tests available to students. Some might not allow it. If you use a past test inappropriately, you may be violating your institution's code of conduct. This could mean failing a course—and losing your athletic eligibility. ⊠

Cooperative learning
Studying with people

As a student athlete, you may thrive on competition. Consider the idea that you can thrive in the classroom without competing against your fellow students. In fact, one way to balance the demands of course work and athletics is to *cooperate* with classmates by joining a study group. Think of your study group as a team dedicated to academic success.

As social animals, humans draw strength from groups. If you skip a solo study session, no one else will know. If you declare your intention to study with others who are depending on you, your intention gains strength.

Look for dedicated students. Find students who pay attention, ask questions, and take notes during class. Invite them to join your study group.

You can recruit group members by posting a note on a bulletin board, in a team locker room, or in the academic athletic support center. A benefit of this method is that you reach many people. However, it can take time, and you have little control over who applies to join your group.

Another option is to recruit in specific settings. For example, pass around a sign-up sheet before class. During key events, such as a team meeting, mention your desire to form a study group. Or go directly to your academic athletic advisor and ask for help in establishing a group.

Your instructor or teaching assistant might also help you identify students who are reliable and willing to study with you on a regular basis.

Balance common interests with diversity. To multiply the benefits of working with study groups, seek out people of other cultures, ethnic groups, and sports—or no sport at all. You can get a whole new perspective on the world, along with some valued new friends. And you can experience what it's like to be part of a diverse team. That's an important asset in today's job market.

Get to know other student athletes in your classes, especially those from other teams. If these students have different travel schedules than yours, create a group to share notes. When one of you travels, the others become responsible for documenting what happened in class.

Remember certain pitfalls involved in studying with people who are similar to you. Studying with friends is fine. But if your shared interests are beer and jokes, then avoid studying together. Fellow student athletes can be supportive, but they might not share your level of academic focus.

Sometimes having a person in a study group who has no interest in sports can help you stay grounded in the primary purpose of attending college—earning a degree. If you do form study groups with nonathletes, be honest about your schedule and how much you will be able to contribute.

Do a trial run. Ask two or three people to get together for a snack and talk about group goals, meeting times, and other logistics. You don't have to make an immediate commitment.

Test the group first by planning a one-time session. If that session works, plan another. After a few successful sessions, you can schedule regular meetings.

Set an agenda for each meeting. Create activities to do as a group. (For suggestions, keep reading.) Set approximate time limits for each activity and determine a quitting time for the meeting. End with assignments for all members.

Test each other by asking questions. Group members can agree to bring 5 to 10 sample test questions to each meeting. Then you can all take the test made up from these questions.

Practice teaching each other. Teaching is a great way to learn something. Turn the material you're studying into a list of topics and assign a specific topic to each person, who will then teach it to the group.

When you teach something, you naturally assume a teacher's attitude ("I know this"), as opposed to a student's attitude ("I still have to learn this"). The vocalization involved in teaching further reinforces the concepts.

Compare notes. Make sure that you all heard the same thing in class and that you all recorded the important

Ways to predict test questions

Predicting test questions can save review time. Making predictions can be fun, too—especially when they turn out to be accurate.

Ask your instructor. Do this early in the term so you can be alert for possible test questions throughout the course. Some specific questions to ask are:

- What course material will the test cover—readings, lectures, lab sessions, or a combination?

- Will the test be cumulative, or will it cover just the most recent material you've studied?

- Will the test focus on facts and details or major themes and relationships?

- Will the test call on you to solve problems or apply concepts?

- What types of questions will be on the test—true/false, multiple choice, short-answer, essay?

- Will you have choices about which questions to answer?

- Will your teacher write and score the test—or will a teaching assistant perform those tasks?

Put yourself in the instructor's shoes. If you were teaching the course, what information would you want students to take away? What kinds of questions would you put on an exam? Make up practice test questions and then answer them.

Save all quizzes, papers, lab sheets, and graded materials of any kind. Quiz questions have a way of reappearing, in slightly altered form, on final exams.

---

information. Ask others to help explain material in your notes that is confusing to you.

Brainstorm test questions. Set aside 5 to 10 minutes of each study session to brainstorm possible test questions. You can add these to the "Test questions" section of your notebook.

Work in small groups at a computer to review a course. One person can operate the keyboard while another person dictates summaries of lectures and assigned readings. Together, group members can check facts by consulting textbooks, lecture notes, and class handouts.

Create wall-sized mind maps or concept maps to summarize a textbook or series of lectures. Work on large sheets of butcher paper, or tape together pieces of construction paper.

Pair off to do "book reports." One person can summarize a reading assignment. The other person can act like an interviewer on a talk show, posing questions and asking for further clarification.

Ask each member to contribute. Recognize signs that group members are not contributing in equal ways. For instance, someone in your group might consistently fail to prepare for meetings or feel that he has nothing to contribute. Other members might dominate the group discussions.

As a group, brainstorm ways to get unprepared members involved. Reel in a dominating member by reminding him about the importance of hearing everyone's voice. ⊠

journal entry 16

Intention Statement

In the space below, outline a plan to form a study group. Explain the steps you will take to get the group organized and set a first meeting date.

I intend to . . .

_____

_____

_____

_____

Now describe the reward you anticipate for fulfilling this intention.

_____

_____

_____

What to do during the test

Prepare yourself for the test by arriving early. That often leaves time to do a relaxation exercise. While you're waiting for the test to begin and talking with classmates, avoid the question "How much did you study for the test?" This question might fuel anxious thoughts that you didn't study enough.

As you begin

Ask the teacher or test administrator if you can use scratch paper during the test. If you use a separate sheet of paper without permission, you might appear to be cheating. If you get permission, use this paper to jot down memory aids, formulas, equations, facts, or other material you know you'll need and might forget. An alternative is to make quick notes in the margins of the test sheet.

Pay attention to verbal directions given as a test is distributed. Then scan the whole test immediately. Evaluate the importance of each section. Notice how many points each part of the test is worth and estimate how much time you'll need for each section, using its point value as your guide. For example, don't budget 20 percent of your time for a section that is worth only 10 percent of the points.

Read the directions slowly. Then reread them. It can be agonizing to discover that you lost points on a test merely because you failed to follow the directions. When the directions are confusing, ask to have them clarified.

Now you are ready to begin the test. If necessary, allow yourself a minute or two of "panic" time. Notice any tension you feel, and apply one of the techniques explained in the article "Let go of test anxiety" later in this chapter.

Answer the easiest, shortest questions first. This gives you the experience of success. It also stimulates associations and prepares you for more difficult questions. Pace yourself and watch the time. If you can't think of an answer, move on. Follow your time plan.

If you are unable to determine the answer to a test question, keep an eye out throughout the test for context clues that may remind you of the correct answer, or provide you with evidence to eliminate wrong answers.

Multiple choice questions

- *Answer each question in your head first.* Do this before you look at the possible answers. If you come up with an answer that you're confident is right, look for that answer in the list of choices.

- *Read all possible answers before selecting one.* Sometimes two answers will be similar and only one will be correct.

- *Test each possible answer.* Remember that multiple choice questions consist of two parts: the stem (an incomplete statement at the beginning) and a list of possible answers. Each answer, when combined with the stem, makes a complete statement that is either true or false. When you combine the stem with each possible answer, you are turning each multiple choice question into a small series of true/false questions. Choose the answer that makes a true statement.

- *Eliminate incorrect answers.* Cross off the answers that are clearly *not* correct. The answer you cannot eliminate is probably the best choice.

True/false questions

- *Read the entire question.* Separate the statement into its grammatical parts—individual clauses and phrases—and then test each one. If any part is false, then the entire statement is false.

- *Look for qualifiers.* These include words such as *most, sometimes,* or *rarely.* Absolute qualifiers such as *all, always,* or *never* generally indicate a false statement.

- *Find the devil in the details.* Double-check each number, fact, and date in a true/false statement. Look for numbers that have been transposed or facts that have been slightly altered. These are signals of a false statement.

- *Watch for negatives.* Look for words such as *not* and *cannot.* Read the sentence without these words and see if you come up with a true or false statement. Then reinsert the negative words and see if the statement makes more sense. Watch especially for sentences with two negative words. As in math operations, two negatives cancel each other out: *We cannot say that Chekov never succeeded at short story writing means the same as Chekov succeeded at short story writing.*

Computer-graded tests

- Make sure that the answer you mark corresponds to the question you are answering.
- Check the test booklet against the answer sheet whenever you switch sections and whenever you come to the top of a column.
- Erase stray marks; they can look like answers.
- If you change an answer, be sure to erase the wrong answer completely, removing all pencil marking completely.

Open-book tests

- Carefully organize your notes, readings, and any other materials you plan to consult when writing answers.
- Write down any formulas you will need on a separate sheet of paper.
- Bookmark the table of contents and index in each of your textbooks.
- Place Post-it Notes and Index Flags or paper clips on other important pages of books (pages with tables, for instance). Don't waste time flipping through the pages.
- Create an informal table of contents or index for the notes you took in class.
- Predict which material will be covered on the test and highlight relevant sections in your readings and notes.

Short-answer/fill-in-the-blank tests

- Concentrate on key words and facts. Be brief.
- Overlearn material. When you know a subject backward and forward, you can answer this type of question almost as fast as you can write.

Matching tests

-  Begin by reading through each column, starting with the one with fewer items. Check the number of items

in each column to see if they're equal. If they're not, look for an item in one column that you can match with two or more items in the other column.

- Look for any items with similar wording and make special note of the differences between these items.
- Match words that are similar grammatically. For example, match verbs with verbs and nouns with nouns.
- When matching individual words with phrases, first read a phrase. Then look for the word that logically completes the phrase.
- Cross out items in each column when you are through with them.

Essay questions

Managing your time is crucial to answering essay questions. Note how many questions you have to answer and monitor your progress during the test period. Writing shorter answers and completing all of the questions on an essay test will probably yield a better score than leaving some questions blank.

Find out what an essay question is asking—precisely. If a question asks you to *compare* the ideas of Sigmund Freud and Karl Marx, no matter how eloquently you *explain* them, you are on a one-way trip to No Credit City.

Before you write, make a quick outline. An outline can help speed up the writing of your detailed answer. You're less likely to leave out important facts. And if you don't have time to finish your answer, your outline could win

Words to watch for in essay questions

The following words are commonly found in essay test questions. If you want to do well on essay tests, study this list thoroughly. Know these words backward and forward. To heighten your awareness of them, underline the words when you see them in a test question.

Analyze: Break into separate parts and discuss, examine, or interpret each part. Then give your opinion.

Compare: Examine two or more items. Identify similarities and differences.

Contrast: Show differences. Set in opposition.

Criticize: Make judgments. Evaluate comparative worth. Criticism often involves analysis.

Define: Explain the exact meaning—usually, a meaning specific to the course or subject. Definitions are usually short.

Describe: Give a detailed account. Make a picture with words. List characteristics, qualities, and parts.

Discuss: Consider and debate or argue the pros and cons of an issue. Write about any conflict. Compare and contrast.

Explain: Make an idea clear. Show logically how a concept is developed. Give the reasons for an event.

Prove: Support with facts (especially facts presented in class or in the text).

Relate: Show the connections between ideas or events. Provide a larger context for seeing the big picture.

State: Explain precisely.

Summarize: Give a brief, condensed account. Include conclusions. Avoid unnecessary details.

Trace: Show the order of events or the progress of a subject or event.

If any of these terms are still unclear to you, consult an unabridged dictionary.

Review these key words and other helpful vocabulary terms by using the online flash cards at

masterstudent.college.hmco.com

---

you some points. To use test time efficiently, keep your outline brief. Focus on key words to use in your answer.

Suppose that you're asked to write a one-paragraph answer to this question: "Define the term *mental disorder* and give some examples." Following is an outline for a possible answer.

Disorder = Problem interferes with daily life
Problem with thought
Example: Schizophrenia
Problem with feeling
Example: Depression
Problem with behavior
Example: Eating disorder

And here is an answer based on that outline:

We can define mental disorder as any problem with thought, feeling, or behavior that interferes with a person's ability to carry out the tasks of daily life. For example, symptoms of schizophrenia include hallucinations, which are a form of distorted thinking. Depression involves persistent feelings of sadness. Finally, eating disorders such as bulimia are characterized by behaviors that can be self-destructive.

Introduce your answer by getting to the point. General statements such as "There are many interesting

facets to this difficult question" can cause acute irritation for teachers grading dozens of tests.

One way to get to the point is to begin your answer with part of the question. Suppose the question is "Discuss how increasing the city police budget might or might not contribute to a decrease in street crime." Your first sentence might be "An increase in police expenditures will not have a significant effect on street crime for the following reasons." Your position is clear. You are on your way to an answer.

When you expand your answer with supporting ideas and facts, start out with the most solid points. Don't try for drama by saving the best points for last. You might run out of time before you get them down on paper.

Write legibly. Grading essay questions is in large part a subjective process. Sloppy, difficult-to-read handwriting might actually lower your grade.

Write on one side of the paper only. If you write on both sides of the paper, writing will show through and obscure the writing on the other side. If necessary, use the blank side to add points you missed. Leave a generous left-hand margin and plenty of space between your answers, in case you want to add to them later.

Finally, if you have time, review your answers for grammar and spelling errors, clarity, and legibility. ⊠

The test isn't over until . . .

Many students believe that a test is over as soon as they turn in the answer sheet. Consider another point of view: You're not done with a test until you know the answer to any question that you missed—and why you missed it.

When you discover what questions you missed and understand the reasons for lost points, you learn something. And you greatly increase your odds of achieving better scores later in the course.

To get the most value from any test, take control of what you do at two critical points: the time immediately following the test, and the time when the test is returned to you.

Immediately following the test. Sit down in a quiet place and take a few minutes to write some Discovery Statements related to your experience of taking the test. Doing this while the test is still fresh in your mind increases the value of this technique. Describe how you felt about taking the test, how effective your review strategies were, and whether you accurately predicted the questions that appeared on the test.

Follow up with an Intention Statement. State what, if anything, you will do differently to prepare for the next test. If the test revealed any gaps in your knowledge, list follow-up questions to ask in class.

When the test is returned. When a returned test includes a teacher's comments, view this document as a treasure-trove of intellectual gold.

First, make sure that the point totals add up correctly and double-check for any other errors in grading. Even the best teachers make an occasional mistake.

Next, ask these questions:

- On what material did the teacher base test questions—readings, lectures, discussions, or other class activities?

- What types of questions appeared in the test—objective (such as matching items, true/false questions, or multiple choice), short-answer, or essay?

- What types of questions did you miss?

- Can you learn anything from the instructor's comments that will help you prepare for the next test?

Also see if you can correct any answers that lost points. To do this, carefully analyze the source of your errors and find a solution. Consult the following chart for help.

Source of test error	Possible solutions
Study errors—studying material that was not included on the test, or spending too little time on material that *did* appear on the test	• Ask your teacher about specific topics that will be included on a test. • Practice predicting test questions. • Form a study group with class members to create mock tests.
Careless errors, such as skipping or misreading directions	• Read and follow directions more carefully–especially when tests are divided into several sections with different directions. • Set aside time during the next test to proofread your answers.
Concept errors—mistakes made when you do not understand the underlying principles needed to answer a question or solve a problem	• Look for patterns in the questions you missed. • Make sure that you complete all assigned readings, attend all lectures, and show up for laboratory sessions. • Ask your teacher for help with specific questions.
Application errors—mistakes made when you understand underlying principles but fail to apply them correctly	• Rewrite your answers correctly. • When studying, spend more time on solving sample problems. • Predict application questions that will appear in future tests and practice answering them.
Test mechanics errors—missing more questions in certain parts of the test than others, changing correct answers to incorrect ones at the last minute, leaving items blank, miscopying answers from scratch paper to the answer sheet	• Set time limits for taking each section of a test and stick to them. • Proofread your test answers carefully. • Look for patterns in the kind of answers you change at the last minute. • Change answers only if you can state a clear and compelling reason to do so.

Integrity in test taking
The costs of cheating

Cheating on tests can be a tempting choice. But before you do it, consider the potential costs.

We lose money. Getting an education costs a lot of money. Cheating sabotages our purchase by reducing the amount that we learn. Even when education is paid for by scholarship, cheating reduces the value of the money granted.

Fear of getting caught promotes stress. For student athletes, the stress is especially great. Cheating could mean that we are ineligible for several competitions. We may even be dismissed from a team and lose our athletic eligibility altogether. An athletic scholarship could be reduced or cancelled. The resulting financial loss can bring a college career to an abrupt end.

Another source of fear is the impact of cheating on the people who trust us. Parents, coaches, and teammates who relied on our contribution may be devastated.

Violating our values promotes stress. Even if we don't get caught cheating, we can feel stress about violating our own ethical standards. Student athletes already face the stress of training and competition. Cheating adds a whole other level of unnecessary tension, raising stress to levels that can compromise health.

Cheating on tests can make it easier to violate our integrity again. Think about the first time you competed in front of a large crowd. You might have felt excited—even a little frightened. Now, competing in front of a huge, raucous group of fans may be second nature to you. Human beings become comfortable with behaviors that they repeat. Cheating is no exception.

Avoid any activity that creates a suspicion of cheating. Whether it's justified or not, student athletes are scrutinized both on and off the field. Some teachers and students believe that student athletes routinely cheat. Students who don't cheat feel that their academic efforts are cheapened by those who do cheat—or even appear to cheat.

The point is to avoid doing anything that leads to even a suspicion that you are cheating. Come to class and to competition focused on giving your most honest effort.

Cheating lowers our self-concept. Winning at any cost is not winning. The sacrifice to self-esteem is greater than any victory. Whether or not we are fully aware of it, cheating sends us the message that we are not smart enough or responsible enough to make it on our own. We deny ourselves the satisfaction of authentic success. Also, other athletes may avoid us if we cheat, fearing that their own reputation will be tarnished.

Athletes and teams that cheated have been stripped of their glory. These people become the footnotes of sports history, remembered only for their mistakes or ignored and eventually forgotten.

An alternative to cheating is to become a master student athlete. Ways to do this are described on every page of this book. ⊠

> ## Have some FUN!
>
> Contrary to popular belief, finals week does not have to be a drag.
>
> In fact, if you use techniques in this chapter, you might find exam week to be fun. By planning ahead, you will have done most of your studying long before finals arrive. You can feel confident and relaxed.
>
> When you are well prepared for tests, you can even use fun as a technique to enhance your performance. The day before a final, go for a run or play a game of basketball. Take in a movie or a concert. Watch TV. A relaxed brain is a more effective brain. If you have studied for a test, your mind will continue to prepare itself even while you're at the movies.
>
> Get plenty of rest, too. There's no need to cram until 3 a.m. when you have used the techniques in this chapter.
>
> On the first day of finals, you can wake up refreshed, have a good breakfast, and walk into the exam room with a smile on your face. You can also leave with a smile on your face, knowing that you are going to have a fun week. It's your reward for studying regularly throughout the term.
>
> If this kind of exam week sounds inviting, remember that you can begin preparing for it right now.

Let go of test anxiety

A little tension before an athletic competition can motivate you to perform to your potential. In the same way, a little tension before a test is also useful. Sometimes, however, tension is persistent and extreme. It is a symptom of test anxiety, and it can prevent you from doing your best.

Test anxiety has two components: mental and physical. The mental component includes all of your thoughts and worries about your test performance. The physical component includes bodily sensations.

The following techniques can help you deal with both components of stress in any situation—from final exams to the stage fright that comes with competing before a stadium-sized crowd.

Dealing with thoughts

Yell "Stop!" When you notice that your mind is consumed with worries and fears, that your thoughts are spinning out of control, mentally yell "Stop!" If you're in a situation that allows it, yell it out loud. This action is likely to bring your focus back to the present moment and allow you to redirect your thoughts.

Daydream. When you fill your mind with pleasant thoughts, there is no room left for anxiety. Relax completely and take a quick fantasy trip. Close your eyes, free your body of tension, and imagine yourself in a beautiful, peaceful, natural setting. Create as much of the scene as you can. Be specific. Use all of your senses.

For example, you might imagine yourself at a beach. Hear the surf rolling in and the seagulls calling to one another. Feel the sun on your face and the hot sand between your toes. Smell the sea breeze. Taste the salty mist from the surf. Notice the ships on the horizon and the rolling sand dunes. Use all of your senses to create a vivid imaginary trip.

Find a place that works for you and practice getting there. When you become proficient, you can return to it quickly for trips that might last only a few seconds. With practice, you can use this technique even while you are taking a test.

Visualize success. Most of us live up—or down—to our own expectations. If we spend a lot of time mentally rehearsing what it will be like to fail a test, our chances of doing so increase.

Instead, take time to rehearse what it will be like to succeed. Be specific. Create detailed pictures, actions, and even sounds as part of your visualization. If you are able to visit the room where you will take the test, mentally rehearse while you are actually in this room.

Focus. Focus your attention on a specific sensation. During an exam, take a few seconds to listen to sounds—the squeaking of chairs, the scratching of pencils, the muted coughs. Touch the surface of your desk and notice the texture. Concentrate all of your attention on one point. Don't leave room in your mind for anxiety-related thoughts.

Praise yourself. Talk to yourself in a positive way. Many of us take the first opportunity to belittle ourselves: "Way to go, dummy! You don't even know the answer to the first question on the test." We wouldn't dream of treating a friend this way. Yet we do it to ourselves.

An alternative is to give yourself some encouragement. Treat yourself as if you were your own best friend. Consider telling yourself, "I am relaxed. I am doing a great job."

Consider the worst. Rather than trying to put a stop to your worrying, consider the very worst thing that could happen. Take your fear to the limit of absurdity.

Imagine the catastrophic problems that might occur if you were to fail a test. You might say to yourself, "Well, if

I fail this test, I might fail the course, lose my financial aid, and get kicked out of school. Then I won't be able to get a job, so the bank will repossess my car, and I'll start drinking." Keep going until you see the absurdity of your predictions.

After you stop chuckling, you can backtrack to discover a reasonable level of concern. Your worry about failing the entire course if you fail the test might be justified. At that point ask yourself, "Can I live with that?" Unless you are taking a test in parachute packing and the final question involves jumping out of a plane, the answer will almost always be yes. (If the answer is no, use another technique. In fact, use several other techniques.)

Zoom out. When you're in the middle of a test or another situation in which you feel distressed, zoom out. Think like a coach who uses film to see all the movements of a team at once from a distant perspective. In your mind, imagine that you're floating away and viewing the situation as a detached outside observer.

If you're extremely distressed, let your imagination take you even farther. See yourself rising above the scene so that your whole community, city, nation, or planet is within view.

From this larger viewpoint, ask yourself whether this situation is worth worrying about. A negative response is not a license to belittle or avoid problems; it is permission to gain some perspective.

Another option is to zoom out in time. Imagine yourself one week, one month, one year, or one decade from today. Assess how much the current situation will matter when that time comes.

Dealing with physical sensations

Breathe. You can calm physical sensations within your body by focusing your attention on your breathing. Concentrate on the air going in and out of your lungs. Experience it as it passes through your nose and mouth.

If you notice that you are taking short, shallow breaths, begin to take longer and deeper breaths. Imagine your lungs to be a pair of bagpipes. Expand your chest to bring in as much air as possible. Then listen to the plaintive chords as you slowly release the air.

Scan your body. Simple awareness is an effective technique to reduce the tension in your body.

Sit comfortably and close your eyes. Focus your attention on the muscles in your feet and notice if they are relaxed. Tell the muscles in your feet that they can relax.

Move up to your ankles and repeat the procedure. Next go to your calves and thighs and buttocks, telling each

group of muscles to relax. Do the same for your lower back, diaphragm, chest, upper back, neck, shoulders, jaw, face, upper arms, lower arms, fingers, and scalp.

Tense and relax. Find a muscle that is tense and make it even more tense. If your shoulders are tense, pull them back, arch your back, and tense your shoulder muscles even more tightly. Then relax. The net result is that you can be aware of the relaxation and allow yourself to relax even more.

You can use the same procedure with your legs, arms, abdomen, chest, face, and neck. Clench your fists, tighten your jaw, straighten your legs, and tense your abdomen all at once. Then relax and pay close attention to the sensations of relaxation. By paying attention, you can learn to re-create these sensations whenever you choose.

Describe it. Focus your attention on your anxiety. If you are feeling nauseated or if you have a headache, concentrate on that feeling. Describe it to yourself. Tell yourself how large it is, where it is located in your body, what color it is, what shape it is, what texture it is, how much water it might hold if it had volume, and how heavy it is.

As you describe your anxiety in detail, don't resist it. When you completely experience a physical sensation, it will often disappear.

Exercise aerobically. This is one technique that won't work in the classroom. Yet it is an excellent way to reduce body tension. Exercise regularly during the days that you review for a test. See what effect this has on your ability to focus and relax *during* the test. Aerobic exercises include rapid walking, jogging, swimming, bicycling, basketball, and anything else that elevates your heart rate and keeps it elevated.

Get help. When these techniques don't work, get help. Talk about it with your academic athletic advisor or a professional counselor. You don't have to live with anxiety before a test, a competition, a job interview, or any other situation where performance counts. ▨

journal entry 17

Discovery/Intention Statement

Do a timed, four-minute brainstorm of all the reasons, rationalizations, justifications, and excuses you have used to avoid studying. Be creative. List your thoughts in the space below by completing the following Discovery Statement.

I discovered that I . . .

_____
_____
_____
_____
_____
_____
_____
_____
_____
_____
_____
_____
_____
_____

Next , review your list, pick the excuse that you use the most, and circle it. In the space below, write an Intention Statement about what you will do to begin eliminating your favorite excuse. Make this Intention Statement one that you can keep, with a timeline and a reward.

I intend to . . .

_____
_____
_____
_____
_____

exercise 15

TWENTY THINGS I LIKE TO DO

One way to relieve tension is to mentally yell "Stop!" and substitute a pleasant daydream for the stressful thoughts and emotions you are experiencing.

To create a supply of pleasant images to recall during times of stress, conduct an eight-minute brainstorm about things you like to do. Your goal is to generate at least 20 ideas. Time yourself and write as fast as you can in the space below.

_____
_____
_____
_____
_____
_____
_____
_____
_____
_____
_____
_____
_____
_____
_____
_____
_____
_____
_____

When you have completed your list, study it. Pick out two activities that seem especially pleasant and elaborate on them by creating a mind map. Write down all of the memories you have about that activity.

You can use these images to calm yourself in stressful situations.

Overcoming math and science anxiety

$$\sum_{n=1}^{\infty}(-1)^{n}\frac{|\sin(n)|}{n}$$

$$(xy)=\begin{cases}\dfrac{x\cos x}{\sin x}\\1\end{cases}$$

Think of the benefits of overcoming math and science anxiety. More courses, majors, jobs, and careers could open up for you. Speaking the language of math and science can also help you feel at home in a world driven by technology.

Many schools offer courses in overcoming math and science anxiety. It pays to check them out. The following suggestions can also help.

Notice your pictures about math and science.
Sometimes what keeps people from succeeding at math and science is their mental picture of scientists and mathematicians. Often that picture includes a man dressed in a faded plaid shirt, baggy pants, and wingtip shoes. He's got a calculator on his belt and six pencils jammed in his shirt pocket. Such images are far from the truth.

Our mental pictures about math and science can be funny. At the same time, they can have serious effects. For many years, science and math were viewed largely as fields for white males. This picture excluded women and people of color. Promoting success in these subjects for all students is a key step in overcoming racism and sexism.

Get your self-talk out in the open and change it.
When students fear math and science, they often say negative things to themselves about their abilities in these subjects. Many times this self-talk includes statements such as:

- "I'll never be fast enough at solving math problems."

- "I'm one of those people who can't function in a science lab."

- "I'm good with words, so I can't be good with numbers."

Faced with this kind of self-talk, you can take three steps.

First, get a clear picture of such statements. When negative thoughts come to mind, speak them out loud or write them down. Getting self-doubt out into the open makes it easier to refute.

Next, do some critical thinking about these statements. Look for the hidden assumptions they contain. Negative self-statements are usually based on scant evidence. They can often be reduced to two simple ideas: "Everybody else is better at math and science than I am" and "Since I don't understand it right now, I'll never understand it." Both of these statements are illogical.

Finally, start some new self-talk. Use self-statements that affirm your ability to succeed in math and science such as:

- "When learning about math or science, I proceed with patience and confidence."

- "Any confusion I feel now will be resolved."

- "I learn math and science without comparing myself to others."

- "I ask whatever questions are needed to aid my understanding."

- "I am fundamentally OK as a person, even if I make errors in math and science."

- "I can succeed in math and science."

Take a First Step about your current level of knowledge. Before you register for a math or science course, seek out the assigned texts for the class. Look at the kind of material that's covered in early chapters. If that material seems new or difficult for you, see the instructor and express any concerns you have. Ask for suggestions on ways to prepare for the course.

Remember that it's OK to continue your study of math and science from your current level of ability—whatever that level might be.

Choose teachers with care. Whenever possible, find a math or science teacher whose approach matches key aspects of your learning style. Ask around and discover which teachers have a gift for making these subjects understandable.

Of course, you might not always have a choice. Perhaps only one teacher is offering the course you need during a given term. If so, there's still plenty you can learn from this teacher. Consider the possibility that this teacher could open up a whole new way of learning math for you. Also form a study group early in the course and ask for help at the first sign that you're failing to understand an assignment.

Take courses "back to back." Think about math and science in the same way that you think about learning a foreign language. If you take a year off in between Spanish I and Spanish II, you won't expect to gain much fluency. To master a language, you take courses back to back. It works the same way with math and science—foreign languages in themselves.

Beware of short courses. Courses that you take during summer school or another shortened term are—by necessity—condensed. You can find yourself doing far more reading and homework each week than you do in longer courses. If math and science are not your favorite subjects, give yourself the gift of extra course time. Enroll in courses with more calendar days.

Make your text an A priority. Math and science courses are often text-driven. To get the most out of your text, be willing to read each sentence slowly and reread it as needed. A single paragraph might merit 15 or 20 minutes of sustained attention.

Read chapters and sections in order, as they're laid out in the text. To strengthen your understanding of the main concepts, study all tables, charts, graphs, case studies, and sample problems. Read with paper and pencil in hand. Work out examples and copy diagrams, formulas, and equations. Understand each step used in solving a problem or testing a hypothesis.

Participate actively in class. Success in math and science depends on your active involvement. Attending class regularly, completing homework assignments, speaking up when you have a question, and seeking extra help can be crucial.

Some students bemoan that they'll never be any good in math and science and then behave in a way that confirms that belief. Get around this mental trap by giving to math and science at least the same amount of time that you give to other courses. If you want to succeed, make daily contact with these subjects.

Apply what you've learned. Applying strategies that you've already learned in this book will help you in math and science. Use chapter summaries and introductory outlines to organize your learning. Review your notes frequently to transfer information into your long-term memory. Develop a strategy and schedule that work best for you, and make a date with yourself to study.

Use lab sessions to your advantage. Laboratory work is crucial to many science classes. To get the most out of these sessions, prepare. Know in advance what procedures you'll be doing and what materials you'll need. If possible, visit the lab before your assigned time and get to know the territory. Find out where materials are stored and where to dispose of chemicals or specimens. Bring your lab notebook and worksheets to class to record and summarize your findings.

If you're not planning to become a scientist, remember that the main point is to understand the process of science—how scientists observe, collect data, and arrive at conclusions. This is more important than the result of any one experiment.

Develop your skills at taking math and science tests. To prepare for tests, practice working problems under a time limit. Time yourself. Exchange problems with a friend and time each other. You can also do this in a study group.

Ask questions fearlessly. To master math and science, ask whatever questions will aid your understanding. Students come to higher education with widely varying backgrounds in these subjects. Your questions might not be the same as those of other people in your class. Go ahead and ask. ✉

8 reasons to celebrate mistakes

Many of us are haunted by the fear of failure. We dread the thought of making mistakes. We shudder at the missteps that might cost us grades, athletic victories, careers, money, or relationships.

It's possible to take an entirely different attitude toward mistakes. Rather than fearing them, we could actually celebrate them. We could revel in our redundancies, frolic in our failures, and glory in our goof-ups. We could marvel at our mistakes and bark with loud laughter when we "blow it."

History offers plenty of examples of people who found reasons to celebrate their mistakes.

Abraham Lincoln entered military service as a captain, came out a private, and went on to fail in business before becoming one of America's greatest presidents.

Writer Jack London got 600 rejection slips before selling his first story.

More recently, a documentary movie titled *Comedian* documents Jerry Seinfeld's mistakes in creating new material for stand-up performances—even after the success of his television series.

A creative environment is one in which failure is not fatal. Coaches expect that their teams will experience a reasonable number of losses. In the business world, creative managers know that innovation requires risk taking and the chance of making mistakes.

Note: Nothing in this article amounts to an argument in favor of *making* mistakes in the first place. Rather, the intention is to encourage shining a light on mistakes so that we can examine them and fix them. Mistakes that are hidden cannot be corrected. That's the rationale behind each of the following reasons for celebrating mistakes.

1 Celebration allows us to notice the mistake. Celebrating mistakes gets them out into the open. This is the opposite of covering up mistakes or blaming others for them. Hiding mistakes takes a lot of energy—energy that could be channeled into correcting errors.

2 Mistakes are valuable feedback. A manager in a major corporation once made a mistake that cost his company $100,000. He predicted that he would be fired when his boss found out. Instead, his boss responded, "Fire you? I can't afford to do that. I just spent $100,000 training you."

The athlete who works hard in practice and competition is often rewarded with additional playing time, even if that effort doesn't result in victory at first. Coaches recognize that victories come when their athletes make correct and consistent efforts to learn from their mistakes.

Mistakes are part of the learning process. Not only are mistakes usually more interesting than most successes—they're often more instructive.

3 Mistakes demonstrate that we're taking risks. People who play it safe make few mistakes. Making mistakes is evidence that we're stretching to the limit of our abilities—growing, risking, and learning. Fear of making mistakes can paralyze us into inaction. Celebrating mistakes helps us move into gear and get things done. The only sure way to avoid mistakes is to stand on the sidelines and never enter the game.

For learning from your mistake.

4 Celebrating mistakes reminds us that it's OK to make them. When we celebrate, we remind ourselves that the person who made the mistake is not bad—just human.

5 Celebrating mistakes includes everyone. It reminds us that the exclusive club named the Perfect Performance Society has no members. All of us make mistakes. When we notice them, we can work together.

In contrast, blaming people for mistakes isolates people. It prevents cooperative efforts that can improve our circumstances. Blame undercuts team unity and undermines a team's potential for future victories. This applies to teams in the workplace as much as teams on the athletic field.

6 Mistakes occur only when we aim at a clear goal. We can express concern about missing a target only if the target is there in the first place. If there's no target, there's no concern about missing it. Making a mistake affirms something of great value—that we have a goal.

7 Mistakes happen only when we're committed to making things work. Systems work when people are willing to be held accountable. Openly admitting mistakes promotes accountability.

Imagine a school where there's no concern about quality and effectiveness. Instructors usually come to class late. Residence halls are never cleaned, and scholarship checks are always late. The administration is in chronic debt, students seldom pay tuition on time, and no one cares. In this school, the word *mistake* would have little meaning.

Mistakes become apparent only when people are committed to improvement. Mistakes go hand in hand with a commitment to quality.

8 Celebrating mistakes cuts the problem down to size. On top of the mistake itself, there is often an extra layer of regret, worry, and desperation. Not only do people have a problem with the consequences of the mistake—they punish themselves for *making* a mistake in the first place.

When we celebrate our mistakes in the classroom or in competition, we eliminate that extra layer of concern. When our anxiety about making a mistake is behind us, we can get down to the business of correcting the mistake and moving on to our next success.

PRACTICING CRITICAL THINKING

6

Create a short multiple choice test on a topic in a course you're taking right now. Ask several people from the class to take this exam.

Then, as a group, discuss the answer you chose for each question. Also talk about *why* and *how* you chose each answer. The purpose is to identify the strategies that different people use when answering a multiple choice question—especially when they are unsure of the correct answer.

You might discover some test-taking strategies that you could use in the future. List those strategies in the space below.

_____

_____

_____

_____

_____

_____

_____

_____

_____

_____

_____

_____

_____

Repeat this exercise by creating and discussing tests in other formats: short-answer, true/false, and essay.

power process

Detach

This Power Process helps you release the powerful, natural student athlete within you. It is especially useful whenever negative emotions are getting in the way of your education.

Attachments are addictions. When we are attached to something, we think we cannot live without it, just as a drug addict feels he cannot live without drugs. We believe our well-being depends on maintaining our attachments.

We can be attached to just about anything—expectations, ideas, objects, self-perceptions, people, results, rewards. The list is endless.

One person, for example, might be so attached to his car that he takes an accident as a personal attack. Pity the poor unfortunate who backs into this person's car. He might as well back into the owner himself.

Another person might be attached to his sport. His identity and sense of well-being depend on it. He could become depressed if he gets benched or taken out of the starting lineup.

We can be addicted to our emotions as well as to our thoughts. We can identify with our anger so strongly that we are unwilling to let it go. We can also be addicted to our pessimism and reluctant to give it up.

Most of us are addicted, to some extent, to our identities. We are Americans, veterans, high achievers, bowlers, loyal friends, business owners, humanitarians, devoted parents, dancers, hockey fans, or birdwatchers. If we are attached to these roles, they can dictate who we think we are. When these identities are threatened, we might fight for them as if we were defending our lives. The more addicted we are to an identity, the harder we fight to keep it. It's like a drowning man—the more he resists drowning, the more he literally becomes "attached" to his

would-be rescuer, grasping and grabbing, until they both sink.

Ways to recognize an attachment

When we are attached and things don't go our way, we often feel irritated, angry, jealous, confused, fatigued, bored, frightened, or resentful.

Suppose you are attached to getting an A on your physics test. You feel as though your success in life depends on getting an A. It's not just that you want an A. You *need* an A. During the exam, the thought "I must get an A" is in the back of your mind as you begin to work a problem. And the problem is difficult. The first time you read it, you have no idea how to solve it. The second time around, you aren't even sure what it's asking. The more you struggle to understand it, the more confused you get. To top it all off, this problem is worth 40 percent of your score.

As the clock ticks away, you work harder, getting more stuck, while that voice in your head gets louder: "I must get an A. I MUST get an A. I MUST GET AN A!"

At this point, your hands begin to sweat and shake. Your heart is pounding. You feel nauseated. You can't concentrate. You flail about for the answer as if you were drowning. You look up at the clock, sickened by the inexorable sweep of the second hand. You feel doomed.

Now is a time to detach.

Ways to use this process

Rather than perceive unpleasant emotions as liabilities, we can see them as indications that it's time to practice detachment. In times of stress, this might seem like the most difficult thing in the world to do. You can practice a variety of strategies to move toward detachment.

Practice observer consciousness. This is the quiet state above and beyond your usual thoughts, the place where you can be aware of being aware. It's a tranquil spot, apart from your emotions. From here, you can observe yourself objectively, as if you were someone else. Pay attention to your emotions and physical sensations. If you are confused and feeling stuck, tell yourself, "Here I am, confused and stuck." If your palms are sweaty and your stomach is one big knot, admit it.

Practice perspective. Athletes who exhaust their eligibility or suffer a career-ending injury often learn, over time, to experience detachment. From that viewpoint, they can move on to success in other arenas.

You can follow their example now. Put current circumstances into a broader perspective. View personal issues within the larger context of your community, your nation, or your planet. You will likely see them from a different point of view. Imagine the impact your present problems will have 20 or even 100 years from now.

Take a moment to consider the worst that could happen. During that physics exam, notice your attachment to getting an A. Realize that flunking the test will not ruin your life or even your overall experience in higher education. Seeing this helps you put the test in perspective.

Practice breathing. Calm your mind and body with breathing or relaxation techniques. Several are described in the article "Let go of test anxiety."

Note: It might be easier to practice these techniques when you're not feeling strong emotions. To begin, notice your thoughts, behaviors, and feelings during neutral activities, such as watching television or taking a walk.

Practice detaching. The key is to let go of automatic emotional reactions when you don't get what you want.

Rewrite the equation

To further understand this notion of detaching, we can borrow an idea from mathematics. An equation is a set of symbols joined by an equal sign (=) that forms a true statement. Examples are $2 \times 2 = 4$ and $a + b = c$.

Equations also work with words. In fact, our self-image can be thought of as a collection of equations. For example, the thought "I am capable" can be written as the equation "I = capable." "My happiness depends on my success in athletics" can be written as "happiness = athletics." The statement "My well-being depends on my job" becomes "well-being = job." Each equation is a tip-off to an attachment.

Once we discover a hidden equation, we can rewrite it. In the process, we can watch our upsets disappear. The person who gets laid off can change his equation to "my happiness = my happiness." In other words, his happiness does not have to depend on any particular job.

People can rewrite equations under the most extreme circumstances. A man dying from lung cancer spent his last days celebrating his long life. One day his son asked him how he was feeling.

"Oh, I'm great," said the man with cancer. "Your mom and I have been having a wonderful time just rejoicing in the life that we have had together."

"Oh, I'm glad you're doing well," said the man's son. "The prednisone you have been taking must have kicked in again and helped your breathing."

"Well, not exactly. Actually, my body is in terrible shape, and my breathing has been a struggle these last few days. I guess what I'm saying is that my body is not working well at all, but I'm still great."

The dying man rewrote the equation "I = my body." He knew that he had a body and that he was more than his body. This man lived this Power Process and gave his son—the author of this book—an unforgettable lesson about detachment.

Some cautions

Giving up an addiction to being an A student does not mean giving up being an A student. And giving up an addiction to a job doesn't mean getting rid of the job. It means not investing your entire well-being in the grade or the job. Keep your desires and goals alive and healthy while detaching from the compulsion to reach them.

Notice also that detachment is different from denial. Denial implies running away from whatever you find unpleasant. In contrast, detachment includes accepting your emotions and knowing the details of them—down to every last thought and physical sensation involved. It's OK to be angry or sad. Once you accept and fully experience your emotions, you can more easily move beyond them.

Being detached is not the same as being apathetic. We can be 100 percent detached and 100 percent involved at the same time. In fact, our commitment toward achieving a particular result is usually enhanced by being detached from it.

Detach and succeed

When we are detached, we perform better. When we think everything is at stake, the results might suffer. Without anxiety and the need to get an A on the physics test, we are more likely to recognize the problem and remember the solution.

This Power Process is useful when you notice that attachments are keeping you from accomplishing your goals. Behind your attachments is a master student athlete. By detaching, you release your master.

Detach. ❌

put it to work

You can apply many of the techniques discussed in this chapter directly to common situations in the workplace. For example, use the test-taking strategies when you take licensing exams, certification exams, and other tests in your career field. In addition, consider the following suggestions.

Seize opportunities to learn cooperatively. Forming study groups or committees helps you develop important workplace skills. Almost every job is accomplished by the combined efforts of many people. For example, manufacturing a single car calls for the contribution of designers, welders, painters, electricians, marketing executives, computer programmers, and many others.

Perhaps you prefer to complete your assignments by working independently. However, teamwork is often required in the workplace. Joining study groups now, while you are in school, can help you expand your learning styles and succeed in the workplace.

Apply your cooperative learning skills to working on project teams. To create a successful project team at work, combine the individual skills of team members in complementary ways. Major tasks in any project include:

- *Planning*—defining the desired outcomes, setting due dates for each task, and generating commitment to action.

- *Doing*—carrying out assigned tasks.

- *Reflecting*—meeting regularly to discuss what's working well and ways to improve the next phase of the project.

- *Interpreting*—discussing what the team has learned from the project and ways to apply that learning to the whole organization.

Many people are drawn to one of these tasks more than the others. Assign tasks to people based on their strengths and preferences.

One potential trap of working in teams is that one person ends up doing most of the work. This person might feel resentful and complain. If you find yourself in this situation, transform your complaint into a request. Instead of scolding team members for being lazy, request help. Ask team members to take over tasks that you've been doing. Delegate specific jobs.

Manage job stress. The same techniques that help you manage test anxiety can help you manage stress at work. Apply techniques for managing the mental and physical aspects of stress while interviewing for a job, making a presentation, doing a performance review, or carrying out any task that raises your anxiety level.

Celebrate mistakes. Recall a mistake you made at work and then write about it. In a Discovery Statement, describe what you did to create a result you didn't want ("I discovered that I tend to underestimate the number of hours projects take"). Then write an Intention Statement describing something you can do differently in the future ("I intend to keep track of my actual hours on each project so that I can give more accurate estimates").

Go for fun. Finally, see if you can adapt suggestions from "Have some FUN!" to cultivate enjoyment at work. One benefit of career planning (see Chapter Twelve) is finding a job that allows you to follow your interests—in other words, to have fun. Successful people often eliminate the distinction between work and play in their lives. You're more likely to excel professionally when you're having a blast at your job. ▨

Name _____ Date _____/_____/_____

quiz

1. Preparing for tests can include creating review tools. Name at least two of these tools.

2. When answering multiple choice questions, it is better to read all of the possible answers before answering the question in your head. True or False? Explain your answer.

3. The presence of absolute qualifiers, such as *always* or *never,* generally indicates a false statement. True or False? Explain your answer.

4. For answering an essay question, which of the following techniques is least effective?
   (A) Make a quick outline before answering the question.
   (B) Save the best points for last.
   (C) Know standard essay question words.
   (D) Include part of the question in your answer.
   (E) Avoid filler sentences.

5. Grades are:
   (A) A measure of creativity.
   (B) An indication of your ability to contribute to society.
   (C) A measure of intelligence.
   (D) A measure of test performance.
   (E) C and D.

6. Describe how *detachment* differs from *denial*.

7. The suggestion to celebrate mistakes offers a reason to make as many mistakes as possible. True or False? Explain your answer.

8. List three possible activities for a study group.

9. Describe at least three techniques for dealing with the thoughts connected to test anxiety.

10. Describe at least three techniques for dealing with the physical feelings connected to test anxiety.

learning styles application

The questions below will "cycle" you through four styles, or modes, of learning as explained in the article "Learning styles: Discovering how you learn" in Chapter One. Each question will help you explore a different mode. You can answer the questions in any order.

what if
Explain how a suggestion for managing test anxiety could help you manage stress in a situation that you face outside of school.

why
Name at least one benefit you could experience—in addition to better grades—by taking tests more effectively.

how
Of the techniques that you gained from this chapter, choose one that you will use on your next test. Describe exactly how you intend to apply the technique.

what
List three new techniques for reviewing course material or taking tests that you gained from reading this chapter.

master student profile

MIA HAMM

(1972–) Three-time U.S. Soccer Athlete of the Year and core member of the gold medal–winning women's soccer team in the 1996 and 2004 Olympics, she is also the founder of the Mia Hamm Foundation.

Learning how to deal with obstacles on the soccer field will no doubt help you off the field as well. Life, like soccer, isn't always fair. There are tackles from behind, your friends will sometimes let you down, referees miss calls, and sometimes your parents will blame you for things you didn't do. It is how you deal with these hurdles that to a large extent can determine how successful a person you are.

One of the most difficult situations I've ever had to deal with was the death of my brother Garrett. The painful emotional toll it took on my family and me was incredible. I missed the first two games of our Olympic Victory Tour in April 1997 to be with my family, but I knew that even though the game I love paled in importance compared to losing Garrett, I needed to get back on the field. The athletic field is where Garrett and I had so many great moments together, and I knew he would have wanted me out there. I knew also one of the best ways to deal with my grief was to play and to be with my teammates, so I joined the team in Milwaukee for our third game of the tour.

To focus mentally after that ordeal was one of the biggest challenges I've faced, and I must admit I really struggled to cope with my emotions and concentrate on soccer, but my teammates were remarkable in their caring for me and my family. There's no way I could have come back without their support and love, and I will always be grateful.

My first game back was against South Korea, and Milwaukee was deluged by rain. The field was covered in water, and you couldn't kick a ball further than five feet without it stopping dead in a huge puddle. Still, the fans came out. These were the same fans who had helped me organize a charity indoor soccer game the year before in Milwaukee to raise money for bone-marrow research. They packed the stadium despite conditions that might have canceled any other sporting event, and they cheered loudly when we took the field—or the lake, as it were.

The game started, and something amazing happened that I'll remember forever. Just thirty seconds into the match, the ball popped loose in front of the goal and I whacked it into the net. All the emotion from the fans and my teammates and from my ordeal rushed in at once. It was a truly overwhelming experience. I ran toward the stands and slid in the puddles before I was buried underneath a pile of soggy teammates.

It took a good dose of mental toughness combined with the support of my team to get me back on the field. It also showed me that you can overcome even the most tragic events if you put your mind to it and accept help from others. Mental toughness requires great patience and sacrifice. You must be willing to battle through the difficulties even if it's a long, arduous process, like recovering from a serious knee injury. The way I have been taught to regain the mental edge when having troubles is to make life or the game as simple as possible. If you have all these insecurities or frustrations when you step on the field, you are giving yourself a hundred different reasons to fail. Those are pretty tough odds. Focus on what you know you can do.

Source: Pages 38–40 from *Go for the Gold: A Champions Guide to Winning in Soccer and Life* by Mia Hamm and Aaron Heifetz. Copyright ©1999 by Mia Hamm. Reprinted by permission of HarperCollins Publishers, Inc.

For more biographical information about Mia Hamm, visit the Master Student Hall of Fame on the *Becoming a Master Student Athlete* Web site at

masterstudent.college.hmco.com

7

Thinking

I always wanted to be somebody, but I should've been more specific.

LILY TOMLIN

Leadership means getting people to think, believe, see, and do what they might not have without you.

BILL BRADLEY

why
this chapter matters . . .

The ability to think creatively and critically helps you succeed in any course and promotes skills that transfer to training and competition.

what
is included . . .

Critical thinking: A survival skill
Becoming a critical thinker
Finding "aha!": Creativity fuels critical thinking
Ways to create ideas
Uncovering assumptions
Ways to fool yourself: Six common mistakes in logic
Gaining skill at decision making
Four ways to solve problems
"But I don't know what I want to do": Choosing a major
Majors for the taking
Solving math and science problems
Asking questions
Power Process: "Find a bigger problem"
Master Student Profile: Oscar Robertson

how
you can use this chapter . . .

Read, write, speak, and listen more effectively.
Learn strategies to enhance your success in problem solving.
Apply thinking skills to practical decisions such as choosing a major.

as you read, ask yourself
what if . . .

I could solve problems more creatively and make decisions in every area of life with more confidence?

Critical thinking: A survival skill

Society depends on persuasion. Advertisers want us to spend money on their products. Political candidates want us to "buy" their stands on the issues. Teachers want us to agree that their classes are vital to our success. Parents want us to accept their values. Authors want us to read their books. Broadcasters want us to spend our time in front of the radio or television, consuming their programs and not those of the competition. The business of persuasion has an impact on all of us.

A typical American sees thousands of television commercials each year. And that's just one medium of communication. Add to that the writers and speakers who enter our lives through radio shows, magazines, books, billboards, brochures, Internet sites, and fund-raising appeals—all with a product, service, cause, or opinion for us to embrace.

This leaves us with hundreds of choices about what to buy, where to go, and who to be. It's easy to lose our heads in the crosscurrent of competing ideas—unless we develop skills in critical thinking. When we think critically, we can make choices with open eyes.

Uses of critical thinking

Critical thinking underlies reading, writing, speaking, and listening. These are the basic elements of communication—a process that occupies most of our waking hours.

Student athletes depend on critical thinking from moment to moment during training and competition. Ask the quarterback in a football game, the point guard bringing the ball up the court, and the runner deciding when to open up and when to hold back. Even though they are coached, these athletes rely on their own ability to judge a situation and make split-second decisions.

Critical thinking also plays an important part in social change. Consider that the institutions in any society—courts, governments, schools, businesses—are the products of a certain way of thinking. Any organization draws its life from certain assumptions about the way things should be done. Before the institution can change, those assumptions need to be loosened up or reinvented. In many ways, the real location of an institution is inside our heads.

Crises occur when our thinking fails to keep pace with reality. An example is the ecological crisis, which sprang from the assumption that people could pollute the earth, air, and water without long-term consequences. Consider how different our world would be if our leaders had thought like the first female chief of the Cherokees. Asked about the best advice her elders had given her, she said, "Look forward. Turn what has been done into a better path. If you are a leader, think about the impact of your decision on seven generations into the future."

Novelist Ernest Hemingway once said that anyone who wants to be a great writer must have a built-in, shockproof "crap" detector.[1] That inelegant comment points to a basic truth: As critical thinkers, we are constantly on the lookout for thinking that's inaccurate, sloppy, or misleading.

Critical thinking is a skill that will never go out of style. Throughout history, half-truths, faulty assumptions, and other nonsense have at one time been commonly accepted as true. For example:

- Illness results from an imbalance in the four vital fluids: blood, phlegm, water, and bile.

- Caucasians are inherently more intelligent than people of other races.

- Women are incapable of voting intelligently.

- We will never invent anything smaller than a transistor. (That was before the computer chip.)

- Computer technology will usher in the age of the paperless office.

In sports, uncritical thinking created the assumption that athletes would always run faster, throw farther, hit more home runs, and generally outperform their predecessors. Yet this unreasonable expectation has led many notable athletes to use performance-enhancing drugs.

In response to such developments rose the critical thinkers of history. These men and women courageously pointed out that—metaphorically speaking—the emperor had no clothes.

Critical thinking is a path to freedom from half-truths and deception. You have the right to question what you see, hear, and read. Acquiring this ability is one of the major goals of a liberal arts education.

Critical thinking as thorough thinking

For some people, the term *critical thinking* has negative connotations. If you prefer, use the words *thorough thinking* instead. Both terms point to the same array of activities: sorting out conflicting claims, weighing the evidence, letting go of personal biases, and arriving at reasonable views. This adds up to an ongoing conversation, a constant process, not a final product.

This conversation takes time. In many situations, thorough thinking takes time and the willingness to say three subversive words: "I don't know." Thorough thinking is undermined in a society that values quick answers and instant certainty. Successful athletes soon learn about this. A competitive play that works results in an athlete being labeled a "genius." The same play when unsuccessful leads critics to label the player an "idiot." Such snap judgments are often at odds with effective thinking.

Skilled student athletes are thorough thinkers. They distinguish between opinion and fact. They ask powerful questions of their professors, their teammates, and their coaches. They make detailed observations. They uncover assumptions and define their terms. They make assertions carefully, basing them on sound logic and solid evidence. Almost everything that we call *knowledge* is a result of these activities. This means that critical thinking and learning are intimately linked.

It's been said that human beings are rational creatures. Yet no one is born a thorough thinker. This is a learned skill. Use the suggestions in this chapter to claim the thinking powers that are your birthright. The critical thinker is one aspect of the master student athlete who lives inside you. ▨

Becoming a Critical Thinker

Stripped to its essence, critical thinking means asking and answering questions. The four basic questions in the Learning Styles Applications in this book—*Why? What? How?* and *What if?*—are a powerful tool for thinking. As they take you through the cycle of learning, they can also guide you in becoming a critical thinker. This article offers a variety of tools for answering those questions. For more handy implements, see *Becoming a Critical Thinker* by Vincent Ryan Ruggiero.

1 *Why* **am I considering this issue?** Critical thinking and personal passion go together. Begin critical thinking with a question that matters to you. Seek a rationale for your learning. Understand why it is important for you to think about a specific topic. You might want to arrive at a new conclusion, make a prediction, or solve a problem. By finding a personal connection with an issue, your interest in acquiring and retaining new information increases.

2 *What* **are various points of view on this issue?** Imagine Michael Jordan, Sheryl Swoopes, and coach John Wooden gathered together in a room to plan the best basketball offense. Picture Mahatma Gandhi, Fidel Castro, George W. Bush, and Mother Teresa at a United Nations conference on conflict resolution. When seeking out alternative points of view, let such events unfold in your mind.

Dozens of viewpoints exist on every critical issue—ways to regulate collegiate athletics, reduce crime, end world hunger, prevent war, educate our children, and countless others. In fact, few problems allow for any permanent solution. Each generation produces new answers, based on current conditions. Our search for answers is a conversation that spans centuries. On each question, many voices are waiting to be heard.

You can take advantage of this diversity by seeking out alternative views with an open mind. When talking to another person, be willing to walk away with a new point of view—even if it's the one you brought to the table, supported with new evidence. Examining different points of view is an exercise in analysis, which you can do with the suggestions that follow.

Define terms. Imagine two people arguing about whether an employer should limit health care benefits to members of a family. To one person, the word *family* means a mother, father, and children; to the other person, the word *family* applies to any long-term, supportive relationship between people who live together. Chances are, the debate will go nowhere until these people realize that they're defining the same word in different ways.

Conflicts of opinion can often be resolved—or at least clarified—when we define our key terms up front. This is especially true with abstract, emotion-laden terms such as *freedom, peace, progress,* or *justice.* Blood has been shed over the meaning of these words. Define them with care.

Look for assertions. A speaker or writer's key terms occur in a larger context called an assertion. An *assertion* is a complete sentence that directly answers a key question. For example, consider this sentence: "A master is a person who has attained a level of skill that goes beyond technique." This sentence is an assertion that answers an important question: How do we recognize a master?

Look for at least three viewpoints. When asking questions, let go of the temptation to settle for just a single answer. Once you have come up with an answer, say to yourself, "Yes, that is one answer. Now what's another?" Using this approach can sustain honest inquiry, fuel creativity, and lead to conceptual breakthroughs.

Be prepared: The world is complicated, and critical thinking is a complex business. Some of your answers might contradict others. Resist the temptation to have all of your ideas in a neat, orderly bundle.

Practice tolerance. Having opinions about issues is natural. The problem occurs when we become so attached to our current opinions that we refuse to consider others. As an athlete, you know this firsthand. Teams succeed when their members are willing to set aside their differences and agree on strategies to win a competition.

One path to critical thinking is tolerance for a wide range of opinions. Consider ideas that are widely accepted today in Western cultures—for example, civil liberties for people of color and the right of women to vote. These ideas were once considered dangerous. Ideas that seem outlandish today might become widely accepted a century, a decade, or even a year from now. Remembering this can help us practice tolerance for differing opinions today. When doing so, we make room for new ideas that might alter our lives.

3 How well is each point of view supported? Uncritical thinkers shield themselves from new information and ideas. As an alternative, you can follow the example of scientists, who constantly look for evidence that contradicts their theories. The following suggestions can help.

Look for logic and evidence. The aim of using logic is to make statements that are clear, consistent, and coherent. As you list a speaker or writer's assertions, you may find gaps between them—assertions that contradict each other or assumptions that are unfounded. These are errors in logic.

In addition to thinking logically, assess the evidence used to support points of view. Evidence comes in several forms, including facts, expert testimony, and examples. To think critically about evidence, ask questions such as:

- Are all or most of the relevant facts presented?
- Are the facts consistent with each other?
- Are enough examples included to make a solid case for the viewpoint?
- Do the examples truly support the viewpoint?
- Are the examples typical? That is, could the author or speaker support the assertion with other examples that are similar?
- Is the expert credible—truly knowledgeable about the topic?

Consider the source. Look again at that article on the problems of manufacturing cars powered by natural gas; it might have been written by an executive from an oil company. Check out the college administrators who argue for extending the competition season for a sport; they might have a hidden agenda to trim budget deficits by boosting revenue.

This is not to say that we should dismiss the ideas of people who have a vested interest in stating their opinions. Rather, we can take their self-interest into account as we consider their ideas.

Understand before criticizing. Polished debaters can sum up the viewpoints they disagree with—often better than the people who support those viewpoints. Likewise, critical thinkers take the time to understand a point of view before agreeing or disagreeing with it.

Watch for hot spots. Many people have mental "hot spots"—topics that provoke strong opinions and feelings. Examples are abortion, homosexuality, gun control, and the death penalty. In higher education, coaches and faculty members often have different opinions about the role of athletics.

To become more skilled at examining various points of view, notice your own particular hot spots. Make a clear intention to accept your feelings about these topics and to continue using critical thinking techniques.

Be willing to be uncertain. Some of the most profound thinkers have practiced the art of thinking by using a magic sentence: "I'm not sure yet."

Those are words that many people do not like to hear. Our society rewards quick answers and quotable sound bites. We're under considerable pressure to utter the truth in 10 seconds or less.

In such a society, it is courageous and unusual to take the time to pause, to consider many points of view—and to not know. When a society adopts half-truths in a blind rush for certainty, a willingness to embrace uncertainty can move us forward.

4 What if I could combine various points of view or create a new one? Finding the truth is like painting a barn door by throwing open cans of paint at it. Few people who throw at the door miss it entirely. Yet no one can really cover the whole door in one toss.

People who express a viewpoint are seeking truth. Yet no reasonable person claims to cover the whole barn door—to have the Whole Truth about anything. Instead, each viewpoint is one approach among many possible approaches. If you don't think that any one opinion is complete, then it's up to you to combine the perspectives on the issue.

Create a critical thinking "spreadsheet." When you consult authorities with different stands on an issue, you might feel confused about how to sort out, evaluate, and combine their points of view. To overcome confusion, create a kind of spreadsheet. List the authorities across the top of a page and key questions down the left. Then indicate each authority's answer to each question, along with your own answers.

For example, the following spreadsheet clarifies different points of view on the issue of whether to outlaw boxing:

	Medical doctor	Former boxer	Sports journalist	Me
Is boxing a sport?	No	Yes	Yes	Yes
Is boxing dangerous?	Yes	Yes	Yes	Yes
Is boxing more dangerous than other sports?	Yes	No	Yes	No
Can the risk of injury be overcome by proper training?	No	No	No	Yes

Source: Vincent Ryan Ruggiero, *Becoming a Critical Thinker,* Fourth Edition. Copyright © 2002 by Houghton Mifflin Company. Reprinted with permission.

You could state your own viewpoint by combining your answers to the questions in the above spreadsheet: "I favor legalized boxing. Though boxing poses dangers, so do other sports. And as with other sports, the risk of injury can be reduced when boxers get proper training."

Accept your changing perspectives. Researcher William Perry found that students in higher education move through stages of intellectual development.[2] Students in earlier stages tend to think there is only one correct viewpoint on each issue, and they look to their instructors to reveal that truth. Later, students acknowledge a variety of opinions on issues and construct their own viewpoints. That same intellectual development often occurs in student athletes' relationships with their coaches.

Monitor changes in your thinking processes as you combine viewpoints. Distinguish between opinions that you accept from authorities and opinions that are based on your own use of logic and search for evidence. Also look for opinions that result from objective procedures (such as using the four questions in this article) and personal sources (using intuition or "gut feelings"). 🗵

→ Attitudes of a critical thinker

The American Philosophical Association invited a panel of 46 scholars from the United States and Canada to come up with answers to the following two questions: "What is college-level critical thinking?" and "What leads us to conclude that a person is an effective critical thinker?"[3] After two years of work, this panel concluded that critical thinkers share the attitudes summarized in this chart.

Attitude	Sample statement
Truth-seeking	"Let's follow this idea and see where it leads, even if we feel uncomfortable with what we find out."
Open-minded	"I have a point of view on this subject, and I'm anxious to hear yours as well."
Analytical	"Taking a stand on the issue commits me to take some new action."
Systematic	"The speaker made several interesting points, and I'd like to hear some more evidence to support each one."
Self-confident	"After reading the book for the first time, I was confused. I'll be able to understand it after studying the book some more."
Inquisitive	"When I first saw that painting, I wanted to know what was going on in the artist's life when she painted it."
Mature	"I'll wait until I gather some more facts before reaching a conclusion on this issue."

Finding "aha!"
Creativity fuels critical thinking

Central to creative thinking is something called the "aha!" experience. Nineteenth-century poet Emily Dickinson described the aha! this way: "If I feel physically as if the top of my head were taken off, I know that is poetry." Aha! is the burst of creative energy heralded by the arrival of a new, original idea. It is the sudden emergence of a new pattern, a previously undetected relationship, or an unusual combination of familiar elements. It is an exhilarating experience.

Aha! does not always result in a timeless poem or a Nobel Prize. It can be inspired by anything from playing a new riff on a guitar to discovering how to consistently complete a complicated dive off the high platform. A nurse might notice a patient's symptom that everyone else missed. That's an aha! An accountant might discover a tax break for a client. That's an aha! A student athlete, after watching hours of video, might suddenly see a critical weakness in an upcoming opponent. Aha!

The flip side of aha! is following through. Thinking is both fun *and* work. It is effortless and uncomfortable. It's the result of luck and persistence. It involves spontaneity *and* step-by-step procedures, planning *and* action, convergent *and* divergent thinking.

Employers in all fields are desperately seeking those rare people who can find aha! and do something with it. The necessary skills include the ability to spot assumptions, weigh evidence, separate fact from opinion, organize thoughts, and avoid

errors in logic. All this can be demanding work. Just as often, it can be energizing and fun.

This chapter offers you a chance to practice two types of thinking that produce aha!: convergent thinking and divergent thinking. One focuses on finding a single solution to a problem, while the other asks you to consider as many viewpoints as possible.

Convergent thinking involves a narrowing-down process. Out of all the possible viewpoints on an issue or alternative solutions to a problem, you choose the one that is the most reasonable or that provides the most logical basis for action.

Some people see convergent thinking and critical thinking as the same thing. However, there's more to the story. *Divergent* or *creative thinking* involves opening up. Before you choose among viewpoints, generate as many of them as possible. Open up alternatives and consider all of your options. Define problems in different ways. Keep asking questions and looking for answers.

Creative thinking provides the basis for convergent thinking. In other words, one path toward having good ideas is to have *lots* of ideas. Then you can pick and choose from among them, combining and refining them as you see fit.

The key is to make conscious choices about what kind of thinking to do in any given moment. Generally speaking, creative thinking is more appropriate in the early stages of planning and problem solving. Feel free to dwell in this domain for a while. If you narrow down your options too soon, you run the risk of missing an exciting solution or of neglecting a novel viewpoint. Convergent thinking is essential, and you should save it until you have plenty of options on the table.

Remember that creative thinking and convergent thinking take place in a continuous cycle. After you've used convergent thinking to narrow down your options, you can return to creative thinking at any time to generate new ones.

Tangram

A tangram is an ancient Chinese puzzle game that stimulates the "play instinct" so critical to creative thinking. The cat figure above was created by rearranging seven sections of a square. Hundreds of images can be devised in this manner. Playing with tangrams allows us to see relationships we didn't notice before.

The rules of the game are simple: Use these seven pieces to create something that wasn't there before. Be sure to use all seven. You might start by mixing up the pieces and seeing whether you can put them back together to form a square.

Make your own tangram by cutting pieces like those above out of poster board. When you come up with a pattern you like, trace around the outside edges of it and see if a friend can discover how you did it.

Ways to create ideas

Use the following techniques to generate ideas about everything, whether you're studying math problems, remodeling a house, or writing a bestseller. With practice, you can set the stage for creative leaps, jump with style, and land on your feet with brand-new ideas in hand.

Conduct a brainstorm.
Brainstorming is a technique for finding solutions, creating plans, and discovering new ideas. When you are stuck on a problem, brainstorming can break the logjam.

For example, if you run out of money two days before your next room and board athletic scholarship check is available, you can brainstorm ways to make your money last longer. You can also brainstorm ways to pay for your education or manage your time so that you free up extra hours every week.

The purpose of brainstorming is to generate as many solutions as possible. Sometimes the craziest, most outlandish ideas can lead to new ways to solve problems. Use the following steps to experiment.

First, state the issue or problem precisely by writing it down as a question. For example: "What methods and techniques can I use to make certain my scholarship money lasts until the next check is available?"

Next, set a time limit for your brainstorming session. Use a clock to time it to the minute.

Before you begin, sit quietly for a few seconds to collect your thoughts. Then start timing and write as fast as you can. Write down everything. Accept every idea. Quantity, not quality, is the goal.

You can also brainstorm with others. Ask one member of the group to write down solutions. Feed off the ideas of others, and remember to avoid evaluating or judging anyone's idea during the brainstorm. After the session, review, evaluate, and edit. Toss out any truly nutty ideas, but not before you give them a chance. During your brainstorm on budgeting your scholarship money, you might have written "Create a four-year budget for completing school." Impossible? It is likely that your coach, academic advisor, or someone from your school's booster group knows of a person who can help you do just that. Stay open to possibilities. One crazy idea can unleash a flood of other, more workable solutions.

Focus and let go. Focusing attention and letting go are alternating parts of the same process. Intense focus on answering a question taps the resources of your conscious mind. Letting go periodically gives your subconscious mind some time to work.

For example, if you are having difficulty writing a paper at a computer, practice focusing by listening to the sounds as you type. Notice the feel of the keys as you strike them. Be gentle with yourself when you notice that your concentration has lapsed. Practice focusing for short periods at first, then let go by giving yourself a break: Stretch. Go for a walk. Take a short snooze when you are tired of working on a problem. Thomas Edison took frequent naps. Then the light bulb clicked on.

You can experiment with this process on a larger scale. Ask yourself a question as you fall asleep at night. Keep pencil and paper or a recorder near your bed. The moment you wake up, begin writing or speaking and see if an answer to your question emerges.

Cultivate creative serendipity.
The word *serendipity* was coined by the English author Horace Walpole from the title of an ancient Persian fairy tale, "The Three Princes of Serendip." The princes had a knack for making lucky discoveries. Serendipity is that knack, and it

involves more than luck. It is the ability to see something valuable that you weren't looking for.

History is full of serendipitous people. Penicillin, for instance, was discovered "by accident." Scottish scientist Alexander Fleming was growing bacteria in a laboratory petri dish. A spore of *Penicillium notatum,* a kind of mold, blew in the window and landed in the dish, killing the bacteria. Fleming isolated the active ingredient. A few years later, during World War II, it saved thousands of lives.

You can train yourself in the art of serendipity. To begin, multiply your contacts with the world. Meet new people. Read. Go to plays, concerts, art shows, lectures, and movies. Watch television programs you normally wouldn't watch. Read magazines you wouldn't normally read. Play with lots of new ideas.

Also keep your eyes open and expect discoveries. You might find a solution to an accounting problem in a Saturday morning cartoon. You might discover a topic for your term paper at the corner convenience store.

Keep idea files. We all have ideas. People who are viewed as creative are those who treat their ideas with care. That means recognizing them, recording them, and filing them so that you can follow up on them later. Write down powerful quotations, random insights, notes on your reading, and useful ideas you encounter in class. Collect jokes, too.

One way to keep track of ideas is to write them down on 3x5 cards. If you carry 3x5 cards in a pocket or purse, you can record ideas while standing in line or sitting in a waiting room. Invent your own categories to keep cards organized. In addition, keep letter-sized files of important correspondence, e-mails, magazine and newspaper articles, and other material. You can also create idea files on a computer using word processing, outlining, or database software.

Review your files regularly. Some amusing thought that came to you in November might be the perfect solution to a problem in March.

Collect and play with data. Look from all sides at the data you collect. There are many ways to do this.

For example, turn a problem upside down by picking a solution first and then working backward.

Look for the obvious solutions or the obvious "truths" about the problem—then toss them

out. Ask yourself: "Well, I know X is true, but if X were *not* true, what would happen?" Or ask the reverse: "If that *were* true, what would follow next?"

Make imaginary pictures with the data. Condense it. Categorize it. Put it in chronological order. Put it in alphabetical order. Put it in random order. Order it from most to least complex. Reverse all of those orders. Look for opposites.

Put unrelated facts next to each other and invent a relationship between them, even if it seems absurd at first. In *The Act of Creation,* novelist Arthur Koestler says that finding a context in which to combine opposites is the essence of creativity.[4]

Refine ideas and follow through. Your initial inspirations may be gems in the rough. Take the time to polish them. Discover the value that lies hidden within.

Apply critical thinking techniques to refine raw ideas. One way to refine an idea is to simplify it. And if that doesn't work, mess it up. Make it more complex.

Then, when appropriate, take further action. Follow-through is key. Many of us ignore this part of the creative process. How many great moneymaking schemes have we had that we never pursued? How many good ideas have we had for short stories that we never wrote? How many times have we said to ourselves, "You know, what they ought to do is attach two handles to one of those things, paint it orange, and sell it to police departments. They'd make a fortune." And we never realize that we are "they." Genius resides in the follow-through—the application of perspiration to inspiration.

Trust the process. Learn to trust the creative process—even when no answers are in sight. Often we are reluctant to look at problems if no immediate solution is at hand. We grow impatient and tend to avoid frustration by giving up.

Most of us do this to some degree with personal problems. If we are having difficulty with a relationship and don't see a quick resolution, we deny that the problem exists rather than face it. Trust that a solution will show up. Frustration and a feeling of being stuck are often signals that a solution is imminent. ▨

Consider the following argument:

Orca whales mate for life.
Orca whales travel in family groups.
Science has revealed that Orca whales are intelligent.
Therefore, Orca whales should be saved from extinction.

One idea underlies this line of thought:

Any animal that displays significant human characteristics deserves special protection.

Whether or not you agree with this argument, consider for a moment the process of making assumptions. Assumptions are assertions that guide our thinking and behavior. Often these assertions are unconscious. People can remain unaware of their most basic and far-reaching assumptions—the very ideas that shape their lives.

Spotting assumptions can be tricky, since they are usually unstated and offered without evidence. And scores of assumptions can be held at the same time. Those assumptions might even contradict each other, resulting in muddled thinking and confused behavior. This makes uncovering assumptions a feat worthy of the greatest detective.

Letting assumptions remain in our subconscious can erect barriers to our success. Take the person who says, "I don't worry about saving money for the future. I think life is meant to be enjoyed today—not later." This statement rests on at least two assumptions: *saving money is not enjoyable,* and *we can enjoy ourselves only when we're spending money.*

It would be no surprise to find out that this person runs out of money near the end of each month and depends on cash advances from high-interest credit cards. She is shielding herself from some ideas that could erase her debt: Saving money can be a source of satisfaction, and many enjoyable activities cost nothing.

The stakes in uncovering assumptions are high. Prejudice thrives on the beliefs that certain people are inferior or dangerous due to their skin color, ethnic background, or sexual orientation. Those beliefs have led to flawed assumptions such as *mixing the blood of the races will lead to genetically inferior offspring* and *racial integration of the armed forces will lead to the destruction of morale.*

When we remain ignorant of our assumptions, we also make it easier for people with hidden agendas to do our thinking for us. Demagogues and unethical advertisers know that unchallenged assumptions are potent tools for influencing our attitudes and behavior.

Take this claim from an advertisement: "Successful students have large vocabularies, so sign up today for our

Uncovering assumptions

seminar on word power!" Embedded in this sentence are several assumptions. One is that a cause-and-effect relationship exists between a large vocabulary and success in school. Another is that a large vocabulary is the single or most important factor in that success. This claim also assumes that the advertiser's seminar is the best way to develop your vocabulary. In reality, none of these assumptions is necessarily true.

Assertions and opinions flow from our assumptions. Heated conflict and hard feelings often result when people argue on the level of opinions—forgetting that the real conflict lies at the level of their assumptions.

An example is the question about whether the government should legislate and control collegiate athletics. People who advocate such programs often assume that overseeing college sports is an appropriate task for government officials. On the other hand, people who argue against such programs might assume that the government has no business interfering with athletics at all. There's little hope of resolving this conflict of opinion unless we deal with something more basic: our assumptions about the proper role of government.

You can follow a three-step method for testing the validity of any viewpoint. First, look for the assumptions—the assertions implied by that viewpoint. Second, write down these assumptions. Third, see if you can find any exceptions to them. This technique helps detect many errors in logic.

Ways to fool yourself

Six common mistakes in logic

Logic is a branch of philosophy that seeks to distinguish between effective and ineffective reasoning. Students of logic look for valid steps in an *argument*, or a series of assertions. The opening assertions of the argument are the *premises*, and the final assertion is the *conclusion*.

Over the last 2,500 years, specialists in logic have listed some classic land mines in the field of logic—common mistakes that are called *fallacies*. Logical fallacies are listed in just about every logic textbook. Following are six examples. Knowing about them when you string together a bunch of assertions can help you avoid getting fooled.

1 Jump to conclusions. Jumping to conclusions is the only exercise that some lazy thinkers get. This fallacy involves drawing conclusions without sufficient evidence. Take the bank officer who hears about a student failing to pay back an education loan. After that, the officer turns down all loan applications from students. This person has formed a rigid opinion on the basis of hearsay. Jumping to conclusions—also called *hasty generalization*—is at work here.

2 Attack the person. This mistake in logic is common at election time. It can also happen during recruitment for collegiate athletics—for instance, when someone claims that a coach is of questionable character because she isn't married. People who indulge in personal attacks are attempting an intellectual sleight of hand to divert our attention from the truly relevant issues.

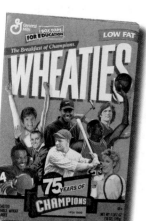

3 Appeal to authority. A professional athlete endorses a brand of breakfast cereal. A famous musician features a soft drink company's product in a rock video. The promotional brochure for an advertising agency lists all of the large companies that have used its services.

In each case, the people involved are trying to win your confidence—and your dollars—by citing authorities. The underlying assumption is usually this: *Famous people and organizations buy our product. Therefore, you should buy it too.* Or *you should accept this idea merely because someone who's well known says it's true.*

Appealing to authority is usually a substitute for producing real evidence. It invites sloppy thinking. When our only evidence for a viewpoint is an appeal to authority, it's time to think more thoroughly.

4 Point to a false cause. The fact that one event follows another does not necessarily mean that the two events have a cause-and-effect relationship. All we can actually say is that the events might be correlated. For example, as children's vocabularies improve, they can get more cavities. This does not mean that cavities are the result of an improved vocabulary! Instead, the increase in cavities is due to other factors, such as physical maturation and changes in diet or personal care.

5 Think in all-or-nothing terms. Consider these statements: *Doctors are greedy. . . . You can't trust politicians. . . . Student athletes these days are just in college to get into the high-paying professional ranks; they lack idealism. . . . Homeless people don't want to work.*

These opinions imply the word *all*. They gloss over individual differences, claiming that all members of a group are exactly alike. They also ignore key facts, for instance, that some doctors volunteer their time at free medical clinics and that many homeless people are children who are too young to work. All-or-nothing thinking is one of the most common errors in logic.

6 Base arguments on emotion. The politician who ends every campaign speech with flag waving and slides of his mother eating apple pie is staking his future on appeals to emotion. Get past the fluff and see if you can uncover any worthwhile ideas. ◪

voices

student

Successful choices are a result of solving a problem, looking at pros and cons, making the decision or choice, and checking how you feel about (and how others will be affected by) this conclusion. This takes concerted effort, but a master student uses this inquisitive, analytical, and open-minded process to gain self-confidence and maturity.

—KRISTINE RUGGLES

Gaining skill at decision making

We make decisions all of the time, whether we realize it or not. Even avoiding decisions is a form of decision making. The student who puts off studying for a test until the last minute might really be saying, "I've decided this course is not important" or "I've decided not to give this course much time."

Decide right now to apply some of the following suggestions, and you can take your overall decision making to new heights of effectiveness.

Recognize decisions. Decisions are more than wishes or desires. There's a world of difference between "I wish I could get better grades" and "I will take more powerful notes, read with greater retention, and review my class notes daily." Decisions are specific and lead to focused action.

When we decide, we narrow down. We give up actions that are inconsistent with our decision. Deciding to eat fruit instead of ice cream for dessert rules out the next trip to the ice cream store.

Determine the decision's importance. Some decisions are trivial: no matter what the outcome, your life is not affected much. Other decisions can shape your circumstances for years—such as the day you choose the school where you'll spend your collegiate athletic career. Devote more time and energy to the decisions with big outcomes.

Clarify your values. When you know specifically what you want from life, making decisions becomes easier. This is especially true when you define your values precisely and put them in writing. Saying that you value education is fine. Now give that declaration some teeth. Note that you value continuous learning as a chance to upgrade your career skills, for instance. That can make registering for next term's classes much easier.

Choose an overall strategy for making the decision. Every time that you make a decision, you use a strategy—even when you're not aware of it. Effective decision makers can articulate and choose from among several strategies. Experiment with these:

- *Find all the available options and choose one deliberately.* Save this strategy for decisions where you have a relatively small number of options, and where each option leads to noticeably different results.

- *Find all the available options and choose one randomly.* This strategy can be risky. Save it for times when your options are basically similar and fairness is the main issue.

- *Limit the options, then choose.* For example, visit many search engines on the World Wide Web and then narrow the list down to two or three that you choose to use regularly.

- *Choose the first acceptable option that you find.* This strategy can work well when you have many options, and when thoroughly researching each option will take too much time or create too little benefit. For instance, when you're writing a paper and are pressed for time, write down the first five facts you find that directly support your thesis. You could look for more facts, but the extra investment of time may not be worth it.

- *Choose to act on someone else's decision.* You use this strategy, for example, when you buy a CD based on a friend's recommendation. A more sophisticated version of this strategy is arbitration, where people who are in conflict agree to act on the decision made by a third party, such as a judge, who listens to each person's case.

Use time as an ally. Sometimes we face dilemmas—situations in which any course of action leads to undesirable consequences. In such cases, consider waiting it out. Do nothing until the circumstances change, making one alternative clearly preferable to another.

Use intuition. Some decisions seem to make themselves. A solution pops into our mind and we gain newfound clarity. Using intuition is not the same as forgetting about the decision or refusing to make it. Intuitive decisions usually arrive after we've gathered the relevant facts and faced a problem for some time.

Act on your decision. There comes a time to move from the realm of discovery and intention to the arena of action. Action is a hallmark of a true decision.

Evaluate your decision. After you act on a decision, observe the consequences over time. Reflect on how well your decision worked and how you might have done it differently. Hindsight can be a source of insight.

Four ways to solve problems

There is a vast literature on problem-solving techniques. Much of it can be traced to American philosopher John Dewey, who devised these steps of effective problem solving:

- Perceive a "felt difficulty" and state it clearly and concisely.

- Invent possible solutions.

- Rationally test each solution by anticipating its possible consequences.

- Act on the preferred solution, evaluate the consequences, and determine whether a new solution is needed.[5]

Much of what you'll read about problem solving amounts to variations on Dewey's steps. Think of problem solving as a process with four P's: Define the *problem*, generate *possibilities*, create a *plan*, and *perform* your plan.

1 Define the problem.
To define a problem effectively, understand what a problem is—a mismatch between what you want and what you have. Problem solving is all about reducing the gap between these two factors.

Start with what you have. Tell the truth about what's present in your life right now, without shame or blame. For example: "I often get sleepy while reading my physics assignments, and after closing the book I cannot remember what I just read."

Next, describe in detail what you want. Go for specifics: "I want to remain alert as I read about physics. I also want to accurately summarize each chapter I read."

Remember that when we define a problem in limiting ways, our solutions merely generate new problems. As Einstein said, "The world we have made is a result of the level of thinking we have done thus far. We cannot solve problems at the same level at which we created them."[6] This idea has many applications for success in school. An example is the student who struggles with note taking. The problem, she thinks, is that her notes are too sketchy. The logical solution, she decides, is to take *more* notes, and her new goal is to write down almost everything her instructors say. No matter how fast and furiously she writes, she cannot capture all of the instructors' comments.

Consider what happens when this student defines the problem in a new way. After more thought, she decides that her dilemma is not the *quantity* of her notes but their *quality*. She adopts a new format for taking notes, dividing her note paper into two columns. In the right-hand column she writes down only the main points of each lecture. And in the left-hand column she notes two or three supporting details for each point.

Over time, this student makes the joyous discovery that there are usually just three or four core ideas to remember from each lecture. She originally thought the solution was to take more notes. What really worked was taking notes in a new way.

2 Generate possibilities.
Now put on your creative thinking hat. Open up. Brainstorm as many possible solutions to the problem as you can. At this stage, quantity counts. As you generate possibilities, gather relevant facts. For example, when you're faced with a dilemma about what courses to take next term, get information on class times, locations, and instructors. If you haven't decided which summer job offer to accept, gather information on salary, benefits, and working conditions.

3 Create a plan.
After rereading your problem definition and list of possible solutions, choose the solution that seems most workable. Think about specific actions that will reduce the gap between what you have and what you want. Visualize the steps you will take to make this solution a reality and arrange them in chronological order. To make your plan even more powerful, put it in writing. Use the guidelines for Intention Statements in the Introduction to this book.

4 Perform your plan.
This step gets you off your chair and out into the world. Now you actually *do* what you have planned. Ultimately, your skill in solving problems lies in how well you perform your plan. Through the quality of your actions, you become the architect of your own success.

Note that the four P's of this problem-solving process closely parallel the four key questions listed in the article "Becoming a critical thinker":

Define the **problem**	**What** is the problem?
Generate **possibilities**	**What if** there are several possible solutions?
Create a **plan**	**How** would this possible solution work?
Perform your plan	**Why** is one solution more workable than another?

When facing problems, experiment with these four P's, and remember that the order of steps is not absolute. Also remember that any solution has the potential to create new problems. If that happens, cycle through the four P's of problem solving again.

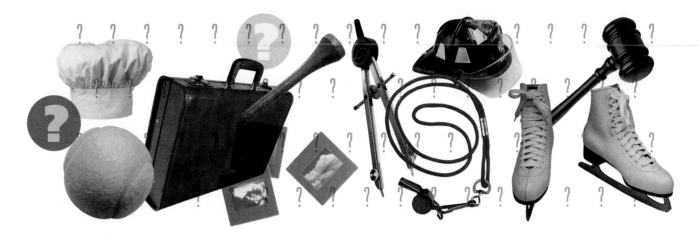

"But I don't know what I want to do"
Choosing a major

As a student athlete, you face challenges in choosing a major that your nonathletic peers may never have to worry about. In addition to finding a major that interests you and meeting its requirements, you need to remain competitive in sports.

Your choice of a major can fall into place once you determine what you want in life. When you see a clear connection between completing school and creating the career and life of your dreams, then the daily tasks of higher education become charged with meaning.

Back up to a bigger picture

Before you choose a major, list your core values, such as contribution to society, wealth, recognition, health, or fun. Also write goals for what you want to accomplish in 5 years, 10 years, or even 50 years from today. After thinking in such big terms, choosing a major can seem like a piece of cake.

Perhaps you participate in sports like baseball, basketball, or football and have dreams of "turning pro." You might feel tempted to ignore other career options. Many student athletes have been so absorbed in sports that they have little work experience and few thoughts about a nonathletic career.

Be careful to avoid limiting yourself. Think about your long-term future. Even if you do make it to a professional level, your athletic career will probably last only a few years. To start sorting out options for the rest of your working life, see "Career planning: Begin the process now" in Chapter Twelve.

Maintain your eligibility

The NCAA has rules for student athletes about making a reasonable rate of academic progress in order to stay eligible for competition. These rules will have an impact on when you declare your major. Get familiar with them now. Meet with your athletic academic advisor to learn exactly what's required of you. Don't get stuck in the position of being forced into a major at the last minute, or of being declared ineligible.

Many schools require all students to take a group of core courses in English composition, speech, literature, mathematics, science, social science, history, and foreign languages. To maintain your eligibility, get started on these courses right away and take them in a logical order. Then you can be ready to focus on your major no later than the beginning of your junior year.

Take steps to choose, now

Students who do not participate in athletics might wait several years to declare their major—or change their major two to three times before graduation. Student athletes who do these things might place their eligibility in jeopardy. Start thinking about your major sooner rather than later.

Even if you say that you're undecided about your major, you probably know a lot about what it is likely to be. To verify this, do a short experiment. Search your school's catalog, online or in print, for a list of available majors. Read through the list two or three times. Then pretend that you have to choose a major today. Write down the first three ideas that come to mind.

The NCAA has rules for student athletes about making a reasonable rate of academic progress in order to stay eligible for competition.

Hold on to this list, which reflects your intuition or "gut wisdom," as you perform the more intellectual task of researching various majors and careers in detail. Your research may lead to a new choice of major—or it may simply confirm one of the majors on your original list.

Test your trial choice

When you've made a trial choice of major, design a series of experiments to test it. For example:

- Study your school's list of required courses for this major, looking for a fit with your interests and long-term goals.

- Visit with instructors who teach courses in the major, asking about required course work and career options in the field.

- Discuss your trial choice with an academic advisor or career counselor.

- Enroll in a course related to your possible major.

- Find a volunteer experience, internship, part-time job, or service learning experience related to the major.

- Meet informally with students who have declared the same major.

- Interview someone who works in a field related to the major.

If these experiences confirm your choice of major, celebrate that fact. If they result in choosing a new major, celebrate that outcome as well.

Ask other people for ideas

Other people might have valuable suggestions about a choice of major or career for you. Ask key people in your life for their ideas. Listen to them with an open mind.

At the same time, release any pressure from family members, coaches, or friends to choose a major or career that fails to interest you. Also avoid choosing a major simply to stay eligible for athletics. If you choose a career based solely on the expectations of other people, you could end up with a job you don't enjoy—and a barrier to your life satisfaction.

Another path to self-knowledge includes questionnaires or inventories that are designed to correlate your interests with specific career choices. Your academic advisor or someone at your school's career planning center can give you more details about these inventories. You might wish to take several of them and meet with an advisor to interpret the results.

Invent a major

When choosing a major, you might not need to limit yourself to those listed in your course catalog. Many schools now have flexible programs that allow for independent study. Through such programs you might be able to combine two existing majors, or invent an entirely new one of your own.

Choose a complementary minor

You can add flexibility to your academic program through your choice of a minor to complement or contrast with your choice of a major. The student who wants to be a minister could opt for a minor in English; all of those courses in composition can help in writing sermons. Or the student with a major in psychology might choose a minor in business administration with the idea of managing a counseling service some day. An effective choice of a minor can expand your skills and career options.

Stay flexible

Many of the majors offered in higher education can help you prepare for several different careers, or for further study in graduate school. One benefit of higher education is mobility—gaining transferable skills that can help you move into a new career field at any time.

Viewing a major as a one-time choice that determines your future can raise your stress levels to artificially high levels. Instead, look at choosing a major as the start of a continuing path of discovery, intention, and action. ✖

The variety of majors available in higher education is staggering. Below, for example, is a list of 100 majors culled from the catalogs of several colleges.

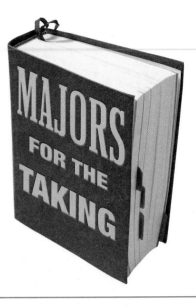

Accounting
Actuarial Science
Advertising
Aerospace Engineering
African American Studies
Agronomy
American Indian Studies
American Studies
Anthropology
Architecture
Art
Astronomy
Biochemistry
Biology
Botany
Broadcast Engineering
Building Construction
Chemical Engineering
Chemistry
Chicano Studies
Child Psychology
Civil Engineering
Clothing Design
Computer Engineering
Construction Management
Corrections Management
Criminal Justice
Dance
Dental Hygiene
Dentistry
Dietetics
Economics
Education
Electrical Engineering
English
Environmental Sciences
Equestrian Studies
Exercise and Sport Science
Family Social Science
Fashion Design and
   Merchandising
Film Studies
Finance
Fisheries and Wildlife
Food Science
Forestry
Geography
Geological Engineering

Geology
Geophysics
Global Studies
Graphic Arts
History
Hospital Administration
Hospitality and Tourism
   Services
Human Resource
   Development
Industrial Psychology
Industrial Technology
Interior Design
International Relations
Jewish Studies
Journalism
Kinesiology
Labor Relations
Latin
Liberal Studies
Library Science
Linguistics
Management Information
   Systems
Marketing
Mass Communication
Mathematics
Mechanical Engineering
Medical Records Services
Medical Technology
Merchandising
Meteorology
Microbiology
Music
Nursing
Personnel Management
Pharmacy
Philosophy
Physical Therapy
Physics
Physiology
Political Science
Psychology
Public Relations
Religious Studies
Retail Merchandising
Scientific and Technical
   Communication

Sociology
Speech and Hearing
   Science
Statistics
Substance Abuse
   Counseling
Theatre Arts
Theology
Urban Studies
Women's Studies
Zoological Sciences

This is not an exhaustive list. You'll find additional examples in your own school catalog.

Many schools also allow for double majors, individually designed majors, interdepartmental majors, and minors in many areas. You have plenty of options for creating a course of study that matches your skills, interests, and passions. ✖

Solving math and science problems

Solving problems is a key part of reading textbooks about math and science. You can approach math and science problems the way rock climbers approach mountains. First, make preparations before you get to the rock (strategies 1–5 below). Then tackle the rock—or problem—itself (strategies 6–10).

1 Review. Review problems you've solved before. Look over additional problems and make up your own variations on them. Work with a classmate and make up problems for each other to solve. The more problems you practice solving, the more you'll feel prepared for new ones. Note: When practicing, time yourself. Sometimes speed counts.

2 Know your terminology. Mathematicians and scientists often borrow words from plain English and assign new meanings to them. For example, the word *work* is usually thought of as referring to a job. For the physicist, *work* means *force multiplied by distance*. To ensure that you understand the terminology used in a problem, see if you can restate the problem in your own words. Translate equations into English sentences. Use 3x5 flash cards to study special terms.

3 Understand formulas. Some students memorize the problems and answers discussed in class—without learning the formulas or general principles behind the problems. This kind of rote learning doesn't allow them to apply the principles or formulas to new problems. If you understand the basic concepts behind these formulas, it is easier to recall them accurately.

4 Use summary sheets. Groups of terms and formulas can be easier to recall if you list them on a sheet of paper or put them on 3x5 cards. Mind map summary sheets allow you to see how various kinds of problems relate to one another. Creating a structure on which you can hang data helps your recall.

5 Use creative visualizations. Before you begin a problem-solving session, take a minute to relax, breathe deeply, and prepare yourself for the task ahead. See yourself solving problems successfully.

6 Survey the territory thoroughly. Read the problem at least twice before you begin. Read slowly. Be sure you understand what is being asked. Let go of the expectation that you'll find the solution right away. Play with possibilities. There's usually more than one way to solve a problem. If you feel stuck, read the problem out loud. Sometimes the sound of your voice will jar loose the solution to a problem.

7 Set up the problem. Survey the problem for all of the givens. Look for what is to be proved or what is to be discovered. Write these down. Before you begin to compute, determine the strategies you will use to arrive at solutions. When solving equations, carry out the algebra as far as you can before plugging in the actual numbers.

8 Draw a picture. Make a diagram. Pictures might show relationships more effectively than words. To keep on track, record your facts in tables. Consider using three columns labeled "What I already know," "What I want to find out," and "What connects the two." This third column is the place to record a formula that can help you solve the problem.

9 Check results. Work problems backwards, then forwards. Take a minute to make sure you kept the units of measurement clear. Say that you're calculating the velocity of an object. If you're measuring distance in meters and time in seconds, then the final velocity should be in meters per second. Also see if you can estimate the answer before you compute it. Then compare your solution to the estimate.

10 Savor the solution. Savor the times when you're getting correct answers to most of the problems in the textbook. Relish the times when you feel relaxed and confident. If you feel math or science anxiety, remember these times.

Asking questions

Thinking is born of questions. Questions open up options that might otherwise remain unexplored. Questions wake up people and lead them to investigate more closely issues and assumptions that had previously gone unchallenged. Questions promote curiosity, create new distinctions, and multiply possibilities. Besides, teachers love them. One of the best ways to develop your relationship with a teacher is to ask a question.

Asking questions is also a great way to improve relationships with friends and coworkers. When you ask a question, you offer a huge gift to people—an opportunity for them to speak their brilliance and for you to listen to their answers.

Students often say, "I don't know what to ask." Following are some ways to construct powerful questions about any subject you study in school, about athletics, or about any other area of your life that you choose to examine.

Let your pen start moving. Sometimes you can access a deeper level of knowledge by taking out your pen, putting it on a piece of paper, and writing down questions—even before you know *what* to write. Don't think. Just watch the paper and notice what appears. The results might be surprising.

Ask about what's missing. Another way to invent useful questions is to notice what's missing from your life and then ask how to supply it. For example, you might

When you ask a question, you offer a huge gift to people—an opportunity for them to speak their brilliance and for you to listen to their answers.

feel overwhelmed by the number of academic, athletic, and social commitments in your schedule. In your journal, you can write, "What's missing is time. How do I create enough time in my day to actually do the things that I say I want to do?"

Pretend to be someone else. Another way to invent questions is first to think of someone you greatly respect. Then pretend you're that person and ask the questions you think *she* would ask.

Begin a general question, then brainstorm endings. By starting with a general question and then brainstorming a long list of endings, you can invent a question that you've never asked before. For example:

What can I do when . . . ? What can I do when an instructor calls on me in class and I have no idea what to say? What can I do when a teacher doesn't show up for class on time? What can I do when I feel overwhelmed with assignments?

How can I . . . ? How can I get just the kind of courses that I want? How can I expand my career options? How can I become much more effective as a student athlete, starting today?

When do I . . . ? When do I decide on a major? When do I transfer to another school? When do I meet with an instructor to discuss an upcoming term paper?

Ask what else you want to know. Many times you can quickly generate questions by simply asking yourself, "What else do I want to know?" Ask this question immediately after you read a paragraph in a book or listen to someone speak.

Start from the assumption that you are brilliant, and begin asking questions that can help you unlock your brilliance. ⬙

voices

student

A master student practices critical thinking. . . . She does not always accept the first answer as the only answer, and constantly questions what is put before her. I am determined to get every ounce of information, to glean and hold onto it, use it, and mature my thinking.

—LYNN LINEBERGER

journal entry 19

Discovery/Intention Statement

Reflect for a moment on your experience with Exercise #16: "Make a trial choice of major." If you had already chosen a major, did it confirm that choice? Did you uncover any new or surprising possibilities for declaring a major?

I discovered that I . . .

_____

_____

_____

_____

Now consider the major that is your current top choice. Think of publications you expect to find, resources you plan to investigate, and people you intend to consult in order to gather more information about this major.

I intend to . . .

_____

_____

_____

_____

_____

Plan to repeat this Journal Entry and the preceding exercise several times. You might find yourself researching several majors and changing your mind. That's fine. The aim is to start thinking about your major now.

exercise 17

EXPLORE EMOTIONAL REACTIONS

Each of us has certain "hot spots"—issues that trigger strong emotional reactions. For some people, these topics include abortion, gay and lesbian rights, capital punishment, and funding for welfare programs. There are many other examples, varying from person to person. Examine your own hot spots by writing a word or short phrase summarizing each issue. Then, describe what you typically say or do when each issue comes up in conversation.

After you have completed your list, think about what you can do to become a more effective thinker when you encounter one of these issues. For example, you could breathe deeply and count to five before you offer your own point of view. Or you might preface your opinion with an objective statement, such as "There are many valid points of view on this issue. Here's the way I see it, and I'm open to your ideas."

exercise 18

TRANSLATING GOALS INTO ACTION

Goal setting is an exercise in decision making and problem solving. Choose one long-range goal such as a personal project or a social change you'd like to help bring about. Examples include learning to scuba dive, eating a more healthful diet, studying to be an astronaut, improving health care for chronically ill children, inventing energy-saving technology, increasing the effectiveness of American schools, and becoming a better parent. List your goal here.

_____

_____

Next, ask yourself: "What specific actions are needed in the short term to meet my long-range goal?" List those actions, focusing on those you could complete in less than one hour or could start in the next 24 hours.

_____

_____

_____

PRACTICING CRITICAL THINKING

7

Statement #2:

_____

_____

_____

_____

_____

_____

_____

Question #2:

_____

_____

_____

_____

_____

_____

_____

The art of asking questions is just as important to critical thinking as answering them. One eye-opening way to create questions is to write something you're sure of and simply put a question mark after it. (You might need to rephrase the question for grammatical sense.) The question you create can lead to others.

For example, someone might say, "I would never take a philosophy course." This person can write "I would never take a philosophy course?" That suggests other questions: "In what ways would taking a philosophy course serve my success in school?" "Could taking a philosophy course help me become a better writer?"

In the space below, write three statements that you accept with certainty. Then rephrase each statement as a question.

Statement #1:

_____

_____

_____

_____

_____

_____

Statement #3:

_____

_____

_____

_____

_____

_____

Question #1:

_____

_____

_____

_____

_____

_____

Question #3:

_____

_____

_____

_____

_____

_____

power process

Find a bigger problem

Most of the time we view problems as barriers. They are a source of inconvenience and annoyance. They get in our way and prevent us from leading happy and productive lives. When we see problems in this way, our goal becomes to eliminate them.

This point of view might be flawed. For one thing, it is impossible to live a life without problems. Besides, they serve a purpose. They are opportunities to participate in life. Problems stimulate us and pull us forward.

When problems are seen in this way, the goal becomes not to eliminate them, but to find the problems that are worthy of us. Worthy problems are those that draw on our talents, move us toward our purpose, and increase our skills. The challenge is to tackle those problems that provide the greatest benefits for others and ourselves. Viewed in this way, problems give meaning to our lives.

Problems fill the available space

Problems seem to follow the same law of physics that gases do: They expand to fill whatever space is available. If your only problem for the entire day is to write a follow-up

Worthy problems are those that draw on our talents, move us toward our purpose, and increase our skills.

letter to a job interview, you can spend the whole day finding paper and pen, thinking about what you're going to say, writing the letter, finding an envelope and stamp, going to the post office—and then thinking about all of the things you forgot to say.

If, on that same day, you also need to go food shopping, the problem of the letter shrinks to make room for a trip to the grocery. If you also need to meet with your coach to discuss your role in an upcoming competition, it's amazing how quickly and easily the letter and the grocery shopping tasks are finished.

One way to handle little problems is to find bigger ones. Remember that the smaller problems still need to be solved. The goal is to do it with less time and energy.

Play full out

When we take on a big problem, we play full out. We do justice to our potentials. We're awake, alert, and engaged.

Bigger problems are not in short supply. Consider world hunger. Every minute of every day, people die because they don't have enough to eat. Also consider nuclear war, which threatens to end life on the planet. Child abuse, environmental pollution, human rights violations, drug abuse, street crime, energy shortages, poverty, and wars throughout the world await your attention and involvement.

and success. Playing full out means living your life as if your life depended on it.

You can make a difference

Perhaps a little voice in your mind is saying, "That's crazy. I can't do anything about global problems" or "Everyone knows that hunger has always been around and always will be, and there is nothing anyone can do about it."

These thoughts prevent you from taking on bigger problems.

Realize that you *can* make a difference. Your thoughts and actions can change the quality of life for your family, your friends, and perhaps everyone on the planet. And no matter what, playing full out will change the quality of *your* life.

One way to find problems that are worthy of your talents and energies is to take on bigger ones. Find a problem that you are sure you cannot handle—then take responsibility for it. Become a leader. Tune in to the needs of your teammates, your classmates, your fellow citizens, and your fellow inhabitants of this precious planet. Then notice how your other problems dwindle in importance—or even vanish. ◪

Playing full out means living your life as if your life depended on it.

Considering such problems does not have to be depressing. In fact, it can be energizing—a reason for getting up in the morning. Taking on a huge project is a tool for creating passion and purpose.

Some people spend vast amounts of time in activities they consider boring: their jobs, their hobbies, their relationships. They find themselves going through the motions, doing the same walk-on part day after day without passion or intensity. In the same way, some student athletes are just content to be on the field. They don't really pursue winning. Writer Henry David Thoreau described this kind of existence as "lives of quiet desperation."

Playing full out in life and athletics enables you to experience a whole new level of commitment, passion,

exercise 19

FIX-THE-WORLD BRAINSTORM

This exercise works well with four to six people. Pick a major world problem such as hunger, nuclear proliferation, poverty, terrorism, overpopulation, or pollution. Then conduct a 10-minute brainstorm about the steps an individual could take to contribute to solving the problem.

Use the brainstorming techniques explained earlier in this chapter. Remember not to evaluate or judge the solutions during the process. The purpose of a brainstorm is to generate a flow of ideas and record them all.

After the brainstorming session, discuss the process and the solutions that it generated. Did you feel any energy from the group? Was a long list of ideas generated? Are several of them worth pursuing?

put it to work

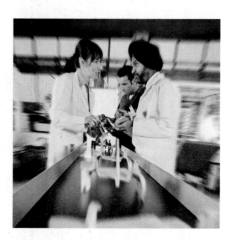

Strategies for creative and critical thinking can assist you in developing new products and services in the workplace. Some examples follow.

State the obvious and go for the opposite. One way to generate a burst of creativity followed by critical thinking is to take an idea that seems obvious and state its opposite. Then see if you can find evidence to support the opposite idea.

This principle has been used with great success in business. An example comes from Jan Carlzon, former president of the Scandinavian Airline SAS. Carlzon questioned an "obvious" truth—that upper management in any company should make most of the decisions. He went for the opposite idea and allowed rank-and-file employees to make daily decisions that directly affected customers. If a customer got bumped from a flight, an SAS counter clerk could decide on the spot whether to pay the customer's hotel bill for the night or find the customer an alternative flight on a competitor's airline. After implementing this policy, SAS's business grew dramatically.[7]

Find a smaller problem. After reading the Power Process: "Find a bigger problem," consider the merits of the opposite strategy. For example, you might feel overwhelmed with managing a complex, year-long project at work. One response is to give up—to quit. Another is to resign yourself to drudgery and dive into the project with a deep sigh, always feeling a monumental weight on your shoulders.

"Find a smaller problem" offers an alternative: Just divide a huge project into many small jobs. Rather than worry about the project as a whole, turn your full attention to a small, specific task until it is complete. Do the same with the next small task, and the next. Just handle the details, one after another, until the project is finished.

The role of planning is critical. "Find a smaller problem" is not a suggestion to fill your days with busywork. When you plan effectively, the small jobs you do are critical to the success of the bigger project.

Experiment with the decreasing options technique. The decreasing options technique (DOT) is a decision-making strategy. It allows you to rank a large pool of ideas created by groups of people in meetings. Before you put DOT in action, go to an office supply store and get a package of several hundred adhesive dots—small stickers that can be attached to a sheet of paper. Then follow these steps:

- *Ask meeting participants to brainstorm solutions to a problem.* Permit all ideas to be expressed. Don't edit them yet. To save time, ask participants to submit ideas before the meeting takes place. That way you can summarize and post ideas ahead of time.

- *Summarize each idea in a single word or phrase on a large sheet of paper.* Write letters that are big enough to be seen across the meeting room. Place only one idea on each sheet of paper.

- *Post the sheets where all meeting participants can see them.*

- *Do an initial review of the ideas.* Ask participants if they can eliminate some ideas as obviously unworkable. Also group similar ideas together and eliminate duplications.

- *"Dot" ideas.* Give each participant a handful of sticker dots. Then ask participants to go around the room and place an adhesive dot next to the ideas that they consider most important.

- *Discuss the most important ideas.* Stand back and review the ideas. The high-priority concerns of the group will stand out clearly as the sheets with the most dots. Now you can bring these important ideas to the discussion table.

You can also use the DOT method online with bulletin boards or "virtual" meetings. Participants can use e-mail or networking software to post their ideas and manipulate computer graphics that look like sticker dots. ▨

Name _____ Date _____/_____/_____

quiz

1. List four questions that can guide you on your path to becoming a critical thinker.

2. Explain what is meant in this chapter by aha!

3. Define *serendipity* and give an example.

4. List and briefly describe three ways to create ideas.

5. Student athletes face special challenges in choosing a major. True or False? Explain your answer.

6. According to the text, *critical thinking* and *thorough thinking* are two distinct and different activities. True or False? Explain your answer.

7. Define *all-or-nothing thinking* and give an example.

8. Explain the suggestion "watch for hot spots" and describe its connection to critical thinking.

9. Name at least one fallacy involved in this statement: "Everyone who's ever visited this school has agreed that it's the best in the state."

10. List the four suggested steps for problem solving and give an example of each step.

learning styles application

The questions below will "cycle" you through four styles, or modes, of learning as explained in the article "Learning styles: Discovering how you learn" in Chapter One. Each question will help you explore a different mode. You can answer the questions in any order.

what if *Explain how you would modify a technique from this chapter to make it a more effective tool for decision making—or describe an original technique of your own.*

why *Think of a major decision you face right now and put it into the form of a question. Possible examples are: "What major will I declare?" or "What is my top priority goal for this year?"*

how *Briefly describe how you will use a technique from this chapter to make a major decision.*

what *List a technique from this chapter that could help you make a major decision you face right now (such as the decision you list under Why?).*

master student

profile

OSCAR ROBERTSON

(1938–   ) Voted "Player of the Century" by the National Association of Basketball Coaches, he has also distinguished himself as a labor leader, an entrepreneur in the business world, and a community activist.

ndianapolis Crispus Attucks High School was an all-black school, literally built to keep us segregated from white students. Ironically, as a result we had a tremendous faculty, many with advanced degrees. They could not get jobs in white schools. And our head coach, Ray Crowe, insisted on high academic standards. If you didn't pass, you didn't play. There were plenty of candidates eager to take your place.

Coach Crowe also taught us a valuable life lesson. We knew we started every game at a disadvantage. But we kept our emotions under control while still playing with passion and intensity. We would not let hostile crowds or blatantly biased officiating take us out of our game.

After we had won two consecutive state titles, going undefeated my senior year, I was named Indiana's "Mr. Basketball" and was the most heavily-recruited player in the nation. Having graduated in the top 10% of my class, I made it clear to recruiters I was just as serious about academics as athletics. Schools who did not take me equally seriously were eliminated from consideration.

University of Cincinnati had an excellent academic reputation, and it also had a co-op program with local businesses. Periods of classroom study alternated with periods of on-the-job training, for which you got paid. When UC's basketball team became successful, the NCAA quickly put a stop to my participation in the co-op program.

I was basically a shy country boy— our family was from Tennessee—and I was not on a mission to desegregate the athletic program at UC or anywhere else. But, along with four other black athletes, that is basically what I did.

As an athlete, you always have to be aware of what you say and do, where you are seen, and who you hang out with. As a young black male in Indianapolis, I had to be conscious of even more stringent limitations based on the color of my skin. I hoped Cincinnati might offer a more enlightened environment. But black athletes were discouraged from entering a bar where other players hung out. A graduate student wrote the school newspaper saying it was insulting to the university to import black student-athletes. While most professors graded students on the quality of their work, it seemed that some were determined to *prevent* black students from graduating. One economics professor told me flat-out that I could not pass. So I had to take the exam from a teacher in another department just to prove I could do the work.

On road trips, especially in the South, there were hotels where I could not stay with the rest of the team, and arenas where I encountered a great deal of racial hostility. The school had prior knowledge of these conditions, and I wondered why they would place me in such situations.

Early in my career at UC, I met a former pro baseball player named Austin Tillotson, who became a mentor and is a friend to this day. When I described my frustrations with the University, he just gave me a bitter laugh and said, "Man. Black people don't go to school here."

Given the conditions I've described, I thought many times about transferring to another school. But I remembered what Coach Crowe had taught us, and I was driven to succeed. On one occasion, I amazed a lot of people when I took a marketing exam and scored higher than the tutor assigned to me! In retrospect, I'm glad I hung in there. There were a few bumps, but I graduated on time with the rest of my class, earning a B.S. in Business Administration with a concentration in accounting. Earning that degree was as important as anything I achieved on the basketball court. ☒

By Oscar Robertson with Michael O'Daniel.

For more biographical information about Oscar Robertson, visit the Master Student Hall of Fame on the *Becoming a Master Student Athlete* Web site at

(masterstudent.college.hmco.com)

8

Communicating

Listening means trying to see the problem the way the speaker sees it—which means not sympathy, which is feeling for him, but empathy, which is feeling with him.

S. I. HAYAKAWA

You have two ears and one mouth. Remember to use them in more or less that proportion.

PAULA BERN

why
this chapter matters . . .

Your communication abilities—
including your skills at listening,
speaking, and writing—are as
important to your long-term success
as your technical skills.

what
is included . . .

Communicating creates our world
The communication loop: Listening
The communication loop: Sending
Communicating with coaches and
  with instructors
Staying cool in the spotlight
The fine art of conflict management
Communicating for powerful
  workplace teams
Relationships can work
Relationships change
7 steps to effective complaints
Three phases of effective writing
Phase 1: Getting ready to write
Phase 2: Writing a first draft
Phase 3: Revising your draft
Giving credit where credit is due
Writing and delivering speeches
Power Process: "Employ your word"
Master Student Profile: Sheryl Swoopes

how
you can use this chapter . . .

Listen, speak, and write more
  effectively.
Prevent and resolve conflict with other
  people.
Experience more satisfying
  relationships in all areas of your life.

as you read, ask yourself
what if . . .

I could use my capacity to make and
  keep agreements as a tool for
  creating my future?

Communicating creates our world

Certain things are real for us because we can see them, touch them, hear them, smell them, or taste them. Books, pencils, tables, chairs, and food all are real in this sense. They enter our world in a straightforward, uncomplicated way.

Many other aspects of our lives, however, do not have this kind of reality. None of us can point to a *purpose*, for example. Nor would a purpose step up and introduce itself or buy us lunch. The same is true about other abstract concepts, such as *quality, intelligence, love, trust, sportsmanship, human rights*, or *student success*.

Concepts such as these shape our experience of life. Yet they don't really exist until we talk about them. These concepts come alive for us only to the degree that we define and discuss them. Communicating brings our world into being.

According to communication theorist Lee Thayer, there are two basic life processes. One is acquiring and processing energy. The other is acquiring and processing information, also known as communication.[1] From this point of view, communicating is just as fundamental to life as eating.

Through communication, we take raw impressions and organize them into meaningful patterns. With our senses, we perceive sights, sounds, and other sensations. However, none of our sense organs is capable of perceiving *meaning*. We create meaning by finding patterns in our sensations and communicating them.

In our daily contact with other people and mass media, we are exposed to hundreds of messages. Yet the obstacles to receiving those messages accurately are numerous. For one thing, only a small percentage of communication is verbal. We also send messages with our bodies and with the tone of our voice. Throw in a few other factors, such as a hot room or screaming fans, and it's a wonder we communicate at all.

Another problem is that the message sent is often not the message received. Even the simplest message can get muddled. For some, the word *ball* conjures up the image of a round object used to play a sport. Others might visualize a fancy dance attended by ladies and gentlemen in formal clothing. If a simple word concept like this can be misunderstood, it's easy to see how complex ideas can wreak havoc.

Written communication adds a whole other set of variables. When you speak, you supplement the meaning of your words with the power of body language and voice inflection. When you write, those nonverbal elements are absent. Instead, you depend on your skills at word choice, sentence construction, and punctuation to get your message across. The choices that you make in these areas can serve as an aid—or a hindrance—to communication. Such difficulties are never fully overcome. You can get past many of them by having a sincere intention to understand other people—and by experimenting with suggestions in this chapter. ▧

journal entry 20

Discovery/Intention Statement

Think of a time when you experienced an emotionally charged conflict with another person. Were you able to resolve this dispute effectively? If so, list below the strategies you used. If not, describe what you could have done differently.

I discovered that I . . .

_____

_____

Now scan this chapter for ideas that can help you get your feelings across more skillfully in similar situations. List at least four ideas here, along with the page numbers where you can read more about them.

Strategy   *Page number*

_____

_____

_____

_____

Describe an upcoming situation in which you intend to apply these techniques. If possible, choose a situation that will occur within the next week.

I intend to . . .

_____

_____

_____

_____

The communication loop

One effective way to improve your ability to communicate is to be aware of when you are the receiver and when you are the sender. If you are receiving (listening), just receive. Avoid switching into the sending (talking) mode. When you are sending, stick with it until you are finished.

If the other person is trying to send a message when you want to be the sender, you have at least three choices: Stop sending and be the receiver, stop sending and leave, or ask the other person to stop sending so that you can send. It is ineffective to try to send and receive at the same time. This becomes clear when we look at what happens in a conversation. When we talk, we put thoughts into words. Words are a code for what we experience. This is called *encoding*. The person who receives the message takes our words and translates them into his own experience. This is called *decoding*.

A conversation between two people is like a communication between two telegraph operators. One encodes a message and sends it over the wire. The operator at the other end receives the coded signal, decodes it, evaluates it, and sends back another coded message. The first operator decodes this message and sends another. The cycle continues. The messages look like this:

1 ..—..—.-.-   3 —.—..— OPERATOR 1

2 —.-..-..   4 -..-—...-. OPERATOR 2

This encoding-decoding loop is most effective when we continually switch roles. One minute we send, the next we receive. If both operators send at the same time, neither knows what the other one sent. Neither can reply. Communication works best when each of us has plenty of time to receive what others send—that is, to listen—and the opportunity to send a complete message when it's our turn.

Communication is often garbled when we try to send and receive messages at the same time.

THE COMMUNICATION LOOP

Listening

You observe a person in a conversation who is not talking. Is he listening? Maybe. Maybe not. He might be preparing his response or daydreaming.

Listening is not easy. Doing it effectively requires concentration and energy.

It's worth it. Listening well promotes success in school and in athletics: more powerful notes, more productive study groups, and better relationships with students, instructors, coaches, and teammates. A skilled listener is appreciated by friends, family, and coworkers. People love a good listener.

To be a good listener, choose to listen. Once you've made this choice, you can use the following techniques to listen more effectively—especially in times of high emotional tension.

Nonverbal listening

Be quiet. Silence is more than staying quiet while someone is speaking. Allowing several seconds to pass before you begin to talk gives the speaker time to catch his breath and gather his thoughts. He might want to continue. Someone who talks nonstop might fear he will lose the floor if he pauses.

If the message being sent is complete, this short break gives you time to form your response and helps you avoid the biggest barrier to listening—listening with your answer running. If you make up a response before the person is finished, you might miss the end of the message—which is often the main point.

Maintain eye contact. Look at the other person while he speaks. Doing so demonstrates your attentiveness and helps keep your mind from wandering. Your eyes also let you "listen" to body language and behavior.

This idea is not an absolute. While maintaining eye contact is important in some cultures, people from other cultures are uncomfortable with sustained eye contact. Also, some people learn primarily by hearing; they can listen more effectively by turning off the visual input once in a while. Keep in mind the differences among people.

Display openness. You can communicate openness by means of your facial expression and body position. Uncross your arms and legs. Sit up straight. Face the other person and remove any physical barriers between you, such as a pile of books.

Listen without response. This doesn't mean that you should never respond. Rather, wait for an appropriate moment to respond. Avoid interrupting with your own stories, opinions, suggestions, and comments.

Watch your nonverbal responses, too. A look of "Good grief!" from you can deter the other person from finishing his message.

Send acknowledgments. Let the speaker know periodically that you are still there. Words and nonverbal gestures of acknowledgment convey to the speaker that you are interested and that you are receiving his message. These include "Umhum," "OK," "Yes," and head nods. Remember that you can send these acknowledgments even when you disagree with the speaker.

A skilled listener is appreciated by friends, family, and coworkers. People love a good listener.

Verbal listening

Feed back meaning. Paraphrase the communication. This does not mean parroting what another person says. Instead, briefly summarize. Feed back what you see as the essence of that person's message: "Let me see if I understood what you said . . ." or "What I'm hearing you say is. . . ." (Psychotherapist Carl Rogers referred to this technique as *reflection*.[2]) Often, the other person will say, "No, that's not what I meant. What I said was. . . ."

If you don't understand the message, be persistent—and concise. This is not a time to stop the other person by talking on and on about what you think you heard.

Listen beyond words. Be aware of nonverbal messages and behavior. You might point out that the speaker's body language seems to be the exact opposite of his words. For example: "I noticed you said you are excited, but you look bored."

Keep in mind that the same nonverbal behavior can have different meanings, depending on the listener's cultural background. Someone who looks bored might simply be listening in a different way. Listen not only to the words but also to the emotion behind the words. Sometimes that emotional message is more important than the verbal content.

Take care of yourself. People seek good listeners, and there are times when you don't want to listen. You might be distracted with your own concerns. Be honest. Don't pretend to listen. You can say, "What you're telling me is important, and I'm pressed for time right now. Can we set aside another time to talk about this?"

Listen for requests. "This class is a waste of my time." "Our instructor talks too fast." An effective way to listen to such complaints is to look for the request hidden in them.

"This class is a waste of my time" can be heard as "Please tell me what I'll gain if I participate actively in class." "The instructor talks too fast" might be asking "What strategies can I use to take notes when the instructor covers material rapidly?"

Viewing complaints as requests gives us more choices. Rather than responding with defensiveness ("What does he know anyway?"), resignation ("It's always been this way and always will be"), or indifference ("It's not my job"), we can decide whether to grant the request or help the person translate his own complaint into an action plan.

THE COMMUNICATION LOOP
Sending

We have been talking with people for years, and we usually manage to get our messages across. There are times, though, when we don't. Often, these times are emotionally charged.

Described below are four techniques for delivering a message through tears, laughter, fist pounding, or hugging.

Replace "You" messages with "I" messages. When conflict occurs, we often make statements about the other person, or "You" messages:

"You are rude."
"You make me mad."
"You must be crazy."
"You don't love me anymore."

This kind of communication results in defensiveness. The responses might be:

"I am not rude."
"I don't care."

"No, *you* are crazy."
"No, *you* don't love *me!*"

"You" messages are hard to listen to. They label, judge, blame, and assume things that might or might not be true. They demand rebuttal. Even praise can sometimes be an ineffective "You" message. "You" messages don't work.

When communication is emotionally charged, psychologist Thomas Gordon suggests that you consider limiting your statements to descriptions about yourself.[3] Replace "You" messages with "I" messages.

"You are rude" might become "I feel upset."
"You make me mad" could be "I feel angry."
"You must be crazy" can be "I don't understand."
"You don't love me anymore" could become "I'm afraid we're drifting apart."

Suppose a teammate asks you to meet him to get in some extra practice on making foul shots in basketball. You turn down the chance to see a movie with friends, drive over to campus, and wait. No teammate. You try to call him on his cell phone. All you get is a voice mail greeting. After a half hour goes by, you drive home, perplexed and worried. The next day, you see your teammate downtown.

"What happened?" you ask.
"I just couldn't make it."
"You are a rude person," you reply.

Look for the facts, the observable behavior. Everyone will agree that your friend asked you to practice with him

---

▶ Five ways to say "I"

An "I" message can include any or all of the following five elements. Be careful when including the last two, since they can contain hidden judgments or threats.

Observations. Describe the facts—the indisputable, observable realities. Talk about what you—or anyone else—can see, hear, smell, taste, or touch. Avoid judgments, interpretations, or opinions. Instead of saying, "You're a slob," say, "Last night's lasagna pan was still on the stove this morning."

Feelings. Describe your own feelings. It is easier to listen to "I feel frustrated" than to "You never help me." Stating how you feel about another's actions can be valuable feedback for that person.

Wants. You are far more likely to get what you want if you *say* what you want. If someone doesn't know what you

want, he doesn't have a chance to help you get it. Ask clearly. Avoid demanding or using the word *need*. Most people like to feel helpful, not obligated. Instead of saying, "Do the dishes when it's your turn, or else!" say, "I want to divide the housework fairly."

Thoughts. Communicate your thoughts, and use caution. Beginning your statement with the word "I" doesn't make it an "I" message. "I think you are a slob" is a "You" judgment in disguise. Instead, say, "I'd have more time to study if I didn't have to clean up so often."

Intentions. The last part of an "I" message is a statement about what you intend to do. Have a plan that doesn't depend on the other person. For example, instead of "From now on we're going to split the dishwashing evenly," you could say, "I intend to do my share of the housework and leave the rest."

---

and that he did not show up. But the idea that he is rude is not a fact—it's a judgment.

He might go on to say, "I called your home and no one answered. My mom had a stroke and was rushed to Valley View. I had to stay by her side. I couldn't even call you because they won't let you use a cell phone in the room with all the electronic equipment that is around. Besides, to tell you the truth, I was just so distressed about my mom, I couldn't think of anything else." Your judgment no longer fits.

When you saw your friend, you might have said, "I waited and waited at the gym. I was worried about you. I didn't get a call. I felt angry and hurt. I don't want to waste my time. Next time, you can call me when your schedule changes."

"I" messages don't judge, blame, criticize, or insult. They don't invite the other person to counterattack with more of the same. "I" messages are also more accurate. They report our own thoughts and feelings.

At first, "I" messages might feel uncomfortable or seem forced. That's OK. Use the five ways to say "I" explained on page 204.

your words. Your posture, the way you dress, how often you shower, and even the poster hanging on your wall can negate your words before you say them.

Most nonverbal behavior is unconscious. We can learn to be aware of it and choose our nonverbal messages. When we know what we want to say and are committed to getting it across, our inflections, gestures, and words work together and send a unified message.

Notice barriers to sending messages. Sometimes fear stops us from sending messages. We are afraid of other people's reactions, sometimes justifiably.

Assumptions can also be used as excuses for not sending messages. "He already knows this," we tell ourselves.

Predictions of failure can be barriers to sending, too. "He won't listen," we say.

Or we might predict, "He'll never do anything about it, even if I tell him." Again, making assumptions can defeat your message before you send it.

It's easy to make excuses for not communicating. If you have fear or some other concern about sending a message, be aware of it. Tact is a virtue; letting fear

Remember that questions are not always questions. We use questions that aren't questions to sneak our opinions and requests into conversations. "Doesn't it upset you?" means "It upsets me," and "Shouldn't we hang the picture over here?" means "I want to hang the picture over here."

Communication improves when we say, "I'm upset" and "Let's hang the picture over here."

Choose nonverbal messages. How you say something can be more important than what you say. Your tone of voice and gestures add up to a silent message that you send. This message can support, modify, or contradict

prevent communication is not.

Realize that you can communicate tactfully even with your concerns. You can choose to make them a part of the message: "I am going to tell you how I feel, and I'm afraid that you will think it's stupid."

Talking to someone when you don't want to could be a matter of educational survival. A short talk with an advisor, a teacher, a friend, or a family member might solve a problem that could jeopardize your education. ⬙

Communicating with coaches and with instructors

Bridging the cultures of athletics and academics

You may feel that communicating with coaches and communicating with instructors are games with contradictory rules. And it's no wonder. According to researcher Martha Sparent, the life of a student athlete is dualistic.[4] With coaches, you deal in specific instructions and clear distinctions between right and wrong. With your instructors, you enter an academic culture that encourages creativity, independent decisions, and differences in opinion.

Yet this dualism is a recent invention. To the ancient Greeks—inventors of the Olympics—it was unknown. The legendary Odysseus, for example, could wrestle almost any opponent to the ground. He was also a skilled orator and could be moved to tears by poetry. The Greek ideal was superior performance in all areas of life, and they had a single word for it—*arête*, or excellence.

There's a saying: "When the mind is tired, work the body; when the body is tired, work the mind." This statement points to the possibility of balancing academics and athletics. You can see the world of coaches and the world of instructors as distinct—and complementary. A key to mastery is clearly identifying and respecting their differences.

Respond to differences in roles. The role of an instructor is to help you master a specific subject matter. When you communicate with an instructor, be prepared to respond as an independent adult, with material read and studied. Bring an open mind to class and ask questions freely. Think critically about the course, take part in discussions, and be prepared to make your own decisions.

When communicating with a coach, acknowledge this person's role as an expert and authority. As a student athlete, your job is to contribute to a greater whole—perhaps to a goal that's larger than you currently see. Your coach operates with a bigger picture and becomes the ultimate decision maker. Keep your comments specific, clear, and to the point. Focus on trusting your coach's plan and following instructions.

Look for common ground. Although coaches and instructors serve different roles, they have a common purpose—to promote your success. Avoid pitting these people against each other. Coaches know about the pressures facing student athletes. They want you to succeed both on and off the field. Ask them for guidance in completing your course work.

Likewise, avoid making any assumptions about instructors' attitudes toward student athletes. They may even be athletic fans. Start from the premise that they want you to achieve academic excellence. Participate actively in class and visit instructors during office hours. Getting to know a teacher outside of class could lead to a job contact, a favorable recommendation—and perhaps a lifelong friendship.

Plan for the long term. Using time management suggestions from Chapter Two, create a plan for meeting your academic and your athletic goals. For example, plot out major class assignments in one color on weekly and monthly calendars. In a second color, plot out your practice and competition schedule, including travel times. Long-term planning will expose "crunches" in your schedule.

journal entry 21

Discovery/Intention Statement

Think about one of your relationships for a few minutes. It can involve a parent, sibling, spouse, child, friend, hairdresser, or anyone else. In the space below, write down some things that are not working in the relationship. What bugs you? What do you find irritating or unsatisfying?

I discovered that . . .

_____

_____

_____

_____

_____

_____

Now think for a moment about what you want from this relationship. More attention? Less nagging? More openness, trust, financial security, or freedom? Choose a suggestion from this chapter and describe how you could use it to make the relationship work.

I intend to . . .

_____

_____

_____

_____

_____

_____

_____

Negotiate solutions. When planning reveals a possible breakdown in your schedule, take the next step. Communicate with everyone concerned.

If an away competition date conflicts with an exam, speak to your instructor at the beginning of the term. Instead of making demands, politely suggest some alternatives. For example, ask if you can take the exam a couple of hours before you depart. Or suggest that an academic advisor or coach proctor the exam while your team travels. Perhaps the instructor can fax the exam to your hotel, and you can fax the completed exam back to the instructor's office.

Do everything in your power to avoid surprising your instructors or your coaches. Spot potential problems and show up with solutions. Long before any conflict develops, you can often negotiate an option that leads to "win-win."

Staying cool in the spotlight

Coping with high visibility and the media

Being in collegiate athletics has been compared to living in a fishbowl. Every move you make, it seems, can be observed. If you perform well, you make the news. If you perform poorly, you also make the news. Your behavior in any setting could lead to a story that hits the front page of tomorrow's newspaper or leads off tonight's television news.

Your skills in coping with media scrutiny can have lasting effects on your life. While your reputation as an athlete depends on how you perform in competition, your reputation as a person may hinge on how you perform in front of the camera.

You can learn to handle high visibility with grace. Remember that many schools provide student athletes with training in media relations.

See yourself as a representative. In the public eye, you represent your team, your coach, and your entire school. Simply remembering this fact can guide your words and actions while you're in the spotlight.

Assume that you are always "on the record." Television, newspaper, and radio reporters may be anxious to contact you. In fact, you might find them waiting outside your classroom or dormitory.

Remember that *anything* you say to a reporter could potentially be broadcasted or published. There is no such thing as being "off the record"—that is, speaking to a reporter simply to provide background information.

In fact, you may be on the record even when you're not standing directly in front of a reporter. Zoom lenses and high-tech microphones can capture your words and actions from a distance.

Get permissions for interviews. Do interviews only with reporters who are cleared through your media relations or sports information director. If reporters contact you directly, refer them to your athletic department first.

During an interview, remember that you have choices. Set a time limit and stick to it. If you're uncomfortable with a reporter's tone, politely end the interview and follow up with your coach.

Take time to prepare a response. When talking with reporters, do not feel obligated to give instant answers— or any answers at all. If you are uncertain about how to answer a question, politely say that you have no comment to make yet. Practice this response now, before you meet an intimidating reporter who fires a question at you and demands an immediate reply.

When you do choose to answer a reporter's question, take a moment to pause. Make sure you understand the question. Then mentally prepare your ideas and provide a thoughtful response.

Stay positive. When speaking publicly, stay upbeat and focus on yourself rather than others. In the spirit of taking a First Step, talk objectively about your strengths and areas for improvement. When referring to your teammates, praise their efforts even if their performance is off.

Reporters might try to trick you into making a negative comment about a school, a competing team, or your own teammates. Be careful. Remember that such comments can easily be misquoted or misrepresented.

Fans and boosters may also approach you with questions and comments. Many will be congratulatory or encouraging. However, be prepared for comments that are cynical or mean-spirited. It may be best not to reply.

Keep inside information on the inside. Avoid talking about competitive strategies or player injuries. Athletes who divulge this information could unwittingly assist people who want to bet on sports—a violation of NCAA rules. In addition, revealing a teammate's injury can violate the Health Insurance Portability and Accountability Act (HIPAA), a federal law.

Put yourself in the reporter's place. Keep in mind that reporters work under pressure. Most of them simply want to meet their deadlines and do their job well. Help them out by being friendly and preparing some short, positive anecdotes about yourself. ⊠

Conflict management is one of the most practical skills you'll ever learn. Following are several strategies that can help. To bring these ideas to life, think of ways to apply them to a current conflict in your life.

The fine art of conflict management

State the problem openly. Using "I" messages as explained earlier in this chapter, state the problem. Allow the other person in a particular conflict to do the same. You might have different perceptions. This is the time to define the conflict clearly. It's hard to fix something unless everyone agrees on what's broken.

Focus on solutions. After stating the problem, dream up as many solutions as you can. Choose one solution that is most acceptable to everyone involved and implement it. Agree on who is going to do what by when. Then keep your agreements and evaluate the effectiveness of your solution. If it works, pat yourselves on the back. If not, implement a new solution.

Step back from the conflict. Define the conflict as a team problem to be solved, not as a contest to be won. Detach. Let go of being "right" and aim for being effective instead.

Commit to the relationship. The thorniest conflicts usually arise between people who genuinely care for each other, such as teammates. We're less likely to be in conflict when the relationship doesn't matter to us.

Begin by affirming your commitment to the other person: "I care about you, and I want this relationship to last. So I'm willing to do whatever it takes to resolve this problem."

Back up to common ground. Conflict heightens the differences between people. When this happens, it's easy to forget how much we still agree with each other.

As a first step in managing conflict, back up to common ground. List all of the points on which you are *not* in conflict. Often, such a list puts the problem in perspective and paves the way for a solution.

Slow down the communication. In times of great conflict, people often talk all at once. Words fly like speeding bullets and no one is really listening.

When this happens, choose either to listen or to talk— not both at the same time. Slow down the pace of the conversation.

To slow down the communication even more, take a break. Depending upon the level of conflict, that might mean anything from a few minutes to a few days.

Be a complete listener. People will often stop short of their true message. Encourage them to continue by asking for it: "Anything else that you want to say about that? Is something more on your mind right now?"

Use a mediator. Even an untrained mediator— someone who's not a party to the conflict—can do much to decrease tension. Mediators can help all those involved get their points of view across. In this case, the mediator's role is not to give advice but to keep the discussion on track and moving toward a solution.

Allow for cultural differences. People respond to conflict in different ways, depending on their cultural background. Some stand close, speak loudly, and make direct eye contact. Other people avert their eyes, mute their voices, and increase physical distance.

When it seems to you that other people are sidestepping or escalating a conflict, consider whether your reaction is based on cultural bias.

Apologize or ask for forgiveness. Conflict often arises from our own errors. We can acknowledge this fact, apologize, and ask for forgiveness. The payoff is an end to conflict.

Write a message and send it. What can be difficult to say to another person face to face might be effectively communicated in writing. When people in conflict write letters or e-mail messages to each other, they automatically apply many of the suggestions in this article. Writing is a way to slow down the communication and ensure that only one person at a time is sending a message.

When writing, make clear what you are *not* saying: "I am saying that I want to be alone for a few days. I am *not* saying that I want you to stay away forever." Saying what you are *not* saying is often useful in face-to-face communication as well.

Before you send your message, put yourself in the place of the person who will receive it. Imagine how your comments could be misinterpreted. Then rewrite your letter, correcting any wording that is open to misinterpretation.

Write a message and don't send it. Write the nastiest, meanest letter you can imagine. Let all of your frustration, anger, and venom flow onto the page. Then take the message and destroy it. Chances are that you've calmed down and are ready to engage in skillful conflict management.

Note: If you're writing while using e-mail software, do not insert the complete address of the recipient. This will prevent you from accidentally sending the message.

Permit emotion. Crying is OK. Feeling angry is often appropriate. Allowing other people to see the strength of our feelings can go a long way toward clearing up the conflict. Emotion is part of life.

Allow the full range of your feelings. Often what's on the far side of anger is love. When we clear out the resentment and hostility, we might find genuine compassion in its place.

Record the disagreement. With the agreement of all parties involved, make an audio or video recording of your conversation. Later, play back the recording and review your side of the conversation. Look for any ways that you perpetuated the upset. Spot anything you did or said to move the problem toward a solution.

In the midst of a raging argument, when emotions run high, it's almost impossible to see ourselves objectively. Let the camera or microphone be your unbiased observer.

Agree to disagree. Sometimes we say all we have to say. We do all of the problem solving we can do. We get all points of view across. And the conflict still remains, staring us right in the face.

What's left is to recognize that honest disagreement is a fact of life. We can peacefully coexist with other people—and respect them—even though we don't agree on fundamental issues. Conflict can be accepted even when it is not resolved.

Do nothing. Sometimes we worsen a conflict by insisting that it be solved immediately. An alternative is to sit tight and wait things out. Some conflicts resolve themselves with the passage of time.

See the conflict within you. When we're angry or upset, we can take a minute to look inside. Perhaps we were ready to take offense, waiting to pounce on something the other person said. Or maybe the other person is simply saying what we don't want to admit is true.

When these things happen, we can shine a light on our own thinking. A simple spot check might help the conflict disappear—right before our eyes.

Networking—communicating to create your future

You have a valuable tool for achieving your immediate and long-term goals. That tool is networking.

As a student athlete, you gain public visibility and a chance to meet leaders in the community. Now is a time to build key relationships and make contacts for the future—for your career after college and beyond athletics. The people you meet now can open doors to opportunities that influence the course of your entire life.

Your network can begin with coaches. Those who have worked in the field for a number of years often have extensive networks of their own that can help you. This is especially true if you aspire to become a coach yourself or to participate in professional athletics. Accessing your coach's contacts can offer a short path to a powerful network.

Make sure that your coaches know about your career plans. Armed with that information, coaches can connect you with colleagues, boosters, and fans who know about your field. One of them may become a mentor or even hire you some day.

Faculty members, academic athletic advisors, and other university staff members have their own networks as well. Build relationships with them *before* you are faced with a delicate situation, such as asking to adjust the due date for an assignment that conflicts with an athletic competition. Often teachers feel pressured to grant a favor when they have no real connection to a student athlete.

Remember that simply being enrolled in a course does not create a relationship. Use the suggestions in this chapter to build a bridge to faculty members before you intend to cross it.

Communicating for powerful workplace teams

As a student athlete, you are developing highly transferable skills in teamwork. In fact, teamwork gives you a chance to practice all the communication skills explored in this chapter.

Teams abound in the workplace. To research their book *When Teams Work Best*, Frank LaFasto and Carl Larson studied 600 teams. These ranged from the Mount Everest climbing team to the collaborations that produced the Boeing 747 airplane—the world's largest aircraft and a product of 75,000 blueprints.[5]

People talk about *empowering* teams. You might wonder how to make that happen. One answer is to take your cue from the word *power* and use the Power Processes in this book. Following are examples of ways to apply four of them in workplace teams. Use your creative thinking skills to invent applications for the rest of the Power Processes.

Discover what you want. When forming a team, look for a fit between individual goals and the team's mission. Team members might want formal recognition for taking part in the project and meeting its objectives. People naturally ask, "What's in this for me?" Provide answers to that question. Emphasize the chance to develop marketable skills by joining the team.

Ideas are tools. People who want a team to succeed will treat its ideas as tools. Instead of automatically looking for what's wrong with a proposal, look for potential applications. Even a proposal that seems outlandish at first might become workable with a few

In an empowered team, all ideas are welcome, problems are freely admitted, and any item is open for discussion.

modifications. In an empowered team, all ideas are welcome, problems are freely admitted, and any item is open for discussion.

Be here now. Concentration and focused attention are attributes of effective students—and effective teams. When a team tries to tackle too many problems or achieve too many goals, it gets distracted. Members can forget the team's purpose and lose their enthusiasm for the project. You can help restore focus by asking: What is the single most important goal that our team can meet? And what is the single most important thing we can do *now* to meet that goal?

Notice your pictures. While you are in school, seize opportunities to work collaboratively. Form study groups. Enroll in classes that include group projects. Show up for your next job with teamwork skills. Some of your coworkers may be skeptical about the value of teams. By demonstrating your abilities, you can help them to form new pictures of a high-performing team. ⊠

You deserve compliments

For some people, compliments are more difficult to accept than criticisms. Here are some hints for handling compliments.

Accept the compliment. People sometimes respond to praise with "Oh, it's really nothing" or "This old thing? I've had it for years." This type of response undermines both you and the person who sent the compliment.

Choose another time to deliver your own compliments. Automatically returning a compliment can appear suspiciously polite and insincere.

Let the compliment stand. "Do you really think so?" questions the integrity of the message. It can also sound as if you're fishing for more compliments.

Accepting compliments is not the same as being conceited. If you're in doubt about how to respond, just smile and say "Thank you!" This simple response affirms the compliment along with the person who delivered it.

You are worthy and capable. Allow people to acknowledge that.

→ Hazing

Hazing is not limited to Greek-letter organizations. It also happens among student athletes. Some of them defend it in theory as a simple, foolish prank that builds team unity. In practice, hazing often becomes abusive, humiliating, and dangerous. Examples include verbal harassment, beating, forced consumption of vile substances, and sexual violation.

In a national survey of hazing in NCAA sports teams, researchers at Alfred University discovered that:

- Over 250,000 collegiate student athletes underwent hazing.
- One in five of these students was subjected to potentially illegal hazing activities, such as being kidnapped, tied up, and abandoned.
- Half were forced to take part in drinking contests or alcohol-related hazing.
- Two-thirds were subjected to humiliation, including being deprived of food and sleep.[6]

Students have died during hazing. It is now illegal in 42 states.

Students who initiate hazing can be suspended or permanently dismissed from school. These students may face legal charges as well—even if hazing victims agreed to participate in the activity. Antihazing laws typically state that such consent cannot be used as a defense.

To determine whether an activity is hazing, ask the following questions (adapted from Sigma Alpha Epsilon, *Death by Hazing*):

- Is alcohol involved?
- Do active and current members of the group refuse to participate in the activity with the new members?
- Does the activity involve emotional or physical abuse?
- Is there risk of injury?
- Would you hesitate to inform your parents, teachers, and school administrators about the activity?
- Are you uncomfortable with the activity being reported in the news?

When your answer to any of these questions is yes, the activity is probably hazing. If you're unsure, contact an advisor or coach.

Hazing will stop only when the culture that supports it dies. Be part of the solution: Refuse to haze.

WRITE AN "I" MESSAGE

First, pick something about school that irritates you. Then pretend that you are talking to the person who is associated with this irritation. In the space below, write down what you would say to this person as a "You" message.

_____

_____

_____

_____

_____

_____

Now write the same complaint as an "I" message. Include at least the first three elements suggested in "Five ways to say 'I.'"

_____

_____

_____

_____

_____

_____

_____

_____

voices

student

I used to be a very shy person who didn't communicate or participate in class or out of class; after I read this chapter and started to use some of the techniques this book offers, I have accomplished my goal of becoming more communicative.

—BRITTANY SCHULTZ

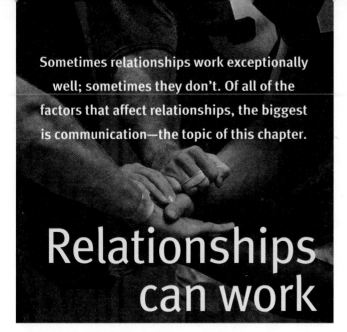

Sometimes relationships work exceptionally well; sometimes they don't. Of all of the factors that affect relationships, the biggest is communication—the topic of this chapter.

Relationships can work

Do tell the truth. Life is complicated when you don't. For example, if you think a friend or teammate is addicted to drugs, tell him so in a nonjudgmental way.

Do support others. Encourage fellow students to reach their goals and be successful. Respect their study time. Help them stay focused.

Don't pry. Being a good listener is invitation enough for classmates to share their problems, feelings, and personal goals.

Don't borrow—too much. Some people have difficulty saying no and resent lending things. Keep borrowing to a minimum.

Do divide chores. Whether it's a class project or a household chore, do your part.

Don't gripe. Gripers usually just want everyone to know how unhappy they are. Sharing a problem is an appropriate way to start the search for a solution.

Do get involved. Go beyond athletics. Study at the library, eat at the cafeteria, or relax at the student union. You might be surprised at how many friends, athletes and nonathletes, you can make.

Don't brag. Other students are turned off by constant references to your money or your athletic abilities. There is a difference between sharing excitement and being obnoxious.

Do detach. Allow others to accept responsibility for their problems. Pitying them, getting upset along with them, or taking over for them is not helpful.

Do allow people to be upset. Trying to joke people out of their upset denies their feelings. Allow them to express their emotions.

Do ask for help. You are not alone. People often respond to a genuine request for help.

Do share yourself. When we brood on negative thoughts, we lose perspective. And when we keep joys to ourselves, we diminish our satisfaction. Imagine a community in which people freely and lovingly speak their minds—without fear or defensiveness. That can be your community.

Don't preach. This piece of advice might seem funny at the end of a list of do's and don'ts. Sometimes people ask for advice. It's OK to share your values and opinions. It's *not* OK to pretend that you know what's best for someone else. ✉

Relationships change

Relationships grow and die. Friends transfer schools and graduate. Lovers and spouses leave. Children grow up and move away. Parents die. Star athletes eventually retire. All of these events can lead to pain.

Pain is a part of living. You can learn how to deal with it in several ways.

Feel the feeling—and stay active. It is appropriate to be miserable when you are. It is also possible to go to class, study, work, eat, and feel miserable at the same time.

Do anything. Exercise. Mop the kitchen floor. Clean out your dresser drawers. Iron your shirts. This sounds ridiculous, and it works.

Use the Power Processes. Experience a barrier and "be here now" with it. Surrender to your emotions, and then detach. Yes, it can be difficult to practice the Power Processes at times like this. And when your practice becomes this intense, it can yield the most learning.

Writing about your feelings and what you're learning through the pain can also bring perspective. Your journal is one friend who is on call 24 hours each day, every day of the year.

Connect with people. Talking to people is a way of healing. If friends and family members can't help, contact a counselor.

Remember that pain passes. One case disappeared in 4 hours and 12 minutes. There's no need to let a broken heart stop your life. Though you can find abundant advice on the subject, just remember: "This, too, shall pass." ✉

7 steps to effective complaints

Sometimes relationship building involves making a complaint. Whining, blaming, pouting, kicking, and spitting usually don't get results. Here are some guidelines for complaining effectively.

1 Go to the source. Start with the person who is most directly involved with the problem.

2 Present the facts without blaming anyone. Your complaint will carry more weight if you document the facts. Keep track of names and dates. Note what actions were promised and what results actually occurred.

3 Go up the ladder to people with more responsibility. If you don't get satisfaction at the first level, go to that person's direct supervisor.

4 Ask for commitments. When you find someone who is willing to solve your problem, get him to say exactly what he is going to do and when.

5 Use available support. Contact consumer groups of the Better Business Bureau. Ask city council members, county commissioners, state legislators, and senators and representatives. All of them want your vote, so they may be eager to help.

6 Take legal action, if necessary. Small-claims court is relatively inexpensive, and you don't have to hire a lawyer. These courts can handle cases involving small amounts of money (usually up to a few thousand dollars). Legal aid offices on campus or in the community can sometimes answer questions.

If your complaint is based on a practice or procedure of your school's athletics department, contact your student athlete advisory committee or a similar group. This committee includes student athletes who advocate for their peers.

7 Don't give up. Assume that others are on your team. Many people are out there to help you. State what you intend to do and ask for their partnership. ⊠

→ Criticism really can be constructive

As a student athlete you will receive criticism from your coach, your parents, your teammates, your friends, the fans. Some of the criticism will be accurate. Some of it will be worthless. Here are some ways to get value from it.

Take it seriously. A humorous reaction on your part can be mistaken for a lack of concern. In the competitive atmosphere of collegiate athletics, coaches and competitors may find it difficult to be lighthearted when they think that criticism is warranted.

React to criticism with acceptance. You can disagree with criticism and still accept it calmly.

Keep it in perspective. Avoid blowing the criticism out of proportion. The purpose of criticism is only to generate positive change.

Listen without defensiveness. You can't hear the criticism if you're busy framing your rebuttal.

Consider the source. A coach, teacher, or seasoned athlete could offer feedback based on a wealth of experience and expertise.

V.I.P.'S (VERY IMPORTANT PERSONS)

Step 1 Under the column below titled "Name," write the names of at least seven people who have positively influenced your life. They might be relatives, friends, teachers, or perhaps persons you have never met. (Complete each step before moving on.)

Step 2 In the next column, rate your gratitude for this person's influence (from 1 to 5, with 1 being a little grateful and 5 being extremely grateful).

Step 3 In the third column, rate how fully you have communicated your appreciation to this person (again, 1 to 5, with 1 being not communicated and 5 being fully communicated).

Step 4 In the final column, put a U to indicate the persons with whom you have unfinished business (such as an important communication that you have not yet sent).

	Name	*Grateful (1–5)*	*Communicated (1–5)*	*U*
1.				
2.				
3.				
4.				
5.				
6.				
7.				

Step 5 Now select two persons with U's beside their names and write them a letter. Express the love, tenderness, and joy you feel toward them. Tell them exactly how they have helped change your life and how glad you are that they did.

Step 6 You also have an impact on others. Make a list of people whose lives you have influenced. Consider sharing with these people why you enjoy being a part of their lives.

_____
_____
_____
_____
_____
_____
_____
_____

Three phases of effective writing

Writing is a way to learn. You can literally write your way into a subject. Through writing, you can get a much clearer picture of what you know, what you don't know, and where to look for the missing pieces.

This chapter outlines a three-phase process for writing any paper or speech:

1. Getting ready to write
2. Writing a first draft
3. Revising your draft

Even though the following articles lay out a step-by-step process, remember that writing is highly personal. You might go through the steps in a different order or find yourself working on several at once.

Note: For specific suggestions on ways to write more efficiently with word processing software, see Chapter Ten: Technology.

PHASE ONE
Getting ready to write

List and schedule writing tasks

You can divide the ultimate goal—a finished paper—into smaller steps, such as those listed below. Set a due date for each step. Start with the date your paper is due and work backward to the present.

Generate ideas for a topic

Brainstorm with a group. There's no need to create in isolation. Forget the myth of the lonely, frustrated artist hashing out his ideas alone in a dimly lit Paris café. You can harness the energy and the natural creative power of a group to assist you. For ideas about ways to brainstorm, see Chapter Seven: Thinking.

Speak it. To get ideas flowing, start talking. Admit your confusion or lack of a clear idea. Then just speak. By putting your thoughts into words, you'll start thinking more clearly. Novelist E. M. Forster said, "'Speak before you think' is creation's motto."[7]

Use free writing. Free writing, a technique championed by writing teacher Peter Elbow, sends a depth probe into your creative mind.[8] There's only one rule in free writing: Write without stopping. Set a time limit— say, 10 minutes—and keep your pencil in motion or your fingers dancing across the keyboard the whole time.

Ignore the urge to stop and rewrite, even if you think what you've written isn't very good. You can revise later. For now, just keep writing and let the ideas flow. Experiment with free writing as soon as your instructor assigns a paper.

Refine initial ideas

Select a topic and working title. Using your instructor's guidelines for the paper or speech, write down a list of topics that interest you. Write as many of these as you can think of in two minutes. Then choose one. If you can't decide, use scissors to cut your list into single items, put them in a box, and pull one out. To avoid getting stuck on this step, set a precise timeline: "I will choose a topic by 4 p.m. on Wednesday."

The most common pitfall is selecting a topic that's too broad. "Harriet Tubman" is not a useful topic for your American history paper. Instead, consider "Harriet Tubman's activities as a Union spy during the Civil War." Your topic statement can function as a working title.

Write a thesis statement. Clarify what you want to say by summarizing it in one concise sentence. This sentence, called a thesis statement, refines your working title. It also helps in making a preliminary outline.

You might write a thesis statement such as "Harriet Tubman's activities with the Underground Railroad led to a relationship with the Union army during the Civil War." A statement that's clear and to the point can make your paper easier to write. Remember, you can always rewrite your thesis statement as you learn more about your topic.

A thesis statement is different from a topic statement. Like newspaper headlines, a thesis statement makes an assertion or describes an action. It is expressed in a complete sentence, including a verb. "Diversity" is a topic. "Cultural diversity is valuable" is a thesis statement.

Consider your purpose

If you want someone to think differently, make your writing clear and logical. Support your assertions with evidence. If you want someone to feel differently, consider crafting a story. Write about a character your audience can empathize with, and tell how he resolves a problem that they can relate to. And if your purpose is to move the reader into action, explain exactly what steps to take and offer solid benefits for doing so.

To clarify your purpose, state it in one sentence. For example, "The purpose of this paper is to define the term *success* in such a clear and convincing way that I win a scholarship from Houghton Mifflin."

Do initial research

At this stage, the objective of your research is not to uncover specific facts about your topic. That comes later. First, you want to gain an overview of the subject.

Outline

An outline is a kind of map. When you follow a map, you avoid getting lost. Likewise, an outline keeps you from wandering off the topic.

To start an outline, gather a stack of 3x5 cards and brainstorm ideas you want to include in your paper. Write one phrase or sentence per card.

Then experiment with the cards. Group them into separate stacks, each stack representing one major category. After that, arrange the stacks in order. Finally, arrange the cards within each stack in a logical order. Rearrange them until you discover an organization that you like.

If you write on a computer, consider using outlining software. These programs allow you to record and rearrange ideas on the screen, much like the way you'd create and shuffle 3x5 cards.

After you write the first draft of your outline, test it. Make sure that each word relates directly to your statement of purpose.

Do in-depth research

A common mistake that beginning writers make is to hold their noses, close their eyes, and jump into the writing process with both feet first—and few facts. Avoid this temptation by gathering more information than you think you can use.

You can begin writing even before your research is complete. The act of writing creates ideas and reveals areas where more research is needed.

For effective research strategies, see Chapter Four: Reading and Chapter Five: Notes.

Sense the time to begin writing

Finding a natural place to begin is one signal to start writing. This is not to say that the skies will suddenly open up and your completed paper, flanked by trumpeting angels, will appear before your eyes. You might instead get a strong sense of how to write just one small section of your paper or speech. When this happens, write.

PHASE TWO
Writing a first draft

If you've planned your writing project and completed your research, you've already done much of the hard work. Now you can relax into writing your first draft.

To create your draft, gather your notes and arrange them to follow your outline. Then write about the ideas in your notes. Write in paragraphs, one idea per paragraph. If you have organized your notes logically, related facts will appear close to each other. As you complete this task, keep the following suggestions in mind.

Remember that the first draft is not for keeps. Don't worry about grammar, punctuation, or spelling as you write your first draft. Write freely, as if you were explaining the subject to a friend. Let the words flow. The very act of writing will release creative energy. It's perfectly all right to crank out a draft that you heavily rewrite or even throw away. The purpose of a first draft is merely to have something to work with—period. For most of us, that's a heck of a lot better than facing a blank page. You will revise this rough draft several times, so don't be concerned if it seems rough or choppy.

Keep in mind that you don't have to follow your outline from beginning to end. Some professional writers prefer to write the last chapter of a novel or the last scene of a play first. With the ending firmly in mind, they can then guide the reader through all of the incidents that lead up to it. You might feel more comfortable with certain aspects of your topic than with others. Dive in where you feel most comfortable.

Be yourself. Let go of the urge to sound "official" or "scholarly," and write in a natural voice instead. Address your thoughts not to the teacher but to an intelligent student or someone you care about. Visualize this person and choose the three or four most important things you'd say to him about the topic. This helps you avoid the temptation to write merely to impress.

Let your inner writer take over. There might be times when ideas come to you spontaneously—when thoughts flow from your head to your hand without conscious effort. This is a "natural high," similar to states that accomplished athletes, musicians, and artists have described. Writer Natalie Goldberg says that during such moments you are in touch with your "inner writer."[9] Often, those moments come just after a period of feeling stuck. Welcome getting stuck. A breakthrough is not far behind.

Ease into it. Some people find that it works well to forget the word *writing*. Instead, they ease into the task with activities that help generate ideas. You can free-associate, cluster, meditate, daydream, doodle, draw diagrams, visualize the event you want to describe, talk into a voice recorder—anything that gets you started.

Get physical. Writing is physical, like jogging or playing tennis. You can move your body in ways that are in tune with the flow of your ideas. While working on the first draft, take breaks. Go for a walk. Speak or sing your ideas out loud. From time to time, practice relaxation techniques and breathe deeply.

Use affirmations and visualizations. Write with the idea that the finished paper or speech is inside you, waiting to be released. Affirmations and visualizations can help you with this. Imagine what your finished paper will look like. Visualize the reaction of audience members after you've given your speech.

Then create statements that affirm your abilities. For example: "I express myself clearly and persuasively." "I am using an effective process to write my paper." "I will be pleased with the results."

Hide it in your drawer for a while. Schedule time for rewrites before you begin, and schedule at least one day in between revisions so that you can let the material sit. On Tuesday night, you might think your writing sings the song of beautiful language. On Wednesday, you will see that those same words, such as the phrase "sings the song of beautiful language," belong in the trash basket. Give yourself time to step back from your material so you can view it with fresh eyes before revising.

PHASE THREE
Revising your draft

One definition of a writer is simply anyone who rewrites. Some people who write for a living will rewrite a piece seven, eight, or even more times.

Ernest Hemingway rewrote the last page of A Farewell to Arms 39 times before he was satisfied with it. When asked what the most difficult part of this process was, he simply said, "Getting the words right."[10]

Keep in mind the saying "Write in haste, revise at leisure." When you revise, slow down and take a microscope to your work. One guideline is to allow 50 percent of writing time for planning, research, and writing the first draft. Then give the remaining 50 percent to revising.

An effective way to revise your paper is to read it out loud. The eyes tend to fill in the blanks in our own writing. The combination of voice and ears forces us to pay attention to the details.

Another technique is to have a friend look over your paper. This is never a substitute for your own review, but a friend can often see things you miss.

Cut

Writer Theodore Cheney suggests that an efficient way to begin revising is to cut the passages that don't contribute to your purpose.[11] It might not pay to polish individual words, phrases, and sentences now—especially if you end up deleting them later. Focus instead on deciding which words you want to keep and which ones you want to let go.

Look for excess baggage. Avoid at all costs and at all times the really, really terrible mistake of using way too many unnecessary words, a mistake that some student writers often make when they sit down to write papers for the various courses in which they participate at the fine institutions of higher learning that they are fortunate enough to attend. (Example: The previous sentence could be edited to "Avoid unnecessary words.")

Approach your rough draft as if it were a chunk of granite from which you will chisel the final product. In the end, much of your first draft will be lying on the floor. What is left will be the clean, clear, polished product.

For maximum efficiency, make the larger cuts first—sections, chapters, pages. Then go for the smaller cuts—paragraphs, sentences, phrases, words.

Note: You might want to keep a file of deleted writings to save for future use.

Paste

In deleting passages, you've probably removed some of the original transitions and connecting ideas from your draft. The next task is to rearrange what's left of your paper or speech so that it flows logically. Look for consistency within paragraphs and for transitions from paragraph to paragraph and section to section. If your draft doesn't hang together, reorder your ideas.

Fix

Now it's time to look at individual words and phrases.

In general, rely on nouns and verbs. Using too many adjectives and adverbs weakens your message and adds bulk to your writing. Write about the details and be specific. Also, use the active rather than the passive voice.

Instead of writing in the passive voice:
A project was initiated.

You can use the active voice:
The research team began a project.

Instead of writing verbosely:
After making a timely arrival and perspicaciously observing the unfolding events, I emerged totally and gloriously victorious.

You can write to the point, as Julius Caesar did:
I came, I saw, I conquered.

Instead of writing vaguely:
The speaker made effective use of the television medium, asking in no uncertain terms that we change our belief systems.

You can write specifically:
The reformed criminal stared straight into the television camera and shouted, "Take a good look at what you're doing! Will it get you what you really want?"

Also, define any terms that the reader might not know, putting them in plain English whenever you can.

Prepare

In a sense, any paper is a sales effort. If you hand in a paper with wrinkled jeans, its hair tangled and unwashed and its shoes untied, your instructor is less likely to buy it. To avoid this situation, format your paper following accepted standards for margin widths, endnotes, title pages, and other details.

Ask your instructor for specific instructions on how to cite the sources used in writing your paper. You can find useful guidelines in the *MLA Handbook for Writers of Research Papers,* a book from the Modern Language Association. Also visit the MLA Web site at **http://www. mla.org/style_faq.**

If you "cut and paste" material from a Web page directly into your paper, be sure to place that material in quotation marks and cite the source. And before referencing an e-mail message, verify the sender's identity.

Use quality paper for your final version. For an even more professional appearance, bind your paper with a paper or plastic cover.

Proof

As you ease down the homestretch, read your revised paper one more time. This time, go for the big picture and look for:

- A clear thesis statement.
- Sentences that introduce your topic, guide the reader through the major sections of your paper, and summarize your conclusions.
- Details—such as quotations, examples, and statistics—that support your conclusions.
- Lean sentences that have been purged of needless words.
- Plenty of action verbs and concrete, specific nouns.

Finally, look over your paper with an eye for spelling and grammar mistakes.

When you're through proofreading, take a minute to savor the result. You've just witnessed something of a miracle—the mind attaining clarity and resolution. That's the aha! in writing. ❇

Giving credit where credit is due

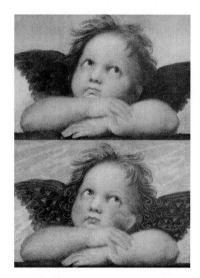

Avoiding the high cost of PLAGIARISM

There's a branch of law known as *intellectual property*. This field is based on the idea that original works—such as speeches, publications, and works of art—are not free for the taking. Anyone who borrows from these works is obligated to acknowledge the work's creator. This is the purpose behind copyrights, patents, and trademarks.

Using another person's words or pictures without giving proper credit is called *plagiarism*. This is a real concern for anyone who writes, including students. Plagiarism amounts to stealing someone else's work and claiming it as your own—the equivalent of cheating on a test.

Higher education consists of a community of scholars who trust each other to speak and write with integrity. Plagiarism undermines this trust. The consequences can range from a failing grade to expulsion from school.

There are several ways to avoid plagiarism when writing.

If your writing includes a passage, identifiable phrase, sequence of ideas, or visual image created by another person, be sure to acknowledge this fact.

Also be careful as you take notes. Clearly distinguish your own ideas from the ideas of others. If you use a direct quote from another writer or speaker, put that person's words in quotation marks. Also note details about the source of the quotation: author, publication title, publisher, date, and page number. Many instructors will require you to add endnotes to your paper with this information, so include it with each quotation in your notes. Ask your instructor for examples of the format to use for endnotes.

If you do research online, you might find yourself copying sentences or paragraphs from a Web page and pasting them directly into your notes. This is the same as taking direct quotes from your source. To avoid plagiarism, identify such passages in an obvious way. Besides enclosing them in quotation marks, you could format them in a different font or color. Also capture relevant information about the Web page where the passages originally appeared: author, title, sponsoring organization, URL, publication date, revision date, and date that you accessed that page. For more information crediting Internet sources, go online to the Modern Language Association's Web site at **http://www. mla. org/publications/style/style_faq/style_faq4**.

Instead of using a direct quote, you might choose to paraphrase an author's words. Paraphrasing means restating the original passage in different words, usually making it shorter and simpler. Paraphrase with care. Students who copy a passage word for word and then just rearrange or delete a few phrases are running a serious risk of plagiarism. Consider this paragraph:

> *Higher education also offers you the chance to learn how to learn. In fact, that's the subject of this book. Employers value the person who is a "quick study" when it comes to learning a new job. That makes your ability to learn a marketable skill.*

Following is an improper paraphrase of that passage:

> *With higher education comes the chance to learn how to learn. Employers value the person who is a "quick study" when it comes to learning a new job. Your ability to learn is a marketable skill.*

A better paraphrase of the same passage would be:

> *The author notes that when we learn how to learn, we gain a skill that is valued by employers.*

Be sure to credit paraphrases in the same way that you credit direct quotes.

When you use the same sequence of ideas as one of your sources—even if you haven't summarized, paraphrased, or quoted—cite that source.

Finally, submit only your own original work, not materials that have been written or revised by someone else.

Out of a concern for avoiding plagiarism, some students go overboard in crediting their sources. You do not need to credit wording that's wholly your own. Nor do you need to credit general ideas. For example, the suggestion that people use a to-do list to plan their time is a general idea. When you use your own words to describe to-do lists, there's no need to credit a source. But if you borrow someone else's words or images to explain this idea, do give credit. ⊠

Writing and delivering speeches

Polishing your speaking and presentation skills can also help you think on your feet and communicate clearly. These are skills that you can use in competition, in any course, and in any career you choose.

Organize your presentation

To make an effective speech, be precise about your purpose and main point, or thesis. Speeches can inform, persuade, motivate, or entertain. Choose what you want to do, let your audience know what your intention is, and state your thesis early on.

Time yourself as you practice your presentation. Be brief, be seated, and leave your listeners wanting more.

Writing a speech is similar to writing a paper. Speeches are usually organized in three main parts: the introduction, the main body, and the conclusion.

Write the introduction. Rambling speeches with no clear point or organization put audiences to sleep. Solve this problem with your introduction. The following

introduction, for example, reveals the thesis and exactly what's coming. The speech will have three distinct parts, each in logical order:

> *Dog fighting is a cruel sport. I intend to describe exactly what happens to the animals, tell you who is doing this, and show you how you can stop this inhumane practice.*

Whenever possible, talk about things that hold your interest. Include your personal experiences and start with a bang! Consider this introduction to a speech on the subject of performance-enhancing drugs:

> *I'm very honored to be here with you today. I intend to talk about performance-enhancing drugs and intercollegiate athletic records. First, I want to outline the extent of this problem; then I will discuss some basic assumptions concerning performance-enhancing drugs and effects on recent world records. Finally I will propose some solutions.*

You can almost hear the snores from the audience. Following is a rewrite:

> *More athletic world records have been set in the past 5 years than in the past 20 years in swimming, track and field, baseball, and weightlifting. And there is evidence that new performance-enhancing drugs are created each year. I'm here to talk about the connection between these two facts.*

Write the main body. The main body of your speech is the content, which accounts for 70 to 90 percent of most speeches. In the main body, you develop your ideas in much the same way that you develop a written paper.

In speeches, transitions are especially important. Give your audience a signal when you change points, using meaningful pauses and verbal emphasis as well as transitional phrases: "On the other hand, until the public realizes what is happening to these athletes . . ." or "The second reason the use of performance-enhancing drugs persists is. . . ."

In long speeches, recap from time to time and preview what's to come. Use facts, descriptions, expert opinions, and statistics to hold your audience's attention.

Write the conclusion. At the end of the speech, summarize your points and draw your conclusion. You started with a bang; now finish with drama. The first and last parts of a speech are the most important. Make it clear to your audience when you've reached the end. Avoid endings such as "This is the end of my speech." A simple standby is "So in conclusion, I want to reiterate three points: First. . . ." When you are finished, stop talking.

Create speaking notes. Some professional speakers recommend writing out your speech in full, then putting key words or main points on a few 3x5 cards. Number the cards so that if you drop them, you can quickly put them in order again. As you finish the information on each card, move it to the back of the pile. Write information clearly and in letters large enough to be seen from a distance.

The disadvantage of the 3x5 card system is that it involves card shuffling. Some speakers prefer to use standard outlined notes. Another option is mind mapping. Even an hour-long speech can be mapped on one sheet of paper. You can also use memory techniques to memorize the outline of your speech.

Practice your presentation

The key to successful public speaking is practice.

Use your "speaker's voice." When you practice, do so in a loud voice. Your voice sounds different when you talk loudly, and this can be unnerving. Get used to it early on.

Practice in the room in which you will deliver your speech. Hear what your voice sounds like over a sound system. If you can't practice your speech in the actual room, at least visit the site ahead of time. Also make sure that the materials you will need for your speech, such as an overhead projector and screen, will be available when you want them.

Make a recording. Many schools have recording equipment available for student use. Use it while you practice, then view the finished recording to evaluate your presentation.

Listen for repeated phrases. Examples include *you know, kind of, really,* plus any little *uh*'s, *umm*'s, and *ah*'s. To get rid of these, tell yourself that you intend to notice every time they pop up in your daily speech. When you hear them, remind yourself that you don't use those words anymore.

Keep practicing until you know your material inside and out. Avoid speaking word for word, as if you were

reading a script. When you know your material well, you can deliver it in a natural way.

Deliver your presentation

Before you begin, get the audience's attention. If people are still filing into the room or adjusting their seats, they're not ready to listen. When all eyes are on you, then begin.

Deal with stage fright by noticing it. Experience stage fright fully. When you do, it often becomes less persistent. Notice all of your thoughts and feelings, then gently release them.

Project your voice. When you speak, talk loudly enough to be heard. Avoid leaning over your notes or the podium.

Maintain eye contact. Find a few friendly faces around the room and imagine that you are talking to each person individually.

Notice your nonverbal communication. Be aware of what your body is telling your audience. Contrived or staged gestures will look dishonest. Be natural. If you don't know what to do with your hands, notice that. Then don't do anything with them.

Notice the time. You can increase the impact of your words by keeping track of the time during your speech. Better to end early than run late.

Pause when appropriate. Beginners sometimes feel that they have to fill every moment with the sound of their voice. Release that expectation. Give your listeners a chance to make notes and absorb what you say.

Have fun. One way to feel at ease while speaking is to look at your audience and imagine everyone dressed as clowns. Chances are that if you lighten up and enjoy your presentation, so will they.

Reflect on your presentation

Review and reflect upon your performance. Did you finish on time? Did you cover all of the points you intended to cover? Was the audience attentive? Did you handle any nervousness effectively?

Welcome evaluation from others. Most of us find it difficult to hear criticism about our speaking. Be aware of resisting such criticism and then let go of your resistance. Listening to feedback will increase your skill. ⬔

PRACTICING CRITICAL THINKING

8

Discuss a controversial issue of your choosing with a small group of classmates. At several points in your discussion, stop to evaluate your group's critical thinking. Answer the following questions in writing.

Are we staying open to opposing ideas, even if we initially disagree with them?

_____

_____

_____

_____

_____

Are we asking for evidence for each key assertion?

_____

_____

_____

_____

_____

Are we adequately summarizing one another's point of view before analyzing it?

_____

_____

_____

_____

_____

Are we foreseeing the possible consequences of taking a particular stand on any issue?

_____

_____

_____

_____

_____

Are we considering more than one solution to problems?

_____

_____

_____

_____

_____

Are we willing to change our stands on issues or suspend judgment when appropriate?

_____

_____

_____

_____

_____

Are we being systematic as we consider the issues?

_____

_____

_____

_____

_____

power process

Employ your word

When you speak and give your word, you are creating—literally. Your speaking brings life to your values. In large part, others know who you are by the words you speak and the agreements you make. You can learn who you are by observing which commitments you choose to make and which ones you choose to avoid.

Your word makes things happen. Circumstances, events, and attitudes fall into place. The resources needed to accomplish whatever was promised become available. When you give your word, all this comes about.

The person you are right now is, for the most part, a result of the choices and agreements you've made in your life up to this point. Your future is determined largely by the choices and agreements you will make from this point on. By making and keeping agreements, you employ your word to create your future.

The world works by agreement

There are over six billion people on planet Earth. We live on different continents and in different nations, and we communicate in different languages. We have diverse political ideologies and subscribe to various social and moral codes.

This complex planetary network is held together by people keeping their word. Agreements minimize confusion, prevent social turmoil, and keep order. Projects are finished, goods are exchanged, and treaties are made. People, organizations, and nations know what to expect when agreements are kept. When people keep their word, the world works. Agreements are the foundation of many things that we often take for granted. Language, our basic tool of communication, works only because we agree about the meanings of words. A pencil is a pencil only because everyone agrees to call a thin, wood-covered column of graphite a pencil. We could just as easily call them ziddles. Then you might hear someone say, "Do you have an extra ziddle? I forgot mine."

Money exists only by agreement. If we leave a $100 Monopoly bill (play money) on a park bench next to a real $100 bill (backed by the United States Treasury), one is more likely to disappear than the other. The only important difference between the two pieces of paper is that everyone agrees that one can be exchanged for goods and services and the other cannot. Shopkeepers will sell merchandise for the "real" $100 bill because they trust a continuing agreement.

Relationships work by agreement

Relationships are built on agreements. They begin with our most intimate personal contacts and move through all levels of families, organizations, communities, and nations.

When we break a promise to be faithful to a spouse, to help a friend move to a new apartment, or to pay a bill on time, relationships are strained and the consequences can be painful. When we keep our word, relationships are more likely to be satisfying and harmonious. Expectations of trust and accountability develop. Others are more likely to keep their promises to us.

Perhaps our most important relationship is the one we have with ourselves. Trusting ourselves to keep our word is enlivening. As we experience success, our self-confidence increases.

When we commit to complete a class assignment and then keep our word, our understanding of the subject improves. So does our grade. We experience satisfaction and success. If we break our word, we create a gap in our learning, a lower grade, and possibly negative feelings.

Ways to make and keep agreements

Being cautious about making agreements can improve the quality of our lives. Making only those promises that we fully intend to keep improves the likelihood of reaching our goals. We can ask ourselves what level of commitment we have to a particular promise.

At the same time, if we are willing to take risks, we can open new doors and increase our possibilities for success. The only way to ensure that we keep all of our agreements is either to make none or to make only those that are absolutely guaranteed. In either case, we are probably cheating ourselves. Some of the most powerful promises we can make are those that we have no idea how to keep. We can stretch ourselves and set goals that are both high and realistic.

If we break an agreement, we can choose to be gentle with ourselves. We can be courageous, quickly admit our mistake to the people involved, and consider ways to deal with the consequences.

Examining our agreements can improve our effectiveness. Perhaps we took on too much—or too little. Perhaps we did not use all the resources that were available to us—or we used too many. Perhaps we did not fully understand what we were promising. When we learn from both our mistakes and our successes, we can become more effective at employing our word.

Move up the ladder of powerful speaking

The words used to talk about whether or not something will happen fall into several different levels. We can think of each level as one rung on a ladder—the ladder of powerful speaking. As we move up the ladder, our speaking becomes more effective.

Obligation. The lowest rung on the ladder is *obligation.* Words used at this level include *I should, he ought to,*

By making and keeping agreements, you employ your word to create your future.

someone better, *they need to, I must,* and *I had to.* Speaking this way implies that people and circumstances other than ourselves are in control of our lives. When we live at the level of obligation, we often feel passive and helpless to change anything.

Note: When we move to the next rung, we leave behind obligation and advance to self-responsibility. All of the rungs work together to reinforce this characteristic.

Possibility. The next rung up is *possibility.* At this level, we examine new options. We play with new ideas, possible solutions, and alternative courses of action. As we do, we learn that we can make choices that dramatically affect the quality of our lives. We are not the victims of circumstance. Phrases that signal this level include *I might, I could, I'll consider, I hope to,* and *maybe.*

Preference. From possibility we can move up to *preference.* Here we begin the process of choice. The words *I prefer* signal that we're moving toward one set of possibilities over another, perhaps setting the stage for eventual action.

Passion. Above preference is a rung called *passion.* Again, certain words signal this level: *I want to, I'm really excited to do that, I can't wait.* Possibility and passion are both exciting places to be. Even at these levels, though, we're still far from action. Many of us want to achieve lots of things and have no specific plan for doing so.

Planning. Action comes with the next rung—*planning.* When people use phrases such as *I intend to, my goal is to, I plan to,* and *I'll try like mad to,* they're at the level of planning. The Intention Statements you write in this book are examples of planning.

Promising. The highest rung on the ladder is *promising.* This is where the power of your word really comes into play. At this level, it's common to use phrases such as these: *I will, I promise to, I am committed, you can count on it.* This is where we bridge from possibility and planning to action. Promising brings with it all of the rewards of employing your word. ▧

put it to work

The techniques described in this chapter have many direct applications in the workplace. According to the National Association of Colleges and Employers, verbal and written communication tops the list of skills that companies look for in college graduates.[12]

Reread specific articles with the workplace in mind.
Simply by remembering to separate the processes of sending and receiving, you can immediately improve your relationships with both supervisors and employees. Use ideas from "Writing and delivering speeches" to craft presentations that persuade your supervisor to increase your department budget—or give you a raise.

If you get into a personal conflict with a coworker, reread the article "The fine art of conflict management" and choose a suggestion to apply. As you read, visualize the suggestion working for you.

Use ideas from "Relationships can work" to stay in contact with coworkers as they change jobs or move to new companies. These people could be in a position to hire you some day.

Make effective presentations with visuals.
Presentations often include visuals such as overhead transparencies, flip charts, or "slides" created with presentation software. These can reinforce your main points and help your audience understand how your presentation is organized. In addition, visuals can serve as your speaking notes.

Use visuals to *complement* rather than *replace* your speaking. If you use too many visuals—or visuals that are too complex—your audience might focus on them and forget about you. To avoid this fate:

- Limit the amount of text on each visual. Stick to key words presented in short sentences and bulleted or numbered lists. Use a consistent set of plain fonts that are large enough for all audience members to see.
- Stick with a simple, coherent color scheme. Use light-colored text on a dark background, or dark text on a light background.
- Use consistent terminology in your speaking, your handouts, and your visuals. Inconsistency can lead people to feel lost or to question your credibility.
- Proofread your visuals for spelling and other mechanical errors.

Write for workplace audiences. Good writing is a marketable skill. To verify this, flip through the help wanted section in a large Sunday newspaper. Note how many job descriptions call for good writing skills. Writing techniques can assist you in preparing memos, reports, e-mail messages, and Web sites.

Jakob Nielsen, author of *Designing Web Usability: The Practice of Simplicity*, suggests that effectively written Web pages are:

- *Concise*—free of needless words and organized so that the main point of each section and paragraph comes at the beginning.
- *Scannable*—prepared with subheadings and visuals that allow readers to skim and quickly find what they need.
- *Objective*—packed with credible facts and free of "hype," that is, vague claims presented without evidence.[13]

These three guidelines can assist you in *all* forms of business writing.

Work effectively in teams. According to authors Frank LaFasto and Carl Larson, the most common barrier to effective teamwork is an atmosphere of defensiveness. Team members can solve this problem by communicating in specific ways: creating an environment in which all opinions are valued; resolving personal conflicts actively rather than ignoring them; staying focused on relevant problems rather than side issues; choosing leaders who allow all opinions to be expressed and keep the team focused; using a simple and clear process for decision making, allowing people to take immediate action without excess paperwork or time-wasting procedures; defining the team's outcome clearly and how individual team members can contribute directly to that outcome.[14]

Name _____ Date _____/_____/_____

1. According to the text, effective communication involves switching back and forth between two primary roles. Name those roles and describe each one in a sentence.

2. Give two examples of ways to display openness while you listen.

3. The suggested techniques for verbal listening include which of the following?

   (A) Parrot exactly what another person says.
   (B) Pay attention to the speaker's words and not the emotions behind the words.
   (C) Always put your own concerns aside in order to listen attentively.
   (D) Look for the requests hidden in complaints.

4. As a student athlete, what you say in an interview reflects only on you. True or False? Explain your answer.

5. List the five parts of an "I" message (the five ways to say "I").

6. One suggestion for conflict resolution is to write a nasty message. True or False? Explain your answer.

7. Which of the following is an effective thesis statement? Explain your answer.

   (A) Two types of thinking.
   (B) Critical thinking and creative thinking go hand in hand.
   (C) The relationship between critical thinking and creative thinking.

8. Define *plagiarism* and explain ways to avoid it.

9. Describe at least three techniques for practicing and delivering a speech.

10. What characteristic distinguishes the top five rungs of the ladder of powerful speaking from the bottom rung?

learning styles application

The questions below will "cycle" you through four styles, or modes, of learning as explained in the article "Learning styles: Discovering how you learn" in Chapter One. Each question will help you explore a different mode. You can answer the questions in any order.

what if *After reading this chapter, will you generally approach conflict management in a different way? Briefly explain your answer.*

why *Think of a conflict you are experiencing right now with an important person in your life. (If you cannot think of one, recall a conflict you've experienced in the past.) Do you think that any of the suggestions in this chapter could help you resolve this conflict? Briefly explain your answer.*

how *Describe when and where you plan to use a suggestion from this chapter to resolve a conflict with another person.*

what *Choose a specific suggestion from this chapter that could help you resolve a conflict you are experiencing right now with another person.*

master student

profile

SHERYL SWOOPES

(1971–   ) Honored in her college and professional career and three-time Olympic gold medalist, she helped the WNBA's Houston Comets to four consecutive championship titles while serving as a role model for other single mothers in the league.

When I went back to play for the Houston Comets six weeks after my son was born, there wasn't a single person I could talk to who had gone through that exactly. Other women who have had kids said, "It's going to take you at least a year to recuperate." But it wasn't about proving them wrong. I was doing it for me. I wouldn't do anything to jeopardize my health or my baby's, and if the doctor says, "Sheryl, you can't play anymore," then I won't continue to do what I'm doing. My number-one priority is taking care of my child. This wasn't something I planned—I didn't know it was going to happen. But now people can look at me and say, "Sheryl's a great mother and she still has her career."

I grew up in a single-parent home, and it was very difficult at times, because we didn't have the money to do things that a lot of [our] friends were able to do. My mother worked three jobs, and we sometimes needed public assistance. But even then, my mom was determined to give us all the things we needed in life and was willing to make the sacrifices that

were necessary to achieve that. She wanted all of her kids to be the best we could possibly be. Her steadfastness and determination brought me to where I am today—she is the reason why I am successful.

It's funny that I ended up playing basketball because, growing up in Brownfield, Texas, I always wanted to be a cheerleader. I used to put on makeup with my cousin, cheer for my brothers at games, and even perform for the family. But I never tried out for the squad because we didn't have the money to buy the uniforms and pom-poms. So I began to play basketball since my two older brothers played, using an old bicycle tire rim placed on top of a pole for the hoop. At first they didn't let me play, saying, "Sheryl, basketball is for boys." And when I did get to play, they were very hard on me, knocking me down and playing keep-away. But they were good teachers. Gradually, my shooting and dribbling got better. During junior high, I spent three nights a week playing hoops at the high school with the boys. I rarely got picked at first, and when I did, the guys almost never passed me the ball. And then they would humor me by handing me the ball and saying, "Let her shoot." But all of this just made me work even harder. I learned that no matter what anybody tells me, as long as I believe it can be done, then I'm going to do it.

It is upsetting for me to hear about dads who tell their daughters they shouldn't play basketball and that they should be cheerleaders, ballerinas, or piano players instead. Girls need to hear that it's okay to play basketball or any other "boy's" sport and that they can be feminine at the same time. Kids used to call me a tomboy because I played basketball. But once I got older, I learned that I could wear makeup and dresses and still play basketball. It's okay to be on the court and be pretty. It's okay to be strong and shop at the mall.

One of the best feelings I have ever had was at our first exhibition game at the University of Georgia. I saw a little girl smiling and waving at our team. She was wearing a red jersey. Number 7. "Swoopes" was on the back. I will never forget the sight—it was so gratifying and so moving that it caused a few tears to roll out of my eyes. ◪

From Christina Lessa, *Women Who Win in Sport and in Life.* Copyright 1998 by Christina Lessa. Reprinted by permission of Universe Publishing.

For more biographical information about Sheryl Swoopes, visit the Master Student Hall of Fame on the *Becoming a Master Student Athlete* Web site at

masterstudent.college.hmco.com

9

Diversity

Candor is a compliment; it implies equality. It's how true friends talk.

PEGGY NOONAN

Labels are for filing. Labels are for clothing. Labels are not for people.

MARTINA NAVRATILOVA

why
this chapter matters . . .

You're likely to learn and work with people from many different cultures.

what
is included . . .

Living with diversity
Diversity is real—and valuable
Communicating across cultures
Overcome stereotypes with critical thinking
Students with learning disabilities: Ask for what you want
Dealing with sexism and sexual harassment
We are all leaders
Power Process: "Choose your conversations and your community"
Master Student Profile: Dat Nguyen

how
you can use this chapter . . .

Study, train, and compete effectively with people of different racial and ethnic groups.
Gain skills to succeed in a multicultural work force.
Choose conversations that promote your success.

as you read, ask yourself
what if . . .

I could create positive relationships with teammates, classmates, or coworkers of any race, ethnic group, or culture?

Living with diversity

Those of us who can study, work, and live with people from other cultures, economic classes, and races can enjoy more success at school, on the job, and in our neighborhoods. Sharing in this success means learning new ways to think, speak, and act. Learning about diversity opens up a myriad of possibilities—an education in itself. At first, this can seem challenging or even painful. It can also be exciting, enriching, and affirming.

Your fellow student athletes will come from different neighborhoods, different states, and different countries. You may be surprised at how many of these students have backgrounds and preferences that are much like your own. You may also encounter vast differences in culture—variations in clothing, diet, language, values, and expectations about higher education.

If you learn to thrive in the midst of this diversity, you'll help to create cohesive teams. You'll also gain a skill that promotes your success in the workplace.

The cultures of the world meet daily. Several forces are shrinking our globe. One is the growth of a world economy. Another is the "electronic village" forged across nations by newspapers, radios, televisions, telephones, fax machines, and computers.

We have an opportunity to benefit from this change instead of merely reacting to it. At one time, only sociologists and futurists talked about the meeting of cultures. Now all of us can enter this conversation. We can value cultural diversity and learn how to thrive with it.

Embracing diversity means overcoming the long history of racism, prejudice, and fear of differences among people. There are no quick fixes or easy answers on this path. Each suggestion in this chapter is merely a starting point. Continue to experiment and see what works for you. As you read, constantly ask yourself: "How can I use this material to live and work more effectively in a diverse world?" The answers could change your life. ⊠

journal entry 22

Discovery/Intention Statement

Briefly describe an incident in which you were discriminated against because you differed in some way from the other people involved. This could be any kind of difference, such as hair length, style of clothing, political affiliation, religion, skin color, sexual orientation, age, gender, economic status, or accent.

I discovered that I . . .

_____

_____

_____

Scan this chapter for ideas that could help you respond more effectively to discrimination, whether it occurs to you or someone else. List at least five ideas that you intend to explore in more detail, along with their associated page numbers.

Strategy   *Page number*

_____

_____

_____

_____

_____

Schedule a time to explore these techniques in more detail. Also describe a situation coming up this term in which you could apply them.

I intend to . . .

_____

_____

_____

_____

_____

_____

Diversity is real— and valuable

We have always lived with people of different races and cultures. Many of us come from families who immigrated to the United States or Canada just two or three generations ago. The things we eat, the tools we use, and the words we speak are a cultural tapestry woven by many different peoples.

Think about a common daily routine. A typical American citizen awakens in a bed (an invention from the Near East). After dressing in clothes (often designed in Italy), she slips on a pair of athletic shoes (made in England), slices a banana (grown in Honduras) on her bowl (made in China) of cereal, and brews coffee (shipped from Nicaragua). After breakfast, she reads the morning newspaper (printed by a process invented in Germany on paper, which was first made in China). Then she flips on a CD player (made in Japan) and listens to music (performed by a band from Cuba). Multiculturalism refers to racial and ethnic diversity— and many other kinds of diversity as well.

As anthropologist Dorothy Lee reminds us, culture is simply one society's solutions to perennial human problems, such as how to worship, celebrate, resolve conflict, work, think, and learn.[1] Culture is a set of learned behaviors—a broader concept than race, which refers to the biological makeup of people.

Multiculturalism refers to racial and ethnic diversity—and many other kinds of diversity as well.

From this standpoint, we can speak of the culture of large corporations or the culture of the fine arts. There are the cultures of men and women; heterosexual, homosexual, and bisexual people; and older and younger people. There are differences between urban and rural dwellers, between able-bodied people and those with disabilities, and between people from two-parent families and people from single-parent families. Diversity in religion is a factor, too. This can be especially difficult to accept, since many people identify strongly with their faith.

In some respects, culture can be compared to an iceberg. Only parts of any given culture—such as language patterns or distinctive apparel—exist on a visible level. Just as most of an iceberg lies under water and out of sight, many aspects of culture lie beneath our conscious awareness.

This invisible realm includes assumptions about the meanings of amateurism and professionalism, beauty and friendship, and sin and justice. Also submerged here are approaches to problem solving, interpretations of eye contact and body language, and patterns of supervisor and employee relationships.

People can differ in countless ways—race, gender, ethnic group, sexual orientation, and more. The suggestions offered in this chapter can help you respond effectively to the many kinds of diversity you'll encounter. Higher education can help reinforce an attitude of tolerance, open-mindedness, and respect for individual differences.

Discrimination is also real. The ability to live with diversity is now more critical than ever. Racism, homophobia, and other forms of discrimination undermine our safety. According to the FBI, a total of 7,462 hate crimes took place in the United States during 2002. About 49 percent of those crimes were based on race, and nearly 17 percent were based on sexual orientation.[2]

Of course, discrimination can be far more subtle than hate crimes. Consider how you would respond to the following situations:

- Members of a sociology class are debating the merits of reforming the state's welfare system. The instructor calls on a student from a reservation and says, "Tell us. What's the Native American perspective on this issue anyway?" Here the student is being typecast as a spokesperson for her entire ethnic group.

- A student athlete reveals that he is gay. His teammates react with fear of sexual advances—even though none take place. This athlete finds himself socially isolated, sitting alone on the team bus during travel to competitions.

- Students in a mass media communications class are learning to think critically about television programs. They're talking about a situation comedy set in an urban high-rise apartment building with mostly African American residents. "Man, they really whitewashed that show," says one student. "It's mostly about inner-city black people, but they didn't show anybody on welfare, doing drugs, or joining gangs." The student's comment perpetuates common racial stereotypes.

- On the first day of the term, students taking English composition enter a class taught by a professor from Puerto Rico. One of the students asks the professor, "Am I in the right class? Maybe there's been a mistake. I thought this was supposed to be an English class, not a Spanish class." The student assumed that only Caucasian people are qualified to teach English courses.

Racism involves the power to define reality, to enshrine a particular set of biases. The operating assumption is that differences mean deficits.

When racism lives, we all lose—even those groups with social and political power. We lose the ability to make friends and to function effectively on teams. We crush human potential. People without the skills to bridge cultures are already at a disadvantage.

Higher education offers a chance to change this. Collegiate academic and athletic environments can become cultural laboratories—places where people of diverse races and cultures can meet in an atmosphere of tolerance.

Diversity is valuable. Synergy is the idea that the whole is more than the sum of its parts. Consider some examples: A symphony orchestra consists of many different instruments; when played together, their effect is multiplied many times. A football team has members with different specialties; when their talents are combined, they can win a league championship.

Diversity in a society offers another example of synergy. It takes no more energy to believe that differences enrich us than it does to believe that differences endanger us. Embracing diversity adds value to any organization and can be far more exciting than just meeting the minimum requirements for affirmative action.

Today we are waking up not only to the *fact* of diversity but also to the *value* of diversity. Biologists tell us that diversity of animal species benefits our ecology. The same idea applies to the human species. Through education our goal can be to see that we are all part of a complex world—that our own culture is different from, not better than, others. Knowing this, we can stop saying, "This is *the* way to work, learn, relate to others, and view the world." Instead, we can say, "Here is the way I have been doing it. I would also like to see your way."

The fact of diversity also represents opportunity in the workplace. Understanding cultural differences—internationally and domestically—can help you to embrace new viewpoints that lead to profitable solutions. Organizations that are attuned to diversity are more likely to prosper in the global marketplace.

Accepting diversity does not mean ignoring the differences among cultures and becoming part of a faceless "melting pot." Instead, we can evolve into a mosaic—a piece of art in which each element maintains its individuality and blends with others to form a harmonious whole.

Learning to live with diversity is a process of returning to "beginner's mind," a place where we question our biases and assumptions. This is a magical place, a place of fresh perspectives and new options. It takes courage to dwell in beginner's mind—courage to go outside the confines of our own culture and world-view. It can feel uncomfortable at first. Yet there are lasting rewards to gain.

As you read the following articles, look to yourself. This chapter aims to help you examine your own biases. With self-awareness, you can go beyond them.

> *Higher education can help reinforce an attitude of tolerance, open-mindedness, and respect for individual differences.*

voices

student

A master student tries on other people's skin, and it is not judgmental. We are all different and a master student accepts that diversity.

—LYNN LINEBERGER

Communicating across cultures

Communicating across cultures begins with a desire to create understanding. Use the following strategies to back up that desire with knowledge and skill. If you truly value cultural diversity, you can create even more ways to build bridges between people.

Learn about other cultures.
The greater our knowledge of other cultures, the easier it is for us to be tolerant. The more we explore our differences, the more we can discover our similarities.

Begin with an intention to increase your knowledge of other cultures. You can start with athletics. Consider the diversity of sports offered at the collegiate level. Football, basketball, baseball, and soccer teams develop cadres of devoted fans. Yet college athletes can also compete in cross country, track, lacrosse, rowing, hockey, swimming, bowling, skiing, softball, volleyball, tennis, water polo, golf, wrestling, and more. Each sport can develop its own culture. Practice initiating a conversation with an athlete whose sport differs from your own. You'll develop skills that can eventually help you reach out to members of different racial and ethnic groups.

You might find yourself fascinated by a particular culture. Consider learning as much about it as possible. Immerse yourself in that culture. Read novels, see plays, go to concerts, listen to music, look at art, take courses, learn the language. Find opportunities to speak with members of that culture. Your quest for knowledge will be an opening to new conversations.

Look for common ground.
Some goals cross culture lines. Most people want health, physical safety, economic security, education, loving relationships, and job satisfaction. To promote cultural understanding, we can become aware of and celebrate our differences. We can also return to our common ground.

Athletics provides a shared set of skills, goals, and rules despite the cultural differences among individual athletes. Practice looking for additional common ground. Do this through volunteering, serving on committees, or joining study groups—any activity in which people from other cultures are also involved. Then your understanding of other people unfolds in a natural, spontaneous way. The key is to honor the differences among people while remembering what we have in common.

Assume differences in meaning.
After first speaking to someone from another culture, don't assume that you've been understood or that you fully understand the other person. Check it out. Verify what you think you said or heard.

If you're speaking to someone who doesn't understand English well, keep the following ideas in mind:

- Speak slowly and distinctly, but don't shout or overexaggerate your words.
- To clarify your statement, don't repeat individual words over and over again. Restate your entire message in simple, direct language. Avoid slang.
- Use gestures to accompany your words.
- Since English courses for non-native speakers often emphasize written English, write down what you're saying.
- Stay calm and avoid sending nonverbal messages that you're frustrated.

Look for individuals, not group representatives.
Sometimes the way we speak glosses over differences among individuals and reinforces stereotypes. For example, a student worried about her grade in math expresses concern over "all those Asian students who are skewing the class curve." Or a Caucasian music major assumes that her African American classmate knows a lot about jazz. We can avoid such errors by seeing people as individuals—not spokespersons for an entire group.

Find a translator, mediator, or model.
People who move with ease in two or more cultures can help us greatly. Diane de Anda, a professor at the University of

California, Los Angeles, speaks of three kinds of people who can communicate across cultures. She calls them *translators, mediators,* and *models.*[3]

A *translator* is someone who is truly bicultural—a person who relates skillfully to people in a mainstream culture and people from a contrasting culture. This person can share her own experiences in overcoming discrimination, learning another language or dialect, and coping with stress. She can point out differences in meaning between cultures and help resolve conflict.

Mediators are people who belong to the dominant or mainstream culture. Unlike translators, they might not be bicultural. However, mediators value diversity and are committed to cultural understanding. Often they are teachers, counselors, tutors, mentors, or social workers.

Models are members of a culture who are positive examples. Models include students from any racial or cultural group who participate in class and demonstrate effective study habits. Models can also include entertainers, athletes, and community leaders.

Your school might have people who serve these functions, even if they're not labeled translators, mediators, or models. Some schools have mentor or "bridge" programs that pair new students with teachers of the same race or culture. Students in these programs get coaching in study skills and life skills; they also develop friendships with possible role models. Ask your athletic academic advisor about such programs.

Develop support systems. Many students find that their social adjustment affects their academic performance. Students with strong support systems—such as families, friends, churches, teammates, self-help groups, and mentors—are using a powerful strategy for success in school. As an exercise, list the support systems that you rely on right now. Also list new support systems you could develop.

Support systems can help you bridge culture gaps. With a strong base of support in your own group, you can feel more confident in meeting people outside that group.

Ask for help. If you're unsure about how well you're communicating, ask questions: "I don't know how to make this idea clear for you. How might I communicate better?" "When you look away from me during our conversation, I feel uneasy. Is there something else we need to talk about?" "When you don't ask questions, I wonder if I am being clear. Do you want any more explanation?" Questions such as these can get cultural differences out in the open in a constructive way.

Remember diversity when managing conflict. While in school or on the job, you might come into conflict with a person from another culture. Conflict is

challenging enough to manage when it occurs between members of the same culture. When conflict gets enmeshed with cultural differences, the situation can become even more difficult.

Fortunately, many of the guidelines for managing conflict offered in Chapter Eight apply across cultures. Also keep the following suggestions in mind:

- *Keep your temper in check.* People from other cultures might shrink from displays of sudden, negative emotion—for example, shouting or pointing.

- *Deliver your criticisms in private.* People in many Asian and Middle Eastern cultures place value on "saving face" in public.

- *Give the other person space.* Standing too close can be seen as a gesture of intimidation.

- *Address people as equals.* For example, don't offer the other person a chair so that she can sit while you stand and talk.

- *Stick to the point.* When feeling angry or afraid, you might talk more than usual. A person from another culture—especially one who's learning your language—might find it hard to take in everything you're saying. Pause from time to time so that others can ask clarifying questions.

- *Be patient.* This guideline applies especially when you're a manager or supervisor. People from other cultures might find it difficult to speak candidly with someone they view as an authority figure. Encourage others to speak. Allowing periods of silence might help.

- *Take time to comment when others do well.* However, avoid excessive compliments. People from other cultures might be uncomfortable with public praise and even question your sincerity.

Change the institution. As a student athlete, you might see people of color ignored in class or on a team. You might see people of certain ethnic groups passed over in opportunities to compete, get a job, or join school organizations. And you might see gay and lesbian students ridiculed or even threatened with violence. One way to stop such actions is to point them out to an appropriate authority. ⬚

Overcome stereotypes with critical thinking

Consider these assertions: "Student athletes barely get by in the classroom." "Female athletes are lesbians." "African Americans don't make good quarterbacks."

These are examples of stereotyping—generalizing about a group of people based on the behavior of isolated group members. The word *stereotype* originally referred to a method used by printers to produce duplicate pages of text. This usage still rings true. When we stereotype, we gloss over individual differences and assume that every member of a group is the same.

Stereotypes infiltrate every dimension of human individuality. People are stereotyped on the basis of their race, ethnic group, religion, sexual orientation, political affiliation, geographic location, job, age, gender, IQ, height, or hobby. We stereotype people based on everything from the color of their hair to the year of their car.

In themselves, generalizations are neither good nor bad. In fact, they are essential. Mentally sorting people, events, and objects into groups allows us to make sense of the world. But when we unconsciously make generalizations that rigidly divide the people of the world into "us" versus "them," we fall into errors in thinking that create intolerance.

As a student athlete, you may already know about stereotyping. Perhaps you've heard a general education geology course referred to as "rocks for jocks." Or on the first day of class, maybe a professor walked up to you and said, "I don't give special favors to athletes, so don't ask for any." Reflecting on your reactions to such statements helps you understand the feelings of women, people with disabilities, people of color, and others who have suffered from stereotypes.

One powerful solution to stereotyping is critical thinking, including the strategies that follow.

Look for errors in logic. Some of the most common errors are:

- *Selective perception.* Stereotypes can literally change the way we see the world. If we assume that home-less people are lazy, for instance, then we tend to notice only the examples that support our opinion. Stories about homeless people who are too young or too ill to work will probably escape our attention.

- *Self-fulfilling prophecy.* When we interact with people based on stereotypes, we set them up to act in ways that confirm our thinking. For example, when people of color were denied access to higher education based on stereotypes about their intelligence, they were deprived of opportunities to demonstrate their intellectual gifts.

- *Self-justification.* Stereotypes can allow people to play the role of a victim and skirt responsibility for their lives. An unemployed white male might believe that affirmative action programs are making it impossible for him to get a job—even as he overlooks his own lack of experience or qualifications. That's another example of stereotyping.

Create categories in a more flexible way. Stereotyping has been described as a case of "hardening of the categories." Avoid this problem by making your categories larger: Instead of seeing people based on their skin color, you could look at them on the basis of their heredity. (People of all races share most of the same genes.) Or make your categories smaller. Instead of talking about "religious extremists," look for subgroups among the people who adopt a certain religion. Distinguish between groups that advocate violence and those that shun it.

Test your generalizations about people through action. You can do this by actually meeting people of other cultures. It's easy to believe almost anything about certain groups of people as long as we never deal directly with individuals. Inaccurate pictures tend to die when people from different cultures and life experiences study together, work together, and live together. Consider joining a school or community organization that will put you in contact with a broad spectrum of people and expand your perspectives. Your rewards will include a more global perspective and an ability to thrive in a multicultural world. ✖

Basketball star "Magic" Johnson, swimmer Greg Louganis, and actress Whoopi Goldberg are living proof that no learning disability has to stand between you and excellence. Like many other high achievers, these people faced diagnoses of dyslexia, attention-deficit/hyperactivity disorder, and other learning disabilities.[4]

Ask for what you want

Students with learning disabilities

Remember that people diagnosed with learning disabilities can still display a wide range of abilities. These include visual/spatial intelligence, bodily/kinesthetic intelligence, and other aptitudes identified in the theory of multiple intelligences. (See Chapter One for more information.)

Learn about your diagnosis. If you've been diagnosed with a learning disability, find out everything you can about it. Talk to the psychologist or other expert who made the diagnosis. Ask about the extent of the disability and specific strategies that can help you deal with it. Be prepared to clearly explain your disability to coaches, teachers, and peers.

If you have not been diagnosed but have consistent patterns in problems with learning, ask your academic-athletic advisor about getting evaluated for learning disabilities. Your athletic department may have funds to pay for this service. Some schools offer evaluations for reduced rates through their departments of psychology or education.

Be sure to document your diagnosis. Get it in writing from a qualified professional such as a neurologist or psychologist. Having this document can help you access services for people with learning disabilities and back up your requests for accommodations, as explained below.

Know your legal rights. Equal opportunity for people with disabilities is the law. In particular, know your rights under the Rehabilitation Act of 1973 (especially Section 504) and the Americans with Disabilities Act (ADA) of 1990. These laws protect the civil rights of people with disabilities. They also require colleges and universities to provide certain services to people with learning disabilities.

In addition, learn about the Family Educational Rights and Privacy Act (FERPA) of 1974. This law guards the confidentiality of your medical records, including those about learning disabilities.

Connect with campus services. Resources exist on campus to support your success in school. Ask your coach or academic athletic advisor where to find services for students with learning disabilities. Many schools offer tutoring, audio recordings of textbooks, note-taking services, and technology such as personal digital assistants that you may find useful. Ask about any extra fees for such services. (Services required by Section 504 and the ADA should be free to you.)

Ask for reasonable accommodations. You can legally ask for certain accommodations based on a learning disability. Examples might include: extra time to complete exams; individually proctored exams; having exam questions read orally; permission to answer essay questions by typing on a computer rather than writing by hand; adjusting course assignments or requirements for a major.

This is where you'll need to keep careful records and get appropriate permissions. Accommodations that are not formally approved by your school might violate NCAA rules.

Learn to advocate for yourself. Under the law, colleges and universities have flexibility in choosing what accommodations to provide. You might need to negotiate for what you want.

Changing just a few words can make the difference between asking for what you want and apologizing for it. When people refer to disabilities, you might hear words such as *special treatment* and *adaptation*. Experiment with using *adjustment* and *alternative* instead. The difference between these terms is equality. Asking for an adjustment in an assignment is a request to produce equal work—not for a favor that "waters down" your academic experience. ◪

Dealing with sexism and sexual harassment

Sexism and sexual harassment are real. They are terms for events that occur in schools and workplaces every year. Nearly all of these incidents are illegal or violate organizational policies.

In the United States, women make up the majority of first-year students in higher education. Yet until the early nineteenth century, they were banned from colleges and universities. Today women in higher education still encounter bias based on gender.

This bias can take many forms. For example, instructors might gloss over the contributions of women. Students in philosophy class might never hear of a woman named Hypatia, an ancient Greek philosopher and mathematician. Those majoring in computer science might never learn about Grace Hopper, who developed a computer language named COBOL. And your art history textbook might not mention the Mexican painter Frida Kahlo or the American painter Georgia O'Keeffe.

Though men can be subjects of sexism and sexual harassment, women are more likely to experience this form of discrimination. Even the most well-intentioned people can behave in ways that hurt or discount women. Sexism takes place when:

- Instructors use only masculine pronouns—*he, his,* and *him*—to refer to both men and women.

- Career counselors hint that careers in mathematics and science are not appropriate for women.

- Women are not called on in class, their comments are ignored, or they are overly praised for answering the simplest questions.

- Examples given in a textbook or lecture assign women only to traditionally "female" roles—wife, mother, day care provider, elementary school teacher, nurse, and the like.

- Men assume that female athletes are lesbians.

- People see the accomplishments of female athletes as less important than those of male athletes.

Many kinds of behavior—both verbal and physical—fall under the title of sexual harassment. This kind of discrimination involves unwelcome sexual conduct. Examples of such conduct in a school setting are:

- Sexual touching or advances.

- Any other unwanted touch.

- Unwanted verbal intimacy.

- Sexual graffiti.

- Displaying or distributing sexually explicit materials.

- Sexual gestures and jokes.

- Pressure for sexual favors.

- Talking about personal sexual activity.

Sexual Harassment: It's Not Academic, a pamphlet from the U.S. Department of Education, quotes a woman who experienced sexual harassment in higher education: "The financial officer made it clear that I could get the money I needed if I slept with him."

That's an example of *quid pro quo harassment.* This legal term applies when an educational decision depends on submitting to unwelcome sexual conduct. *Hostile environment harassment* takes place when such incidents are severe, persistent, or pervasive.

The feminist movement has raised our awareness about discrimination against women. We can now respond to sexism and sexual harassment in the places we live, work, and go to school. Specific strategies follow.

Point out sexist language and behavior. When you see examples of sexism, point them out. Your message can be more effective if you use "I" messages instead of personal attacks, as explained in the Communicating chapter. Indicate the specific statements and behaviors that you consider sexist—for example, spreading rumors about someone's sexual activity, rating a person's sexual performance, or making derogatory comments about an athlete's sexual orientation.

Keep in mind that men can also be subjected to sexism, ranging from antagonistic humor to exclusion from jobs that have traditionally been done by women.

Observe your own language and behavior.
Looking for sexist behavior in others is effective. Detecting it in yourself can be just as powerful. Write a Discovery Statement about specific comments that could be interpreted as sexist. Then notice if you've ever said any of these things. Also ask people you know to point out occasions when you use similar statements. Follow up with an Intention Statement that describes how you plan to change your speaking or behavior.

You can also write Discovery Statements about the current level of intimacy (physical and verbal) in any of your relationships at home, work, or school. Be sure that any increase in the level of intimacy is mutually agreed upon.

Encourage support for women.
Through networks, women can join to overcome the effects of sexism. Strategies include study groups for women, women's job networks, and professional organizations, such as Women in Communications. Other examples are counseling services and health centers for women, family planning agencies, and rape prevention centers. Check your school catalog and library to see if any of these services are available at your school.

Even the most well-intentioned people can behave in ways that hurt or discount women.

Set limits.
Women, value yourselves. Recognize your right to an education without the distraction of inappropriate and invasive behavior. Trust your judgment about when your privacy or your rights are being violated. Decide now what kind of sexual comments and actions you're uncomfortable with—and refuse to put up with them. Challenge your teammates and your fellow male athletes to excel in a mutually respectful way.

If you are sexually harassed, take action.
Some key federal legislation protects the rights of women. One is Title VII of the Civil Rights Act of 1964. Guidelines for interpreting this law offer the following definition of harassment.

Unwelcome sexual advances, requests for sexual favors, and other verbal or physical conduct of a sexual nature constitute sexual harassment when:

1. *Submission to this conduct becomes a condition of employment.*
2. *Women's response to such conduct is used as a basis for employment decisions.*
3. *This conduct interferes with work performance or creates an offensive work environment.*

The law also states that schools must take action to prevent sexual harassment.

All universities and most athletics departments have specific policies regarding sexual harassment. Become familiar with these. Policies usually include specific consequences that involve eligibility, team membership, and suspension as well as potential university-wide penalties.

Another relevant law is Title IX of the Education Amendments of 1972. This act bans discrimination against students and employees on the basis of gender. It applies to any educational program receiving federal funds, including intercollegiate athletics programs.

If you believe that you've been sexually harassed, report the incident to a school official. This person can be a teacher, athletics administrator, or campus security officer. Check to see if your school has someone specially designated to handle your complaint, such as an affirmative action officer or Title IX coordinator.

You can also file a complaint with the Office of Civil Rights (OCR), a federal agency that enforces Title IX. In your complaint, include your name, address, and daytime phone number, along with the date of the incident and a description of it. Do this within 180 days of the incident. You can contact the OCR at 1-800-421-3481 or go to the agency's Web site at **http://bcol01.ed.gov/CFAPPS/OCR/contactus.cfm**.

Your community might also offer resources to protect against sexual discrimination. Examples are public interest law firms, legal aid societies, and unions that employ lawyers to represent students. ▨

We are all leaders

No matter our station in life, at some point most of us become leaders.

Many people mistakenly think that leaders are only those with formal titles such as *supervisor* or *manager*. In fact, effective leaders often have no such titles. Like Mahatma Gandhi, some people change the face of the world without ever reaching a formal leadership position.

While many of us will never become so well known, we all have the capacity to make significant changes in the world around us. Through our actions and words we constantly influence what happens in our classrooms, offices, communities, families, and teams. We are all leaders, even if sometimes we are unconscious of that fact.

In fact, it is impossible to escape leadership. Every time you speak, you lead others in some way. Every time you take action, you lead others through your example. Every time you ask someone to do something, you are in essence leading that person. Leadership becomes more effective when it is consciously applied.

Be willing to be uncomfortable. Leadership is a courageous act. Leaders often are not appreciated or even liked. They can feel isolated, cut off from their colleagues. This can sometimes lead to self-doubt and even fear.

Before you take on a leadership role, be aware that you might experience such feelings. Also remember that none of them needs to stop you from leading.

Allow mistakes. The more important and influential you are, the more likely it is that your mistakes will have huge consequences. The anchor man on a relay could drop the baton and lose a championship meet. The chief financial officer for a large company can make a mistake that costs thousands or even millions of dollars. As commander in chief of the armed forces, the president of a country can make a decision that costs thousands of lives.

At the same time, these people are in a position to make huge changes for the better—to save thousands of dollars or lives through their power, skill, and influence.

People in leadership positions can become paralyzed and ineffective if they fear making a mistake. It's necessary for them to act even when information is incomplete or when they know a catastrophic mistake is a possible outcome.

Take on big projects. Leaders make promises. Tackle projects that stretch you to your limits—projects that are worthy of your time and talents. Consider taking on the biggest project you can think of—winning a national championship, eliminating nuclear weapons, wiping out poverty, promoting universal literacy. Even if you miss a big goal, moving toward it will change you and everyone who moves into action with you.

Provide feedback. An effective leader is a mirror to others. Share what you see. Talk with others about what they are doing effectively—*and* what they are doing ineffectively.

Some people feel awkward about getting feedback. You can help by giving it with skill. Use "I" messages as explained in Chapter Eight: Communicating. And when people complete a task effectively, point that out as well.

Paint a vision. There's a biblical saying: "Without vision, the people perish." Long-term goals usually involve many intermediate steps. Unless we're reminded of the purpose for those day-to-day actions, our work can feel like a grind. Leadership is the art of helping others lift their eyes to the horizon—keeping them in touch with the ultimate value and purpose of a project. Keeping the vision alive helps spirits soar again.

Model your values. "Be the change you want to see" is a useful motto for leaders. Perhaps you want to see integrity, focused attention, and productivity in the people around you. Begin by modeling these qualities yourself. Be on time to practice. Display sportsmanship. Listen attentively, give positive feedback to your coaches, and participate in community service projects.

Make requests—lots of them. An effective leader is a request machine. Making requests—both large and small—is an act of respect. When we ask a lot from others, we demonstrate our respect for them and our confidence in their abilities.

Follow up. What we don't inspect, people don't respect. When other people agree to do a job for you, follow up to see how it is going. This can be done in a way that communicates your respect and interest—not your fear that the project might flounder. Don't simply ask, "Did you get done?" Instead, say, "How is it going?" If the answer indicates confusion or frustration, ask what the problem is and perhaps how you can be of assistance.

Focus on the problem, not the person. A skier who misses a gate doesn't do it on purpose. The golfer who slices a tee shot doesn't do it on purpose. Focus on the problem. Most people will join you in searching for solutions if your focus is on the problem, not on what they did wrong.

Acknowledge others. Express genuine appreciation for the efforts of others. When you're congratulated, share the credit. Similarly, it takes a team to win, not just an individual. No captain, no goalie, no anchor runner or swimmer, and no project leader wins based on an individual performance.

Delegate. Be willing to admit that you cannot do some things on your own. Take on projects that are important to you. Then find people who can lead the effort.

We often see delegation as a tool that's available only to those above us in the chain of command. Actually, delegating up or across an organization can be just as effective. Consider delegating a project to your boss. That is, ask her to take on a job that you'd like to see accomplished. This might be a job that you cannot do, given your position in the company.

Listen. Sometimes it seems that effective leaders talk a lot. Chances are, they also listen a lot. As a leader, be aware of what other people are thinking, feeling, and wanting. Listen fully to their concerns and joys. Practice critical listening. Before you criticize their views or make personal judgments, take the time to understand what's going on inside them.

This is not merely a personal favor to the people you work with. The more you know about your teammates, coworkers, or classmates, the more effectively you can lead them.

Tackle projects that stretch you to your limits— projects that are worthy of your time and talents.

Practice. Leadership is an acquired skill. No one is born knowing how to make requests, give feedback, create budgets, do long-range planning, or delegate tasks. We learn these things over time, with practice, by seeing what works and what doesn't. Look for opportunities to learn leadership.

Each summer, the NCAA's Leadership Conference provides student athletes from around the country with the skills and experiences they need to return to their campuses and become team leaders. Other organizations also sponsor seminars and workshops to get you headed in the leadership direction. One is the CHAMPS (Challenging Athletes' Minds for Personal Success) Life Skills programs for student athletes. This program involves specific commitments to academic success, athletic achievement, career planning, personal development, and community service.

At times, leadership is a matter of trial and error and even flying by the seat of your pants. You might sometimes feel that you don't know what you're doing. That's OK. A powerful course of action can be discovered in midstream. You can *act* as a leader even when you don't *feel* like a leader.

Look for areas in which you can make a difference and experiment with these strategies. Right now there's something worth doing that calls for your leadership. Take action and others will join you. ◩

Discovery/Intention Statement

There are things we think about telling people, but don't. Examine your relationships and complete the following statements.

I discovered that I am not communicating about . . .

_____

_____

with . . .

_____

_____

I discovered that I am not communicating about . . .

_____

_____

with . . .

_____

_____

I discovered that I am not communicating about . . .

_____

_____

with . . .

_____

_____

Now choose one idea from this chapter that can open communication with these people in these areas. Describe below how you will use this idea.

I intend to . . .

_____

_____

_____

_____

Discovery Statement

In the space below, describe the circumstances of a conversation you had today and summarize its content.

_____

_____

_____

_____

_____

Now reflect on this conversation. Determine whether it aligned with your values and goals.

I discovered that . . .

_____

_____

_____

_____

_____

_____

voices

student

The whole concept of choosing your conversations to be successful was probably the most useful for me in the book. I discovered that the people and conversations I chose to surround myself were getting me nowhere, fast! As soon as I made the change to choose my conversations around everyone, I noticed a difference in myself and my motivation to succeed in school.

—MARIA MARTINEZ

PRACTICING CRITICAL THINKING

9

Write down the first words that come to mind when you hear the terms listed below. Do this now.

musician

_____

_____

homeless people

_____

_____

football players

_____

_____

computer programmers

_____

_____

disabled person

_____

_____

_____

retired person

_____

_____

_____

adult learner

_____

_____

Next, exchange your responses to this exercise with a friend. Did you discover stereotypes or other examples of bias? What counts as evidence of bias? Summarize your answers here.

_____

_____

_____

_____

_____

_____

_____

_____

_____

_____

power process

Choose your conversations and your community

onversations can exist in many forms. One involves people talking out loud to each other. At other times, the conversation takes place inside our own heads, and we call it thinking. We even have a conversation when we read a magazine or a book, plan a strategy for an athletic competition, watch television or a movie, or write an e-mail or a report. These observations lead to three discoveries that touch every aspect of our lives.

Conversations shape our lives

One is that conversations exercise incredible power over what we think, feel, and do. We become our conversations. They shape our attitudes, our decisions, our opinions, our emotions, and our actions. Each of these is primarily the result of what we say over and over again, to ourselves and to others. If you want clues as to what a person will be like tomorrow, listen to what she's talking about today.

Conversation is constant

This leads to a second discovery. Given that conversations are so powerful, it's amazing that few people act on this fact. Most of us swim in a constant sea of conversations, almost none of which we carefully and thoughtfully choose.

Consider how this works. It begins when we pick up the morning paper. The articles on the front page invite us to a conversation about current events. Often the headlines speak of war, famine, unemployment figures, and other species of disaster. The advertisements start up a conversation about fantastic products for us to buy. They talk about hundreds of ways for us to part with our money.

That's not all. If we flip on the radio or television, or if we surf the Web, millions of other conversations await us. Thanks to modern digital technology, many of these conversations take place in CD-quality sound, high-resolution images, and living color 24 hours each day.

Something happens when we tune in to conversation in any of its forms. We give someone else permission to dramatically influence our thoughts—the conversation in our heads. When we watch a movie, scenes from that movie become the images in our minds. When we read a book, passages from that book become the voice in our heads. It's possible to let this happen dozens of times each day without realizing it.

You have a choice

The real power of this process lies in a third discovery: We can choose our conversations. Certain conversations create real value for us. They give us fuel for reaching our goals. Others distract us from what we want. They might even create lasting unhappiness and frustration.

We can choose more of the conversations that exhilarate and sustain us, those that re-create us as winners. Sometimes we can't control the outward circumstances of our lives. Yet no matter what happens, we can retain the right to choose our conversations.

Suppose that you meet with an instructor to ask about some guidelines for writing a term paper. She launches into a tirade about your writing skills and lack of preparation for higher education. This presents you with several options. One is to talk about what a jerk the instructor is and give up on the idea of learning to

write well. Another option is to refocus the conversation on what you can do to improve your writing skills, such as working with a writing tutor or taking a basic composition class. These two sets of conversations will have vastly different consequences for your success in school.

In a similar way, a coach might give you tough feedback after you competed in a way that was not up to your usual standards. Again, you have options. You can say nasty things about the coach. Or you can watch the video of the competition, analyze your performance, and look for ways to improve it. These internal conversations are likely to have much different outcomes.

The conversations you have are dramatically influenced by the people you associate with. If you want to change your attitudes about almost anything—prejudice, politics, religion, humor—choose your conversations by choosing your community. Spend time with people who speak about and live consistently with the attitudes you value. Use conversations to change habits. Use conversations to create new options in your life.

A big part of this Power Process is choosing *not* to participate in certain conversations. Sometimes we find ourselves in conversations that are not empowering— gripe sessions, gossip, and the like. Or we can let our conversations become one-dimensional and dwell on a single subject, such as athletics. That's a time for us to switch the conversation channel. It can be as simple as changing the subject, politely offering a new point of view, or excusing ourselves and walking away.

Some conversations are about antagonism. Instead of resolving conflict, they fan the flames of prejudice, half-truths, and misunderstanding. We can begin taking charge of these conversations by noticing where they start and choosing ways to change them.

Go for balance

One immediate way to take charge of any conversation is to notice its *time frame*—whether the conversation dwells on the past, the present, or the future.

Conversations about the past can be fun and valuable. When we focus exclusively on the past, however, we can end up rehashing the same incidents over and over again. Our future could become little more than a minor variation of what has already occurred in our lives.

Conversations with a focus on the future can also be empowering. A problem arises if these conversations focus on worst-case scenarios about what could go wrong next week, next month, or next year. Having too many of these conversations can add a baseline of worry and fear to our lives.

As an alternative, we can choose to have constructive

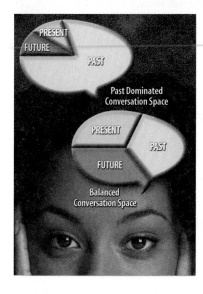

conversations about the present as well as the past and future. Conversations about the past can dwell on what we learn from our experiences. Conversations about the present can focus on what we currently love about our lives and on ways to solve problems. Instead of worrying about the future, we can use our planning skills to set goals that we feel passionately about and consider ways to prevent potential problems. In looking for ways to balance our conversations, we can also select among four categories of *topics:* things, other people, ourselves, and relationships. Most conversations fall into one of these categories.

Many people talk about things (cars, houses, trips, football games, weather) or gossip about others (politicians, actors, neighbors, kids, coworkers) far more than they talk about anything else. To create more balance in your conversations, remember the other two categories of topics. Talk about yourself—your heartfelt desires, fears, and joys—and about ways to create more loving relationships as well.

Conversations promote success

Excelling in higher education means allowing plenty of time for conversations that start in class and continue in your reading and your notes. Extend those conversations by visiting with your instructors during their office hours, talking to classmates, and forming study groups.

Right now you're holding a conversation about student success. This conversation has a big red cover that features the words *Becoming a Master Student Athlete.* Its chapters invite you to 12 subconversations that can make a real difference in what you get in exchange for your hard-earned tuition money.

When we choose our conversations, we discover a tool of unsurpassed power. This tool has the capacity to remake our thoughts—and thus our lives. It's as simple as choosing the next article you read or the next topic you discuss with a friend.

Begin applying this Power Process today. Start choosing your conversations and watch what happens. ⧗

put it to work

By 2008, the U.S. Department of Labor predicts that 27 percent of the total U.S. civilian work force will be either African American, Hispanic, or Asian. Your next boss or coworker could be a person whose life experience and view of the world differs radically from yours.

Geert Hofstede, a Dutch psychologist and author of *Culture's Consequences: Comparing Values, Behaviors, Institutions and Organizations Across Nations*, identifies several core dimensions of cultural difference. Keeping them in mind can help you prevent and resolve conflict with coworkers on project teams.

Power-distance. If you observe teams from cultures based on high power-distance, you will see clear differences in status and power between team members. Some people will clearly function as leaders and others as followers. Compare such teams to those from low power-distance cultures, in which people function basically as equals and decisions are based on consensus. To cope with these differences, ask your team leader to clarify roles. Explain how members are expected to participate in decision making and how their performance will be evaluated.

Supervision. Some of your teammates might do what they can to avoid uncertainty. They focus on details, expect close supervision, and prefer clearly defined tasks with specific due dates. In contrast, other team members might want less supervision rather than more, preferring to work independently. Your team can function more effectively when you look for such differences and tailor assignments to individual preferences.

Individual and collective orientations. People from many Western cultures value individual achievement, competition, and personal recognition. These workers might clash with people from Latin American and Asian cultures that emphasize group cohesion and cooperation.

If you lead a team marked by this cultural difference, take action to balance these differences. When

supervising workers who are motivated by competition, acknowledge their achievements—and remind them that they are members of a group with a shared goal.

Long-term and short-term orientations. Some workers like to lift their eyes to the horizon and set goals to meet over several years or decades. Their orientation leads them to value patience, and they might be willing to make sacrifices now for long-term gains later. On the other hand, workers with a short-term orientation value immediate results and might quickly tire of long-range planning.

By recognizing this difference in orientation up front, you can make it work for you. Ask workers with a long-term orientation to craft a mission statement, list of core values, and five-year plan for your organization. Leave the details of implementing the plan to team members with a short-term orientation. These workers can focus on the month-by-month and week-by-week tasks that lead to achieving long-range goals. ⚵

Name _____ Date _____/_____/_____

1. Racial, ethnic, and other kinds of diversity have become key factors in our lives only in the last decade or two. True or False? Explain your answer.

2. Define the term *culture* and give three examples of different cultures.

3. List three strategies for communicating across cultures.

4. Give two examples of sexist behavior that could take place in higher education.

5. Define the terms *translator, mediator,* and *model* as explained in this chapter.

6. Describe at least one way to overcome stereotypes with critical thinking.

7. List three guidelines for resolving conflict with a person from another culture.

8. Summarize the three key discoveries presented in the Power Process: "Choose your conversations."

9. List three strategies for creating balance in your conversations.

10. Few of us get the chance to be leaders. True or False? Explain your answer.

learning styles application

The questions below will "cycle" you through four styles, or modes, of learning as explained in the article "Learning styles: Discovering how you learn" in Chapter One. Each question will help you explore a different mode. You can answer the questions in any order.

what if *Describe one action you could take to reduce racism in your community.*

why *Describe an example of discrimination or sexual harassment you've personally experienced or witnessed.*

how *Briefly describe how you will respond differently to incidents of discrimination or sexual harassment after reading this chapter.*

what *List two or three of the most valuable suggestions you gained from this chapter for overcoming discrimination or sexual harassment.*

master student profile

DAT NGUYEN

(1975–   ) Highly decorated in his career at Texas A&M University, and the first Vietnamese player in the NFL, his hard work and discipline has led to success academically—he started graduate work while in his final year of eligibility—and professionally.

Like many of their fellow Vietnamese countrymen and women fleeing Vietnam in the 1970s, Dat Nguyen's parents found opportunity in the shrimp industry and related businesses on the Texas gulf coast. Through hard work and careful planning for the future, they provided Dat and his siblings with a deep legacy of industriousness and love of family. But Dat saw that hard work alone did not necessarily provide his family members with the level of respect they deserved. The influx of so many new immigrants of Vietnamese heritage into the Texas gulf coast area meant that many more people were competing for jobs. Some Texans saw that the competitive Vietnamese-Americans posed a threat to their livelihood. They responded in ways that Dat found confusing and hurtful.

On the football field Dat discovered that his talented play temporarily suspended any feelings of ill will toward him and the heritage he represented. Football not only earned him personal success, but it also provided respect for other members of his family, especially his parents.

But at home he was still Dat the son, not the football star. His parents spoke little English, which suited them fine among their Vietnamese-American friends. But in dealing with the extended world of a primarily English-speaking nation, they relied on Dat and his sister to serve as translators. Their own background did not include Americans' passion for football. They were perplexed that so many people were interested in their son dedicating his time and effort to playing a game. Working in the family restaurant or in the local shrimp business could provide Dat with all he really needed.

Dat found that he was unprepared for the interest in him on his arrival on the Texas A&M campus. This sudden rush to celebrity status was not easily comparable to his past experience in high school, when only a few newspapers called to ask questions about his athletic performance. Dat believed, as his parents had taught him, that there is never any reason to disregard the needs of others. He did his best to please everyone. But there just did not seem to be enough hours in the day to accommodate everyone, and at an academically competitive university, sometimes balancing his commitments was tough. Completing assignments and keeping up with classes was difficult when coupled with travel schedules, practice, interviews with the media, and spending time with friends.

When a progress report came in showing that his work was slipping, Dat's advisor got involved. He had seen other athletes struggle as a result of being away from home. He knew that unlike in Rockport, Dat did not have the ever-present support system of his parents and siblings to keep him grounded. He tracked Dat down. One day he pulled him into his office. When confronted with the potential outcome of continued poor performance, Dat became determined.

His advisor asked one question: "Do I need to call your parents?"

Dat quickly responded, "No, this will never happen again. I will not dishonor my mother and father."

Dat bought a planner and learned how to use it to manage his commitments to his coursework as well as his athletics, and to accommodate requests for interviews. From that point forward the only comments received from any of Dat's professors were that he was an outstanding example of what a student athlete should be: hardworking, inquisitive, and trustworthy. ✕

Written from interviews conducted by Karl Mooney.

For more biographical information about Dat Nguyen, visit the Master Student Hall of Fame on the *Becoming a Master Student Athlete* Web site at

masterstudent.college.hmco.com

10

Technology

Nothing will work unless you do.

JOHN WOODEN

The test of the machine is the satisfaction it gives you. There isn't any other test.

ROBERT PIRSIG

why
this chapter matters . . .

Your skill with information technology might be as critical to your success as the ability to read, write, listen, and speak well.

what
is included . . .

Technology, satisfaction, and success
Connect to cyberspace
Finding what you want on the Internet
Thinking critically about information on the Internet
Using technology to manage time and money
Write e-mail that gets results
Becoming an online learner
Library—the buried treasure
Power Process: "Risk being a fool"
Master Student Profile: Rick Hansen

how
you can use this chapter . . .

Become an effective learner when you go online.
Find useful, accurate information on the Internet—and filter out irrelevant content.
Take part in online communities that promote your success.

as you read, ask yourself

what if . . .

I could stay up-to-date with information technology and use it with confidence to achieve my goals?

Technology, satisfaction, and success

Information technology pervades our lives. Computers are not only found on our desktops, in our libraries, and on our laps. They are embedded in cars, appliances, automatic teller machines, grocery checkout lanes, and sometimes—given the latest advances in medical technology—the human body.

Several years ago, the Massachusetts Institute of Technology made headlines by making the content for all of its courses available on the Internet. At the time, this event seemed exotic. Today it is not far from the norm on many campuses.

Courses in higher education are no longer divided into separate categories—distance learning (delivered exclusively over the Internet) versus traditional courses (delivered by human beings standing in front of a classroom). A new model has emerged: the hybrid course that combines online instruction with class meetings and textbooks. Course management software such as WebCT and Blackboard creates virtual classrooms—sites on the World Wide Web where a teacher can post a syllabus, readings, announcements, tests, grades, and a digital "drop box" for student assignments. Digital discussions and debates can also take place via computer bulletin boards, chat rooms, and two-way audio and visual connections. In this chapter, the term *online learning* refers to all of these tools. You can use information technology to succeed in school, advance in your career, and achieve many other goals. Besides helping you complete your course work, computer applications can assist you in creating calendars, setting goals, and managing to-do lists. Other applications will help you crunch numbers, maintain mailing lists, send and receive faxes, manage your finances, stay abreast of the news, and connect you to people and organizations across the world. In addition, you can edit photos, create videos, produce audio files, and launch a personal Web site that introduces you to the worldwide online community.

There's more to technology savvy than just showing up on campus with your own computer or locating your school's computer labs. Knowing which hardware to use is an essential starting point. Mastering software applications such as word processing, databases, and spreadsheets will also help you succeed with technology in the classroom and in the workplace.

At the same time, succeeding with technology is not about becoming a "hacker" or an expert on the latest digital gadgets. Even students who major in computer science can fumble when it comes to online learning.

The bigger picture is that higher education offers you the chance to integrate technology with your own method of processing information. ⊠

journal entry 25

Discovery/Intention Statement

Recall an incident when you felt frustrated during an attempt to use computer-based technology to complete a course assignment. Briefly describe what happened.

I discovered that I . . .

_____

_____

_____

_____

Now skim this chapter for at least five ideas that you intend to explore in more detail—suggestions that could help you become a powerful online learner. Summarize each suggestion in a short phrase and list the page where you found it.

Strategy	Page number

Finally, describe a situation coming up this term—preferably within the next week—in which you could apply several of the suggestions you just listed.

I intend to . . .

_____

_____

_____

_____

Connect to cyberspace

You can take two paths to accessing information technology in higher education. One is through the resources offered by your school. The other is through your own technology resources, including a personal computer.

Your school's resources. Pose the following questions to advisors, librarians, and the staff of your campus computer center. These are especially useful questions to ask when applying to a college or university, or when transferring to a new school.

- Does the school require a level of computer competency for graduation or for completing specific majors?

- How many public access computers are available on campus?

- Are discounts available for students who want to buy a computer through the school?

- Does the school loan or lease computers to students?

- What computer support and troubleshooting services are available on campus?

- What library resources are available online, and are they accessible from remote locations?

- Can students receive credit for courses taken online from other schools?

- Is the school catalog available online?

- Can students access grades and other personal information online?

- Can students register for classes, drop classes, and add classes online?

- Can students handle financial transactions online—for example, tuition payments, financial aid, and bookstore purchases?

- Are students allowed to create personal Web pages and online portfolios?

- Do faculty members distribute course materials online and accept assignments submitted via e-mail?

- Does tuition include a technology fee? If so, what services does it cover?

- Does the campus provide high-speed Internet connections in residence halls and class buildings?

- Does the campus charge for printing from public access computers?

- Does the campus regularly update its own information technology?

Be sure to check out the technology resources available to you as a student athlete. At some schools, athletic departments furnish their students with laptops that are equipped for wireless Internet connection. A laptop can be a lifesaver when you need to complete assignments while traveling for competition. Ask a technician how to configure the computer so that it can connect to wireless networks and hotel data ports across the country.

Your personal resources. Many campuses have computer labs with equipment that's available to students for free. These labs can get crowded, especially during finals week or when other major assignments are due in large courses. To maintain your access to computers, find several sources of public computers on campus and check their availability.

With some creative thinking, you might find even more possibilities. A library on campus or in your community might offer public access. Some students get permission to use computers at their workplace after hours. Perhaps a friend or family member would be willing to loan you a computer or offer you computer time at his home. If you choose one of these options, be realistic about the number of hours that the computer will be available to you.

You might find that it's more convenient to buy your own computer and peripheral equipment. Find out whether your campus bookstore or another outlet on campus sells computer hardware at a student discount. Also ask about getting an extended warranty with technical support. Other options include leasing a computer or buying a used one.

To make an informed purchase, take your time. Start by contacting an admissions counselor or academic advisor at your school and asking the following questions.

Should I get a laptop computer or a desktop computer? Laptop computers have the obvious advantage of portability. They also take up less space—a key consideration if you live in a dorm room. Yet laptops tend to be more fragile and more expensive than desktop computers.

Also, the portability of laptop computers makes them easy targets for thieves. If you get one, keep it in a secure place or always carry it with you in public. Don't leave your computer unattended, even for a few seconds. Treat your laptop the same way that you treat your wallet or purse. Your computer dealer can give you information about security devices for laptops. These include locks and software that identifies the Internet addresses of stolen computers when thieves use them to go online.

What platform will work better for me—Windows or Macintosh? The majority of personal computers used in higher education and business settings are Windows-based. However, most campuses accommodate Macintoshes. You might also find that students with certain majors—such as art, music, or video production—favor Macintoshes. Ask your academic advisor for guidance in this area. If you use a Macintosh, look for software that freely exchanges files with Windows.

What hardware specifications should my computer meet? To find a personal computer that supports your academic success, think about technical specifications. These are the requirements that computers must meet in order to connect to the campus network and run software applications commonly used by students. In particular, ask about requirements for your computer's:

- *Operating system*, the built-in software that keeps track of computer files and allows you to run software applications. Be sure to keep the CDs that contain backup of files of your operating system software and upgrades.

- *Processor*, the piece of hardware that actually carries out the operating system's commands. Processor speed is measured in megahertz (MHz) or gigahertz (GHz). One GHz is about the same as 1,000 MHz. The higher this rating, the faster your computer will run.

- *Random access memory (RAM)*, a temporary storage area for data that you're actively using, such as word processing or database files. RAM is measured in megabytes (MB). Get as much RAM as you can afford. The extra memory helps your computer run faster and allows you to open up more software applications at once.

- *Hard drive*, which stores the operating system along with all of the other files you save and use. Space on a hard drive is measured in gigabytes (GB). One gigabyte equals about 1,000 megabytes.

- *Ethernet card*, sometimes called a network adapter or network interface card (NIC). This allows you to connect your computer to campus networks and the Internet. The speed of an Ethernet card is measured in megabits per second (Mbps). Find out what speed is recommended for your campus.

- *Optical drive*, a piece of equipment built into newer computers, though you can buy it separately. An optical drive allows you to read and write data to compact discs (CDs), digital video discs (DVDs), or

both. Use optical drives to make backup copies of all your working files. Another option is to use an Iomega Zip drive and Zip disks to create backups.

What software do I need to successfully complete course work? Many students find that a package—including a word processor as well as spreadsheet, database, and presentation software—meets their needs. Find out what's recommended for your campus. Again, check with your campus bookstore to see if student discounts are offered on software packages. Also ask whether your school provides software to access the Internet (e-mail and Web browsers) and to protect your computer from viruses. ✖

→ Overcoming technophobia

If you are experiencing technophobia (fear of technology, including computers), this is a wonderful time to overcome it. You can start with these strategies:

- Get in touch with the benefits of technology. Being comfortable with computers can give you an edge in almost every aspect of being a student, from doing library research to planning your career. In the eyes of many employers, experience with computers is sometimes a necessity and almost always a plus.

- Sign up for a computer class for beginners.

- Ask questions. When it comes to computers, there truly aren't any "dumb" questions.

- Find a competent teacher—someone who remembers what it was like to know nothing about computers.

- Just experiment. Sit down, do something, and see what happens. Short of dropping a computer or hitting it with a hammer, you can't hurt the thing.

- Remember that computers are not always user-friendly—at least not yet. Learning how to use them takes patience and time. Knowing this up front can put you at ease and prepare you for the cyberspace adventures ahead.

- Also remind yourself of past successes in making transitions. As far as technology is concerned, this includes everything from writing with a pen to driving a car. You're already mastering a major life change—the transition to higher education. In doing so, you've shown that you have what it takes to tame any technology that enters your life.

Finding what you want on the Internet

Imagine a library with millions of books—a place where anyone can bring in materials and place them on any shelf or even toss them randomly on the floor. That's something like the way information accumulates on the Internet. Finding your way through this maze can be a challenge. But it's worth it.

Experiment with different search tools. When searching the Internet—especially the World Wide Web—you can use several tools:

- *Directories* offer extensive lists of Web pages, all grouped by topic—a "table of contents" for the Web.

- *Search engines* scan millions of Web pages in the same way that a human indexer reviews hundreds of book pages.

- *Meta search engines* draw on the capabilities of several search engines at once—similar to scanning several book indexes at the same time.

Each search site has different features. Some combine aspects of directories and search engines. Look for links on each search site that explain how to use advanced search capabilities. In any case, find a few search sites you like and use them consistently. That way you get to know each one well and capitalize on its strengths.

Treat searches as dialogues with your computer. Even though you're dealing with a machine, you can treat computer-based searches as a series of questions and answers. When doing research, start with a question you want to answer, such as "What mutual funds invest in bonds issued by the U.S. Treasury?" Write the question out as precisely as you can.

Next, identify the key words in this question—for example, *mutual funds, bonds,* and *U.S. Treasury.* Type these words into the blank box that appears on your search site's main page. Be sure you spell your key words correctly. Hit the return key or "Search" button on the screen and wait for your computer to answer with a "hit list" of relevant Web pages.

Check three to five of these pages to see if they include answers to your original question. If not, rephrase your question and search again with different key words.

Use search tricks. Boolean operators include the words *AND, OR,* and *NOT.* For example, if you type *portfolios AND résumés,* you'll get a list of Web sites that refer to both portfolios and résumés. *Portfolios OR résumés* will give you sites that refer to either topic. *Portfolios NOT résumés* will give you sites that relate only to portfolios. With some search tools, a plus sign (+) functions like the term *AND.* A minus sign (–) functions in the same way as the term *NOT.*

Knowing some other nifty shortcuts can help you save research time. You should bookmark Web sites that you visit frequently. Also, restrict your search to specific types of files, such as audio or video files, images, or newsgroup postings.

Put quotation marks around key words that you want to appear all together and in a specific order on Web pages. For example, using the key words *online learning skills* might return a list of sites about general learning skills as well as sites devoted specifically to online learning. Enclosing those words in quotation marks (*"online learning skills"*) will yield only the pages where all three of them appear together—an exact match for your key words.

After performing one key word search, open up a new window and search again using different key words. Compare the search results listed in the two windows.

Scrutinize search results. The Web pages listed at the top of your search results might not be the most suitable ones for your purpose. Many search engines generate revenue by prominently displaying the Web sites of their advertisers. The most useful search tools clearly separate these listings from the rest of their results.

Dig into the "invisible Web." As you use the Web for research, remember that some pages elude conventional search engines. Examples are pages that are searchable only *within* a particular Web site—for example, databases that you can access exclusively from the U.S. Census Bureau site. A popular name for this group of "hidden" pages is the *invisible Web.* Check out search sites that mine all of those hard-to-find pages—for example, *Invisible-Web.net* (www.invisible-web.net) and *The Invisible Web* (www.invisibleweb.com).

Thinking critically about information on the Internet

Sources of information on the Internet range from the reputable (such as the Library of Congress) to the flamboyant (such as the *National Enquirer*). This fact underscores the need for thinking critically about everything you see online. Long before the Internet, critical thinking created value in every form of communication. Typos, mistakes, rumors, and downright lies can easily creep into print publications and television programs. Newspaper, magazine, and book publishers often employ fact checkers, editors, and lawyers to screen out errors and scrutinize questionable material before publication.

However, authors of Web pages and other Internet sources might not have these resources or choose to use them. People are free to post anything on the Internet, and this can include outdated facts as well as intentional misinformation. Do not assume that Internet content is more accurate or current than what you find in print.

Taking a few simple precautions when you surf the Internet can keep you from crashing onto the rocky shore of misinformation.

Distinguish between ideas and information. To think more powerfully about what you find on the Internet, remember the difference between information and ideas. For example, consider the following sentence: *Nelson Mandela became president of South Africa in 1994.* That statement provides information about South Africa. In contrast, the following sentence states an idea: *Nelson Mandela's presidency means that apartheid has no future in South Africa.*

Information refers to facts that can be verified by independent observers. *Ideas* are interpretations or opinions based on facts. These include statements of opinion and value judgments. Several people with the same information might adopt different ideas based on that information.

People who speak of the Internet as the "information superhighway" often forget to make the distinction between information and ideas. Don't assume that an idea is more current, reasonable, or accurate just because you find it on the Internet. Apply your critical thinking skills to all published material—print and online.

Look for overall quality. To begin thinking critically about a Web site, step back and examine the features of that site in general. Notice the effectiveness of the text and visuals as a whole. Also note how well the site is organized and whether you can navigate the site's features with ease. Look for the date that crucial information was posted, and determine how often the site is updated.

Next, take a more detailed look at the site's content. Link between several of the site's pages and look for consistency of facts, quality of information, and competency with grammar and spelling.

Also evaluate the site's links to related Web pages. Look for links to pages of reputable organizations. Click on a few of those links. If they lead you to dead ends, this might indicate a site that's not updated often—one that's not a reliable source for late-breaking information.

Look at the source. Think about the credibility of the person or organization that posts a Web site. Look for a list of author credentials and publications.

Notice evidence of bias or special interest. Perhaps the site's sponsoring organization wants you to buy a service, a product, or a point of view. If so, determine whether this fact colors the ideas and information posted on the Web site.

The domain in the Uniform Resource Locator (URL) for a Web site can give you clues about sources of information and possible bias. For example, distinguish between information from a for-profit commercial enterprise (URL ending in .com), a nonprofit organization (.org), a government agency (.gov), and a school, college, or university (.edu). In addition, reputable sites usually include a way for you to contact the author or sponsoring organization outside the Internet, including a mailing address and phone number.

Look for documentation. When you encounter an assertion on a Web page or some other Internet resource, note the types and quality of the evidence offered. Look for credible examples, quotations from authorities in the field, documented statistics, or summaries of scientific studies. Also look for source notes, bibliographies, or another way to find the original sources of information on your own.

Set an example. In the midst of the Internet's chaotic growth, you can light a path of rationality. Whether you're sending a short e-mail message or building a massive Web site, bring your own critical thinking skills into play. Every word and image that you send down the wires to the Web can display the hallmarks of critical thinking—sound logic, credible evidence, and respect for your audience.

Using technology to manage time and money

When it comes to managing your time and financial resources, your computer can become as valuable as your calendar and your checkbook.

In addition, gaining experience with time management, project planning, and financial software now—while you are in school—can give you additional skills to list on your résumé. Get started with the following options.

Set and meet goals. Review your responses to the goal-setting exercises in Chapter Two of this book. Take your written goals—long-term, mid-term, and short-term—and key them into a word processing file or database file. Open up this file every day to review your goals and track your progress toward meeting them.

Since success hinges on keeping goals fresh in your memory, print out a copy of your goals file each time you update it. You might wish to post your printout in a visible place, such as in your study area, on your refrigerator, or even next to a bathroom mirror.

In addition to lists of goals, keep files of inspirational quotes, stories, articles, and images.

Another key to goal achievement is asking other people to hold you accountable. Consider sending e-mail messages to friends and family members about your goals. Ask these people to check in with you periodically as key due dates approach, inquire about your progress, and send notes of encouragement.

Save yourself a trip or phone call. The Web offers sites that allow you to manage your bank account, get stock quotes, place classified ads for items you want to sell, book airline reservations, and buy almost anything. Use these sites to reduce shopping time, eliminate errands, and get discounts on purchases.

Also employ technology to decrease phone time and avoid long-distance charges. Use e-mail and real time online chatting software to stay in contact with friends, family members, classmates, and teachers.

Manage calendars, contacts, and projects. Software can help you create and edit calendars and to-do lists on

your computer. Typically, these applications also allow you to store contact information—mailing addresses, phone numbers, and e-mail addresses—for the key people in your life. To find such products, search the Web using the key words *contact management, project management, time management,* and *software.*

Also use your computer to prevent the snafus that can result when you want to coordinate your calendar with those of several other people. This is often a necessity in completing group projects. Consider creating an area on the Web where group members can post messages, share files, and access an online calendar that shows scheduled events. One option is the *calendar* link at www.yahoo.com. You can search the Web for more sites of this type.

Project planning software offers a way to coordinate the work of many people working in teams. Look for features that allow you to create sophisticated timelines such as Gantt, PERT (Program Evaluation Review Technique), and CPM (Critical Path Method) charts. These display a list of tasks, the estimated duration of each task, and the person responsible for completing it.

Crunch numbers and manage money. Many students can benefit from crunching numbers on a computer with spreadsheets such as Excel. This type of computer software allows you to create and alter budgets of any size. By plugging in numbers based on assumptions about the future, you can quickly create many scenarios for future income and expenses. Quicken and similar products include spreadsheets and other features that can help you manage personal and organizational finances.

Employ a personal digital assistant (PDA). These devices—also called *palmtops* or *pocket PCs*—are handheld computers designed to replace paper-based calendars and planning systems. Many PDAs are small enough to fit in a pocket or purse. You can use them to list appointments and view your schedule in a daily, weekly, or monthly format. If you have a recurring event, such as a meeting that takes place at the same time every week, you can just enter it once and watch it show up automatically on your PDA.

Using a PDA, you can also take notes, create contact lists, manage to-do lists, and keep track of personal expenses. Capabilities for connecting to the Internet and sending e-mail are becoming standard features as well. In addition, PDAs come with software for exchanging files with a personal computer. This allows you to store essential information—such as appointments, to-do lists, and contacts—in a form that's even more portable than a laptop computer.

Some Web sites allow you to download content that is formatted specifically for PDAs. Perhaps some of your online course material will be available in this way.

Before you invest in a PDA, consider its price and potential value. Talk to people who use PDAs and ask about their experience with these devices. You might find a PDA's capabilities to be nice but not essential for the way you work. And after seeing a PDA's small screen size, you might prefer a paper calendar printed in a larger format.

To enter information in a PDA, you'll need to use a tiny onscreen keyboard or a stylus that requires you to form handwritten letters and numbers in a special way. An alternative available with many PDAs is a portable keyboard that you can fold up and store in a briefcase or backpack.

If you do decide to use a PDA, allow for a learning curve. It takes some time to master these time-management devices.

→ Ways to waste time with your computer

Stay alert for the following computer-based time-wasters.

Trial-and-error learning. Flying by the seat of your pants as you learn the computer sometimes works well. In other cases, you can save critical hours by spending a few minutes reading the instructions or by taking a computer class.

Hours that evaporate while you play. When cruising the Internet or playing computer games, you might find that a whole morning, afternoon, or evening has disappeared into the digital void. If you start losing too much time to computer play, set a specific time to end the fun before you start. Or consider playing a computer game for 20 minutes as a reward for completing your homework.

Endless revising. Computers make it easy to revise your writing, and you might feel tempted to keep fiddling with a paper to the point that you miss your deadline. Experiment with dictating your revisions or marking them on hard copy with a red pencil.

Losing data. It's been said that the two most important words about using a computer are *save* and *backup*. This refers to the fact that power surges and loss of electricity can destroy data. Most computer users can tell stories about losing many hours of work in a millisecond. To prevent this fate, take three simple but powerful steps. First, while you're creating or editing a computer file, save your work every few minutes. Your computer manual will explain how. (Some software does this automatically.)

Second, make backup copies of your files on separate storage media, such as Zip disks or CDs. Having backups promotes peace of mind. Should your computer files ever be lost or damaged, you'll avoid the countless hours of re-creating your work from scratch.

Finally, make sure that the computer you're working on has software to detect viruses and repair the damage they can do. Update this software regularly.

Crashing and freezing. Your computer might *crash* or *freeze*—that is, suddenly quit or refuse to respond to anything that you type. Find out how to shut down and restart the computer if this happens.

Getting "spammed." *Spam* is the Internet equivalent of junk mail—unwanted messages that show up in your e-mail inbox. To reduce spam, be selective in giving out your e-mail address. Also check with your Internet service provider for help in minimizing spam.

One more caution. Don't expect your life to slow down or your grades to soar right after you start using a time-management application or other new software. Becoming more productive can take several weeks. And there's always more to learn.

Computers can perform many tasks with dizzying speed. What they *don't* do is write papers, create ideas, read textbooks, or attend classes. For those tasks, human beings are irreplaceable.

Write e-mail that gets results

Target your audience. Be conscious of the amount of e-mail that busy people receive. Send e-mail messages only to the people who need them, and only when necessary.

Write an informative subject line. Rather than writing a generic description, include a capsule summary of your message. "Biology 100 Report due next Tuesday" packs more information than "Report." If your message is urgent, include that word in the subject line as well. Your teachers might require a specific format for the subject line of e-mail messages you send to them. Follow those instructions.

Think short. Keep your subject line short, your paragraphs short, and your message as a whole short. Most people don't want to read long documents on a computer screen.

Put the point first. To make sure your point gets across, put it at the top of the first paragraph. If your message will take up more than one screen's worth of text, break it up into short sections and add a heading for each section. Then pack those headlines with the important ideas.

Consider how long your message might be stored. Your message could dwell in a recipient's in-basket for weeks or months. Edit sentences written in the heat of a strong emotion—sentences that you might regret later. Also remember that it's easy to send a message to the wrong person. Don't include a statement in any e-mail that would embarrass you if this should happen.

Review your message. Every message you send—even the shortest, most informal message—says something about your attention to detail. Before you hit the "send" button, proofread. Before sending a long message, ask someone else to review it.

Use text formatting carefully. Boldface, italics, underlining, smart quotes, and other formatting options might not transfer well across e-mail programs. If your message will be widely circulated, use generic characters that any computer can read.

For example, use asterisks to *emphasize* words. Place titles within plain quotation marks. Don't indent the first line of a paragraph. Instead, insert a "hard return"—a blank line—between paragraphs. Use two hyphens (--) in place of a dash (—). Avoid using special symbols such as ©; instead, use an alternative such as (c).

Test attachments. If you plan to send an attachment, do a dry run first. You might find that it takes a couple of tries to send attachments in a format that your recipient can read. For instructions on how to prepare files as attachments, see the help feature in your e-mail program.

Note: Attachments sometimes come with computer viruses that can damage your hard disk. Open attachments only from people you know, and use antivirus software. Forward attachments with extreme care.

Reply promptly and consciously. Provide context. If you're responding to a question from a previous e-mail, include that question in your response.

Be aware of everyone who will receive your reply. If you hit the "reply to all" button, your response will go to all of the people who received the original message—including those on the "cc" (carbon copy) line. Instead, you might want to reply to just one or two of these people.

Forward messages selectively. Think twice before forwarding generic messages from other sources—cartoons, joke files, political diatribes, and "inspirational" readings. Your recipients might already have an in-basket overflowing with e-mail. Such forwarded messages might be viewed as irritating clutter.

Protect your privacy. Any competent hacker can intercept a private message. Treat all online communication as public communication. Include only content that you're willing to circulate widely, and share personal data with caution. Before sending, ask yourself: "What would be the costs if this information were made public?"

Stay on top of your in-box. Read and respond to new messages promptly. Identify messages that you might refer to again. Sort these by date received, subject, or sender—whatever will help you retrieve them later. Consider printing out essential messages, such as schedules and lists of assignments. Most e-mail programs provide an option to save messages into folders for future reference. Use this option to organize messages that you send and receive. However, if there's little chance that you will refer to a message in the future, delete it now. Tame the e-mail tiger. ✉

Becoming an online learner

Set yourself up for successful online learning by using specific strategies before courses begin. Also consider new ways to complete your online course work, and expand your learning strategies as a whole to include technology.

Before courses begin

Take a first step about technology. Before you begin your next experience with online learning, practice telling the truth about your current skills in this area. The Master Student Web site has a special tool for this purpose. Go online to **masterstudent.college.hmco.com** and look for a link to the E-Learning Readiness Self-Assessment.

Do a trial run with course technology. Most online courses have been created using course management software like WebCT or Blackboard. You do not need to install this software to access the online course, but you will need to know the procedure, access code, and password to get into the online course site. Get the details and then verify your access to course Web sites—*before* the first assignment is due.

Locate support services. If you feel intimidated by technology, remember that there are living, breathing human beings who can help. Possibilities include instructors, people who staff computer labs, librarians, and on-campus technical support services.

Locate helpful people and services before courses begin. Post their phone numbers next to your computer or in another place you can easily find them when hardware or software breaks down.

Develop a contingency plan. Murphy's Law of Computer Crashes states that technology tends to break down at the moment that you most need it. You might not find this piece of folklore to be true, but it's still wise to prepare for it in advance:

- Identify several on-campus computer labs with the technology you need.
- Find a technology buddy in each of your classes—someone who can update you on assignments and contact the instructor if you lose Internet access.
- Set up a backup e-mail account in case your Internet service provider goes offline. Many Web sites offer this service for free.

- Get complete contact information—address and office phone and fax numbers—for your instructors.
- Keep extra printer supplies—paper and toner or ink cartridges—always on hand. Don't run out of either on the day that a paper is due.

Set up files. Before classes meet, create a separate folder for each class on your computer's hard disk. Give each folder a meaningful name, such as *biology-spring2007*. Place all files related to a course in the appropriate folder. Doing this can save you from one of the main technology-related time-wasters—searching for lost files.

During your online courses

Manage your time. Some students act as if they have all the time in the world to complete their online assignments. The temptation to procrastinate can be strongest with courses that take place mostly or totally online. Such courses can become invisible in your weekly academic schedule, creating the possibility of late-semester all-nighters for completing last-minute work.

Early in the term, create a detailed timeline with a due date for each assignment. Break big assignments into smaller steps and schedule a due date for each step. If possible, submit online assignments early. Staying ahead of the game will help you avoid an all-nighter at the computer during finals week.

The earlier you clarify expectations for online course-work, the greater your opportunities to succeed. When you receive an online assignment, e-mail questions immediately. If you want to meet with an instructor in person, request an appointment several days in advance. In addition, download or print out online course materials as soon as they're posted on the class Web site. These materials might not be available later in the term.

Consider scheduling times in your daily or weekly calendar to complete online course work. Give these scheduled sessions the same priority as regular classroom meetings. At these times, check for announcements relating to assignments, tests, and other course events.

Ask for feedback. To get the most from online learning, request feedback from your instructor via e-mail. When appropriate, ask for conferences by phone or in person as well. Be sure to check with your instructor to see how he wants e-mail messages from online course students to be addressed. Many teachers use a standard subject area format so that e-mails from online students can be quickly and easily recognized.

Merging technology and learning strategies

Create course glossaries. One way to review for tests is to create and maintain a glossary of key terms for each of your courses. Every time you encounter a key word or technical term in your course notes or textbooks, key that word into a word processing or database file. Create a separate file for each of your courses. For each term, write a definition and a sentence using the word in context. Sort the terms in alphabetical order.

Update your glossary files once weekly, based on that week's class work and assigned readings. Each time you update a glossary file, print it out. Keep a current printout in your backpack or briefcase to study on the go.

Capture your notes on disk. Software offers many possibilities for organizing and reviewing the notes you take when listening to lectures or studying textbooks. For example, take lecture notes directly on a laptop, or take handwritten notes and key them into your computer after class. Divide your notes into sections, then write a heading to capture the main point of each section. For greater depth of detail, use several levels of headings ranging from major to minor. To save time when you review, display the headings and scan them as you would scan the headlines in a newspaper.

Also use drawing and painting tools to create maps, charts, diagrams, and other visuals that enhance your notes. Look for personal digital assistants that can convert your handwritten notes into text that can be uploaded to your personal computer.

Reflect on your learning. After completing online courses, take time to evaluate the experience. Write about what you liked, what you didn't like, and what you can do to become a more effective online learner. Go beyond the technology and focus on the outcomes—the knowledge and skills you gained. When you create ways to make online education work, you gain another option for lifelong learning. ⊠

EVALUATE SEARCH SITES

Use a computer to access several popular search sites on the Web. Possibilities include:

Alta Vista	www.altavista.com
Ask Jeeves	www.ask.com
Dogpile	www.dogpile.com
Excite	www.excite.com
Google	www.google.com
HotBot	www.hotbot.com
The Invisible Web	www.invisibleweb.com
Yahoo	www.yahoo.com

Choose a specific topic that you'd like to research—preferably one related to a paper or other assignment that you will complete this term. Identify key words for this topic and enter them in several search sites. (Open up a different window in your browser for each site.) Be sure to use the same key words each time that you search.

Next, evaluate the search sites by comparing the results that you got and the following factors:

- Simplicity of the site's design and use.
- Number of results you got.
- Presence of duplicate results.
- Quality of results—that is, their relevance to your topic.
- Number of sponsored results (links to the search site's advertisers or paid sponsors) and how clearly these results are identified.
- Number of results that are "dead" links (leading you to inactive Web sites).
- Options for doing advanced searches and the ease of using those options.

Based on your evaluation, list your favorite search sites here:

_____

_____

_____

_____

_____

_____

_____

STAYING MOTIVATED WITH TECHNOLOGY

This exercise demonstrates one way that you can use technology to transform data into useful information and strategies for action. There are six steps. Allow about one hour to complete the exercise.

1. Use a Web browser such as Netscape Navigator or Microsoft Internet Explorer to access the Web site for one of your courses. (Ask your instructor whether you need a password and user ID to do this.)

2. Once you've accessed the site, find the course syllabus or another document that lists assignments, topics to be covered in class, and information about upcoming tests.

3. Copy the syllabus information and paste it into a blank word processing file. Then make this document your own by adding notes. Highlight key information and include any ideas that can help you succeed in the course. For example, you could put due dates for assignments and test dates in boldface. You could also list questions that you want to ask the instructor or specific steps that you plan to take in completing an assignment.

4. Next, write a goal that describes a lasting benefit you want to gain from this course. Focus on a specific body of information you'd like to remember after the course is over, or on a job skill you'd like to acquire. Add your goal to the file you've created and highlight it in boldface or a bright color. Refer to this goal if you ever feel stuck or discouraged while taking the course.

5. List specifically what you will do to meet your course goal. Examples include forming a study group or searching for Web sites that are relevant to the course.

6. Finally, identify specific people who can help you succeed in the course and meet the goal you just created. For instance, highlight contact information (e-mail address, phone number, and office hours and location) for your instructor. Also add contact information for other students in the class—people who can share notes with you, take part in a study group, or assist you in any other way to meet your course goal. Consider adding their e-mail addresses to the address book in your e-mail software.

→ Staying up-to-date with technology

Computer technology is so dynamic that statements made about it can become outdated almost instantaneously. What once seemed like remote possibilities—such as Web-based television and Internet connection via cable television lines—quickly became realities. To get the most value from emerging technology, adopt the following habits that can help you to stay up-to-date.

Read. Much of the hottest information about new technology still appears in print. Several magazines and periodicals are devoted to emerging technology. For example, the *Chronicle of Higher Education* regularly includes articles about new technology and its implications for vocational schools, colleges, and universities. *Wired* magazine covers digital technology and popular culture. Many such magazines have related Web sites.

Go to the Internet. Search engines and directories often highlight Web sites that cover the latest technology developments. To find basic information, do a search using the key words *Internet tutorial* or *technology tutorial*.

Hang out with those who know. Seek out people who seem technologically savvy. Go to computer stores and browse among the displays and new products. Talk with the salespeople and ask about what's new. Investigate computer clubs at your school or in your community. Talk to knowledgeable people at on-campus computer labs. Look for a student-friendly help desk or links to technical support on your school's Web site.

Look beyond personal computers. Watch for continuing innovation in other forms of digital technology. These include new capabilities for DVDs, PDAs, cellular phones with an Internet connection, and watches and other small devices with computing and communication capabilities.

Go back to your purpose. Technology can add value to your life—and can also complicate it. Laptops and PDAs make it possible for you to work all of the time, anywhere. Cell phones and text messaging create the risk of interruption at any moment. That might not be what you want. Consider the purposes and values served by the technology in your life. Machines exist to serve you—not the other way around.

Library
the buried treasure

Knowing ways to unearth a library's treasures can enhance your writing, boost your presentation skills, help you plan your career, and enable you to continue learning for the rest of your life.

In the early days of the Internet, researchers used to distinguish between sources published in print and sources published online. Today that distinction no longer holds so tightly.

In addition to housing print and audiovisual materials, many libraries give you access to online sources—including special databases that are not available on the Web. Also remember that much published material is available only in print, not on the Internet. Books—a form of information technology that's been with us for centuries—still have something to offer.

Remember the best library resource.
Libraries give you access to one resource that goes beyond the pages of a book or a site on the Web. That resource is a living person called a librarian.

Librarians have different specialties. Start with a reference librarian, who can usually tell you whether the library has the material that you want or direct you to another source, such as a business, community agency, or government office. Librarians are trained explorers who can guide you on your expedition into the information jungle. Asking them for help can save you hours.

Take a tour.
Libraries—from the smallest one in your hometown to the Smithsonian in Washington, D.C.—consist of just three basic elements:

- *Catalogs*—Online databases that list all of the library's accessible sources.
- *Collections*—Materials, such as periodicals (magazines and newspapers), books, audiovisual materials, and materials available from other collections via interlibrary loans.
- *Computer resources*—Internet access; connections to campus-wide computer networks; and databases stored on CD-ROMs, CDs, DVDs, or online. Through your library, you might have access to databases that are available only by subscription. Ask a librarian for a list of these and about how to access them.

Take some time to investigate all three elements of your campus or community library. Start with a library orientation session or tour. Step into each room and ask about what's available there. Find out whether the library houses any special collections or provides access to primary sources that are related to your major.

Search the catalog.
A library's catalog lists the materials available in its collections. These listings used to be kept on index cards. Today, libraries catalog their materials on computers; some even include listings for several libraries. To find materials in a library's collections, do a keyword search—much like using a search engine on the Internet. The catalog is an alphabetical listing that is cross-referenced by subject, author, and title. Each listing carries the author's name, the title, the publisher, the date of publication, the number of pages and illustrations, the Library of Congress or Dewey decimal system number (for locating materials), and sometimes a brief description of the material. Some catalogs let you see if a book or periodical is on the shelf or checked out—and even allow you to put a hold on the materials you want.

Inspect the collection.
When inspecting a library's collections, look for materials such as the following:

- *Encyclopedias*—Leading print encyclopedias include *Encyclopaedia Britannica*. Specialized encyclopedias cover many fields and include, for example, *Encyclopedia of Psychology, Encyclopedia of the Biological Sciences,* and *Encyclopedia of Asian History*.
- *Biographies*—Read accounts of people's lives in biographical works such as *Who's Who, Dictionary of American Biography,* and *Biography Index: A Cumulative Index to Biographical Material in Books and Magazines*.
- *Critical works*—Read what scholars have to say about works of art and literature in *Oxford Companion* volumes (such as *Oxford Companion to Art* and *Oxford Companion to African American Literature*).
- *Statistics and government documents*—Among many useful sources are *Statistical Abstract of the United States, Handbook of Labor Statistics, Occupational Outlook Handbook,* and U.S. Census publications.

- *Almanacs, atlases, and gazetteers*—For population statistics and boundary changes, see *The World Almanac, Countries of the World,* or *Information Please.*

- *Dictionaries*—Consult *American Heritage Dictionary of the English Language, Oxford English Dictionary,* and other specialized dictionaries such as *Dictionary of Literary Terms and Literary Theory* and *Dictionary of the Social Sciences.*

- *Indexes and databases*—Databases contain publication information and an abstract, or sometimes the full text, of an article, available for downloading or printing from your computer. Your library houses print and CD-ROM databases and subscribes to some online databases; others are accessible through online library catalogs or Web links.

- *Reference works in specific subject areas*—These cover a vast range. Examples include the *Oxford Companion to Art, Encyclopedia of the Biological Sciences,* and *Concise Oxford Companion to Classical Literature.*

- *Periodical articles*—Find articles in periodicals (works issued periodically, such as scholarly journals, magazines, and newspapers) by using a periodical index. Use electronic indexes for recent works, print indexes for earlier works—especially for works written before 1980. Check to see which services your library subscribes to and the dates the indexes cover. Indexes might provide abstracts; some, such as Lexis-Nexis Academic Universe, Infotrac, OCLC FirstSearch, and New York Times Ondisc, provide the full text of articles. You might be able to access such indexes from a computer in your dorm room or apartment. Ask a librarian for more details.

Access computer resources. Many libraries offer computers with Internet access. These computers are often available on a first-come, first-served basis, for free or for a nominal cost.

Also remember that the Web gives you access to the online resources of many libraries. Some useful sites are: Library of Congress (**http://lcweb.loc.gov**), Smithsonian Institution Libraries (**http://www.sil.si.edu/**), New York Public Library (**http://www.nypl.org/**), Internet Public Library (**http://www.ipl.org**), and WWW Virtual Library (**http://www.vlib.org**).[1]

Gain information literacy. *Information literacy* is the ability to locate, evaluate, use, and document sources of ideas and facts. Considering the variety of materials available at modern, fully equipped libraries, improving your ability to access information efficiently will help promote your success in school.

Start with the distinction between primary and secondary sources. *Primary sources* are often the researcher's dream. These are firsthand materials such as personal journals, letters, speeches, reports of scientific research, scholarly articles, field observations, archeological digs, and original works of art.

Secondary sources explain and comment on primary sources. Examples are nationally circulated newspapers such as the *Washington Post, New York Times,* and *Los Angeles Times.* Magazines with wide circulation but substantial treatment of current issues—such as the *Atlantic Monthly* and *Scientific American*—are secondary sources. So are general reference works such as the *Encyclopedia Britannica.*

Secondary sources are useful places to start your research by getting an overview of your topic. They might even be all you need for informal research. Other research projects in higher education—major papers, presentations, theses, or manuscripts you want to publish—will call on you to find primary sources.

Once you find the sources you want, inspect each one. With print sources, look at the preface, publication data, table of contents, bibliography, glossary, endnotes, and index. (Nonprint materials, including online documents, often include similar types of information.) Also scan any headings, subheadings, and summaries. If you have time, read a chapter or section. Then evaluate sources according to their:

- *Relevance*—Look for sources that deal directly with your research questions. If you're in doubt about the relevance of a particular source, ask yourself: "Will this material help me achieve the purpose of my research and support my thesis?"

- *Currentness*—Notice the published date of your source material (usually found in the front matter on the copyright page). If your topic is time-sensitive, set some guidelines about how current you want your sources to be.

- *Credibility*—Scan the source for biographical information about the author. Look for education, training, and work experience that qualifies this person to publish on the topic. Also notice any possible sources of bias, such as political affiliations or funding sources that might color the author's point of view.

The process of research is like climbing Mount Everest. You'll make observations, gather facts, trek into unfamiliar intellectual terrain, and ascend from one plateau of insight to another.

Keen researchers see facts and relationships. They focus their attention on the details, then discover unifying patterns. Far from being a mere academic exercise, library research can evolve into a path of continual discovery. ⬕

REVISIT YOUR GOALS, TAKE TWO

One powerful way to achieve any goal is periodically to step back from your day-to-day activities and assess your progress in meeting that goal. This is especially important with goals that can take years to achieve.

Exercise #6: "Get real with your goals" (on page 60) asked you to focus on one long-term goal and create a detailed plan to achieve it—including short-term and mid-term goals related to the long-term goal. Exercise #14: "Revisit your goals" (on page 142) asked you to revisit the same long-term goal and determine its continuing relevance to your life.

You can now take another opportunity to sustain this process. Before you begin, take a few minutes to read your responses to those previous exercises. Then complete the following steps.

1. Rewrite your long-term goal in the space below. If you would like to reword it, feel free to do so.

_____

_____

_____

2. Next, ask yourself how you feel about this goal. Is your enthusiasm still high? On a scale of 1 to 10 (with 10 as the highest level of commitment), rate your current interest in achieving this goal.

_____

_____

3. If your level of commitment is 5 or less, you might want to drop the goal and replace it with a new one. To set a new goal, just turn back to Exercise #6 and do it again. Also release any self-judgment about dropping your original long-term goal. Letting go of one long-term goal creates space in your life to set and achieve a new one.

4. If you're committed to the goal you listed in step 1, consider whether you're still on track to achieve it. Have you met any of the short-term goals you'll need in order to achieve this long-term goal? If so, list your completed goals here:

_____

_____

_____

Before going on to the next step, take a minute to congratulate yourself. Celebrate your success in achieving the goals you just listed.

5. Finally, consider any adjustments you'd like to make to your plan. For example, write additional short-term or mid-term goals that will take you closer to your long-term goal. Or cross out any goals that you no longer see as necessary. Make a clean copy of your current plan in the space below.

Long-term goal from step 1 above (to achieve within your lifetime):

_____

_____

_____

Supporting mid-term goals (to achieve in one to five years):

_____

_____

_____

_____

_____

Supporting short-term goals (to achieve within the coming year):

_____

_____

_____

_____

_____

Read the following two passages. Each makes a prediction about how computer technology could change our society over the next two decades.

Passage #1

Today's technology could evolve into a source of increasing tranquility. Software will search Web sites specifically for news and other information that interests you, screening out hordes of irrelevant data. Cell phones will give way to portable personal communicators that are completely voice-activated and small enough to wear on a necklace or wrist band. Desktop and laptop computers will disappear from most homes as separate pieces of technology. Instead, computer chips will be embedded into most home appliances. Large, flat-panel screens—also voice-activated—will serve as a combination television, movie screen, and monitor for viewing Internet content. Rather than commuting to offices or schools, most people will work and educate themselves at home, leading to a slower, more relaxed pace of life.

Passage #2

We are on the verge of social disruption caused by technology. Advances in robotics will lead to machines that replace factory workers. White-collar workers of every variety will experience the same fate. Sophisticated automatic teller machines (ATMs) will completely replace human bank tellers. Most of the services now offered by travel agents, lawyers, accountants, tax preparers, investment advisors, and teachers will be automated in similar ways. Currently, people in these jobs stake their careers on access to special bodies of knowledge. In the future, thanks to easy-to-use software and vast digital libraries, this knowledge will be freely available to almost anyone. Many jobs will simply disappear, and it's not certain what will replace them. Massive unemployment could result in higher crime rates and urban decay along with record levels of suicide, alcoholism, and other drug addiction.

Assess the claims and evidence presented in the above passages. Then, in the space below, write a one-paragraph response—a prediction of your own about the future impact of technology. Be sure to include evidence to back up your prediction.

_____

_____

_____

_____

_____

_____

_____

_____

_____

_____

_____

_____

_____

_____

_____

_____

_____

_____

Share your responses to this exercise on the Web and see what other students predict. Go online to

masterstudent.college.hmco.com

power process

Risk being a fool

A powerful person has the courage to take risks. And taking risks means being willing to fail sometimes—even to be a fool. This idea can work for you because you already are a fool.

Don't be upset. All of us are fools at one time or another. There are no exceptions. If you doubt it, think back to that stupid thing you did just a few days ago. You know the one. Yes . . . *that* one. It was embarrassing and you tried to hide it. You pretended you weren't a fool. This happens to everyone.

People who insist that they have never been fools are perhaps the biggest fools of all. We are all fallible human beings. Most of us, however, spend too much time and energy trying to hide our fool-hood. No one is really tricked by this—not even ourselves. And whenever we pretend to be something we're not, we miss part of life.

For example, many of us never dance because we don't want to risk looking ridiculous. We're not wrong. We probably would look ridiculous. That's the secret of risking being a fool.

It's OK to look ridiculous while dancing. It's all right to sound silly when singing to your kids. Sometimes it's OK to be absurd. It comes with taking risks.

Taking risks is not being foolhardy

Sometimes it's not OK to be absurd. This Power Process comes with a warning label: Taking risks does *not* mean escaping responsibility for our actions. "Risk being a fool" is not a suggestion to get drunk at a party and make a fool of yourself. It is not a suggestion to act the fool by disrupting class. It is not a suggestion to be foolhardy or to "fool around."

"Risk being a fool" means recognizing that foolishness—along with dignity, courage, cowardice, grace, clumsiness, and other qualities—is a human characteristic. We all share it. You might as well risk being a fool because you already are one, and nothing in the world can change that. Why not enjoy it once in a while? Consider the case of the person who won't dance because he's afraid he'll look foolish. This same person will spend an afternoon tripping over his feet on a basketball court. If you say that his jump shot from the top of the key looks like a circus accident, he might even agree.

"So what?" he might say. "I'm no Michael Jordan." He's right. On the basketball court, he is willing to risk looking like a fool in order to enjoy the game.

He is no Fred Astaire, either. For some reason, that bothers him. The result is that he misses the fun of dancing. (Dancing badly is as much fun as shooting baskets badly—and maybe a lot more fun.)

There's one sure-fire way to avoid any risk of being a fool, and that's to avoid life. The writer who never finishes a book will never have to worry about getting negative reviews. The center fielder who sits out every game is safe from making any errors. And the comedian who never performs in front of an audience is certain to avoid telling jokes that fall flat. The possibility of succeeding at any venture increases when we're comfortable with making mistakes—that is, with the risk of being a fool.

Look at courage in a new way

Again, remember the warning label. This Power Process does not suggest that the way to be happy in life is to do

The possibility of succeeding at any venture increases when we're comfortable with making mistakes— that is, with the risk of being a fool.

things badly. Courage involves the willingness to face danger and risk failure. Mediocrity is not the goal. The point is that mastery in most activities calls for the willingness to do something new, to fail, to make corrections, to fail again, and so on. On the way to becoming a good writer, be willing to be a bad writer.

Consider these revised clichés: Anything worth doing is worth doing badly at first. Practice makes improvement. If at first you don't fail, try again.

Most artists and athletes have learned the secret of being foolish. Comedians are especially well versed in this art. All of us know how it feels to tell a joke and get complete silence. We truly look and feel like fools. Professional comedians risk feeling that way for a living. Being funny is not enough for success in the comedy business. A comedian must have the courage to face failure.

Courage is an old-fashioned word for an old-fashioned virtue. Traditionally, people have reserved that word for

illustrious acts of exceptional people—the campaigns of generals and the missions of heroes.

This concept of courage is fine. At the same time, it can be limiting and can prevent us from seeing courage in everyday actions. Courage is the kindergartner who, with heart pounding, waves good-bye to his parents and boards the bus for his first day of school. Courage is the 40-year-old who registers for college courses after being away from the classroom for 20 years.

For a student, the willingness to take risks means the willingness to experiment with new skills, to achieve personal growth, and sometimes to fail. The rewards of risk taking include expanded creativity, more satisfying self-expression, and more joy.

An experiment for you

Here's an experiment you can conduct to experience the joys of risk taking. The next time you take a risk and end up doing something silly or stupid, allow yourself to be totally aware of your reaction. Don't deny it. Don't cover it up. Notice everything about the feeling, including the physical sensations and thoughts that come with it. Acknowledge the foolishness. Be exactly who you are. Explore all of the emotions, images, and sensations surrounding your experience.

Also remember that we can act independently of our feelings. Courage is not the absence of fear but the willingness to take risks even when we feel fear. We can be keenly homesick and still register for classes. We can tremble at the thought of speaking in public yet still walk up to the microphone.

When we fully experience it, the fear of taking risks loses its power. Then we have the freedom to expand and grow. ◪

voices

student

I am someone who is shy, so I am always afraid of what people think of me. "Risk being a fool" taught me that this thought could prevent me from succeeding. I learned that in order to discover yourself, you have to take risks. I will be more willing to feel uncomfortable in order to learn about myself.

—STEVE TRAN

put it to work

Having a working knowledge of information technology will be an asset as you enter the workplace or change jobs.

However, the phrase *working knowledge* can have many different definitions over time, depending on the current state of technology and your personal goals.

You can use the cycle of discovery, intention, and action explained in this book to integrate technology continuously with your interests and career path. The idea is to continuously keep your technology skills updated for the workplace.

Step 1: Discover what you know about technology. Consider the following levels of knowledge and skill related to personal computers:

Discussing technology. People with this level of knowledge can walk into a computer store and describe what kind of hardware and software they want for home or professional use.

Performing basic functions. Examples are turning the computer off and on, opening and closing windows on a computer desktop, managing files and folders, installing software, and making backup copies of working files.

Finding information. This cluster of skills enables you to search the Internet or a library catalog to locate sources that can help you answer a specific question.

Creating and editing documents and presentations. With these types of skills, you can:

- Use a word processor to write a memo, letter, report, or research paper.

- Use a database program to organize bodies of data such as a mailing list.

- Use a spreadsheet to manage your household finances, track business expenses for your job, or run your own business.

- Use presentation software to create supporting visuals for a speech or a class you plan to teach.

Functioning in online communities. Included at this stage is the ability to use e-mail with attachments, listservs, newsgroups, chat rooms, and instant messaging software.

After reviewing the above list, write in a personal journal about your current skill with technology. Describe your strengths, along with any significant gaps in your knowledge or ability.

Step 2: Clarify your intentions for learning about technology. Next, describe what you'd like to be able to do with computer technology that you can't do now. Consider the skills you'll want to gain in order to meet your current career goals. Talk to people working in your chosen field and ask them how they use technology in their day-to-day work. Follow up by writing specifically about what you intend to learn.

Step 3: Act on your intentions. Find sources of information, ideas, and personal support as you act on your intentions to learn about technology. Options include:

- Books, periodicals, and Web sites about technology. These are available for people at all levels of technological savvy—from first-time computer users to management information specialists.

- Help screens and tutorials included with personal computer software.

- Courses offered through your school, workplace, library, or another community organization.

- A technology mentor—someone who can clearly answer your technology questions, demonstrate the skills you want to gain, and coach you as you sit at the keyboard.

Note: Plan to cycle through the above three suggestions many times in your career. Consider doing them every year to review your knowledge and update your technology skills for the workplace.

Name _____ Date _____/_____/_____

1. List three strategies that you can use before courses begin to promote your success as an online learner.

2. Give an example of treating an Internet search as a dialogue with your computer.

3. In general, you can assume that information you find on the Internet is more current and accurate than information you find in print materials. True or False? Explain your answer.

4. The Power Process in this chapter distinguishes between "being a fool" and "being foolhardy." Explain this distinction by giving an example.

5. Define the term *information literacy*.

6. List four strategies for writing effective e-mail messages.

7. Explain how the domain in the Uniform Resource Locator (URL) for a Web site can give you clues about sources of possible bias.

8. State the distinction between *ideas* and *information* given in this chapter and explain how it relates to thinking critically about Internet content.

9. A technology contingency plan can include:
   (A) Identifying on-campus computer labs with the technology you need.
   (B) Setting up a backup e-mail account in case your Internet service provider goes offline.
   (C) Getting complete contact information—address and office phone and fax numbers—for your instructors.
   (D) All of the above.

10. List three ways to manage your time effectively while interacting with online course content.

learning styles application

The questions below will "cycle" you through four styles, or modes, of learning as explained in the article "Learning styles: Discovering how you learn" in Chapter One. Each question will help you explore a different mode. You can answer the questions in any order.

what if *Explain how a technique from this chapter could help you succeed as a user of technology in the workplace.*

why *Name at least one benefit you could experience in school by gaining more skills with information technology. Examples of these skills include conducting Internet searches, studying online course material, accessing library materials, and joining online communities.*

how *Of the techniques you gained from this chapter, choose one that you will use. Describe exactly how you intend to apply the technique.*

what *List three techniques from this chapter that could significantly improve your skills as an online learner.*

master student

profile

RICK HANSEN

(1957–   ) World-class athlete and president and CEO of Rick Hansen Man in Motion Foundation, he wheeled over 40,000 kilometres around the world, raising millions of dollars and a public awareness of the potential of people with disabilities.

was optimistic, but I wasn't stupid. All my life I'd felt that if you worked hard enough you could get what you wanted. I wanted to walk again. I was working my butt off—and there was no improvement. Worse, than that, nobody would tell me anything, not even my friends, the student nurses.

So I broke into the files to find out.

I picked a time at night when no one was in the nurses' station, wheeled in, hauled out the drawer with the H files in it and read mine. It said, "Acute paralysis, secondary to thoracic spine 10 and 12 fracture"—10 and 12, as I discovered later, meaning the two points of fracture on the spinal cord.

I put the file back, closed the drawer and wheeled out. Then I went looking for a nurse and asked her what "acute" meant. "Serious," she said. So now I know: the kid who believed he could do anything was a serious paraplegic.

The educational process was painfully slow, and it came in stages. My thinking was being shaped by my experiences, and I was making progress. I was learning to do some things on my own. But I was still going about it the wrong way. I still didn't appreciate the things I could do. Instead I was focusing on the things I couldn't do.

Then I burned my foot.

It was June of 1975, my grad year. By that time I was beginning to discover that competitive sports, like girls, weren't really out of the question. A man named Stan Stronge had lured me into wheelchair sports . . . and there I was in Montreal, a third-string basketballer in the Canadian Wheelchair Games.

It was really an eye-opener. I was tremendously impressed by the sheer athletic ability of these people. I'd had a wonderful time, and now I was in the shower still half asleep from a late night, racing to make the plane home. So I turned on the hot water tap, expecting it to take a while for it to heat as it did at home, and dozed off. It came out hot from the start. My left foot was under the spout, and because I had no feeling in my legs I couldn't feel the flesh scalding.

There was no permanent damage, but in the month it took for the foot to heal, I was hit with a whole new set of frustrations—and a new appreciation of the things I'd been able to do before it happened. I'd made gains, gains that I'd taken for granted. I could drive, so I had transportation. I had crutches and braces, so I wasn't bound to the chair. Now those edges were gone.

I could drive, but with the wound on the foot I couldn't get the braces on, which meant using the chair all the time if I wanted to get anywhere,

and in the house the wheelchair was worse than useless. I wasn't just back to square one. It was worse than that, because I'd had a taste of what I could accomplish myself. Now my family had to help me everywhere. And again, I came to expect it.

One day I drove up to the house and honked the horn for [my brother] Brad to come and help me into the house. Without the braces I couldn't do it myself. He'd already helped me from the house to the truck when I [had] left. Now I was back, and ready to go in.

"There in a minute!" he yelled. "I'm busy."

Busy? What did he mean busy? . . . I was furious. And suddenly it hit me. "Hey! You don't need these guys. You can do it yourself." . . . I was mad because I needed someone again. I was dependent again because I didn't have the braces. When I had [the braces] I could do things. And if I could do some things, maybe I could do others. ◪

Excerpt from *Rick Hansen: Man in Motion* by Rick Hansen and Jim Taylor. Published 1987 by Douglas & McIntyre, Ltd. Reprinted by permission of the publisher.

For more biographical information about Rick Hansen, visit the Master Student Hall of Fame on the *Becoming a Master Student Athlete* Web site at

masterstudent.college.hmco.com

11

Health

To be somebody you must last.

RUTH GORDON

Early in my career, I decided I never wanted to get out of shape.

CAL RIPKIN, JR.

why

this chapter matters ...

Preserving your physical and mental health over the long term involves more than training for collegiate competition.

what

is included ...

Thinking about health
Take care of your machine
Your machine: Fuel it
Your machine: Move it
Your machine: Rest it
Your machine: Observe it
Your machine: Protect it
The experts recommend—seven dietary guidelines
Developing self-esteem
Emotional pain is not a sickness
Suicide
Alcohol, tobacco, and drugs: The truth
Seeing the full scope of addiction
Warning: Advertising can be dangerous to your health
Power Process: "Surrender"
Master Student Profile: Wilma Rudolph

how

you can use this chapter ...

Maintain physical and mental energy by treating your body as an incredible machine.
Choose ways to fuel, move, rest, observe, and protect your machine.
Develop self-esteem while considering the impact of alcohol and other drugs on your academic and athletic performance.

as you read, ask yourself

what if ...

I could meet the demands of my daily life with energy and optimism to spare?

Thinking about health

If you want to experience greater health, start by exercising some tissue that lies between your ears—the organ called your brain. Often the path to greater health starts not with new food or aerobic activity but with a change in thinking.

Consider the power of beliefs. Some of them erect barriers to higher levels of health: "Your health is programmed by your heredity." "Some people are just low on energy." "Healthful food doesn't taste very good." "Over the long run, people just don't change their health-related behaviors."

To create new possibilities for your life, consider some alternate ideas.

First, health is a continuum. On one end of that continuum is a death that comes too early. On the other end is a long life filled with satisfying athletic achievement, work, and fulfilling relationships. Many people exist between those extremes at a point we might call average. Most of the time they're not sick. And most of the time they're not truly thriving, either.

Second, health changes. Health is not a fixed state. In fact, health fluctuates from year to year, day to day, and moment to moment.

Third, you can take charge of your health. Changes in your health can occur by chance. Or they can occur largely by choice, as you take conscious control of habits.

When you enrolled in college, you entered an advanced arena of competition, both athletically and academically. The games move faster. The players are bigger, stronger, and smarter. Initially you may doubt your ability to match up to many of them. The health habits that you've relied on in the past may not work at this level.

Those habits can be changed. And you already have at your disposal a powerful tool for changing habits—the cycle of discovery, intention, and action that's central to this book. By reading and doing this chapter, you can use this tool to take your health to a new level. As you do, remember that physical fitness alone does not guarantee victory in competition. To maximize your athletic and academic success, choose habits that promote your physical *and* your mental health.

You don't have to accept these ideas just because they're printed here. Test them as you would any other idea in this book. The proof lies not on the page but in your life—in the level of health that you create, starting today. ◪

journal entry 26

Discovery/Intention Statement

In the space below, make a quick list of your activities during the last 48 hours, including any physical activities and the foods you ate at each meal. Circle any activities on your list that promoted your health. Underline any activities that could detract from your health.

I discovered that I . . .

_____

_____

_____

_____

Next, scan this chapter for at least five strategies you can use immediately to sustain any behaviors you just circled—or to change any behavior you underlined. List the strategies you want to read about in more detail and their associated page numbers.

Strategy   *Page number*

_____

_____

_____

_____

_____

_____

Finally, describe how you can use these strategies to achieve a health-related goal that matters to you. Choose a goal—such as sleeping better, losing weight, or having more energy—that will significantly raise the quality of your life.

I intend to . . .

_____

_____

_____

Some people are offended by the notion that the human body is a machine.

Take care of your machine

This analogy is made with great respect for our bodies, and with the understanding that we are also more than our bodies.

Our machines are truly incredible. They often continue to operate despite abuse. Throughout our athletic experiences we may pollute them, dent them, run them too hard, let them sit idle for years, even wreck them. At times we try to fuel our machines with food that has little or no nutritional value. We pollute them with empty calories and expose them to unnecessary risks of illnesses or accidents. And still our incredible machines continue to run—most of the time. Ironically, we can also take excellent care of our machines, only to have them quit on us just when we need them most.

It's amazing that we often take better care of our cars, dishwashers, air conditioners, and furnaces than we do of our bodies. This is true even for many athletes.

When we buy a car or a new appliance, we generally look at the owner's manual. We study it to find out just how this new machine works. We make sure we understand all of its features and what is needed to properly maintain it.

You can spend at least as much time learning about your own health as you do reading the owner's manual for a new car. Before participating in a sport, for example, evaluate your skills and desire to compete. Find out what the sport requires and consider how your machine could work effectively within that setting.

It would be easier if each of us received an owner's manual for our body at the moment of birth. Unfortunately, no such manual exists. Our challenge is to create a personal guidebook to health based on our own observations, studies, and experiences. To an extent greater than most of us imagine, we choose our level of health. We can promote our health by taking definite steps.

The suggestions in this chapter are accepted by many experts on health. Study them as if they were an owner's manual for a priceless machine—one that can't be replaced, one that your life depends on. That machine is your body. ◪

To an extent greater than most of us imagine, we choose our level of health.

YOUR MACHINE
Fuel it

It's a cliché, and it's true: You are what you eat. What you eat can have immediate and long-term effects on your academic and athletic performance. That giant jelly donut can make you drowsy within minutes. A steady diet of them can affect the amount of energy you have to meet the demands of classes, family members, jobs, practice, competition, and other commitments.

As a student athlete you need a healthful diet to maintain a healthy body and perform to your potential. It is important that you eat before you are hungry and drink before you are thirsty. Fuel your machine in a way that converts food into energy when you need it.

Start with widely accepted guidelines. Hundreds of books are written about nutrition. One says don't drink milk. Another says buy a cow. This debate can be confusing. There is, however, wide agreement among nutritional scientists. A list of dietary guidelines was developed by the U.S. government and is updated every five years (see "The experts recommend—seven dietary guidelines" on page 284 in this chapter). Though you might find a more healthful diet, you can do well by starting with these guidelines.

In addition, seek out nutritional wisdom geared specifically to student athletes. Many collegiate athletics programs have staff members who can provide sound nutritional advice. You can also get current guidelines from the National Collegiate Athletic Association (NCAA)

→ Prevent and treat eating disorders

Eating disorders involve overeating or extreme reduction of food intake, as well as irrational concern about body shape or weight. Student athletes who participate in sports that emphasize appearance and minimum body fat are the most susceptible to eating disorders. Women are much more likely to develop these disorders than men.

Bulimia involves cycles of excessive eating and forced purges. A person with this disorder might gorge on a pizza, donuts, and ice cream and then force herself to vomit. Or she might compensate for overeating with excessive use of laxatives, enemas, or diuretics. *Anorexia nervosa* is a potentially fatal illness marked by self-starvation, either through extended fasts or by eating only one food for weeks at a time.

A related disorder among student athletes is obligatory exercise—overdoing a workout regimen to continually lose weight and achieve an "athletic" appearance. Athletes who fail to balance the calories that they burn off with the calories they consume can harm their health.

Eating disorders are not due to a failure of willpower. Instead, these are real illnesses in which harmful patterns of eating take on a life of their own. Coaches who emphasize low body fat and a childlike appearance may contribute to higher rates of eating disorders.

Eating disorders can lead to many complications, including life-threatening heart conditions and kidney failure. Many people with eating disorders also struggle with depression, substance abuse, and anxiety.

These disorders require immediate treatment to stabilize health. This is usually followed by continuing medical care, counseling, and medication to promote a full recovery.

If you're worried about having an eating disorder, seek help. Your coach, teammates, and friends are resources. So is your campus health service and local public health clinic.

Also watch for possible signs of an eating disorder in someone else. People with these disorders frequently criticize their body. They may also:

- Immediately leave the table after eating.
- Complain often of feeling cold.
- Use laxatives frequently.
- Exercise compulsively and excessively.
- Fast for long periods or eat only one meal per day.

If you think that someone might have an eating disorder, approach this person in a nonthreatening way. State what you have observed and share your concerns. Don't be surprised if the person denies the problem. If you're concerned about another athlete, talk to a coach or trainer. Make sure proper care is provided.

To learn more, contact the National Eating Disorders Association at 1-800-931-2237 and online at **http://www.nationaleatingdisorders.org**. For more information about athletes and eating disorders, go to the ANRED (Anorexia Nervosa and Related Eating Disorders, Inc.) Web site at **http://www.anred.com/ath_intro.html**.

online at **http://www1.ncaa.org/eprise/main/ membership/ed_outreach/nutrition-performance/ index.html.**

Avoid fad diets. If you are overweight, avoid people who make claims about a quick fix. Even if that "Lose 20 pounds in 20 days!" diet works at first, you're likely to gain the weight back. Remember, fluctuation of your weight is likely to result in inconsistent performance.

For example, think critically about low-carbohydrate plans such as the Atkins diet. These plans can lead to significant weight loss in the short term. However, research undercuts claims for long-term benefits. The "drop-out" rate for the Atkins diet is comparable to that of other diets.[1] Many people simply find these plans too difficult to sustain. In addition, low-carbohydrate diets focus on meat and dairy products with high levels of saturated fat, which can increase the risk of heart disease and several forms of cancer. The formula for weight loss is simple, though not always easy: Eat better food, eat less food, and exercise regularly.

To find safe weight-loss programs, visit your team doctor or trainer, or your campus health service. Look for a program that provides peer support for you. Enlist a teammate who can do the program with you.

Take time to enjoy your food. Eating can be one of life's greatest pleasures. If you eat slowly and savor each bite, you can be satisfied with smaller portions. Use mealtimes as a chance to relax, reduce stress, and connect with people.

YOUR MACHINE
Move it

E xercise offers a way to perform better at whatever you do. Your brain usually functions best when the rest of your body is in shape.

Physical activity promotes weight control. It also helps to prevent heart disease, control cholesterol levels and diabetes, and slow the bone loss that comes with aging. In addition, exercise can lower the risk of certain cancers and reduce anxiety and depression.

If you want to lose weight, do it safely and effectively. Work with a professional who can properly assess your metabolism, your body structure, your needs, and your diet. This person can guide you to an appropriate exercise regimen.

You can make real progress in a matter of weeks. Remember that dieting alone doesn't create lean muscles

and a strong heart. The only way to get leaner is by moving.

You don't have to train for the Boston Marathon, however. It's not even smart, unless you're already in great shape. Even on those days when you are unable to do your regular exercise, consider those activities that you can do to help you stay in shape. Some activity is better than none.

Your body requires that you burn 2,000 to 3,500 calories a week to achieve cardiovascular health. During preseason workouts, you might burn twice that many calories. To avoid weight loss that could create a health risk, you may need to counter your calorie burning with extra amounts of healthful foods. The NCAA offers a list of foods that you can carry around campus with you and munch on whenever you like. You can find this list online at **http://www1.ncaa.org/eprise/main/membership/ ed_outreach/nutrition-performance/student/ nutrition.html.**

Look for exercise facilities on campus, especially during the off-season or during holidays when a coach is not available to supervise your workouts. Before your season ends or you leave campus, work with your weight coach and nutritionist to set up an eating and exercise program that you can follow until you come back to school. Back at home, check into programs from your local recreation and parks department. They might offer classes in aerobics, swimming, volleyball, basketball, golf, tennis, and other sports. There is always a way to stay in shape.

Before beginning any vigorous exercise program, consult a health care professional. As a student athlete you will have to pass a physical. Be completely honest with the team doctor who is evaluating you. Failure to disclose your health history could lead to damaging results during intense workouts and competitions.

YOUR MACHINE
Rest it

A lack of sleep combined with high levels of stress can decrease your immunity to illness and impair your performance in school. You can avoid this fate. Take specific steps to keep your machine rested and relaxed.

Promote sound sleep. To cope with academic and athletic demands, you might be tempted to cut back drastically on your sleep once in a while. You might pull an all-nighter before exams. Or nervousness might keep you awake the night before a competition. If you have trouble falling asleep, experiment with the following suggestions:

- Avoid naps during the daytime.

- Monitor your caffeine intake, especially in the afternoon and evening.

- Take a relaxing warm bath, or a shower, just before bed.

- Keep your sleeping room cool.

- When you are at home, sleep in the same place each night. When you're there, your body gets the message "It's time to go to sleep."

- Practice relaxation techniques while lying in bed. A simple one is to count your breaths and release distracting thoughts as they arise.

- Get up and study or do something else until you're tired.

- Do not focus on controversial or competitive situations that could create mental stress.

- See a doctor if sleeplessness persists.

How much sleep is enough? Your body knows when it's tired. Look for signs of depression, irritability, and other emotional problems. Lack of sleep can interfere with your memory, concentration, and ability to compete. The solution is a good night's sleep.

As a student athlete, you may find it necessary to get more sleep at certain times of the year. When your sport is in its competitive season, you might feel tired often. You may also find that traveling across time zones to compete disrupts your sleep. When you return to campus, you are then expected to immediately resume your old clock schedule.

Don't try to solve these problems by depending on brief catnaps. Make the time for regular, sound sleep. If you find this difficult, read Chapter Two: Planning for some time-management ideas. Depriving yourself of sleep is a choice you can avoid.

Manage stress. Athletic victories are often achieved by the slimmest of margins. When pressure to win in that environment is combined with expectations to excel academically, student athletes can experience levels of stress that they are unable to manage.

Stress is not always harmful. It can result from pleasant experiences as well as unpleasant ones. The excitement of a new term—new classes, instructors, coaches, classmates, and teammates—can be fun and stressful at the same time.

Oddly enough, your body perceives excitement in almost the same way that it perceives fear. Both emotions produce rapid heart rates, increased adrenaline flow, and muscle contractions. Both emotions produce stress.

Stress, at appropriate times and at manageable levels, is normal and useful. It can sharpen our awareness and boost our energy just when we need it the most. When stress persists or becomes excessive, it is harmful.

Your stress level is probably too high if you consistently experience any of the following symptoms: irritability; depression; low productivity; strained relationships with your teammates and coaches, your coworkers, or your friends and family; health problems such as an upset stomach, frequent colds, and a low energy level; a pattern of avoiding tasks; difficulty falling asleep or staying asleep; feeling burned out at home or at work; feeling tense, nervous, or fearful.

Stress has both mental and physical components. The mental components include thoughts that promote fear and anxiety; the physical components include illnesses and muscle tension. To see how these interact, consider stress in the context of athletics. Anxiety can lead you to focus mentally on your opponent more than your own performance. At the same time, you may feel "tight" physically—your muscles just won't respond as you want them to do. Competitive efforts combined with such stress rarely result in success.

The fact that stress has two main elements points to several broad strategies for managing it:

- *Deal with stressful thoughts by releasing irrational beliefs.* According to Martin Seligman and other cognitive psychologists, stress results not from events in our lives but from the way we *think* about those events.[2] If we believe that people should always behave in exactly the way we expect them to, for instance, we set ourselves up for stress. Noticing these beliefs and replacing them with more rational ones (such as *I can control my own behavior but not the behavior of others*) can reduce stress significantly.

- *Deal with stressful thoughts by releasing them altogether.* One technique, called visualization therapy, offers a way to release distressing thoughts. While visualizing, you meditate on an upcoming event, vividly imagining several scenarios that might occur. As distracting thoughts fall away, you can see yourself responding effectively in each one. Throughout the actual experience you can remain alert and relaxed with few, if any, surprises.

- *Counter the physical element of stress.* Options include breathing exercises, relaxation techniques, yoga, and therapeutic bodywork such as massage.

Many athletics departments and university counseling centers offer training in the techniques listed above. You can also learn them through health maintenance organizations, YMCAs or YWCAs, and community education programs.

In addition, use this book. It includes relaxation and breathing exercises, along with empowering ways to think about the events in your life. You may find that many of the Power Processes and the techniques for letting go of test anxiety (see Chapter Six: Tests) have a positive impact on your academic and athletic efforts.

Know when to get professional help. If the above stress-management techniques don't work within a few weeks, get help. See your team doctor, a psychologist who is connected with the athletics department, or a counselor at your student health service. Stress management is a well-researched field. There is no need to continue to have a pain in your neck, a knot in your stomach, cold feet, or other symptoms of tension. Relax and win.

YOUR MACHINE
Observe it

A skilled mechanic is an expert on a particular type of automobile. As an athlete, you can become an expert on your machine. You are more likely to notice changes in your body before anyone else does. Pay attention to even subtle changes. They are often your first clue to the need for medical treatment.

Watch for the following signs:

- Weight loss of more than 10 pounds in 10 weeks with no apparent cause.

- A sore, scab, or ulcer that does not heal in three weeks.

- An irregular or fluttering heartbeat.

- Leg cramps that do not go away.

- A skin blemish or mole that bleeds, itches, or changes size, shape, or color.

- Persistent or severe headaches.

- Sudden vomiting that is not preceded by nausea.

- Fainting spells.

- Double vision.

- Difficulty swallowing.

- Persistent hoarseness or a nagging cough.

- Blood that is coughed up or vomited.

- Shortness of breath for no apparent reason.
- Persistent indigestion or abdominal pain.
- A change in normal bowel habits, such as alternating diarrhea and constipation.
- Black and tarry bowel movements.
- Rectal bleeding.
- Pink, red, or unusually cloudy urine.
- Discomfort or difficulty when urinating or during sexual intercourse.
- Lumps or thickening in a breast.
- Vaginal bleeding between menstrual periods.

This is not a complete list. Any change in your body's regular functioning calls for a careful evaluation.

If you experience symptoms such as those listed above, consult your team trainer or doctor immediately. Do this even if the problem seems minor. Without timely and proper treatment, a minor illness or injury can lead to major problems. Remember that your school might cancel your athletic scholarship if you fail to follow the advice of your trainer and team doctor.

At some point in your athletic experience you will be injured. Physical injuries can also take their mental toll on student athletes and hurt their academic performance. The way you deal with injury is likely to determine how much you will hurt, and for how long. The sooner you react to your body's messages, the sooner you can recover and return to peak performance.

You may feel soreness as your body adjusts to a training regimen, especially before a season begins. Keep in mind that soreness and injury are distinctly different. You can distinguish between the two by carefully observing your body over time. If you are uncertain about what you're feeling, talk to your team trainer and doctor. Get answers and take responsible action.

YOUR MACHINE
Protect it

Protect against sexually transmitted diseases.
Choices about sex can be life altering. Sex is a basic human drive, and it can be wonderful. In certain conditions, sex can also be hazardous to your health. It pays to be clear about the pitfalls, including sexually transmitted diseases and unwanted pregnancies.

Technically, anyone who has sex is at risk of getting a sexually transmitted disease (STD). Without treatment,

journal entry 27

Discovery/Intention Statement

For three minutes, brainstorm things you can do during the next month to improve the ways that you fuel, move, rest, and observe your body. Write your ideas in the space below. Use additional paper if needed.

I discovered that I . . .

_____

_____

_____

_____

_____

_____

Next, pick three of your ideas that you can begin to use or practice this week. Write an Intention Statement below about how and when you intend to use these ideas.

I intend to . . .

_____

_____

_____

_____

_____

_____

some of these diseases can lead to blindness, infertility, cancer, heart disease, or even death. Sometimes there are no signs or symptoms of an STD; the only way to tell if you're infected is to be tested by a health care professional.

STDs are often spread through body fluids that are exchanged during sex—semen, vaginal secretions, and blood. Some STDs, such as herpes and genital warts, are spread by direct contact with infected skin. Human immunodeficiency virus (HIV) can be spread in other ways as well.

There are more than 25 kinds of STDs, including chlamydia, gonorrhea ("clap"), syphilis, genital warts, genital herpes, and trichomoniasis. Hepatitis can also be spread through sexual contact. STDs are the most common contagious diseases in the United States.

HIV is one of the most serious STDs, and it is different from the others in several respects. HIV is the virus that causes acquired immune deficiency syndrome (AIDS). AIDS is the last stage of HIV infection. A person with AIDS has an immune system that is weakened to the point of having difficulty in fighting off many kinds of infections and cancers.

Someone infected with HIV might feel no symptoms for months—sometimes years. Many times, those who are spreading HIV don't even know that they have it.

HIV/AIDS is not transmitted just through unprotected sexual contact. It can be transmitted by shared needles or equipment used to inject drugs. The virus can also be passed from an infected pregnant woman to her fetus during pregnancy or delivery, or through breast-feeding after delivery. Before 1985, HIV was sometimes spread through contaminated blood transfusions. Since March 1985, blood supplies have been screened for HIV, and blood transfusion is no longer considered a means of HIV infection.

Although the disease was initially prevalent in this country among male homosexuals, HIV/AIDS is becoming increasingly common among heterosexuals. HIV/AIDS cases among women have been rising steadily, and it is predicted to become one of the five leading causes of death among women.

Public hysteria and misinformation about HIV/AIDS still flourish. You cannot get HIV/AIDS from touching, kissing, hugging, food, coughs, mosquitoes, toilet seats, hot tubs, or swimming pools.

Being infected with HIV is not a death sentence. There are medical treatments that can slow down the rate at which HIV weakens the immune system. Some of the illnesses associated with AIDS can be prevented or treated, although AIDS itself is not curable. Some people live with HIV for years without developing AIDS, and people with AIDS might live for years after developing the condition. As with other chronic illnesses, early detection and early entry into medical care offers more options for treatment and a longer life.

STDs other than AIDS and herpes can be cured, if treated early. Prevention is better. Remember these guidelines:

- *Abstain from sex, or have sex exclusively with one person who is free of infection and has no other sex partners.* This is the only way to be absolutely safe from STDs.

- *Talk about STDs.* Ask sex partners if they have an STD. Tell your partner if you have one.

- *Recognize the symptoms of STDs in yourself and others.* Symptoms include swollen glands with fever and aching; itching around the vagina; vaginal discharge; pain during sex or when urinating; sore throat following oral sex; anal pain after anal sex; sores, blisters, scabs, or warts on the genitals, anus, tongue, or throat; rashes on the palms of your hands or soles of your feet; dark urine; loose and light-colored stools; and unexplained fatigue, weight loss, and night sweats.

- *Avoid injecting illegal drugs.* Sharing needles or other paraphernalia with other drug users is a behavior that can spread STDs.

- *Take action soon after you have sex.* Urinate soon after you have sex and wash your genitals with soap and water.

- *See a doctor to get checked for STDs twice each year.* If you have sex with several different people, get checked for STDs even if you have no symptoms. The more people you have sex with, the greater your risk. You are at risk even if you have sex only once with one person who is infected.

- *Use condoms.* Male condoms are thin latex membranes stretched over the penis prior to intercourse. (Female condoms are an option, but they are not as effective as male condoms.) Condoms prevent semen from entering the vagina. Both women and men can carry them and insist that they be used. Use a condom every time you have sex, and for any type of sex—oral, vaginal, or anal. Use latex condoms—not lambskin.

Note: Do not use spermicides containing nonoxynol-9. Also avoid lubricants, condoms, and other sex products with nonoxynol-9. At one time, researchers thought that this ingredient could help prevent STDs. New studies indicate that nonoxynol-9 can irritate the vagina and cervix, which actually increases the risk of STDs.

Remember that having multiple sex partners puts you at risk for STDs, even if you use condoms. While condoms can be effective, they are not guaranteed to work all of the time. Condoms can break, leak, or slip off. In addition, condoms cannot protect you from STDs that are spread by contact with herpes sores or warts.

If you think you have an STD, call your medical health care professional, campus health service, or local public health clinic. Seek counseling and further testing to find out if you are really infected. Early entry into treatment might prevent serious health problems. To avoid infecting other people, abstain from sex until you are treated and cured.

Protect against unwanted pregnancy. Following is some information that can help you and your partner avoid unwanted pregnancy. This is not a complete list of options, so be sure to supplement it with information from your medical health care professional.

Total abstinence and sterilization are the most effective methods of birth control. Other methods can fail. Also, many forms of birth control do not protect against STDs, including AIDS.

Abstinence is choosing not to have intercourse. You might feel pressured to change your mind about this choice. Keep in mind that, contrary to popular belief, many people exist happily without sexual intercourse. In addition, remember that abstinence as a means of birth control is guaranteed only when it is practiced without exception.

The "pill" is a synthetic hormone that "tells" a woman's body not to produce eggs. To be effective, it must be taken every day for 21 days a month. Birth control pills must be prescribed by a medical health care professional; the type of pill and the dose needed vary from one woman to the next. Side effects sometimes include slight nausea, breast tenderness, weight gain from water retention, and moodiness.

Some women choose not to take the pill due to increased risks of heart disease, including high blood pressure, blood clots, and breast or endometrial cancer. If you have a history of any of these conditions, see a doctor before taking the pill. If you are over age 35 and smoke, also see your doctor before using this form of birth control.

A contraceptive injection (Depo-Provera) into the buttocks or arm muscle is administered by a doctor or nurse every three months. This hormone prevents pregnancy by decreasing ovulation, preventing sperm from reaching the egg, and preventing a fertilized egg from implanting in the uterus. Unlike the pill, this method requires little effort: Women simply need an injection every three months. Side effects can include irregular periods, weight gain, and breast tenderness.

The *contraceptive implant device* (Norplant) is a small contraceptive inserted under the skin of a woman's upper arm. This device releases a steady stream of the hormone progestin (one of the hormones in the pill). Side effects can include inflammation or infection at the site of the implant, menstrual cycle changes, weight gain, and breast tenderness. **Note:** This device was taken off the market in July 2002. If you are using this form of birth control, see your doctor to talk about other options.

An *intrauterine device* (IUD) is a small metal or plastic device that is inserted in the uterus and left there for one to 10 years. It prevents fertilized eggs from developing. Side effects might include heavier menstrual flow, anemia, pelvic infection, perforation of the cervix or uterus, or septic abortion.

One brand of IUD—the Dalkon Shield—was taken off the market in 1975 after it was associated with pelvic infection, infertility, and some deaths. Today, IUDs rarely lead to serious complications. Possible side effects include increased risk of pelvic inflammatory disease, perforation of the uterus, abnormal bleeding, and cramps.

A *diaphragm* is a shallow rubber dome that is covered with a spermicide (sperm-killing cream) and inserted in the vagina. It fits over the cervix, which is the opening of the uterus, and prevents sperm from getting to the egg. A trained medical health care professional must measure and fit the diaphragm. It must be inserted before intercourse and left in place for six to eight hours after intercourse. It is more than 80 percent effective.

The *cervical cap* is a soft rubber cup that fits snugly around the cervix. Available by prescription only, it is also used with spermicide. Wearing it for more than 48 hours is not recommended due to a low risk of toxic shock syndrome.

A *sponge* works something like a diaphragm. It is effective for 24 hours. The sponge has been unavailable since 1995 when its only producer stopped making it. However, the sponge still has federal approval and might be marketed in the future.

The *hormonal vaginal contraceptive ring* (NuvaRing) releases the hormones progestin and estrogen from a ring placed inside the vagina and around the cervix. A woman removes the ring during her period and then puts in a new ring. This form of birth control is available only by prescription.

Foams, creams, tablets, suppositories, and *jellies* are chemicals that are placed in the vagina before intercourse and prevent sperm from getting to the egg.

When used carefully and consistently, *male condoms* offer a safe method of birth control. Latex condoms work the best for reducing the risk of STDs. Do not use male condoms with oil-based lubricants such as petroleum jelly, lotions, or baby oil, all of which can lead to breakage.

The *female condom* is a sheath of lubricated poly-urethane with a ring on each end that is inserted into the vagina. This is a relatively new form of contraception, and not many studies exist to document its effectiveness. Ask your doctor for the latest information.

The *rhythm method* involves avoiding intercourse during ovulation. The problem with this method is that it is difficult to know for sure when a woman is ovulating.

Natural family planning is based on looking for specific signs of fertility in a woman. (This is not to be confused with the rhythm method.) There are no side effects with natural family planning, and this method is gaining acceptance. Before you consider it, however, talk to a qualified instructor.

Douching is flushing the vagina with water or another liquid after intercourse. Do not use it for birth control. Even if a woman douches immediately after intercourse, this method is ineffective. Sperm are quicker than humans.

Withdrawal is the act of removing the penis before ejaculation occurs. This is also ineffective, since sperm can be present in pre-ejaculation fluid.

Sterilization is a permanent form of birth control, and one to avoid if you still want to have children.

All of these methods vary in effectiveness. Of course, abstinence is 100 percent effective in preventing pregnancy when practiced faithfully, and sterilization is nearly 100 percent effective. Methods that deliver extra hormones to a woman—through pills, injections, or implants—are typically rated 95 to 99 percent effective, as is the IUD. Condoms for both women and men are less effective—around 80 percent.

However, effectiveness rates can only be estimated. The actual effectiveness of most contraceptive methods depends on many factors—for example, the health of the people using them, the number of sex partners, and the frequency of sexual activity. Effectiveness also depends on how carefully and consistently the methods are used.

Protect against rape. Rape and other forms of sexual assault are all too common at vocational schools, colleges, and universities. People often hesitate to report rape for many reasons, such as fear, embarrassment, and concerns about credibility. Both women and men can be rape victims. And both can take steps to prevent rape:

- Get together with a group of people and take a tour of the school grounds. Make a special note of danger spots, such as unlighted paths and

→ **Stay up-to-date on STDs**

Our knowledge of HIV/AIDS and other STDs is changing constantly. For the latest statistics and information on prevention, check these resources from the Centers for Disease Control:

- National STD and AIDS Hot Line, 1-800-342-2437; Spanish, 1-800-344-7432; TTY, 1-800-243-7889
- Division of HIV/AIDS Prevention, http://www.cdc.gov/hiv/dhap.htm
- Division of STD Prevention, http://www.cdc.gov/nchstp/dstd/dstdp.html

You can also call your state health department.

unguarded buildings. Keep in mind that rape can occur during daylight and in well-lit places.

- Ask if your school has escort services for people taking evening classes. These might include personal escorts, car escorts, or both. If you do take an evening class, ask if there are security officers on duty before and after the class.

- Avoid practicing alone or going to the locker room alone. Stay with a group and keep track of one another. Don't just wait for someone to come out of the locker room alone or to return from a solo cross-country run.

- Take a course or seminar on self-defense and rape prevention. To find out where these courses are being held, check with your student counseling service, community education center, or local library.

- If you are raped, get help. Resources include the nearest rape crisis center, hospital, student health service, and police station. Your team doctor or trainer can also help. Report the crime as soon as you can, and also arrange for follow-up counseling.

Date rape—the act of forcing sex on a date—is the most common form of rape among college students. Date rape is rape. It is a crime.

It is particularly dangerous when neither the victim nor the perpetrator realizes that a crime has taken place. Drugs such as rohypnol and GHB (gamma hydroxy-butyrate) have been used to facilitate date rape. These drugs, often given to people without their knowledge, reduce resistance to sexual advances and produce an amnesia-like effect. People who have taken these drugs might not remember the circumstances that led to their being raped.

You have the right to refuse to have sex with anyone, including dates. You also have the right to refuse sex with your partner, fiancé(e), or spouse. Protect yourself by communicating clearly what you want and don't want. Be cautious about using alcohol or drugs, and be wary of dates who get drunk or high. You can also provide your own transportation on dates and avoid going to secluded places with people you don't know well.

Forcing someone to have sex is *never* acceptable—under any circumstances. Anyone who commits rape has to live with the pain of the victim, the reactions of friends and family, and the legal system. Student athletes convicted of rape also have to face their teammates and coaches. These students will be declared ineligible and suspended from school.

Not all people who commit a rape have their name made public. However, a student athlete who commits rape will almost certainly be in the news. Student athletes are public figures, and even a false accusation of rape can damage your reputation. Avoid putting yourself in any situation where someone could make an accusation against you.

Protect against accidents. Disabling injuries and death can occur in the haven called the home and in car accidents. To reduce the odds of such accidents, remember the following:

- Don't drive after drinking alcohol or using psychoactive drugs.

- Drive with the realization that other drivers are possibly preoccupied, intoxicated, or careless.

- Identify a designated driver—someone who will abstain from alcohol for the entire evening. Prevent even a mildly intoxicated person from driving.

- Put poisons out of reach of children, and label poisons clearly. Poisoning takes a larger toll on people aged 15 to 45 than on children.

- Keep stairs, halls, doorways, and other pathways clear of shoes, newspapers, and other clutter.

- Don't smoke in bed.

- Don't let candles burn unattended.

- Keep children away from hot stoves, and turn pot handles inward.

- Check electrical cords for fraying, loose connections, or breaks in insulation. Don't overload extension cords.

- Keep a fire extinguisher handy.

- Watch for ways that an infant or a toddler could suffocate or choke: small objects that can be swallowed, old refrigerators or freezers that can act as air-tight prisons, unattended or unfenced swimming pools, kerosene heaters in tightly closed rooms, and plastic kitchen or clothing bags.

- Install smoke detectors where you live and work. Most of these run on batteries that need occasional replacement. Follow the manufacturer's guidelines. ⊠

The experts recommend— seven dietary guidelines

1 Choose a variety of fruits, vegetables, and grains daily, especially whole grains. Eating plenty of fruits, vegetables, and grains of different kinds can help protect you against many chronic diseases. Remember that whole grains provide more fiber and other nutrients than processed grains. For those who eat little meat, combining whole grains with legumes (dried beans and soy products) will provide important nutrients.

2 Keep food safe to eat. Wash hands and cooking surfaces often. Separate raw, cooked, and ready-to-eat foods while shopping, preparing, or storing. Read labels for instructions on preparing foods, and refrigerate perishable foods promptly. When serving, keep hot foods hot and cold foods cold. If you're in doubt about the safety of a food, throw it out.

When you are traveling or participating in a competition, find out what food will be available. You may need to provide your own nutritious snacks. Wash them and prepare or package them in bite-sized morsels. That way you can eat them gradually.

3 Choose a diet that is low in saturated fat and cholesterol and moderate in total fat. Limit solid fats, such as butter, hard margarines, lard, and partially hydrogenated shortenings. Use canola or olive oils and a heart-healthy spread as a substitute. Talk to your team trainer or doctor about the fat and carbohydrate content of foods. Find out what to eat and what to avoid.

4 Choose beverages and foods to moderate your intake of sugars. Get most of your calories from whole grains, fruits, and vegetables; low-fat or nonfat dairy products; and lean meats or meat substitutes. Don't let soft drinks or sweets crowd out other foods you need to maintain health. Drink water often. Also consider your need for hydrating beverages that can replace lost salt and other nutrients.

5 Choose and prepare foods with a level of salt that is appropriate to your athletic activity. Many people need to reduce their risk of high blood pressure by consuming less salt. To do this, read labels and find foods lower in sodium.

Remember that your body does need salt to function normally. Athletes lose higher than average levels of salt through perspiration and urination.

Some athletes run the risk of hyponatremia—a low concentration of sodium in the blood. Symptoms include nausea, muscle cramps, disorientation, slurred speech, confusion and unusual behavior. Athletes who train and compete in hot, humid conditions have an increased risk of hyponatremia. Minor symptoms can be treated with salty foods and a hydrating sports drink. Severe symptoms call for medical treatment. If left untreated, an athlete with severe hyponatremia can suffer seizures, coma, or even death.

6 If you drink alcoholic beverages, do so in moderation and absolutely not while you are in season. Alcoholic beverages supply calories but few nutrients. Excessive alcohol consumption affects judgment and can lead to dependency. It also reduces the sense of pain and can lead to severe injury as well as increase the risk of motor vehicle crashes and other injuries, violence, suicide, high blood pressure, stroke, and certain types of cancer. If you choose to drink alcoholic beverages, consume them only in moderation—up to one drink per day for women or two drinks per day for men. Drink with meals to slow alcohol absorption.

7 Aim for a healthy weight. Determine how you can achieve and maintain a healthy weight that is appropriate for your body size and your regular athletic activities. Consume nutritious foods that provide more than empty calories and convert to high levels of energy.[5]

Developing self-esteem

The challenges of higher education can put self-esteem at risk. A demanding course schedule, financial concerns, new social settings, and the pressure to succeed can all test your ability to adapt and change. It's no wonder that some student athletes feel performance anxiety in class or in competition.

During the past 30 years, psychologists have produced key studies about *self-efficacy*. This term refers to your belief in your ability to determine the outcomes of events—especially outcomes that are strongly influenced by your own behavior. A strong sense of self-efficacy allows you to tackle problems with confidence, set long-term goals, and see difficult tasks as creative challenges rather than potential disasters.

The field of self-efficacy research is closely associated with psychologist Albert Bandura of Stanford University.[6] While self-esteem refers to an overall impression of your abilities, self-efficacy points to specific factors that influence the ways you think, feel, and act. According to Bandura, self-efficacy has several sources. You can use specific strategies to strengthen them.

Set up situations in which you can win

Start by planning scenarios in which you can succeed. Recognize that pretest and pregame jitters are normal. Imagine that you will do everything right in each of these scenarios. Bandura calls these "mastery situations." For example, set yourself up for success by breaking a big project down into small, doable tasks. Then tackle and complete the first task. This accomplishment can help you move on to the next task with higher self-efficacy. Success breeds more success.

Set goals with care

If you want to boost self-efficacy, also be picky about your goals. According to the research, goals that you find easy to meet will not boost your self-efficacy. Instead, set goals that call on you to overcome obstacles, make persistent effort, and even fail occasionally.

At the same time, it's important to avoid situations in which you are *often* likely to fail. Setting goals that you have little chance to meet can undermine your self-efficacy. Ideal goals are both challenging *and* achievable.

For example, set careful goals when responding to injury. Remember that athletes are susceptible to failure when they return to competition too early after an injury. Following the advice of your trainer or team doctor, set reasonable goals that permit enough time for you to heal. Even when you return to practice and competition, gauge your ability to perform at your preinjured level. Set goals based on what your body tells you.

Adopt a model

In self-efficacy research, the word *model* has a special definition. This term refers to someone who is similar to you in key ways, and who succeeds in the kinds of situations in which you want to succeed.

To find a model, look for teammates and other students with whom you have a lot in common—and who have mastered the skills that you want to acquire. Your models need not be athletes. By demonstrating excellence in any area that matters to you, these people hold out a real possibility of success for you.

Change the conversation about yourself

Monitor what you say and think about yourself. Remember that this self-talk might be so habitual that you don't even notice it. Whether you are fully aware of them or not, your thoughts can make or break your sense of self-efficacy. Your thoughts largely create your sense of being a winner or a loser.

Pay close attention and notice when you speak or think negatively about yourself. Telling the truth about your weaknesses is one thing. Consistently underrating yourself is another. In the conversation about yourself, go for balance. Tell the truth about the times you set a goal and miss it. Also take the time to write and speak a plan about the goals you meet and what works well in your life.

People with a strong sense of self-efficacy attribute their failures to skills that they currently lack—and that they can acquire in the future. This approach chooses not to look on failures as permanent, personal defects. Rather than saying "I just don't have what it takes to become a skilled test taker," say "I can adopt techniques to help me remember key facts even when I feel stressed."

Interpret stress in a new way

Achieving your goals might place you right in the middle of situations in which you feel stress. You might find yourself meeting new people, leading a meeting, speaking in public, or doing something else that you've never done before. That can feel scary.

Remember that stress comes in two forms—thoughts and physical sensations. Thoughts can include mental pictures of yourself making mistakes or being publicly humiliated after a loss. You might say to yourself, "This is the worst possible thing that could happen to me." Sensations can include shortness of breath, dry mouth, knots in the stomach, tingling feelings, headaches, and other forms of discomfort.

The way you interpret stress as you become aware of it can make a big difference in your sense of self-efficacy. During moments when you want to do well, see if you can focus your attention. Rather than attaching negative interpretations to your experience of stress, simply notice your thoughts and sensations. Release them instead of dwelling on them or trying to resist them.

As you observe yourself over time, you might find that the physical sensations associated with your sense of stress and your sense of excitement are largely the same. Instead of viewing these sensations as signs of impending doom, see them as a boost of energy and enthusiasm that you can channel into performing well.

Compare yourself to yourself

Our own failures are often more dramatic to us than the failures of others, and our own successes are often more invisible. When we're unsure of ourselves, we can look in any direction and see people who seem more competent and more confident than we do. When we start the comparison game, we open the door to self-doubt.

Athletes often have difficulty doing this. The news media and the public measure success by wins and losses. However, you can describe yourself in positive and encouraging terms. Instead of talking about what you can't do, describe how you plan to achieve your goals by doing something differently in your training or competition.

Measure success in terms of self-improvement rather than of triumphs over others. Take time to note any progress you've made toward your goals over time. Write Discovery Statements about that progress. Celebrate your success in any area of life, no matter how small that success might seem.

There is a way to play the comparison game and win: Instead of comparing yourself to others, compare yourself to yourself.

Soak in the acknowledgments of others

Instead of deflecting compliments ("It was nothing"), fully receive the positive things that others say about you ("Thank you"). Also take public credit for your successes. "Well, I was just lucky" can change to "I worked hard to achieve that goal." Be prepared to give thoughtful responses that accurately describe what you did to succeed. You'll create a model for others to follow. ⬤

Emotional pain is not a sickness

Emotional pain has gotten a bad name. This type of slander is undeserved. There is nothing wrong with feeling bad. It's OK to feel miserable, depressed, sad, upset, angry, dejected, gloomy, or unhappy.

Athletes are likely to experience emotional highs and lows. You've probably seen a team take the lead in the waning moments of a contest. The athletes literally jump for joy. Then, in the flash of a few seconds, the opposition snatches the victory with a miracle play. Exuberance becomes despair.

It might not be pleasant to feel bad, but it can be good for you. Often, the appropriate way to feel is bad. When you leave a place you love, sadness is natural. When a loved coach decides to retire, you may feel miserable.

Unless you are suicidally depressed, it is almost impossible to feel too bad. Feeling bad for too long can be a problem. If depression, sadness, or anger persists, get help. Otherwise, allow yourself to experience these emotions. They're usually appropriate and necessary for personal growth.

When a loved one dies, it is fine to grieve. The grief might appear in the form of depression, sadness, or anger. There is nothing wrong with emotional pain. It is natural, and it doesn't have to be fixed.

Sometimes feeling bad becomes a problem. It can happen when you don't allow yourself to feel bad at the outset. The next time you feel rotten, go ahead and feel rotten. It will pass—and probably more quickly if you don't fight it or try to ignore it.

Allowing yourself to feel bad might even help you get smart. Harvey Jackins, a psychotherapist, bases his work on this premise.[7] Jackins believes that when people fully experience and release their emotions, they also remove

> *There is nothing wrong with emotional pain. It is natural, and it doesn't have to be fixed.*

blocks to their thinking and clear a path for profound personal insights. And Daniel Goleman, author of *Emotional Intelligence,* asserts that being attuned to feelings can lead to sounder personal decisions.[8]

Following are some good ways to feel bad.

Don't worry about reasons. Sometimes we allow ourselves to feel bad if we have a good reason. For example: "Well, I feel very sad, but that is because I just found out my best friend is moving to Europe." It's all right to know the reason why you are sad, and it is fine *not* to know. You can feel bad for no apparent reason. The reason doesn't matter.

Set a time limit. If you are concerned about feeling bad, if you are worried that you need to "fix it," give yourself a little time. You might even ask your coach for time away from your sport.

Before you force yourself not to feel the way you feel, set a time limit. Say to yourself, "I am going to give myself until Monday at noon, and if I don't feel better by then, I am going to try to fix myself."

Sometimes it is appropriate to fix the situation associated with a bad feeling. There might be a problem that needs a solution. Feeling bad can motivate you to solve the problem. And sometimes it helps just to feel bad for a while.

Reassure others. If you feel bad, talk to someone about it—a friend, family member, coach, or athletic advisor. Sometimes other people will have a hard time letting you feel bad. They might be worried that they did something wrong and want to make it better. They want you to quit feeling bad. Tell them you will. Assure them that you will feel good again, but that for right now, you just want to feel bad.

This is no joke. Sometimes students think that this whole idea of allowing yourself to feel bad is a joke, reverse psychology, or something else. It isn't. This suggestion is based on the notion that good mental health is possible only if you allow yourself to feel the full range of your emotions.

Suicide

Suicide is one of the leading causes of death among students.

You are likely to meet someone who attempts suicide. Student athletes face media scrutiny, pressure to win, self-doubt in the face of competition, and the despondency that comes with injury or retirement from sport.

When athletes base their sense of self-worth on the outcomes of their sport, they are vulnerable to depression, anxiety, and suicide.

Recognize danger signals

Talking about suicide. People who attempt suicide might say things like "I just don't want to live anymore. I'm a loser." Or "I want you to know that no matter what happens, I've always loved you." Or "Tomorrow night at 7:30 I'm going to end it all."

Planning for it. People planning suicide will sometimes put their affairs in order. They might close bank accounts, give away or sell precious possessions, or make or update a will.

Having a history of previous attempts. Some estimates suggest that up to 50 percent of the people who kill themselves have attempted suicide at least once before.

Dwelling on problems. Expressing extreme helplessness or hopelessness about solving problems can indicate that someone might be considering suicide.

Feeling depressed. Although not everyone who is depressed attempts suicide, almost everyone who attempts suicide feels depressed.

Take prompt action

Suicide can be prevented. If you suspect that one of your classmates or teammates is considering suicide, do whatever it takes to ensure the person's safety. Let this person know that you will persist until you are certain that she's safe. Any of the following actions can help.

Take it seriously. Taking suicidal comments seriously is especially important when you hear them from young adults. Suicide threats are more common in this age group and might be dismissed as "normal." Err on the side of being too careful rather than on the side of being negligent.

Listen fully. Encourage the person at risk to express thoughts and feelings appropriately. If she claims that she doesn't want to talk, be inviting, be assertive, and be persistent. Be totally committed to listening.

Speak powerfully. Let the person at risk know that you care. Trying to talk someone out of suicide or minimizing problems is generally useless. Acknowledge that problems are serious *and* that they can be solved. Point out that suicide is a permanent solution to a temporary problem—and that help is available.

Get professional help. Suggest that the person see a mental health professional. If she resists help, offer to schedule the appointment for her and to take her to it. If this fails, get others involved, including the depressed person's family or school personnel.

Remove access to firearms. Most suicides are attempted with guns. Get rid of any that might be around. Also remove dangerous drugs and razors.

Ask the person to sign a "no-suicide contract." Get a promise, in writing, that the person will not hurt herself before speaking to you. A written promise can provide the "excuse" she needs not to take action.

Handle an emergency. If a situation becomes a crisis, do not leave the person alone. Call a crisis hot line, 911, or a social service agency. If necessary, take the person to the nearest hospital emergency room, clinic, or police station.

Follow up. Someone in danger of attempting suicide might resist further help even if your first intervention succeeds. Ask this person if she's keeping counseling appointments and taking prescribed medication. Help this person apply strategies for solving problems. Stay in touch.

Take care of yourself

If you ever begin to think about committing suicide, remember that you can apply any of the above suggestions to yourself. If you're at risk, grant yourself the same compassion that you'd extend to another person.

Find out more on this topic from the American Foundation for Suicide Prevention at 1-888-333-AFSP or **http://www.afsp.org**. ✉

Alcohol, tobacco, and drugs: The truth

The truth is that getting high can be fun. In our culture, and especially in our media, getting high has become synonymous with having a good time. Even if you don't smoke, drink, or use other drugs, you are certain to come in contact with people who do.

We are a drug-using society. Of course, some of those uses are therapeutic and lawful, including drugs that are taken as prescribed by a doctor or psychologist. The problem comes when we turn to drugs as *the* solution to any problem, even before seeking professional guidance. Are you uncomfortable? Often the first response is "Take something." When faced with a problem, ignore potential solutions and go directly for the chemical fix.

There is a big payoff in using alcohol, tobacco, caffeine, cocaine, heroin, or other drugs—or people wouldn't do it. The payoff can be direct, such as relaxation, self-confidence, comfort, excitement, or other forms of pleasure. At times the payoff is indirect. People use drugs to avoid rejection, mask emotional pain, win peer group acceptance, or reject authority.

In addition to the payoffs, there are costs. For some people, the cost is much greater than the payoff. It goes beyond money. Even if drug use doesn't make you broke, it can make you crazy. Drug use can cause you to care about little else except finding more drugs—friends, athletics, classes, work, and family be damned.

Substance abuse—the compulsive use of a chemical in alcohol or drugs resulting in negative consequences—is only part of the picture. People can also relate to food, gambling, money, sex, and even work in compulsive ways.

Some people will stop abusing a substance or activity when the consequences get serious enough. Other people don't stop, even after they get caught. They continue their self-defeating behaviors, no matter the consequences for themselves, their friends, or their families. At that point the problem goes beyond abuse. It's addiction.

With substance addiction, the costs can include overdose, infection, and lowered immunity to disease—all of which can be fatal. Long-term excessive drinking damages every organ system in the human body. Each year, almost 400,000 people die from the effects of cigarette smoking.

Lectures about why to avoid alcohol and drug abuse and addiction can be pointless. Ultimately, people don't take care of their bodies because someone says they should. They might take care of themselves when they see that the costs of using a drug outweighs the payoffs.

The point is this: People are more likely to abstain when they're convinced that using these substances leads to more pain than pleasure over the long run. It's your body. You choose. ✖

Getting high—the costs for student athletes

Getting high can cost you your scholarship, your athletic eligibility, and your chance to complete a college education.

Athletes can now alter their body chemistry in sophisticated and illegal ways. Some people depend on performance-enhancing drugs such as creatine and steroids. Others rely on blood-doping, dietary supplements and even over-the-counter medications.

Today it is harder than ever before to get away with such practices. The NCAA, the United States Olympic Committee, and other athletic organizations are researching illegal ways to enhance performance. They're also stiffening the penalties for illegal substance use and are stepping up their enforcement.

The NCAA publishes a current list of banned drugs. Look for it online at **http://www.ncaa.org/health-safety** and **http://www.drugfreesport.com/rec/**.

Athletic conferences and individual institutions also have their own policies and procedures. Know these and follow them explicitly. A guiding principle for student athletes is that you must get approval from your team trainer or team doctor before you take any medication or supplement, or before you engage in any practice that could alter your physical chemistry.

As a student athlete, you will also be required to sign consent forms for drug testing. Make certain that you understand the drug-testing process. Learn about your rights and responsibilities. Before you get high, consider the costs of testing positive for a banned substance.

→ Some facts . . .

In 2001 the NCAA Committee on Competitive Safeguards and Medical Aspects of Sports conducted its fifth study to measure substance abuse patterns of student athletes at NCAA member institutions. The goal of the NCAA researchers was to secure surveys from 12 percent of the student athlete population. The 2001 data was compared with similar data that was gathered in 1997.

The comparative results were the following:

- Half of all student athletes who continue to use marijuana and /or amphetamines report they have used it 10 or more times.

- Two-thirds of student athletes who reported using alcohol in the last year said they did so two or fewer times a week, with more than half reporting no alcohol consumption before competition.

- Most ergogenic substance and nutritional supplement use starts in high school.

- Over half of those student athletes who used cocaine stated that they did not start until after they were in college.

- While more than half the users of anabolic steroids in 1997 stated they used them for injuries, the majority in 2001 say they use them to improve athletic performance and many use them to improve appearance.

- Use of amphetamines to improve athletic performance was up significantly in the 2001 study.

- Alcohol, cocaine, and marijuana were used for recreational and social reasons.

- Sixty percent of student athletes believe that their use of alcoholic beverages does not affect their athletic performance or their general health.

- One-third of student athletes surveyed stated that they performed poorly in practice or a game due to drinking or drug use.

- Over 50 percent of the student athletes surveyed believe that the NCAA should drug-test student athletes and that current testing deters college athletes from using drugs.

In the United States, substance abuse and addiction take a heavy toll on students in higher education, especially those aged 18 to 24. In this group:

- Thirty-one percent met criteria for a diagnosis of alcohol abuse and 6 percent for a diagnosis of alcohol dependence in the past 12 months, according to questionnaire-based self-reports about their drinking.

- About 25 percent report academic consequences of their drinking, including missing class, falling behind, doing poorly on exams or papers, and receiving lower grades overall.

- 1,400 die each year from alcohol-related unintentional injuries, including motor vehicle crashes.

- 500,000 are unintentionally injured under the influence of alcohol.

- 400,000 had unprotected sex, and more than 100,000 students report having been too intoxicated to know if they consented to having sex.

- 70,000 are victims of alcohol-related sexual assault or date rape.

For related information from the National Institute for Alcohol Abuse and Alcoholism, go online to **http://www.collegedrinkingprevention.gov.**

Sources: R. W. Hingson, T. Heeren, R. C. Zakocs, A. Kopstein, and H. Wechsler, "Magnitude of Alcohol-Related Mortality and Morbidity among U.S. College Students Ages 18-24," *Journal of Studies on Alcohol* 63, no. 2 (2002): 136-144.

H. Wechsler, J. E. Lee, M. Kuo, M. Seibring, T. F. Nelson, and H. P. Lee, "Trends in College Binge Drinking during a Period of Increased Prevention Efforts: Findings from Four Harvard School of Public Health Study Surveys, 1993-2001," *Journal of American College Health* 50, no. 5 (2002): 203-217.

J. R. Knight, H. Wechsler, M. Kuo, M. Seibring, E. R. Weitzman, and M. Schuckit, "Alcohol Abuse and Dependence among U.S. College Students," *Journal of Studies on Alcohol* 63, no. 3 (2002): 263-270.

ADDICTION: HOW DO I KNOW . . . ?

People who have problems with drugs and alcohol are great at hiding that fact from themselves and from others.

The purpose of this exercise is to give you an objective way to look at your relationship with drugs or alcohol. There are signals that indicate when drug or alcohol use has become abusive or even addictive. This exercise can also help you determine if a friend might be addicted.

Answer the following questions quickly and honestly with "yes," "no," or "n/a" (not applicable). If you are concerned about someone else, rephrase each question using that person's name.

_____ Are you worried about your own drug or alcohol use?

_____ Are any of your friends worried about your drug or alcohol use?

_____ Have you ever hidden from a friend, spouse, teammate, or coworker the fact that you were drinking? (Pretended you were sober? Covered up alcohol breath?)

_____ Do you sometimes use alcohol or drugs to escape lows rather than to produce highs?

_____ Have you ever gotten angry when confronted about your use?

_____ Do you brag about how much you consume? ("I drank her under the table.")

_____ Do you think about or do drugs when you are alone?

_____ Do you store up alcohol, drugs, cigarettes, or caffeine (in coffee or soft drinks) to be sure you won't run out?

_____ Does having a party almost always include alcohol or drugs?

_____ Do you try to control your drinking so that it won't be a problem? ("I drink only on weekends now." "I never drink before 5 p.m." "I drink only beer.")

_____ Do you often explain to other people why you are drinking? ("It's my birthday." "We won today." "It's Veterans Day." "It sure is a hot day.")

_____ Have you changed friends to accommodate your drinking? ("She's OK, but she isn't excited about getting high.")

_____ Has your behavior changed in the last several months? (Grades down? Lack of interest in your sport? Change of values or of what you think is moral?)

_____ Do you have medical problems (stomach trouble, malnutrition, liver problems, anemia) that could be related to drinking?

_____ Have you ever decided to quit drugs or alcohol and then changed your mind?

_____ Have you had any fights, accidents, or similar incidents related to drinking or drugs in the last year?

_____ Has your drinking or drug use ever caused a problem at home?

_____ Do you envy people who go overboard with alcohol or drugs?

_____ Have you ever told yourself you can quit at any time?

_____ Have you ever missed school or practice because you had a hangover?

_____ Have you ever had a blackout (a period you can't remember) after drinking?

_____ Do you wish that people would mind their own business when it comes to your use of alcohol or drugs?

_____ Is the cost of alcohol or other drugs taxing your budget or resulting in financial stress?

_____ Do you need increasing amounts of the drug to produce the desired effect?

_____ When you stop taking the drug, do you experience withdrawal?

_____ Do you spend a great deal of time obtaining and using alcohol or other drugs?

_____ Have you used alcohol or another drug when it was physically dangerous to do so (such as when driving a car or working with machines)?

_____ Have you been arrested or had other legal problems resulting from the use of a substance?

Now count the number of questions you answered "yes." If you answered "yes" five or more times, talk with a professional. Five "yes" answers does not necessarily mean that you are addicted. It does point out that alcohol or other drugs are adversely affecting your life. Talk to someone with training in recovery from chemical dependency. Do not rely on the opinion of anyone who lacks such training.

If you filled out this questionnaire about another person and you answered "yes" five or more times, your friend might need help. You probably can't provide that help alone. Seek out a counselor or a support group such as Al-Anon. Call the local Alcoholics Anonymous chapter to find out about an Al-Anon meeting near you.

Seeing the full scope of addiction

Here are some guidelines that can help you decide if addiction is a barrier for you right now. Most addictions share some key features, such as the following: loss of control, pattern of relapses, increased tolerance, and withdrawal.[9]

The same basic features can be present in anything from cocaine use to compulsive gambling. All of this can add up to a continuous cycle of abuse or addiction. These common features prompt many people to call some forms of addiction a disease. If you or someone you love has a problem with addiction, consider getting help. The problem might be your own addiction or perhaps the behavior of someone you love. In any case, consider acting on several of the following suggestions.

Admit the problem. People with active addictions are a varied group—rich and poor, young and old, successful and unsuccessful. Often these people do have one thing in common: They are masters of denial. They deny that they are unhappy. They deny that they have hurt anyone. They are convinced that they can quit any time they want. They sometimes become so adept at hiding the problem from themselves that they die.

Pay attention. If you do use a substance compulsively or behave in compulsive ways, do so with awareness. Then pay attention to the consequences. Act with deliberate decision rather than out of habit or under pressure from others.

Look at the costs. There is always a tradeoff. Drinking 10 beers might result in a temporary high, and you will probably remember that feeling. No one feels great the morning after consuming 10 beers, but it seems easier to forget pain. Often people don't notice how bad alcoholism, drug addiction, or other forms of substance abuse make them feel.

Take responsibility. Nobody plans to become an addict. If you have pneumonia, you can recover without guilt or shame. Approach an addiction in yourself or others in the same way. You can take responsibility for your recovery without blame, shame, or guilt.

Get help. Many people find that they cannot treat addiction on their own. Addictive behaviors are often symptoms of an illness that needs treatment.

Two broad options exist for getting help with addiction. One is the growing self-help movement. The other is formal treatment. People recovering from addiction often combine the two.

Many self-help groups are modeled after Alcoholics Anonymous. AA is made up of recovering alcoholics and addicts. These people understand the problems of abuse firsthand, and they follow a systematic, 12-step approach to living without it. This is one of the oldest and most successful self-help programs in the world. Chapters of AA welcome people from all walks of life, and you don't have to be an alcoholic to attend most meetings. Programs based on AA principles exist for many other forms of addiction as well.

Some people feel uncomfortable with the AA approach. Other resources exist for these people, including private therapy and group therapy. Also investigate organizations such as Women for Sobriety, the Secular Organizations for Sobriety, and Rational Recovery Systems. Use whatever works for you. The Web site for this text has links to organizations that can provide information and aid in recovering from addiction.

Treatment programs are available in almost every community. They might be residential (you live there for weeks or months at a time) or outpatient (you visit several hours a day). Find out where these treatment centers are located by calling a doctor, a mental health professional, or a local hospital. Most head trainers at athletics departments have studied drug and alcohol abuse and addiction and are also willing to give you help.

Alcohol and drug treatments are now covered by many health insurance programs. If you don't have insurance, it is usually possible to arrange some other payment program. Cost is no reason to avoid treatment.

Get help for a friend, teammate, or family member. You might know someone who uses alcohol or other drugs in a way that can lead to serious and sustained negative consequences. If so, you have every right to express your concern to that person. Wait until the person is clear-headed and then mention specific incidents. For example: "Last night you drank five beers when we were at my apartment, and then you wanted to drive home. When I offered to call a cab for you instead, you refused." Also be prepared to offer a source of help, such as the phone number of a local treatment center.

For more information on places to turn for help with addiction, visit

masterstudent.college.hmco.com

journal entry 28

Discovery Statement

If you look and feel healthy, a greater understanding of your body can help you be aware of what you're doing right. If you are not content with your present physical or emotional health, you might discover some ways to adjust your personal habits and increase your sense of well-being.

This exercise is a structured Discovery Statement that allows you to look closely at your health. As with the Discovery Wheel exercise in Chapter One, the usefulness of this exercise will be determined by your honesty and courage.

To begin, draw a simple outline of your body on a separate sheet of paper. You might have positive and negative feelings about various internal and external parts of your body. Label the parts and include a short description of the attributes you like or dislike. For example: straight teeth, fat thighs, clear lungs, double chin, straight posture, etc.

The body you drew substantially reflects your past health practices. To discover how well you take care of your body, on a separate sheet of paper complete the following sentences.

Eating

1. The truth about what I eat is . . .

2. What I know about the way I eat is . . .

3. What I would most like to change about my diet is . . .

4. My eating habits lead me to be . . .

Exercise

1. The way I usually exercise is . . .

2. The last time I did 20 minutes or more of heart/lung (aerobic) exercise was . . .

3. As a result of my physical conditioning I feel . . .

4. And I look . . .

5. It would be easier for me to work out regularly if I . . .

6. The most important benefit for me in exercising more is . . .

Substances

1. My history of cigarette smoking is . . .

2. An objective observer would say my use of alcohol is . . .

3. In the last 10 days the number of alcoholic drinks I have had is . . .

4. I would describe my use of coffee, colas, and other caffeinated drinks as . . .

5. I have used the following illegal drugs in the past week:

6. When it comes to drugs, what I am sometimes concerned about is . . .

7. I take the following prescription drugs:

Relationships

1. Someone who knows me fairly well would say I am emotionally . . .

2. The way I look and feel has affected my relationships by . . .

3. My use of drugs or alcohol has been an issue with . . .

4. The best thing I could do for myself and my relationships would be to . . .

Sleep

1. The number of hours I sleep each night is . . .

2. On weekends I normally sleep . . .

3. I have trouble sleeping when . . .

4. Last night I . . .

5. The night before last I . . .

6. The quality of my sleep is usually . . .

In general

What concerns me more than anything else about my health is . . .

Warning

Advertising can be dangerous to your health

The average American is exposed to hundreds of advertising messages per day. Unless you are stranded on a desert island, you are affected by commercial messages.

Advertising serves a useful function. It helps us make choices about how we spend our money. We can select from an endless array of products and services. Advertising makes us aware of the options.

Advertising space is also expensive, and the messages are carefully crafted to get the most value for the cost. Advertisements can play on our emotions and be dangerously manipulative.

For example, consider the messages that ads convey about your health. Advertising alcohol, tobacco, and pain relievers is a big business. Much of the revenue earned by newspapers, magazines, radio, television, and Web sites comes from advertisements for these products.

Advertising also affects what we eat and drink. The least nutritious foods receive the most advertising money. Ads for alcohol glorify drinking. One of the aims of these ads is to convince heavy drinkers that the amount they drink is normal. Advertisers imply that daily drinking is the norm, pleasant experiences are enhanced by drinking, holidays naturally include alcohol, parties are a flop without it, relationships are more romantic over cocktails, and everybody drinks. Each of these implications is questionable.

Also questionable is the way that sports celebrities and other athletes are used as marketing tools. Advertisers spend millions to place their faces in ads that can distort our perception of a product. Look for commercials that show physically fit people drinking "low-carb" beers. Sometimes images of a product are paired with shots of an athlete in competition. The implication seems to be that alcohol should be part of your training regimen.

In addition, advertising can affect our self-image. A typical advertising message is "You are not OK unless you buy our product." These messages are painstakingly programmed to get us to buy clothes, makeup, and hair products to make us look OK; drugs, alcohol, and food to make us feel OK; perfumes, toothpaste, and deodorants to make us smell OK. Advertising also promotes the idea that buying the right product is essential to having valuable relationships in our lives.

Another problem with advertising involves images of women. The basic message of some ads is that women love to spend hours discussing floor wax, deodorants, tampons, and laundry detergent—and that they think constantly about losing weight and looking sexy. In others ads, women handle everything from kitchen to bedroom to boardroom. These women are Superwomen.

Advertising photography creates illusions. The next time you're in a crowd, notice how few people look like those in the media. Though advertising is making progress in representing racial diversity, it still frequently excludes people of color. If our perceptions were based solely on advertising, we would be hard-pressed to know that our society is racially and ethnically diverse. See how many examples of cultural stereotypes you can find in the ads you encounter this week.

Use advertising as a continual opportunity to develop the qualities of a critical thinker. Be aware of how a multibillion-dollar industry threatens your health and well-being. 🔀

journal entry 29

Discovery/Intention Statement

Think of a time when—after seeing an advertisement or a commercial—you craved a certain food or drink or you really wanted to buy something. Describe how the advertising influenced you.

I discovered that I . . .

_____

_____

_____

Now describe anything you'd like to do differently in the future when you notice that advertising affects you in the way you just described.

I intend to . . .

_____

_____

_____

PRACTICING CRITICAL THINKING

11

This exercise is about clarifying the differences between behaviors and interpretations. A behavior is factual and observable, while an interpretation is subjective and often based on observed behaviors. Understanding this distinction can help you think clearly about your behaviors—including those that affect your emotional health by influencing your key relationships.

For instance, arriving 10 minutes after a lecture starts or pulling a dog's tail are both observable behaviors. In contrast, an interpretation is a conclusion we draw on the basis of the observed behavior: "She's either too rude or too irresponsible to get to a lecture on time." "She hates animals. Just look at how she pulled that dog's tail!" Keep in mind that other interpretations are possible. Perhaps the person's car broke down on the way to the lecture. And maybe the owner of the dog is playing a game that her pet enjoys.

Consider another example. "She shouted at me, left the room, and slammed the door" is a statement that describes behaviors. "She was angry" is one interpretation of the social significance or meaning of the observed behavior.

With this distinction in mind, brainstorm a list of behaviors you have seen in others when they were in conflict with you. Use the space below to record your brainstorm. Afterward, review your list to see if some of the behaviors you noted are actually interpretations.

_____

_____

_____

_____

_____

_____

_____

_____

_____

_____

_____

_____

_____

_____

_____

_____

_____

power process

Surrender

Life can be magnificent and satisfying. It can also be devastating.

Sometimes there is too much pain or confusion. Problems can be too big and too numerous. Life can bring us to our knees in a pitiful, helpless, and hopeless state. A broken relationship with a loved one, a sudden diagnosis of cancer, total frustration with a child's behavior problem, or even the prospect of several long years of school are situations that can leave us feeling overwhelmed—powerless.

In these troubling situations, the first thing we can do is to admit that we don't have the resources to handle the problem. No matter how hard we try and no matter what skills we bring to bear, some problems remain out of our control. When this is the case, we can tell the truth: "It's too big and too mean. I can't handle it."

Releasing control, receiving help

Desperately struggling to control a problem can easily result in the problem's controlling you. Surrender is letting go of being the master in order to avoid becoming the slave.

Once you have acknowledged your lack of control, all that remains is to surrender. Many traditions make note of this. Western religions speak of surrendering to God. Hindus say surrender to the Self. Members of Alcoholics Anonymous talk about turning their lives over to a Higher Power. Agnostics might suggest surrendering to the ultimate source of power. Others might speak of following their intuition, their inner guide, or their conscience. William James wrote about surrender as a part of the conversion experience.[10]

In any case, surrender means being receptive to help. Once we admit that we're at the end of our rope, we open ourselves up to receiving help. We learn that we don't have to go it alone. We find out that other people have faced similar problems and survived. We give up our old habits of thinking and behaving as if we have to be in control of everything. We stop acting as general manager of the universe. We surrender. And that creates a space for something new in our lives.

Surrender works

Surrender works for life's major barriers as well as for its insignificant hassles.

You might say, as you struggle to remember someone's name, "It's on the tip of my tongue." Then you surrender. You give up trying and say, "Oh well, it will come to me later." Then the name pops into your mind.

An alcoholic admits that he just can't control his drinking. This becomes the key that allows him to seek treatment.

A person with multiple sclerosis admits that she's gradually losing the ability to walk. She tells others about this fact. Now the people around her can understand, be supportive, and explore ways to help.

A man is devastated when his girlfriend abandons him. He is a "basket case," unable to work for days. Instead of struggling against this fact, he simply admits the full extent of his pain. In that moment, he is able to trust. He trusts that help will come and that one day he will be OK again. He trusts in his ability to learn and to create a new life. He trusts that new opportunities for love will come his way.

After trying unsuccessfully for years to have a baby, a couple finally surrenders and considers adoption. The woman then conceives in a few months.

After finding out she has terminal cancer, a woman shifts between panic and depression. Nothing seems to console her. Finally, she accepts the truth and stops fighting her tragedy. She surrenders. Now at peace, she invests her remaining years in meaningful moments with the people she loves.

A writer is tackling the first chapter of his novel, feeling totally in control. He has painstakingly outlined the whole plot, recording each character's actions on individual 3x5 cards. Three sentences into his first draft, he finds that he's spending most of his time shuffling cards instead of putting words on paper. Finally, he puts the cards aside, forgets about the outline, and just tells the story. The words start to flow effortlessly, and he loses himself in the act of writing.

In each of these cases, the people involved learned the power of surrendering.

What surrender is not

Surrender is not resignation. It is not a suggestion to quit and do nothing about your problems. You have many skills and resources. Use them. You can apply all of your energy to handling a situation and surrender at the same time. Surrender includes doing whatever you can in a positive, trusting spirit. Giving up is fatalistic and accomplishes nothing. So let go, keep going, and know that the true source of control lies beyond you.

Once we admit that we're at the end of our rope, we open ourselves up to receiving help.

This Power Process says, in effect, don't fight the current. Imagine a person rafting down a flowing river with a rapid current. She's likely to do fine if she surrenders control and lets the raft flow with the current. After all, the current always goes around the rocks. If she tries to fight the current, she could end up in an argument with a rock about where the current is going—and lose.

Detachment helps us surrender

Watching yourself with detachment can help your ability to surrender. Pretend that you are floating away from your body, and then watch what's going on from a distance.

Objectively witness the drama of your life unfolding as if you were watching a play. When you see yourself as part of a much broader perspective, surrender seems obvious and natural.

"Surrender" might seem inconsistent with the Power Process: "I create it all." An old parable says that the Garden of Truth, the grand place everyone wants to enter, is guarded by two monsters—Fear and Paradox. Most of us can see how fear keeps us from getting what we want. The role of paradox might not be as clear.

The word *paradox* refers to a seemingly contradictory statement that might nonetheless be true. It is our difficulty in holding seemingly contradictory thoughts that sometimes keeps us out of the Garden of Truth. If we suspend the sovereignty of logic, we might discover that ideas that seem contradictory can actually coexist. With application, we can see that both "Surrender" and "I create it all" are valuable tools. ◪

put it to work

Suggestions for managing your health can help you achieve the mental and physical energy needed to work to your full capacity. Following are ways to transfer two key topics of this chapter—physical health and substance abuse—to the workplace.

Apply insights from ergonomics. The field of study called *ergonomics* focuses on ways to prevent health problems due to human behavior and workplace conditions. Recently, specialists in ergonomics have developed many suggestions for people who work continually at computers. These people can experience health problems that range from eyestrain and lower back pain to numbness in the arms and wrists.

You can hire specialists in ergonomics to redesign your workspace. That costs money. The following suggestions are free:

- *Rest your eyes.* To prevent eyestrain caused by staring too long at a computer screen, give your eyes rest from time to time. Looking out a window or at another object that is closer or farther away can help by forcing your eyes to readjust their focus. Also, set up your computer away from windows so that you can avoid squinting as you look at the screen.

- *Take breaks.* Get away from the computer. Stretch. Move. Walk, jog, or run.

- *Pay attention to your posture.* To avoid lower back problems, pay attention to your posture as you sit at the computer. Adjust your chair so that you can sit comfortably, with your back relaxed and your spine erect. Placing a pillow or small cushion behind your lower back might help.

- *Type with the keyboard in your lap.* This allows your hands to be lower than your elbows and minimizes the tension in your shoulders.

The idea behind each of the above suggestions is to position yourself so that you remain alert *and* relaxed while you're at the computer. Taking some simple precautions now can help you avoid feeling like a pretzel in a few years.

Remember the toll that addiction to alcohol and other drugs can take on your workplace. Employees who show up to work hung over or "under the influence" are, at the very least, unproductive. If they drive or operate machinery, they are downright dangerous. Use your skill with "I" statements (see Chapter Eight: Communicating) to speak candidly with a colleague about her drinking or drug use problem and offer help.

Name _____ Date _____/_____/_____

1. Explain three ways you can respond effectively if someone you know threatens to commit suicide.

2. The suggestions for building self-efficacy include setting goals with care. Give an example of how student athletes can apply this suggestion.

3. How does the Power Process: "Surrender" differ from giving up?

4. A person infected with HIV might have no symptoms for months—sometimes years. True or False? Explain your answer.

5. Define *date rape* and describe at least two ways to protect yourself against it.

6. List at least three dietary guidelines that can contribute to your health.

7. One of the suggestions for dealing with addiction is "Pay attention." This implies that it's OK to use drugs, as long as you do so with full awareness. True or False? Explain your answer.

8. Name at least three methods for preventing unwanted pregnancy.

9. Sometimes it's a good idea to allow yourself to feel bad for a while. True or False? Explain your answer.

10. Give an example of how advertisements that feature athletes can distort our perception of a product.

learning styles application

The questions below will "cycle" you through four styles, or modes, of learning as explained in the article "Learning styles: Discovering how you learn" in Chapter One. Each question will help you explore a different mode. You can answer the questions in any order.

what if *After using a plan to improve your health based on the suggestions in this chapter, consider how well the plan worked for you. Which actions do you intend to continue on a regular basis? Are there any new actions you intend to take?*

why *Name one specific health benefit you'd like to gain from this chapter. Possibilities include stress reduction, weight loss, or a higher energy level.*

how *Using suggestions from this chapter, create an action plan for meeting an important goal relating to your health. List the actions you will take and set a date for taking each action or beginning a new health habit. (Continue writing on additional paper, if necessary.)*

what *List three suggestions from this chapter that can help you meet an important goal relating to your health.*

master student profile

WILMA RUDOLPH

(1940–1994) In the 1960 Olympics she became the first American woman runner to win three gold medals. These accomplishments came in the face of adversity as she grew up amid poverty and racial discrimination and was the victim of childhood illness.

I **was the first girl out there at** practice and the last one to leave, I loved it so. We had some more of those playday-type meets early that season, and I kept on winning all the races I was in. I felt unbeatable.

Then came the big meet at Tuskegee, Alabama. It was the big meet of the year. Girls from all over the South were invited down there to run, and the competition was the best for high school kids.

All the way down to Alabama, we talked and laughed and had a good time, and Coach Gray would tell us how tough the competition was going to be, especially the girls from Atlanta, Georgia, because they had a lot of black schools down there, and they had these track programs that ran the whole year because of the warm weather.

When we got to the track, these girls from Georgia really looked like runners, but I paid them no mind because, well, I was a little cocky. I did think I could wipe them out because, after all, I had won every single race I had ever been in up to that point. So what happens? I got wiped out. It was the absolute worst experience of my life. I did not win a single race I ran in, nor did I qualify for anything. I was totally crushed. The girls from Georgia won everything. It was the first time I had ever tasted defeat in track, and it left me a total wreck. I can't remember ever being so totally crushed by anything.

After so many easy victories, using natural ability alone, I got a false sense of being unbeatable. But losing to those girls from Georgia, who knew every trick in the book, that was sobering. It brought me back down to earth, and it made me realize that I couldn't do it on natural ability alone, that there was more to track than just running fast. I also realized it was going to test me as a person—could I come back and win again after being so totally crushed by a defeat?

I ran and ran and ran every day, and I acquired this sense of determination, this sense of spirit that I would never, never give up, no matter what else happened. That day at Tuskegee had a tremendous effect on me inside.

Losing as badly as I did had an impact on my personality. Winning all the time in track had given me confidence; I felt like a winner. But I didn't feel like a winner any more after Tuskegee. My confidence was shattered and I was thinking the only way I could put it all together was to get back the next year and wipe them all out.

But looking back on it all, I realized somewhere along the line that to think that way wasn't necessarily right, that it was kind of extreme. I learned a very big lesson for the rest of my life as well. The lesson was, winning is great, sure, but if you are really going to do something in life, the secret is learning how to lose. Nobody goes undefeated all the time. If you can pick up after a crushing defeat, and go on to win again, you are going to be a champion someday. But if losing destroys you, it's all over. You'll never be able to put it all back together again. ◪

From *Wilma* by Wilma Rudolph and Bud Greenspan. Copyright © 1977 by Bud Greenspan. Used by permission of Dutton Signet, a division of Penguin Group (USA), Inc.

For further biographical information about Wilma Rudolph, visit the Master Student Hall of Fame on the *Becoming a Master Student Athlete* Web site at

masterstudent.college.hmco.com

12

What's Next?

Live as if you were to die tomorrow. Learn as if you were to live forever.

GANDHI

I try to keep in mind not what I have accomplished but what I have to accomplish in the future.

JACKIE JOYNER-KERSEE

why
this chapter matters . . .

You can use the techniques introduced in this book to set and achieve goals for the rest of your life.

what
is included . . .

Now that you're done—begin ". . . use the following suggestions to continue . . ."
Transferring to another school
Career planning: Begin the process now
Jumpstart your education with transferable skills
Use résumés and interviews to "hire" an employer
Cruising for jobs on the Internet
Contributing: The art of selfishness
Service learning: The art of learning by contributing
Define your values, align your actions
One set of values
Power Process: "Be it"
Master Student Profile: John Wooden

how
you can use this chapter . . .

Choose the next steps in your education and career.
Experience the joys of contributing.
Use a Power Process that enhances every technique in this book.

as you read, ask yourself
what if . . .

I could create the life of my dreams—starting today?

Now that you're done—begin

If you used this book fully—if you actively partici-pated in reading the contents, writing the journals, doing the exercises, practicing critical thinking, com-pleting the learning styles applications, and applying the suggestions—you have had quite a journey.

Recall some high points of that journey. The first half of this book is about the nuts and bolts of education—the business of acquiring knowledge and skill. It prepares you for the athletic and academic challenges of higher educa-tion. It also suggests that you take a First Step by telling the truth about your skills and setting goals to expand them. Also included are guidelines for planning your time, making your memory more effective, improving your reading skills, taking useful notes, and succeeding at tests.

All of this activity prepares you for another aim of education—generating new knowledge and creating a unique place for yourself in the world. Meeting this aim leads you to the topics in the second half of this book: thinking for yourself, enhancing your communication skills, embracing diversity, mastering technology, and living with vibrant health.

Now what? What's the next step?

As you ponder this question, consider the possibility that you can create the life of your dreams. Your responses to the ideas, exercises, and Journal Entries in this book can lead you to think new thoughts, say new things, and do what you never believed you could do at a level you might have previously thought was impossible. The possibilities are endless. This message is more fundamental than any individual tool or technique you'll ever read about.

There are people who scoff at the suggestion that they can create the life of their dreams. These people have a perspective that is widely shared. Please release it.

You are on the edge of a universe so miraculous and full of wonder that your imagination at its most creative moment cannot encompass it. Paths are open to lead you to worlds beyond your wildest dreams.

If this sounds like a pitch for the latest recreational drug, it might be. That drug is adrenaline, and it is automatically generated by your body when you are learning, growing, taking risks, preparing for competition, and discovering new worlds inside and outside your skin.

One of the first articles in this book is about transitions. You are about to make another transition—not just to ano-ther chapter of this book but to the next chapter of your life. The next pages of your life may include participation in athletics, or in new activities that are equally inspiring. Remember the process of discovery, intention, and action.

This tool can help you master any change and achieve any goal. In the following pages, look for ways to reinforce this process. Use it to choose what's next for you. ⬙

journal entry 30

Discovery/Intention Statement

Complete the following sentences with the first thoughts that come to mind.

From my life, I have discovered that I want . . .

_____

_____

_____

_____

_____

To get what I want from my life, I intend to . . .

_____

_____

_____

_____

_____

voices

student

After reading this book, my professor challenged our class to come up with a list of how we could apply the strategies we learned to promote our success in intercollegiate athletics and in our fu-ture workplace. In reviewing the table of contents, I discovered that almost every skill could be turned into an applicable career tool for both of these areas. I intend to discuss these master stu-dent qualities in my pursuit of improved athletic performances and in an upcoming job interview.

— CALVIN WHITE

"...use the following suggestions to continue..."

Keep a journal. Psychotherapist Ira Progoff based his Intensive Journal System on the idea that regular journaling can be a path to life-changing insights.[1] To begin journaling, consider buying a bound notebook in which to record your private reflections and dreams for the future. Get one that will be worthy of your personal discoveries and intentions. Write in this journal daily. Record what you are learning about yourself and the world.

Write about your hopes, wishes, and goals, including your athletic goals. Keep a record of significant events. Consider using the format of Discovery Statements and Intention Statements that you learned in this book.

Take a workshop. Schooling doesn't have to stop at graduation, and it doesn't have to take place on a campus. In most cities, there are a variety of organizations that sponsor ongoing workshops, covering topics from cosmetology to cosmology. Use workshops to learn skills, understand the world, and discover yourself. You can be trained in cardiopulmonary resuscitation (CPR), attend a lecture on anaerobic training, or take a course on assertiveness training.

Read, watch, and listen. Ask friends and instructors what they are reading. Sample a variety of newspapers and magazines. None of them has all of the truth; most of them have a piece of it. In addition to books, many bookstores and publishing houses offer audio and video recordings on personal growth topics. Record your most exciting discoveries in an idea file. Remember, an exciting discovery can occur as the result of a success or a failure.

Take an unrelated class. Sign up for a class that is totally unrelated to your major. If you are studying to be a coach, take a physics course. If you are going to be a doctor, take a bookkeeping course. Take a course that will help you develop new computer skills and expand your possibilities for online learning.

You can discover a lot about yourself and your intended future when you step out of old patterns. In addition to formal courses offered at your school, check into local community education courses. Offer to volunteer for youth groups and programs. You will be amazed at what you can learn about yourself through the eyes of a child. These offer a low-cost alternative that poses no threat to your grade point average.

Travel. See the world. Visit new neighborhoods. Find out what it looks like inside buildings and cultures that you normally have no reason to enter, museums that you never found interesting before, cities that are out of the way, forests and mountains that lie beyond your old boundaries, and far-off places that require planning and saving to reach. Through organized athletics you may be able to travel to other countries. Don't simply go there to compete. Go there to learn and explore.

Get counseling. Solving emotional problems is not the only reason to visit a counselor or sport psychologist. These people are also excellent resources for personal growth. You can use counseling to look at and talk about yourself in ways that might be uncomfortable for anyone except a trained professional. If you have been involved in a sport that focuses on the team's outcome, you may find it refreshing that counseling offers a chance to focus exclusively on yourself, something that is usually not possible in many normal social settings.

Form a support group. Just as a well-organized study group can promote your success in school, an organized support group can help you reach goals in other areas of your life.

Today, people in support groups help one another lose weight, stay sober, cope with chronic illness, recover from emotional trauma, and overcome drug addiction.

Groups can also brainstorm possibilities for job hunting, career planning, parenting, solving problems in relationships, preparing for athletic competition, promoting spiritual growth—for reaching almost any goal you choose.

Find a mentor—or become one. Seek the counsel of experienced people you respect and admire. Use them as role models. If they are willing, ask them to be sounding boards for your plans and ideas. Many people are flattered to be asked.

You can also become a mentor. If you want to perfect your skills as a master student athlete, teach them to another team member or someone else. Offer to coach another student in study skills in exchange for childcare, free lunches, or something else you value. A mentor relationship can bridge the boundaries of age, race, and culture.

Redo this book. Start by redoing one chapter or maybe just one exercise. If you didn't get everything you wanted from this book, it's never too late.

You can also reread and redo portions that you found valuable. As you plan your career and hunt for jobs, you might find that the Put It to Work articles in each chapter acquire new meaning. Redo the quizzes to test your ability to recall certain information. Redo the exercises that were particularly effective for you. They can work again. Many of the exercises in this book can produce a different result after a few months. You are changing, and your responses change, too.

The Discovery Wheel can be useful in revealing techniques you have actually put into practice. This exercise is available online at **masterstudent.college.hmco.com,** and you can redo it as many times as you like. You can also redo the Journal Entries. If you keep your own journal, refer to it as you rewrite the Journal Entries in this book.

As you redo this book or any part of it, reconsider techniques that you skimmed over or skipped before. They might work for you now. Modify the suggestions or add new ones. Redoing this book can refresh and fine-tune your study habits.

Another way to redo this book is to retake your student success course. People who do this often say that the second time is much different from the first. They pick up ideas and techniques that they missed the first time around and gain deeper insight into things they already know. ▨

DO SOMETHING YOU CAN'T

Few significant accomplishments result when people stick to the familiar. You can accomplish much more than you think you can. Doing something you can't involves taking risks.

This exercise has three parts.

Part 1 Select something that you have never done before, that you don't know how to do, that you are fearful of doing, or that you think you probably can't do. Use the space below to describe the thing you have chosen.

Be smart. Don't pick something that will hurt you physically, such as flying from a third-floor window.

_____

_____

_____

_____

Part 2 Do it. Of course, this is easier to say than to do. This exercise is not about easy. It is about discovering capabilities that stretch your self-image.

In order to accomplish something that is bigger than your self-perceived abilities, use any of the tools you have gained from this book. Develop a plan. Divide and conquer. Stay focused. Use outside resources. Let go of self-destructive thoughts.

Summarize the tools you will use.

_____

_____

_____

_____

Part 3 In the space below, write about the results of this exercise.

_____

_____

_____

_____

Transferring
to another school

Transferring to a different school involves a decision that will have a major impact on your academic and athletic career. This is true at many points in higher education—such as when you're transferring from a two-year to a four-year school, or when you're choosing a graduate school.

Selecting a school for the next step in your higher education is much like choosing a career. First, you define the profile of an ideal prospective school, much as you would that of an ideal job. Next, you create a profile of yourself—your skills, background, experience, learning style, and other preferences. Then you seek a reasonable fit between yourself and your ideal school, just as you seek a fit between yourself and your ideal job.

The following suggestions can assist you in making this important decision.

Know key terms. As you begin researching schools, take a few minutes to review some key terms.

Articulation agreements are official documents that spell out the course equivalents a school accepts.

An *Associate of Arts (A.A.)* or *Associate of Science (A.S.)* is the degree title conferred by many two-year colleges. Having a degree from a two-year college might save you time and money when transferring to another school. It may also assure you of being admitted into a public four-year school that is in the same state as a two-year college. Be sure to ask your academic advisor about transfer preparation guidelines.

Course equivalents are courses you've already taken that another school will accept as meeting its requirements. Since no two schools offer the same curriculum, determining course equivalents is often a matter of interpretation. In some cases, you might be able to persuade a registrar or an admissions office to accept some of your previous courses.

Prerequisites are courses or skills that a school requires students to complete or have before they enter or graduate.

Transfer is an official term for changing schools.

Learn about the different types of schools. Schools differ in countless dimensions. Start by digging up facts in the following areas about each school you're considering. Key factors include: location; reputation; mission or religious affiliation; number of students and their diversity; class sizes; opportunities for contact with instructors; availability of courses, majors, and degrees that interest you; costs for tuition, fees, books, and a residence hall or other housing.

In addition, resources such as counseling centers, computer labs, academic assistance centers, career-planning centers, or job placement offices can be critical to your success in school. Check out the availability of these services at each school you consider.

Also consider admissions criteria. Some schools are highly competitive, admitting only a small percentage of the students who apply each year. Other schools are relatively open, admitting most students with high school diplomas. Schools that practice "enrollment management" may admit students but place limits on the number or type of students enrolled in each major field of study.

Find out the special admission criteria that transferring student athletes must meet. These are likely to be determined by rules from the NCAA or another athletic conference.

Another factor is the availability of financial aid. Organizations such as the NCAA have limits on the number of athletic scholarships that can be awarded for each team. And not every student athlete who receives an athletic scholarship gets a full scholarship.

If athletic scholarships are not available, check to see if you qualify for other types of financial aid that you can accept as a student athlete. In most cases, you can accept grants-in-aid and scholarships from sources other than a college or university athletics department that

- do not have athletics ability as a major criterion,
- do not restrict your attendance to a particular institution, and
- when combined with any athletically related financial aid, do not exceed your annual cost of attendance at a school.

The athletics compliance or financial aid offices at your current and future schools can help. Know exactly what financial aid you are going to receive and what it will provide.

Other questions to ask due to your status as a student athlete are:

- Will transferring lead to any eligibility penalty?
- If I transfer, will I be able to play immediately?
- How stable is the coaching staff at the schools I'm considering?
- Do I see myself fitting in with the other members of another school's team?
- Will transferring to another school improve my chances to play professionally?
- If I transfer, will my parents, other relatives, and friends be able to see me compete?

Meet with your athletic advisor to make sure you know all rules governing transfers and eligibility. Remember that a coach at another school cannot talk to you about transferring until you receive permission from your current school and coach to transfer. Plan to get this permission early on.

Dig up other key facts. Before you transfer to any school or choose a graduate program, gather some facts about you. This includes grades, courses completed, degrees attained, and grade point average (GPA). The head coach at another school may require that your current school send a copy of your academic transcript.

Standardized test scores are also important, such as those for the Scholastic Aptitude Test (SAT), the American College Test (ACT), the Graduate Record Exam (GRE), and any advanced placement tests you've taken.

Also keep a folder of syllabuses from your courses. They can help you get transfer credits that will apply toward your degree and athletic eligibility.

List each school's course requirements. Note all prerequisites, including those required for general education or your proposed major, and any other courses required for graduation. Large universities have staff members who will check the availability of courses in your major, including any graduate courses and advanced

degrees. Find out who these people are and contact them. If you visit another school, meet with them in person.

With your requirements in hand, begin creating a list of course equivalents. Most schools will have specific worksheets for this purpose. A school's registrar, admissions office, or academic athletic advisor can answer questions about how to complete these forms and how your past courses apply to a degree at their school.

Check these sources of information. When researching another school, you can turn to three basic sources of information.

Materials include print sources, such as school catalogs. Also check more general guides, such as *Barron's Profiles of American Colleges, Peterson's National College Data Bank,* or *The Big Book of Minority Opportunities: The Directory of Special Programs for Minority Group Members.* In addition, many schools have sites on the World Wide Web.

You may also want to search the archives of the *NCAA News* or other sports periodicals to learn about a school's past athletic performance and history of rules compliance.

People include instructors, academic advisors, counselors, coaches, and other school staff members. Also seek out current students and future teammates at the schools you are considering. Ask about faculty, coaches, and other staff members. It may be helpful to talk to former students who are now working in your chosen field.

Your own experience includes a visit to the two or three schools on the top of your list. This experience can be more intensive if you work in the surrounding community for a summer or take a course at the school before you transfer.

Put this choice in context. Consider the needs and wishes of your family members. Ask for their guidance and support. If you involve them in any decision about changing schools, they can have more stake in your success.

In addition, consider the purposes, values, and long-term goals you've generated through exercises such as the "Create a lifeline" exercise in Chapter Two and the Journal Entries in this book. All of these can have a bearing on the school you select.

Your experience of a school goes well beyond the facts listed in the catalog. After you gather facts, let them simmer in your subconscious. Then pay attention to your instincts and intuition—your attraction to one school or feelings of hesitation about another.

Finally, just choose. There is no one "right" school for you, and you could probably thrive at many schools (perhaps even your current one). Use the suggestions in this book to practice self-responsibility and take charge of your education—no matter what school you attend. ⊠

Career planning

Begin the process now

A satisfying and lucrative career is often the goal of education. To meet that goal, clearly define your career and your path to entering that career. Then you can plan your education effectively.

Career planning can be the bridge between your dreams and the reality of your future.

There are many effective ways to plan your career. All are based on knowledge of yourself—your skills and interests—and of the skills demanded in the work world. Begin your career-planning adventure now by remembering the following ideas.

Acknowledge what you already know

When students seek to expand their skills, they usually start with finding out things they don't know. That means discovering new strategies for taking notes, reading, writing, managing time, and the other subjects covered in this book.

Career planning is different. Begin by realizing how much you *do* know. You've already made many decisions about your career. This is true for young people who say, "I don't have any idea what I want to be when I grow up." It's also true for midlife career changers.

Consider the student who can't decide if he wants to be a cost accountant or a tax accountant and then jumps to the conclusion that he is totally lost when it comes to career planning. Actually, he's already discovered he *doesn't* want to be a doctor, playwright, or taxicab driver. He knows he likes working with numbers and balancing books.

The same could be said about a student who doesn't know if he wants to be a veterinary assistant or a nurse. He's already ruled out becoming a lawyer, computer programmer, or teacher. He just isn't sure whether he has a bedside manner for horses or for people.

You have probably narrowed your list of career choices to a number of jobs in the same field that draw on the same core skills. Demonstrate this for yourself right now. Find a long list of occupations. (One is published by the U.S. Department of Labor on its Occupational Information Network, online at **http://online.onetcenter.org**.) Using a stack of 3x5 cards, write down 50 to 100 randomly selected job titles, one title per card. Sort through the cards and divide them into two piles. Label one pile "Careers I've Definitely Ruled Out for Now." Label the other pile "Possibilities I'm Willing to Consider."

Students commonly go through a stack of 100 such cards and end up with 95 in the "definitely ruled out" pile and five in the "possibilities" pile. This demonstrates that they already have a career in mind.

Create multiple career paths

As a student athlete, it is important for you to begin career planning as soon as you enter college. Perhaps the first goal that comes to your mind is a career in professional sports. Fine. To maximize your options for the future, also plan for other careers. The few student athletes who are lucky enough "go pro" usually retire with decades left to pursue another career. Mastering the process of planning now allows you to make seamless transitions from one career to another at any stage of life.

Through career planning, you create long-term balance in your life between athletics and goals beyond athletics. Your experience as a student and as an athlete will be a powerful asset in the future, and you will be able to apply that experience to multiple careers. With appropriate training to round out your skills, your job title might be:

- Advertising consultant
- Athletic academic advisor

- Athletic coach
- Community recreation counselor
- Computer programmer
- Corporate fitness instructor
- Dietician
- Executive coach
- Guidance counselor
- Image consultant
- Life coach
- Marketing director
- Occupational therapist
- Personal trainer
- Physical therapist
- Physician assistant
- Public relations director
- Real estate agent
- Sales director
- Sports academy counselor
- Teacher
- Web site manager

These are just a few examples. As a student athlete, you could find a natural fit in many jobs that call for leadership, teamwork, and other skills you're developing.

Discover your skills

The word *job* brings to mind many terms. Among them are *task, role, duty, chore, responsibility,* and *function.* But one word comes closest to the heart of what we do in our jobs. That word is *skill.*

Skills are the core content—the "skeleton"—of any job. A career consists of the skills you use across several jobs in a related field. Learn to talk the language of skills and you'll become an ace career planner. You'll also find it easier to choose your major.

Begin from the perspective that you have many skills. The *Encarta World English* dictionary defines *skill* as "the ability to do something well, usually gained through experience and training."

Note the flexibility in this definition. You can gain skills by taking advanced degrees or spending years in the work force. But there are ways to gain skills other than formal education or professional experience. In fact, *any* activity that you improve with practice can be called a skill. Just

by going to school, relating to people, and pursuing your interests, you're constantly developing skills. If you can run a meeting, organize your study area, plant a garden, comfort a troubled friend, or draw interesting doodles, you've got skills that are worth money.

To learn more, do Exercise #27: "Recognize your skills" on page 311. And to link your skills with possible careers, do the online Skills Search from the Occupational Information Network at **http://online.onetcenter.org**.

Plan by naming names

One key to making your career plan real and to ensuring that you can act on it is naming. You can create a powerful career plan simply by naming names:

- *Name your job.* Take the skills you enjoy using and find out which jobs use them. What are those jobs called? List them. Note that the same job might have different names.

- *Name your company—the agency or organization you want to work for.* If you want to be self-employed or start your own business, name the product or service you'd sell. Also list some possible names for your business.

- *Name your contacts.* Take the list of organizations you just compiled. What people in these organizations are responsible for hiring? List those people and contact them directly. If you choose self-employment, list the names of possible customers or clients. All of these people are job contacts.

  Expand your list of contacts by brainstorming with your family and friends. Come up with a list of names—anyone who can help you with career planning and job hunting. Write each of these names on a 3x5 card or Rolodex card. You can also use a spiral-bound notebook or a computer.

  Next, call the key people on your list. After you speak with them, make brief notes about what you discussed. Also jot down any actions you agreed to take, such as a follow-up call.

  Consider everyone you meet a potential member of your job network. Also be prepared to talk about what you do. Develop a "pitch"—a short statement of your career goal that you can easily share with your contacts. For example: "After I graduate, I plan to work in the travel business. I'm looking for an internship in a travel agency for next summer. Do you know of any agencies that take interns?"

- *Name your location.* Ask if your career choices are consistent with your preferences about where to live and work. For example, someone who wants to make a living as a studio musician might consider living in a large city such as New York or Toronto. This contrasts with the freelance graphic artist who conducts his business mainly by phone, fax, and e-mail. He might be able to live anywhere and still pursue his career.

Ask for assistance

Don't go it alone. Help with career planning is yours for the asking. Taking advantage of these resources can reduce the time, money, and effort it takes to create the career of your dreams.

Start with career-planning books and Web sites. Also take career-planning courses and seminars sponsored by your school. Visit the career-planning and job placement offices on campus. Ask career counselors about skills assessments and help for identifying jobs that call for those skills.

Check out career-planning resources that are specially designed for student athletes. These include athletic academic counselors, coaches, and staff members involved with the CHAMPS/Life Skills program. Many athletic departments offer career-planning workshops for student athletes.

Also connect directly to role models—student athletes who have moved successfully into their dream careers. Learn about their career-planning strategies. Ask if you can "shadow" them on the job to directly observe how their athletic skills are broadened and applied in the workplace.

Test your career choice—
and be willing to change

Once you have a possible career choice in mind, run some informal tests to see if it will work for you. For example:

■ Contact people who are actually doing the job you're researching and ask them what it's like (an *information interview*).

■ Choose an internship or volunteer position in a field that interests you.

■ Get a part-time job in your career field during the off-season or summer.

The people you meet through these experiences are possible sources of recommendations, referrals, and employment in the future.

Keep a log of the activities you perform in these positions and the skills you're developing. Update your records at least once each year. When it comes time to prepare your résumé, you'll be glad you did.

Remember your purpose

While digging deep into the details of career planning, take some time to back up to the big picture. Listing skills, researching jobs, writing résumés—all of this is necessary and useful. At the same time, attending to these tasks can obscure our broadest goals. To get perspective, we can go back to the basics—a life purpose.

Your deepest desire might be to see that hungry children are fed, to make sure that beautiful music keeps getting heard, or to help alcoholics become sober. When such a large purpose is clear, smaller decisions about what to do are often easier.

A life purpose makes a career plan simpler and more effective. It cuts through the stacks of job data and employment figures. Your life purpose is like the guidance system for a rocket. It keeps the plan on target while revealing a path for soaring to the heights.

➔ Twenty-five transferable skills

Use the following list of transferable skills as a starting point for making an inventory of your abilities. There are literally hundreds of transferable skills, so expand this list based on your own lifetime of experiences.

Analyzing	Planning
Budgeting	Problem solving
Coaching	Reading
Consulting	Researching
Decision making	Selling
Editing	Serving customers
Evaluating	Speaking
Interviewing	Supervising
Learning	Thinking critically
Listening	Training
Managing time	Writing
Negotiating	Working on teams
Organizing	

See a career as your creation

Many people approach career planning as if they were panning for gold. They keep sifting through the dirt, clearing the dust, and throwing out the rocks. They are hoping to strike it rich and discover the perfect career.

Other people believe that they'll wake up one morning, see the heavens part, and suddenly know what they're supposed to do. Many of them are still waiting for that magical day to dawn.

We can approach career planning in a different way. Instead of seeing a career as something we discover, we can see it as something we choose. We don't find the right career. We create it.

There's a big difference between these two approaches. Thinking that there's only one "correct" choice for your career can lead to a lot of anxiety: "Did I choose the right one?" "What if I made a mistake?"

Viewing your career as your creation helps you relax. Instead of anguishing over finding the right career, you can stay open to possibilities. Choose one career today, knowing that you can choose again later.[2] ⬙

---

exercise 27

RECOGNIZE YOUR SKILLS

 Student athletes who create a résumé are sometimes concerned about their lack of work experience. They take for granted all the skills they acquire while training and competing. To energize your career plan, start becoming aware of these skills now.

This exercise about discovering your skills includes three steps. Before you begin, gather at least 100 3x5 cards and a pen or pencil. Allow about one hour to complete the exercise.

Step 1

Recall your activities during the past week or month. To refresh your memory, review your responses to the Time Monitor/Time Plan in Chapter Two. (You might even benefit from doing that exercise again.)

List each activity on a separate 3x5 card. Write down as many activities as you can. Include work-related activities, school activities, and hobbies. Some of your cards might read "washed dishes," "tuned up my car," or "tutored a French class."

In addition to daily activities, recall any rewards you've received or recognition of your achievements during the past year. Examples include scholarship awards, athletic awards, or recognitions for volunteer work. Again, list the activities that were involved.

Spend 20 minutes on this step, listing all of the activities you can recall.

Step 2

Next, look over your activity cards. Then take another 20 minutes to list any specialized knowledge or procedures needed to complete those activities. These are your *content skills*. For example, tutoring a French class requires a working knowledge of that language. Tuning a car requires knowing how to adjust a car's timing and replace spark plugs. You could list several content skills for any one activity. Write each skill on a separate card and label it "Content."

Step 3

Go over your activity cards one more time. Look for examples of *transferable skills*. For instance, giving a speech or working as a salesperson in a computer store requires the ability to speak persuasively. That's a transferable skill. Tuning a car means that you can attend to details and troubleshoot. Tutoring in French requires teaching, listening, and speaking skills.

Write each of your transferable skills on a separate card.

Congratulations—you now have a detailed picture of your skills. Keep your lists of content and transferable skills on hand when writing your résumé, preparing for job interviews, and doing other career-planning tasks. As you think of new skills, add them to the lists.

Jumpstart your education with transferable skills

When meeting with an academic advisor, some students say, "I've just been taking general education and liberal arts courses. I haven't got any marketable skills."

Think again. Few words are as widely misunderstood as skill. Defining it carefully can have an immediate and positive impact on your career planning.

Two kinds of skills

One dictionary defines *skill* as "the ability to do something well, usually gained by training or experience." Some skills—such as the ability to repair fiber-optic cables or do brain surgery—are acquired through formal schooling, on-the-job training, or both. These abilities are called *work-content skills*. People with such skills have mastered a specialized body of knowledge needed to do a specific kind of work. Student athletes develop work-content skills in the sports in which they compete.

However, we develop another category of skills through experiences both inside and outside the classroom. We may never receive formal training to develop these abilities. Yet they are key to success in the workplace. These are *transferable skills*. Transferable skills are the kind of abilities that help people thrive in any job—no matter what work-content skills they have.

Perhaps you've heard someone described this way: "She's really smart and knows what she's doing, but she's got lousy people skills." People skills—such as *listening* and *negotiating*—are prime examples of transferable skills. Other examples are analyzing, budgeting, consulting, decision making, editing, evaluating, interviewing, learning, managing time, organizing, planning, reading, researching, problem solving, selling, serving customers, speaking, supervising, thinking critically, training, and writing. As a student athlete, you are developing a number of transferable skills that employers desire. Among them are leading, coaching, working on teams, responding to adversity, following directions, achieving goals, and competing.

Succeeding in many situations

Transferable skills are often invisible to us. The problem begins when we assume that a given skill can only be used in one context, such as being in school, competing in a particular sport, or working at a particular job. Thinking in this way places an artificial limit on our possibilities. As an alternative, think about the things you routinely do to succeed in school and in competition. Analyze your activities to isolate specific skills. Then brainstorm a list of jobs where you could use the same skills.

Consider the task of implementing a workout regimen. This calls for skills such as:

- *Interviewing* people who can help you devise a safe and effective regimen.
- *Researching* using the Internet and campus library to find out what regimens have worked for other people in your sport.
- *Planning* by setting goals for specific aspects of your performance that you want to improve.
- *Managing time* to allow for an effective workout program that will help you meet your goals by your target date.

Now consider the kinds of jobs that draw on these skills. For example, interviewing and research skills could help you enter the field of market research or journalism. Use the same kind of analysis to think about transferring skills from one job to another job. Say that you work part-time as an administrative assistant at a computer dealer that sells a variety of hardware and software. You take phone calls from potential customers, help current customers solve problems using their computers, and attend meetings where your coworkers plan ways to market new products. You are developing skills at *selling*, *serving customers*, and *working on teams* that could help you land a job as a sales representative for a computer manufacturer or software developer. The basic idea is to take a cue from the word *transferable*. Almost any skill you use to succeed in one situation can *transfer* to success in another situation.

The concept of transferable skills creates a powerful link between higher education and the work world. List the specific skills you are developing and ways to transfer them to the work world. Almost everything you do can be applied to your career.

Ask four questions

To experiment further with this concept of transferable skills, ask and answer four questions derived from the Master Student Map.

Why identify my transferable skills? Getting past the "I-don't-have-any-skills" syndrome means that you can approach job hunting with more confidence. As you uncover these hidden assets, your list of qualifications will grow as if by magic. You won't be padding your résumé. You'll simply be telling the full truth about what you can do.

Identifying your transferable skills takes a little time. But the payoffs are numerous. A complete and accurate list of transferable skills can help you land jobs that involve more responsibility, more variety, more freedom to structure your time, and more money.

Transferable skills also help you thrive in the midst of constant change. Technology will continue to upgrade. Ongoing discoveries in many fields could render current knowledge obsolete. Jobs that exist today may disappear in a few years, only to be replaced by entirely new ones. Your keys to prospering in this environment are transferable skills—those that you can carry from one career to another.

What are my transferable skills? Discover your transferable skills by reflecting on key experiences. Recall a time when you performed at the peak of your ability, overcame obstacles, won an award, gained a high grade, or met a significant goal. List the skills you used to create those successes.

Remember that the word *skill* points to something that you do. In your list of transferable skills, start each item with an action verb such as *budget* or *coach*. Or use a closely related part of speech—*budgeting* or *coaching*.

For a more complete picture of your transferable skills, describe the object of your action. Say that one of the skills on your list is *organizing*. This could refer to organizing ideas, organizing people, or organizing objects in a room. Specify the kind of organizing that you like to do.

How do I perform these skills? You can bring your transferable skills into even sharper focus by adding adverbs—words that describe *how* you take action. You might say that you edit *accurately* or learn *quickly*.

In summary, you can use a three-column chart to list your transferable skills. For example:

Verb	Object	Adverb
Organizing	Records	Effectively
Serving	Customers	Courteously
Coordinating	Special events	Efficiently

Add a specific example of each skill to your list, and you're well on the way to an engaging résumé and a winning job interview.

Focus on the skills that you most enjoy using, and look for careers and jobs that directly involve those skills.

What if I could expand my transferable skills? In addition to thinking about the skills you already have, consider the skills you'd like to acquire. Describe them in detail and list experiences that can help you develop them. Possibilities include extracurricular activities, group memberships, internships, volunteer positions, work-study assignments, and other part-time jobs. Throughout this book, *Put It to Work* articles highlight transferable skills you can continue to develop and transfer to the workplace. Let your list of transferable skills grow and develop as you do.

Use the SCANS reports to discover your skills

The U.S. Department of Labor has issued a series of reports created by the Secretary's Commission on Achieving Necessary Skills (SCANS). This influential series of documents lists essential skills for workers in the twenty-first century. Use this list as you assess your current skills and plan to develop new ones.

Basic skills. Read to locate and interpret written information. Write to communicate information. Listen to interpret verbal and nonverbal cues. Use arithmetic to perform basic computations and solve problems.

Thinking. Speak to inform and persuade. Think creatively, make decisions, and solve problems. Create and interpret pictures, graphs, and other visual tools. Choose learning strategies.

Personal qualities. Assess yourself accurately and set goals. Exert sustained effort to meet goals. Speak positively of your abilities. Demonstrate adaptability and empathy in social settings.

Resources. Budget time and money for goal-relevant activities. Allocate materials and facilities. Assign tasks effectively and provide coworkers with feedback.

Interpersonal skills. Participate as a member of a team. Teach others. Serve clients and customers. Exercise leadership. Negotiate to reach agreements. Work with diversity.

Information skills. Acquire and evaluate information. Organize and maintain information. Interpret and communicate information in oral, written, and visual forms. Use computers to process information.

Systems. Explain how social and technical systems operate. Monitor and correct system performance. Redesign to improve systems.

Technology Select and apply appropriate technology to complete tasks. Maintain and troubleshoot technology.[3]

Use résumés and interviews to "hire" an employer

The logical outcome of your career plan is a focused job hunt. To succeed at this task, remember that many job openings are never advertised. Employers typically turn to help wanted listings, résumés, and employment agencies only as a last resort. When jobs open up, they prefer instead to hire people they know—friends and colleagues, or people who walk through the door and prove that they're excellent candidates for available jobs.

Based on these discoveries, career counselor Richard Bolles recommends the following approach to job hunting:[4]

- Discover which skills you want to use in your career.
- Discover which jobs draw on the skills you want to use.
- Interview people who are doing the kind of jobs you'd want to do.
- Research companies you'd like to work for and find out what kinds of problems they face on a daily basis.
- Identify your contacts—a person at each one of these companies who has the power to hire you.
- Arrange an interview with that person, even if the company has no job openings at the moment.
- Stay in contact with the people who interviewed you, knowing that a job opening can occur at any time.

A powerful source of information about new jobs is people—friends, relatives, coworkers, and fellow students. Ask around. Tell everyone you want a job. One of them might be willing to *create* a job for you.

Use résumés to get interviews

If you act on the above list of suggestions, you'll probably meet someone who asks for your résumé. Remember that a résumé is not a dry recitation of facts or a laundry list of previous jobs. Instead, it is a piece of persuasive writing designed to get you to the next step in the hiring process, usually an interview.

Begin your résumé with your name, address, phone number, and e-mail address. Then name your desired job, often called an "objective" or "goal." Follow with the body of your résumé—your skills, work experience, and education. In fact, you can use those last three topics as major headings printed in bold in a larger font.

Write your résumé so that the facts leap off the page. Describe your work experiences in short phrases that start with active verbs: "*Supervised* three people." "*Wrote* two annual reports." Also leave reasonable margins and space between paragraphs.

As you draft your résumé, remember that every organization has problems to solve. Show in your résumé that you know about those problems and can offer your skills as solutions. Whenever you can, give evidence that you used those skills to get measurable results. For example: "Our program reduced the average training time for newly hired people by 25 percent."

Use interviews to screen employers

You might think of job interviews as a time when a potential employer sizes you up and possibly screens you out. Consider another viewpoint—that interviews offer you a chance to size up potential employers and possibly screen *them* out.

To get the most from your interviews, learn everything you can about each organization that interests you. Job interviewers have many standard questions. Most of them boil down to a few major concerns:

- How did you find out about us?
- Would we be comfortable working with you?
- How can you help us?
- Will you learn this job quickly?
- What makes you different from other applicants?

Before your interview, prepare some answers to these questions.

If you get turned down for the job after your interview, don't take it personally. Every interview is a source of feedback about what works—and what doesn't work—in contacting employers. Use that feedback to interview more effectively next time.[5]

Cruising for jobs on the Internet

Modern technology is creating new ways for you to plan your career and find jobs in the future. On the World Wide Web, you can research companies you'd like to work for, read lists of job openings, and post your résumé and a digital recording of yourself. Widespread availability of high-speed Internet access has increased the number of long-distance job interviews being conducted via video conference or in a real time chatroom, and has increased the possibility of sending an electronic portfolio attachment with a résumé.

According to one estimate, about two million people go online every month to hunt for jobs. That's a testament to the potential power of the digital medium and to some of its pitfalls as well. When you're looking for a job, the strength of the Internet—the sheer density of data—can also lead to frustration:

- The haphazard organization of the Internet makes it hard for potential employers to find your résumé when you post it online. The organizations you most want to work for might avoid using the Internet to find job applicants.

- Job openings listed on the Internet can be heavily skewed to certain fields, such as jobs for computer professionals or people in other technical fields.

- Across all fields, the majority of job openings are not listed on the Internet (or in newspaper want ads, for that matter).

The point is that posting a résumé on a Web site will not automatically lead to an e-mail in-basket that's bursting to its digital seams with job offers. For an effective job search, view the Internet as just one resource.

With this caveat in mind, you might choose to post your résumé online and scan Internet job ads. If you do, begin with sites such as that for JobBank USA (**http://www.jobbankusa.com**), which links to over 20 search engines for finding job openings. Also check Career-Builder.com (**http://www.CareerBuilder.com**) for want ads, updated weekly, from major U.S. newspapers.

When responding to ads and posting résumés online, avoid some common mistakes. One is to use word processing software to create lots of fancy formatting for your résumé and then attach it to an e-mail message. Many Web sites are not powerful enough to handle such formatting and will garble your attachments. Instead, skip the word processing and paste your résumé right into an e-mail message. Proofread it one more time before you hit the "send" button.

Some people create personal Web pages to highlight their accomplishments and entice employers. If you go this route, keep your page simple and easy to download. Some Web hosts will want to run banner ads on your page. These ads are widely seen as tacky. Avoid them.

Even if you don't choose to post a digital résumé or Web page, you can access career-planning resources on the Internet. Begin with "gateway" sites that offer organized links to many career-related pages on the World Wide Web. For instance, the Riley Guide (**http://www.rileyguide.com**) gives an overview of job hunting on the Internet.

Also check JobHuntersBible.com (**http://www.jobhuntersbible.com**), a site maintained by Richard Bolles, author of *What Color Is Your Parachute?* This site focuses on effective ways to use the Internet. And for some revealing figures, visit sites such as Salary.com to find out the current pay scales of typical jobs in your field. One way in which the Internet can really help you is in researching organizations before you contact them. Chances are that the company you're interested in has a Web site. Go to the site to gather information, discover the names of key players, and view financial data. Doing so will show potential employers that you've done your homework. That can make a favorable impression and even land you a job. ✉

journal entry 31

Intention Statement

Even if you are not sure of your career preference, write a career plan right now. Include three elements: a career goal, a list of steps you can take to prepare for that career, and a timeline for reaching that career goal.

Your plan might be incomplete or tentative. No problem. You can change this plan later—even throw it out and start all over. Career planning is a continual cycle of discovery, intention, and feedback.

The point is to dive into the process and make career planning a lifelong habit. This habit can radically affect the quality of your life.

You can plan now, with no further research. Go ahead. There's nothing to lose. On a separate sheet of paper, make an outline, do a mind map—use any format you like. Discover what you already know.

Mind map, outline, or write down your career plan now. You can also use a computer for this purpose.

Contributing:
The art of selfishness

This book is about contributing to yourself—about taking care of yourself and fulfilling your own needs. One result of all this successful selfishness is the capacity for giving back to others.

Contributing is what's left to do when your needs are fulfilled. People who are satisfied with life can share that satisfaction with others. It is not easy to contribute to another person's joy until you experience joy yourself.

Contributing is a satisfying activity for its own sake. And its benefits will come back to you. Volunteering your time to a worthy cause can help you develop new skills and make new friends. Through this activity you can explore possible career choices and expand your résumé. This can be especially valuable if your schedule as a student athlete makes it hard to work while you are in school.

Interdependence calls for contributing. Every day we stake our lives on the compassion of other people. When we drive, we depend on the skill of other drivers for our safety. We also depend on the sensibilities of world leaders for our survival. In this interdependent world, there is no such thing as win/lose. If others lose, their loss directly affects us. If we lose, it is more difficult to contribute to others. The only way to win and to get what we want in life is for others to win, also.

A caution. The idea of contributing is not the same as knowing what is best for other people. We can't know. True contributing occurs only after you find out what another person wants or needs and then determine that you can lovingly support his having it.

You can contribute globally and locally. To open up possibilities for contributing, consider the full scope of our international problems. According to the Human Development Report 2003, commissioned by the United Nations, 1.242 million people in the world live on less than one dollar per day.[6]

There are people and organizations devoted to ending global problems. By joining with them, you can help to create a new future for our planet. For example, world hunger groups want you to help feed starving people and inform all of us about the problems of malnutrition, food spoilage, and starvation. These groups include Oxfam America, CARE, and The Hunger Project.

You can also make a difference right in your own backyard. Many people enjoy seeing student athletes in action. By competing, you add something to their lives. At the same time, there's more to contributing than getting headlines and signing autographs. You can give something back to everyone in your community, even those who are not athletics fans.

Find ways to begin. Explore the CHAMPS/Life Skills program offered by the NCAA. It's designed to help student athletes get involved in community service. Many schools have a CHAMPS/Life Skills director. Check for campus departments that connect students to local nonprofit organizations looking for volunteers.

Follow through on your commitments. Set aside regular time in your schedule. You may find that the best time to volunteer is when your sport is not in season. If you do not feel comfortable volunteering by yourself, ask teammates or friends to participate.

Some nonprofit organizations offer a natural fit for student athletes. Examples include Boys and Girls Clubs and Big Brother/Big Sister programs. Also check out local day care centers, hospitals, and parks and recreation centers. You could assist in coaching local high school teams.

Hospitals and hospice programs often depend on volunteer help to supplement patient care provided by the professional staff. Nursing homes welcome visitors who are willing to spend time with residents. Most communities have volunteer-based programs for people living with HIV infection or AIDS.

Tutoring centers offer opportunities for competent students to help non–English-speaking people, grade school and high school students, and illiterate adults.

Political parties, candidates, and special interest groups need volunteers to stuff envelopes, gather petition signatures, distribute literature, and maintain Web sites.

The American Red Cross provides disaster relief. Local community care centers use volunteers to help feed homeless people. Service organizations such as Jaycees, Kiwanis, and Lions want members who are willing to serve others. Churches of all denominations want volunteers to assist with projects for the community and beyond.

Every day you can contribute to the well-being of your family, friends, classmates, teachers, teammates, and opponents. Contributing can become your way of being in the world. ◪

Service learning
The art of learning by contributing

As part of a service-learning project for a sociology course, students volunteer at a community center for older adults. For another service-learning project, history students interview people in veterans' hospitals about their war experiences. These students plan to share their interview results with a psychiatrist on the hospital staff. Meanwhile, business students provide free tax-preparation help at a center for low-income people. Students in graphic arts classes create free promotional materials for charities. Other students staff a food cooperative and community credit union.

These examples of actual projects from the National Service-Learning Clearinghouse demonstrate the working premise of service learning—that volunteer work and other forms of contributing can become a vehicle for higher education.

Service learning generally includes three elements: meaningful community service, a formal academic curriculum, and time for students to reflect on what they learn from service. That reflection can include speeches, journal writing, and research papers.

Service learning creates a win/win scenario. For one thing, students gain the satisfaction of contributing. They also gain experiences that can guide their career choices and help them develop job skills.

At the same time, service learning adds a valuable resource to the community with a handsome return on investment. For example, participants in the Learn and Serve program (administered by the Corporation for National and Community Service) provided community services valued at four times the program cost. When you design a service-learning project, consider these suggestions:

- Work with a community agency that has experience with students. Make sure that the agency has liability insurance to cover volunteers.

- Handle logistics. Integrating service learning into your schedule can call for detailed planning. If your volunteer work takes place off campus, arrange for transportation and allow for travel time.

- Reflect on your service-learning project with a tool you've used throughout this book—the Discovery and Intention Journal Entry system explained in the Introduction. Write Discovery Statements about what you want to gain from service learning and how you feel about what you're doing. Follow up with Intention Statements about what you'll do differently for your next volunteer experience.

- Include ways to evaluate your project. From your Intention Statements, create action goals and outcome goals. *Action goals* state what you plan to do and how many people you intend to serve, for instance, "We plan to provide 100 hours of literacy tutoring to 10 people in the community." *Outcome goals* describe the actual impact that your project will have: "At the end of our project, 60 percent of the people we tutor will be able to write a résumé and fill out a job application." Build numbers into your goals whenever possible. That makes it easier to evaluate the success of your project.

- Create a way to build long-term impact into your project. One potential pitfall of service learning is that the programs are often short-lived. After students pack up and return to campus, programs can die. To avoid this outcome, make sure that other students or community members are willing to step in and take over for you when the semester ends.

- Celebrate mistakes. If your project fails to meet its goals, have a party. State—in writing—the obstacles you encountered and ways to overcome them. The solutions you offer will be worth gold to the people who follow in your footsteps. Sharing the lessons learned from your mistakes is an act of service in itself. ◩

voices

student

I first began working with a local environmental organization in our community during my freshman year. It was intended partly as a way to be more social in a strange, new town, but after a year of service, we now have a university-supported recycling program that services both the students and the local residents.

—MANDY WISCONSIN

PRACTICING CRITICAL THINKING

12

Imagine that you are about to teach a student success course. Analyze the topic of student success and then create a brief outline or syllabus for the course. Choose the main subtopics you will cover, any texts or other materials you will use, and any guest speakers you will invite. Write down your ideas in the space below.

_____

_____

_____

_____

_____

_____

_____

_____

_____

_____

_____

_____

_____

_____

_____

_____

_____

_____

Now reflect on what you just wrote. What results do you want students to achieve in this course? For each result you list, include ways that you as a teacher could help students achieve these results.

_____

_____

_____

_____

_____

_____

_____

_____

_____

_____

_____

_____

_____

_____

_____

_____

_____

_____

_____

_____

Finally, look over the lists you just wrote. Circle any ideas that you can use right now to enhance the value that you take away from this student success course.

PLAN FOR SOPHOMORE-YEAR SUCCESS

If you're a freshman, you can look forward to sophomore year as an opportunity to get a fresh start in higher education. This year could be more hectic than your first year, especially if you redshirted. You might be living off-campus for the first time. Perhaps your athletic performance will start gaining attention from boosters and reporters. You may find that the demands of coursework, training, and competition simply rise to a whole new level during your sophomore year.

Maximize your success by taking time to plan for such changes. Determine what's next for you during your sophomore year. This two-part exercise will help you do that.

Part 1: Take a first-year First Step

You will probably look back in amazement at how fast your freshman year went by. You may also be surprised at how much you learned, both inside and outside the classroom.

In the space below, list three things that you've done well so far during your first year. Examples might include "Took the initiative to meet three new friends" or "Learned an effective way to take notes in class." Write down any success that you find personally significant, now matter how small it might seem to others. Use additional paper as needed.

1. _____

_____

2. _____

_____

3. _____

_____

Now take a moment to write about three things that did not go so well during your weeks or months in college. These could range from simple embarrassing moments to large mistakes. (Remember to keep it light; it's fine to laugh at yourself.) If you set your alarm at 7:00 p.m. instead of 7:00 a.m. on the night before a big test at 8:00 a.m., list that in the space below. Or if you felt a lot of stress during your first competition, describe that feeling.

1. _____

_____

2. _____

3. _____

_____

Part 2: Determine what you want

You've come a long way since first setting foot on campus. Now consider how far you want to go. Take this opportunity to set goals to meet during your sophomore year. See yourself producing new outcomes in your life—creating results that you really want.

As you do this, build on the writing you did in Part 1 of this exercise. Look for ways to maintain the excellence you've demonstrated in your first year, or to change some of the experiences that you didn't like.

As an *athlete*, for example, you might set a goal to always have your head in the games or to boost a first-year student athlete with your encouragement. Complete the following sentence.

As an athlete, I want to . . .

_____

_____

_____

Also determine what you want from *academics*. For instance, you could set a goal to maintain your eligibility or to raise your grade point average to a specific number.

In my academic life, I want to . . .

_____

_____

Remember your *social* life as well. Perhaps you want to resolve a conflict with a roommate or teammate. Or you may want to deepen a bond with someone you already know and make this person a friend for life.

In my social life, I want to . . .

_____

_____

_____

Finally, plan specific actions you can take to meet these three goals. Record these actions in your calendar or to-do list. For more suggestions, review Chapter Two.

Define your values align your actions

One key way to choose what's next in your life is to define your values. Values are the things in life that you want for their own sake. Values influence and guide your choices, including your moment-by-moment choices of what to do and what to have. Your values define who you are and who you want to be.

The subject of values is crucial for student athletes. Today, athletes are constantly challenged to act on the basis of sound values. When they do not, they are criticized or even ridiculed.

Some people are guided by values that they automatically adopt from others or by values that remain largely unconscious. These people could be missing the opportunity to live a life that's truly of their own choosing.

Investing time and energy to define your values is a pivotal suggestion in this book. In fact, *Becoming a Master Student Athlete* is based on a particular value system that underlies suggestions given throughout the book. This system includes the values of:

- Focused attention
- Self-responsibility
- Integrity
- Risk-taking
- Contributing

You'll find these values and related ones directly stated in the Power Processes throughout the text. For instance:

Discover what you want is about the importance of living a purpose-based life.

Ideas are tools points to the benefits of being willing to experiment with new ideas.

Be here now expresses the value of focused attention.

Love your problems (and experience your barriers) is about seeing difficulties as opportunities to develop new skills.

Notice your pictures and let them go is about adopting an attitude of open-mindedness.

I create it all is about taking responsibility for our beliefs and behaviors.

Detach reminds us that our core identity and value as a person does not depend on our possessions, our circumstances, or even our accomplishments.

Find a bigger problem is about offering our lives by contributing to others.

Employ your word expresses the value of making and keeping agreements.

Choose your conversations and your community reminds us of the power of language, and that we can reshape our lives by taking charge of our thoughts.

Risk being a fool is about courage—the willingness to take risks for the sake of learning something new.

Surrender points to the value of human community and the power of asking for help.

Be it is specifically about the power of attitudes—the idea that change proceeds from the inside out as we learn to see ourselves in new ways.

In addition, most of the study skills and life skills you read about in these pages have their source in values. The Time Monitor/Time Plan exercise, for example, calls for focused attention. Even the simple act of sharing your notes with a student who missed a class is an example of contributing.

As you begin to define your values, consider those who have gone before you. In creeds, scriptures, philosophies, myths, and sacred stories, the human race has left a vast and varied record of values. Be willing to look everywhere, including sources that are close to home. The creed of your local church or temple might eloquently describe some of your values—so might the mission statement of your school, company, or club. Another way to define your values is to describe the qualities of people you admire.

Also translate your values into behavior. Though defining your values is powerful, it doesn't guarantee any results. To achieve your goals, take actions that align with your values. ◪

One set of values

Following is a sample list of values. Don't read it with the idea that it is the "right" set of values for you. Instead, use this list as a point of departure in creating your own list.

Value: Be accountable

This means being:

- Honest
- Dependable
- Reliable
- Responsible
- Trustworthy

Being accountable includes making and keeping agreements—operating with integrity.

Value: Be loving

This means being:

- Affectionate
- Equitable
- Dedicated
- Accepting
- Devoted

Being loving includes appreciating ourselves and others—being gentle, considerate, forgiving, respectful, friendly, and courteous. It also includes being nonantagonistic, nonresistant, inclusive, understanding, compassionate, fair, and ethical.

Value: Be self-generating

This means being:

- Self-responsible
- The creator of our internal experiences—regardless of our external circumstances

Being self-generating includes not being a victim and not blaming others. Instead, we choose how to interpret and respond to all stimuli.

Value: Be promotive

This means being:

- Nurturing
- Reasonable
- Contributing
- Judicious
- Frugal
- Cooperative
- Helpful
- Appreciative
- Encouraging

Value: Be candid

This means being:

- Honest
- Sincere
- Authentic
- Free of deceit
- Genuine
- Able to avoid false modesty without arrogance
- Self-expressed
- Frank
- Self-disclosing
- Outspoken
- Open about strengths and weaknesses
- Spontaneous

Value: Be detached

This means being:

- Impartial
- Adaptable
- Unbiased
- Trusting
- Experimental
- Tolerant
- Satisfied
- Willing to surrender
- Patient (not resigned)
- Joyful—fun-loving, humorous, light-hearted, and happy
- Open-minded
- Without distress

Detachment includes being separate from but aware of thoughts, emotions, body, health, accomplishments, relationships, desires, commitments, possessions, values, opinions, roles, and expectations. The opposite of detachment is being addicted (physically or emotionally), dogmatic, bigoted, absolutely certain, prejudiced, anxious, grave, or somber.

Value: Be aware of the possible

This means being:

- Creative
- Holistic
- Imaginative
- Visionary
- Resourceful
- Inquisitive
- Inventive
- Audacious
- Foresighted
- Exploring

Being aware of the possible means expecting great things of ourselves and others.

Value: Be involved

This means being:

- Committed
- Enduring
- Participative
- Courageous
- Focused
- Energetic
- Enthusiastic
- Productive

THE DISCOVERY WHEEL—COMING FULL CIRCLE

Do this exercise online at masterstudent.college.hmco.com

This book doesn't work. It is worthless. Only you can work. Only you can make a difference and use this book to become a more effective student.

The purpose of this book is to give you the opportunity to change your behavior. The fact that something seems like a good idea doesn't necessarily mean that you will put it into practice. This exercise gives you a chance to see what behaviors you have changed on your journey toward becoming a master student.

Answer each question quickly and honestly. Record your results on the Discovery Wheel on this page and then compare it with the one you completed in Chapter One.

The scores on this Discovery Wheel indicate your current strengths and weaknesses on your path toward becoming a master student. The last Journal Entry in this chapter provides an opportunity to write about how you intend to change. As you complete this self-evaluation, keep in mind that your commitment to change allows you to become a master student. *Your scores might be lower here than on your earlier Discovery Wheel.* That's OK. Lower scores might result from increased self-awareness and honesty, and other valuable assets.

Using the total score from each category, shade in each section of the Discovery Wheel. Use different colors, if you want. For example, you could use green to denote areas you want to work on. When you have finished, complete Journal Entry #32 on page 325.

5 points
This statement is always or almost always true of me.

4 points
This statement is often true of me.

3 points
This statement is true of me about half the time.

2 points
This statement is seldom true of me.

1 point
This statement is never or almost never true of me.

1. _____ I enjoy learning.
2. _____ I understand and apply the concept of multiple intelligences.

3. _____ I connect my courses and athletic experiences to my purpose for being in school.
4. _____ I make a habit of assessing my personal strengths and areas for improvement.
5. _____ I am satisfied with how I am progressing toward achieving my academic and athletic goals.
6. _____ I use a knowledge of learning styles to support my success.
7. _____ I am willing to consider any idea that can help me succeed—even if I initially disagree with that idea.
8. _____ I take responsibility for my attitudes.

_____ Total score (1) *Motivation*

1. _____ I set long-term goals and periodically review them.
2. _____ I set short-term goals to support my long-term goals.
3. _____ I write a plan for each day and each week.
4. _____ I assign priorities to what I choose to do each day.
5. _____ I work and socialize with others outside the athletic realm.
6. _____ I schedule my time to effectively balance my academic and athletic commitments.
7. _____ I have adequate time each day to accomplish what I plan.

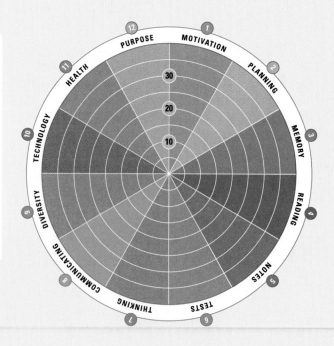

8. _____ I am confident that I will find the resources to finance my education.

_____ **Total score (2) *Planning***

1. _____ I am confident of my ability to remember.
2. _____ I can remember people's names.
3. _____ At the end of a presentation, I can summarize the key points.
4. _____ I apply techniques that enhance my memory skills.
5. _____ I can recall information when I'm under pressure in the classroom or during competition.
6. _____ I remember important information clearly and easily.
7. _____ I can jog my memory when I have difficulty recalling.
8. _____ I can relate new information to what I've already learned.

_____ **Total score (3) *Memory***

1. _____ I preview and review reading assignments.
2. _____ When reading, I ask myself questions about the material.
3. _____ I underline or highlight important passages when reading.
4. _____ When I read, I am alert and awake.
5. _____ I keep up with my reading assignments and other study tasks while I'm on the road.
6. _____ I select a reading strategy to fit the type of material I'm reading.
7. _____ I take effective notes when I read.
8. _____ When I don't understand what I'm reading, I note my questions and find answers.

_____ **Total score (4) *Reading***

1. _____ I take notes during class and other key presentations.
2. _____ When I take notes, I focus my attention.
3. _____ I am aware of various methods for taking notes and choose those that work best for me.
4. _____ When listening, I distinguish important material and note key phrases.
5. _____ I copy down key material that an instructor, coach, or other presenter displays visually—via a chalkboard, overhead projector, or slide presentation.

6. _____ I can put important concepts into my own words.
7. _____ My notes are valuable for review.
8. _____ Before I miss classes due to my athletic schedule, I let instructors know and take responsibility for keeping up with course work and getting notes from other classmates.

_____ **Total score (5) *Notes***

1. _____ I feel confident and calm during an exam.
2. _____ I manage my time during exams and am able to complete them.
3. _____ I am able to predict test questions.
4. _____ I adapt my test-taking strategy to the kind of test I'm taking.
5. _____ I understand what essay questions ask and can answer them completely and accurately.
6. _____ I start reviewing for tests at the beginning of the term.
7. _____ I continue reviewing for tests throughout the term.
8. _____ My sense of personal worth is independent of my test scores, athletic record, or other measures of performance.

_____ **Total score (6) *Tests***

1. _____ I have flashes of insight and often think of solutions to problems at unusual times.
2. _____ I use brainstorming to generate solutions to a variety of problems.
3. _____ When I get stuck on a creative project, I use specific methods to get unstuck.
4. _____ I see problems and tough decisions as opportunities for learning and personal growth.
5. _____ I am willing to consider different points of view and alternative solutions.
6. _____ I can detect common errors in logic.
7. _____ I construct viewpoints by drawing on information and ideas from many sources.
8. _____ As I share my viewpoints with others, I am open to their feedback.

_____ **Total score (7) *Thinking***

1. _____ I am candid with others about who I am, what I feel, and what I want.
2. _____ Other people tell me that I am a good listener.

3. _____ I can communicate my upset and anger without blaming others.

4. _____ I can make friends and create valuable relationships in a new setting.

5. _____ I communicate effectively in a variety of contexts—with classmates, other student athletes, coaches, alumni, and members of the media.

6. _____ I can effectively plan and research a large writing assignment.

7. _____ I create first drafts without criticizing my writing, then edit later for clarity, accuracy, and coherence.

8. _____ I know ways to prepare and deliver effective speeches.

_____ Total score (8) *Communicating*

1. _____ I am aware of my biases and am open to understanding people from other cultures, races, and ethnic groups.

2. _____ I build rewarding relationships with people from other backgrounds.

3. _____ I can point out examples of discrimination and sexual harassment and effectively respond to them.

4. _____ I am learning ways to thrive with diversity—attitudes and behaviors that will support my success in higher education and in my career.

5. _____ I can effectively resolve conflict with people from other cultures.

6. _____ My writing and speaking are free of sexist expressions.

7. _____ I can recognize bias and discrimination in the media.

8. _____ I am aware of the changing demographics in my country and community.

_____ Total score (9) *Diversity*

1. _____ I learn effectively from materials and activities that are posted online.

2. _____ I can efficiently find information on the Internet.

3. _____ I think critically about information and ideas that I access online.

4. _____ I write clear and concise e-mail messages that generate the results I want.

5. _____ My online communication is fair to and respectful of other people.

6. _____ I monitor new technology that can support my success at the collegiate level.

7. _____ I monitor new technology that can support my success in my career.

8. _____ I effectively use libraries to find the resources and information I want.

_____ Total score (10) *Technology*

1. _____ I have enough energy to meet my academic and athletic commitments—while fully enjoying other areas of my life.

2. _____ If the situation calls for it, I have enough reserve energy to put in a long day.

3. _____ The way that I train for athletics supports my long-term health.

4. _____ The way I eat is independent of my feelings of self-worth.

5. _____ I engage in healthy relationships, always mindful of my health and well-being.

6. _____ My emotional health supports my ability to succeed as a student athlete.

7. _____ I notice changes in my physical condition and respond effectively.

8. _____ I am in control of any alcohol or other drugs I put into my body.

_____ Total score (11) *Health*

1. _____ I see learning as a lifelong process.

2. _____ I understand that while not every class I take will relate directly to my specific purpose in college, I can relate all of my experiences in higher education to the rest of my life.

3. _____ My life includes opportunities to contribute to others.

4. _____ I revise my plans as I learn, change, and grow.

5. _____ I am clear about my purpose in life.

6. _____ I know that I am responsible for my own education.

7. _____ I take responsibility for the quality of my life.

8. _____ I am willing to accept challenges even when I'm not sure how to meet them.

_____ Total score (12) *Purpose*

journal entry 32

Discovery/Intention Statement

The purpose of this Journal Entry is to (1) review both of the Discovery Wheels you completed in this book, (2) summarize your insights from doing them, and (3) declare how you will use these insights to promote your continued success in school.

Again, a lower score on the second Discovery Wheel does not necessarily indicate decreased personal effectiveness. Instead, the lower score could result from increased honesty and greater self-awareness.

	Chapter 1	Chapter 12
Motivation		
Time		
Memory		
Reading		
Notes		
Tests		
Thinking		
Communicating		
Diversity		
Technology		
Health		
Purpose		

Comparing the Discovery Wheel in this chapter with the Discovery Wheel in Chapter One, I discovered that I . . .

_____
_____
_____
_____
_____
_____
_____

In the next six months, I intend to review the following articles from this book for additional suggestions I could use:

_____
_____
_____
_____
_____
_____
_____
_____
_____

exercise 30

THIS BOOK SHOUTS, "USE ME!"

Becoming a Master Student Athlete is designed to be used for years. The success strategies presented here are not likely to become habits overnight. There are more suggestions than can be put into action immediately. Some of what is discussed might not apply to your life as a collegiate athlete right now, but it might be just what you could use in a few months.

Plan to keep this book and use it again. Imagine that your book has a mouth. (Visualize the mouth.) Also imagine that it has arms and legs. (Visualize them.)

Now picture your book sitting on a shelf or table that you see every day. Imagine a time when you are having trouble in school and struggling to be successful as a student. Visualize your book jumping up and down, shouting, "Use me! Read me! I might have the solution to your problem, and I know I can help you solve it."

This is a memory technique to remind you to use a resource. Sometimes when you are stuck, all you need is a small push or a list of possible actions. At those times, hear your book shout, "Use me!"

power process

Be it

All of the techniques in this book are enhanced by this Power Process.

To tap into its full benefits, consider that most of our choices in life fall into three categories. We can:

- Increase our material wealth (what we have).
- Improve our skills (what we do).
- Develop our "being" (who we are).

Many people devote their entire lifetime to the first two categories. They act as if they are "human havings" instead of human beings. For them, the quality of life hinges on what they have. They devote most of their waking hours to getting more—more clothes, more cars, more relationships, more degrees, more trophies. "Human havings" define themselves by looking at the circumstances in their lives—what they have.

Some people escape this materialist trap by adding another dimension to their identities. In addition to living as "human havings," they also live as "human doings." They thrive on working hard and doing everything well. They define themselves by how efficiently they do their jobs, how effectively they raise their children, and how actively they participate in clubs and organizations. Their thoughts are constantly about methods, techniques, and skills.

Look beyond doing and having

In addition to focusing on what we have and what we do, we can also focus on our being. While it is impossible to live our lives without having things and doing things, this Power Process suggests that we balance our experience by giving lots of attention to who we are—an aspect of our lives that goes beyond having and doing. Call it soul, passion, purpose, or values. Call it being. This word describes how we see ourselves—our deepest commitments, the ground from which our actions spring.

The realm of being is profound and subtle. It is also difficult to capture in words, though philosophers have tried for centuries. Christian theologian Paul Tillich described this realm when he defined faith as "ultimate commitment" and the "ground of being." In the New Testament, Jesus talked about being when he asked his followers to love God with all of their heart, soul, and mind. An ancient Hindu text also touches on being: "You are what your deep, driving desire is."

If all this seems far removed from taking notes or answering test questions, read on. Consider an example of how "Be it" can assist in career choices. In a letter to her father, a young woman wrote:

We just went to see the Dance Theatre of Harlem. It was great! After the last number, I decided that I want to dance more than anything. I have a great passion to do it, more than anything else I can think or dream of. Dancing is what will make me happy and feel like I can leave this earth when my time comes. It is what I must do. I think that if I never fulfill this passion, I will never feel complete or satisfied with what I have done with my life.

In her heart, this woman *is* a dancer now, even before her formal training is complete. From her passion, desire, commitment, and self-image (her *being*) comes her willingness to take classes and rehearse (*doing*). And from her doing she might eventually *have* a job with a professional dance company.

Picture the result as you begin

The example of the dancer illustrates that once you have a clear picture of what you want to *be,* the things you *do* and *have* fall more naturally into place.

The idea is this: Getting where you want to be by what you do or by what you have is like swimming against the current. Have → do → be is a tough journey. It's much easier to go in the other direction: be → do → have.

Usually, we work against nature by trying to have something or do something before being it. That's hard. All of your deeds (what you do) might not get you where you want to be. Getting all of the right things (what you have) might not get you there either.

Take the person who values athletics and wants to master tennis. He buys an expensive racket and a stylish tennis wardrobe. Yet he still can't return a serve. Merely having the right things doesn't deliver what he values.

Suppose that this person takes a year's worth of tennis lessons. Week after week, he practices doing everything "right." Still, his game doesn't quite make it.

What goes wrong is hard to detect. "He lost the match even though he played a good game," people say. "Something seemed to be wrong. His technique was fine, but each swing was just a little off." Perhaps the source of his problem is that he cannot see himself as ever mastering the game. What he has and what he does are at war with his mental picture of himself.

You can see this happen in other areas of life. Two people tell the same joke in what seems to be the same way. Yet one person brings a smile, while the other person has you laughing so hard your muscles hurt. The difference in how they do the joke is imperceptible. When the successful comedian tells a joke, he does it from his experience of already being funny.

To have and do what you want, be it. Picture the result as you begin. If you can first visualize where you want to

Change the way you see yourself, and watch your actions and results shift as if by magic.

be, if you can go there in your imagination, if you can be it today, you set yourself up to succeed.

Be a master student now

Now relate this Power Process to succeeding in school. All of the techniques in this book can be worthless if you operate with the idea that you are an ineffective student athlete. You might do almost everything this book suggests and still never achieve the success in academics and athletics that you desire.

For example, if you believe that you are stupid in math, you are likely to fail at math. If you believe that you are not skilled at remembering, all of the memory techniques in the world will probably fail to improve your recall. If you don't believe that you can run 100 meters in a time below 10.8 seconds, you will probably perform to that level of expectation. Generally, we don't outperform our self-concept.

If you value success in school, picture yourself as a master student athlete right now. Through higher education you are gaining knowledge and skills that reflect and reinforce this view of yourself.

This principle works in other areas of life. For example, if you value a fulfilling career, picture yourself as already being on a path to a job you love. Use affirmations and visualizations to plant this idea firmly in your mind. Change the way you see yourself, and watch your actions and results shift as if by magic.

While you're at it, remember that "Be it" is not positive thinking or mental cheerleading. This Power Process works well when you take a First Step—when you tell the truth about your current abilities. The very act of accepting who you are and what you can do right now unleashes a powerful force for personal change.

In summary, flow with the natural current of be → do → have. Then watch your circumstances change. If you want it, be it. ⬛

put it to work

Plan for change. Even the most brilliant people can fall flat when predicting trends in business and the workplace. Case in point: Thomas Watson, founder of IBM, said, "I think there's a world market for about five computers."[7] Still, you can benefit from making predictions about changes in the workplace that affect your own employment opportunities. Keep up-to-date with breaking changes as you decide what's next in your career. This is easier to do than ever before, thanks to resources mentioned throughout this book:

- *The Internet.* Use your skills in searching the Internet to find Web sites devoted to your field. Start by keying your job title into a search engine such as Google or Yahoo! Also search for career-related listservs—programs that distribute e-mail messages to groups of people with similar interests.

- *Periodicals.* Read the business sections of the *New York Times* and the *Wall Street Journal*, for example. Most newspapers also have online editions, as do general interest magazines such as *Time* and *Business Week.*

- *Professional associations.* People in similar jobs like to band together and give each other a heads-up on emerging trends—one reason for professional associations. These range from the American Medical Association to the Society of Actuaries. There's bound to be one for people in your field. Ask colleagues and search the Internet. **Note:** Many associations post Web sites and publish newsletters or trade magazines.

- *Conferences and conventions.* Many professional associations sponsor annual meetings. Here's where you can meet people face to face and use your net-

working skills. Print and online publications are powerful sources of news, but sometimes nothing beats plain old schmoozing.

Consider coaching. Consider receiving life coaching as a way to continue the cycle of discovery, intention, and action you started in this book. A life coach is someone with training in counseling or a related field who meets with clients several times per month in person or over the phone. Life coaches can help you define your personal values, align your daily life with those values, write goals and action plans, and create projects that allow you to contribute to others. With the support of a life coach, you can start now to envision the jobs you want to have in 5 years, 10 years, and 20 or more years into the future. You can set comprehensive, long-term goals in every other area of your life as well. Like other professionals, life coaches charge for their services. Fees vary widely. Consider life coaching even if you can afford only a few hours of this service a year.

You can also meet with friends to offer each other free coaching. Start by redoing the exercises and Journal Entries in this book, sharing the results, and inventing new exercises of your own. The results can be dramatic.

Continue the conversation about success. As you begin your life beyond this student success course, continue to engage in a conversation about what you want from your life and how you intend to get it. You can experience success as you define it and live the life of your dreams. ▨

Name _____ Date _____/_____/_____

quiz

1. Explain a benefit of approaching career planning as a process of choice rather than a process of discovery.

2. Explain how *content skills* and *transferable skills* differ.

3. List three factors that are especially important for student athletes to consider before transferring to another school.

4. List three examples of transferable skills that you can develop as a student athlete.

5. Describe the three main types of life choices explained in the Power Process: "Be it."

6. Using the Power Process: "Be it" eliminates the need to take action. True or False? Explain your answer.

7. If your scores are lower on the Discovery Wheel the second time you complete it, that means your study skills have not improved. True or False? Explain your answer.

8. Contributing to others does *not* involve:
   (A) Telling people what is best for them.
   (B) Finding out what people want or need.
   (C) Determining if you can help people get what they want.
   (D) Giving your time, talent, or money.
   (E) Making sure that you experience satisfaction, also.

9. List three ways the Internet can help you in your job search.

10. List at least four ways that you can continue on your path of becoming a master student athlete after completing this book.

learning styles application

The questions below will "cycle" you through four styles, or modes, of learning as explained in the article "Learning styles: Discovering how you learn" in Chapter One. Each question will help you explore a different mode. You can answer the questions in any order.

what if

Consider this statement from the first article in this chapter: "You are on the edge of a universe so miraculous and full of wonder that your imagination at its most creative moment cannot encompass it. Paths are open to lead you to worlds beyond your wildest dreams." If you adopted this statement as a working principle, what would you do differently on a daily basis?

why

Consider your experience with this book and your student success class. Which of your attitudes or actions changed as a result of this experience?

how

List one suggestion from this book that you would like to apply but have not yet acted upon. Describe exactly how you will implement this suggestion.

what

List five suggestions from this book that you've already applied. Rate each suggestion for its effectiveness on a scale of 1 to 5 (1 is most effective, 5 is least effective).

master student profile

JOHN WOODEN

(1910–   ) The most successful coach in college basketball history, he led the UCLA Bruins to ten NCAA championships in his 27 years with the team. His reliance on discipline and fundamentals, as outlined in his Pyramid of Success, encourages achievement both on and off the court.

As a brand-new teacher in 1932 at Kentucky's Dayton High School, I was greatly troubled by the pressure parents put on children in my English classes. Anything less than an A or a B was viewed as failure even if the youngster had worked hard—to the best of his or her ability.

In sports, I had learned painfully that sometimes you're defeated—outscored—even when you do your best. Twice, even though we gave it all we had, my Martinsville Artesians lost the championship game of the Indiana state high school tournament. And yet we were neither losers nor failures. The Indiana State Sycamores had been outscored by Louisville in the 1948 NAIB championship game and yet had every right to be proud of their performance. At UCLA we were on the short end of the score 148 times, including twice in the final seconds of the Final Four. But on those occasions when the Bruins prepared and played to near their potential, I considered them a success. Was there something more I could require of them? I think not.

Likewise, I believed any student in my English class who did his or her best but received a B or a C shouldn't be judged a failure nor made to feel ashamed. Perhaps other students had worked just as hard but were simply better at the subject.

I had not always felt this way. At Martinsville High School, my history teacher, Mr. Scheidler, asked students to write an essay on the question, "What is success?" My answer was the same as everyone else's in class—namely, fame, fortune, and power, or an A in Mr. Scheidler's class.

But over the years my feelings changed. As a teacher, coach, and parent I wanted to come up with a better way than grades or a winning percentage for judging success and failure—something that was both fair and very productive. I remembered what Dad had told me, "Don't worry about being better than somebody else, but never cease trying to be the best *you* can be." At Dayton I began thinking that success should be measured along the lines he described—by one's effort in the classroom, in sports, or in life.

In 1934, after careful consideration for the exact wording, I wrote down my personal definition of success. It is the standard by which I have judged myself and those under my supervision: "Success is peace of mind which is a result of self-satisfaction in knowing you did your best to become the best that you are capable of becoming."

I wanted those under my supervision to understand the highest goal and greatest reward exist in the effort they make to achieve their potential. This is what Cervantes was getting at when he wrote, "The journey is greater than the inn." For me the "journey" is my effort, and it is truly much greater and more rewarding than the "inn" provided by fame or fortune, grades, or victories. So I began teaching this idea to English students, student-athletes, and parents. It wasn't easy then, and it's harder now.

Our society tells us all that matters is, "Who's number one?" By this standard, most of us are losers. I think the opposite is true: we all have the potential to be winners. We may or may not drive a bigger car, get a better grade, or score more points than someone else. But for me the "score" that matters most is the one that measures your effort—and ultimately, only you know the score. ⬩

Source: John Wooden with Steve Jamison, *My Personal Best.* Copyright © 2004 by John Wooden. Reprinted by permission of The McGraw-Hill Companies.

For more biographical information on John Wooden, visit the Master Student Hall of Fame on the *Becoming a Master Student Athlete* Web site at

masterstudent.college.hmco.com

endnotes

Introduction

1. U.S. Department of Labor, Bureau of Labor Statistics, "Education pays . . . ," August 7, 2003, http://www.bls.gov/emp/emptab7.htm (accessed May 3, 2004). Also see National Center for Education Statistics, "Annual Earnings of Young Adults," http://www.nces.ed.gov/programs/coe/2002/section2/indicator16.asp, 2002 (accessed January 13, 2004).
2. Robert Mager, *Preparing Instructional Objectives* (Belmont, CA: Fearon, 1975).
3. Martin E. P. Seligman, *Learned Optimism* (New York: Pocket Books, 1998).
4. James O. Prochaska, John C. Norcross, and Carlo C. DiClemente, *Changing for Good* (New York: Avon, 1994).
5. B. F. Skinner, *Science and Human Behavior* (Boston: Free Press, 1965).
6. Excerpts from *Creating Your Future*. Copyright © 1998 by David B. Ellis. Reprinted by permission of Houghton Mifflin Company. All rights reserved.

chapter 1

1. Carl Rogers, *Freedom to Learn* (Columbus, OH: Merrill, 1969).
2. Ezra Pound, *The ABC of Reading* (New York: New Directions, 1934).
3. David A. Kolb, *Experiential Learning: Experience as the Source of Learning and Development* (Englewood Cliffs, NJ: Prentice-Hall, 1984).
4. Howard Gardner, *Frames of Mind: The Theory of Multiple Intelligences* (New York: Basic Books, 1993).

5. William James, *Pragmatism and Other Essays* (New York: Washington Square, 1963).

chapter 2

1. Alan Lakein, *How to Get Control of Your Time and Your Life* (New York: New American Library, 1973; reissue 1996).
2. Linda Sapadin, with Jack Maguire, *It's About Time! The Six Styles of Procrastination and How to Overcome Them* (New York: Penguin, 1997).
3. Jane B. Burka and Lenora R. Yuen, *Procrastination: Why You Do It, What to Do About It* (Reading, MA: Addison-Wesley, 1983).
4. Stephen R. Covey, *The Seven Habits of Highly Effective People: Restoring the Character Ethic* (New York: Simon & Schuster, 1990).
5. Joe Dominguez and Vicki Robin, *Your Money or Your Life: Transforming Your Relationship with Money and Achieving Financial Independence* (New York: Viking Penguin, 1992).
6. M. A. Just, P. A. Carpenter, T. A. Keller, et al., "Interdependence of Nonoverlapping Cortical Systems in Dual Cognitive Tasks," *NeuroImage* 14, no. 2 (2001): 417-426.

chapter 3

1. Donald Hebb, quoted in D. J. Siegel, "Memory: An Overview," *Journal of the American Academy of Child and Adolescent Psychiatry* 40, no. 9 (2001): 997-1011.
2. David Yukelson, "Teaching Athletes Visualization and Mental Imagery Skills," http://www.mascsa.psu.edu/visualization.html (accessed August 15, 2004).
3. H. Hyden, "Biochemical Aspects of Learning and Memory," in Karl Pribram, ed., *On the Biology of Learning* (New York: Harcourt Brace Jovanovich, 1969)
4. Richard Saul Wurman, *Information Anxiety* (New York: Doubleday, 1989), 59.
5. D. J. Siegel, "Memory: An Overview," *Journal of the American Academy of Child and Adolescent Psychiatry* 40, no. 9 (2001): 997-1011.
6. Daniel L. Schacter, *The Seven Sins of Memory: How the Mind Forgets and Remembers* (Boston: Houghton Mifflin, 2001), 34.
7. John W. Rowe and Robert L. Kahn, *Successful Aging* (New York: Pantheon, 1998).
8. CNN.com, "Ethical Debate over Potential 'Viagra for the Mind,'" March 11, 1999, http://www.cnn.com/SPECIALS/views/y/1999/03/utley.memory.mar11/#1 (accessed April 15, 2002).

chapter 4

1. William Glasser, *Take Effective Control of Your Life* (New York: Harper & Row, 1984).
2. School of Information Management and Systems, University of California, Berkeley, "How Much Information? 2003," October 27, 2003, http://www.sims.berkeley.edu/research/projects/how-much-info-2003/execsum.htm (accessed February 20, 2004).
3. John Morkes and Jakob Nielsen, "Concise, Scannable and Objective: How to Write for the Web," 1997, http://www.useit.com/papers/webwriting/writing.html (accessed February 20, 2004).

chapter 5

1. Walter Pauk and Ross J.Q. Owens, *How to Study in College*, Eighth Edition (Boston: Houghton Mifflin, 2005).
2. Tony Buzan, *Use Both Sides of Your Brain* (New York: Dutton, 1991).

3. Joseph Novak and D. Bob Gowin, *Learning How to Learn* (New York: Cambridge University Press, 1984).

4. David P. Ausubel, *Educational Psychology: A Cognitive View* (New York: Holt, Reinhart, and Winston, 1968.)

chapter 7

1. Quoted in Theodore A. Rees Cheney, *Getting the Words Right: How to Rewrite, Edit and Revise,* reprinted (Cincinnati, OH: Writer's Digest books, 1990).

2. William G. Perry, Jr., *Forms of Intellectual and Ethical Development in the College Years: A Scheme* (New York: Holt, Rinehart, and Winston, 1970).

3. Peter A. Facione, "Critical Thinking: What It Is and Why It Counts." A paper from California Academic Press reprinted at http//www.calpress.com/critical.html

4. Arthur Koestler, *The Act of Creation* (New York: Dell, 1964).

5. John Dewey, *How We Think* (Boston: D.C. Heath, 1910).

6. Quoted in Alice Calaprice, ed., *The Expanded Quotable Einstein* (Princeton, NJ: Princeton University Press, 2000).

7. Jan Carlzon, *Moments of Truth* (New York: HarperCollins, 1989).

chapter 8

1. Lee Thayer, "Communication–Sine Qua Non of the Behavioral Sciences," in *Vistas in Science,* ed. David L. Arm (Albuquerque: University of New Mexico, 1968).

2. Carl Rogers, *On Becoming a Person* (Boston: Houghton Mifflin, 1961).

3. Thomas Gordon, *Parent Effectiveness Training: The Tested New Way to Raise Responsible Children* (New York: New American Library, 1975).

4. Martha E. Sparent, "The Student-Athlete in the Classroom: The Impact of Developmental Issues on College Athletes' Academic Motivation and Performance." *Research & Teaching in Developmental Education* 5, no. 2 (1989): 7-16.

5. LaFasto and Larson refer to their book *When Teams Work Best* in their online article: Center for Association Leadership, "The Zen of Brilliant Teams," http://www.centeronline.org/knowledge/article.cfm?ID=1884&, July 2002 (accessed January 5, 2004).

6. Nadine C. Hoover, Alfred University, "National Survey: Initiation Rites and Athletics for NCAA Sports Teams," Executive Summary, http://www.alfred.edu/sports_hazing/executivesummary.html, August 30, 1999 (accessed October 1, 2004).

7. Quoted in Richard Saul Wurman, Loring Leifer, and David Sume, *Information Anxiety2* (Indianapolis: QUE, 2001), 116.

8. Peter Elbow, *Writing with Power: Techniques for Mastering the Writing Process* (New York: Oxford University Press, 1981).

9. Natalie Goldberg, *Writing Down the Bones: Freeing the Writer Within* (Boston: Shambhala, 1992).

10. Quoted in Theodore Cheney, *Getting the Words Right: How to Revise, Edit and Rewrite* (Cincinnati: Writer's Digest, 1983).

11. Theodore Cheney, *Getting the Words Right: How to Revise, Edit and Rewrite* (Cincinnati: Writer's Digest, 1983).

12. National Association of Colleges and Employers, "Recreate Yourself: From Student to the Perfect Job Candidate," http://www.jobweb.com/joboutlook/2004outlook/outlook5.htm (accessed December 15, 2003).

13. Jakob Nielsen, *Designing Web Usability: The Practice of Simplicity* (Indianapolis: New Riders, 1999).

14. Frank LaFasto and Carl Larson, Center for Association Leadership, "The Zen of Brilliant Teams," http://www.centeronline.org/knowledge/article.cfm?ID=1884&, July 2002 (accessed January 5, 2004).

chapter 9

1. Dorothy Lee, *Freedom and Culture* (Englewood Cliffs, NJ: Prentice-Hall, 1959).

2. Federal Bureau of Investigation, "Uniform Crime Reports," http://www.fbi.gov/ucr/ucr.htm, 2002 (accessed January 12, 2004).

3. Diane de Anda, *Bicultural Socialization: Factors Affecting the Minority Experience* (Washington, DC: National Association of Social Workers, 1984).

4. SchwabLearning.org, "Successful People with Learning Disabilities and AD/HD," http://www.schwablearning.org/articles.asp?r=258&g=3#athletes. (accessed October 7, 2004).

chapter 10

1. From Ann Raimes, *Universal Keys for Writers.* Copyright © 2005 by Houghton Mifflin Company. Reprinted with permission.

chapter 11

1. Frederick F. Samaha, Nayyar Iqbal, and Prakash Seshadri et al., "A Low-Carbohydrate as Compared with a Low-Fat Diet in Severe Obesity," *New England Journal of Medicine* 348, no. 21 (2003): 2074–2081.

2. Martin E. P. Seligman, *Learned Optimism* (New York: Pocket Books, 1998).

3. Commonwealth Fund, "Out of Touch: American Men and the Health Care System," http://www.cmwf.org/programs/women/sandman_outoftouch_374.pdf, March 2000 (accessed January 13, 2004).

4. Agency for Healthcare Research and Quality, "Men, Stay Healthy at Any Age," http://www.ahrq.gov/ppip/healthymen.htm, June 2003 (accessed January 12, 2004).

5. Adapted from *Dietary Guildelines for Americans 2000,* 5th ed., U.S. Department of Agriculture and U.S. Department of Agriculture and U.S. Department of Health and Human Services.

6. Albert Bandura, "Self-Efficacy," in *Encyclopedia of Human Behavior,* vol. 4, ed. V. S. Ramachaudran (New York: Academic Press, 1994), 71–81.

7. Harvey Jackins, *The Benign Reality* (Seattle: Rational Island, 1991).

8. Daniel Goleman, *Emotional Intelligence* (New York: Bantam, 1997).

9. American Psychological Association, *Diagnostic and Statistical Manual of Psychoactive Substance Abuse Disorders* (Washington, D.C.: American Psychological Association, 1994).

10. William James, *The Varieties of Religious Experience: A Study in Human Nature* (New York: Scribner, 1997).

chapter 12

1. Ira Progoff, *At a Journal Workshop* (New York: Dialogue House, 1975).

2. From Dave Ellis, Stan Lankowitz, Ed Stupka, and Doug Toft, *Career Planning,* Third Edition. Copyright © 2003 by Houghton Mifflin Company. Used by permission.

3. Richard Nelson Bolles, *What Color Is Your Parachute?* (Berkeley: Ten Speed Press, updated annually).

4. United Nations Development Programme. *Human Development Report* (New York: Oxford University Press, 2003).

5. United Nations Development Programme. *Human Development Report.* New York: Oxford University Press, 2003.

index

Abbott, Jim, 127
Abbreviations, 134
ABC priority method, 61, 120
Abstinence, 280, 281
Abstract conceptualization, 35, 93
Academic advisors, 9, 11
Academic athletic advisors, 9, 11, 210, 237
Academics, 9, 10, 59
Academic skills, 39, 97
Accident prevention, 283
Acronyms, 100
Acrostics, 100
Action goals, 317
Active experimentation, 35
Active learning, 93
Addiction, 168, 169, 289, 291, 292, 298
Advertisements, 294
Aerobic exercise, 162
Affirmations, 41, 218
Agreements, 224, 225
AIDS, 279, 280, 282
Alcohol abuse, 98, 289, 290, 292, 298
Alcoholics Anonymous (AA), 292
Alumni associations, 11
American Philosophical Association, 179
Anorexia nervosa, 275
Answers, 45
Anxiety
  math and science, 164–165
  methods for overcoming, 43
  over transitions, 10
  public speaking, 222
  test, 161–163
Appeals to authority, 184
Arts resources, 12
Assertions, 177, 183
Assignments, 111, 130, 131
Assistant coaches, 11
Associations, 99
Assumptions, 183
Athletes
  careers related to, 308–309
  choice of majors by, 187–188
  detachments in, 169
  diversity of, 231, 246
  drug use by, 289, 290
  emotions in, 287, 288
  focus on present by, 10
  health issues for, 278–279
  injuries in, 64, 208, 279
  media relations for, 208
  networking by, 210
  nutrition for, 275–276
  overcoming failures as, 69
  regulation of, 12. See also Eligibility
  resources for, 11
  success strategies for, 20, 38
  transferable skills developed from, 309, 312–313
  travel time for, 120
Athletic advisors, 11, 210, 307. See also Academic athletic advisors
Athletic centers, 11
Athletic departments, 11, 239, 278, 310
Athletic financial aid officers, 11
Athletics
  balancing academics and, 9, 10, 59
  mastery in, 27
  organizations governing, 12
  playing full out in, 195

Athletic scholarships, 79, 306–307
Athletics compliance office, 11
Athletics directors, 11
Athletic skills, 38–39
Athletic ticket managers, 11
Attachments, 168–169
Attendance, 9–10, 132, 139–140
Attention, 28, 69
Attitudes
  awareness of, 94–95
  changing your, 41
  of critical thinkers, 179
Auditory learning, 33, 34
Ausubel, David, 143

Balance, 9, 10, 59
Behavior, 15, 295
Behavioral change, 14
Birth control, 281–282
Blackboard, 259
Blame, 145
Boards, 132, 134
Bodily/kinesthetic intelligence, 30
Body awareness, 162
Body language, 131. See also Nonverbal communication
Bolles, Richard Nelson, 97
Boolean terms, 254
Brain, 89, 95, 98, 273
Brainstorming
  to create ideas, 181
  to create to-do list, 61
  to examine goals, 60
  to find solutions, 186, 195
  as memory technique, 95
  for test questions, 155
  for writing topics, 216
Breathing, 162, 169
Budgets, 78
Bulimia, 275
Burka, Jane, 67
Buzan, Tony, 135

Calendars, 74, 257
Careers
  choice of, 310
  planning for, LSI-6, 84, 187, 308–311
  skills for, 31–32, 310
Carlzon, Jan, 196
CHAMPS/Life Skills program, 310, 316
Change, 10, 28, 328
Chapels, 12
Cheating, 160
Cheney, Theodore, 218
Childcare, 12
Classes
  attendance in, 9–10, 132, 139–140
  math and science, 164–165
  online, 259–260
  participation in, 131, 165
  seating in, 130–131
  studying for, 63
  taking unrelated, 304
Coaches
  communicating with, 206, 207
  health issues and, 275
  life, 328
  networking with, 210
  as resource, 11

Collective orientations, 246
Colleges. See Universities/colleges
Communication. See also Listening; Writing
  with coaches and instructors, 206–207
  of complaints, 214
  conversations as, 244–245
  across cultures, 234–235
  function of, 201, 202
  with media, 208
  messages in, 204–205
  networking as, 210
  in relationships, 213, 214, 224–225
  sexist language in, 238–239
Community service, 316, 317
Competence, 28
Complaints, 214
Complements, 211
Compound interest, 79
Computer games, 257
Computer-graded tests, 157
Computers. See also Internet; Technology
  access to, 252–253, 263
  hardware for, 253
  laptop, 252–253
  money management using, 256
  notes on, 134, 138, 260
  research on, 220, 254, 262
  time management using, 64, 256, 257
  wasting time with, 257
Computer software, 253, 259
Concept maps, 143
Concrete experience, 35
Conflict management, 209–210, 235
Convergent thinking, 180
Conversations, 244–245. See also Communication
Cooley, Tatiana, 104
Cooperative learning, 154–155, 170
Cornell notes, 135–137
Counseling, 304
Courage, 29, 266, 267
Covey, Stephen R., 70
Cramming, 43
Creativity, 29, 180
Credit cards, 80–81
Critical thinking
  about information on Internet, 255
  about procrastination, 67
  during classes, 131
  concept maps to promote, 143
  creativity and, 180
  development of, 177–179
  function of, 44, 175–176
  questioning to promote, 191, 193
  at work, 196
Criticism, 139, 214
Cultural diversity. See Diversity

Darrow, Clarence, 97
Darwin, Charles, 97
Date rape, 282–283
Daydreaming, 161
de Anda, Diane, 234–235
Decision-making strategies, 185
Decoding, 202
Decreasing Options Technique (DOT), 196
Delegation, 70–71, 241
Diagrams, in notes, 133
Dickinson, Emily, 180
DiClemente, Carlo, 14

Dictionaries, 117
Dietary guidelines, 284
Diets, 276. *See also* Nutrition
Discomfort, 37, 42
Discovery Statements, 5–7
Discovery Wheel, 22–25, 322
Discrimination, 232–233
Distractions, 131
Divergent thinking. *See* Critical thinking
Diversity
    awareness of, 71
    conflict and, 209
    discrimination and, 232–233
    explanation of, 231, 232
    nonverbal communication and, 203, 246
    stereotypes and, 236
    in study groups, 154
    on teams, 231, 233, 234
    value of, 233
    at work, 246
Dominguez, Joe, 78
Downtime, 73
Drafts, 217–219
Drug abuse, 98, 290–292
    and eligibility, 289
    and work, 298

Eating disorders, 275
Ebbinghaus, Hermann, 137
Ebbinghaus forgetting curve, 137
Editing, 137
Education, 1, 9, 79, 81
Einstein, Albert, 97
Elaboration, 95
Eligibility, 9, 11, 12, 28, 38, 160, 169, 212,
    306–307, 319
E-mail, 258
Emotions, 9, 58, 94, 184, 192, 210, 287
Empowerment, 211
Encoding, 202
Energy, 94
Engagement, 98
English as a second language (ESL) students, 119
English language, 119
Entertainment costs, 78
Enthusiasm, 28
Equations, 169
Ergonomics, 298
Escalante, Jaime, 97
Essay questions, 157–158
Ethernet cards, 253
Evaluation, 60
Evidence, 178
Excuses, 139
Exercise, 98, 162, 276
Experiential learning theory, 36
Eye contact, 203
Eye movement, 115, 132

Fear. *See* Anxiety
Feedback
    importance of, 15, 240–241
    mistakes as, 166
    in online classes, 260
Fill-in-the-blank tests, 157
Financial aid, 79, 306–307
Financial aid officers, 11
Financial aid offices, 12, 307
Financial matters
    cost of attending class, 1, 9, 81
    credit card use, 80–81
    purchasing decisions, 73, 78
    use of technology for, 256, 257
Financial planning, 77–79
First Step technique, 19
Fixations, 115
Flash cards, 96, 153
Fleming, Alexander, 182
Focus, 28, 161, 181

Ford, Henry, 97
Free Application for Federal Student Aid
    (FAFSA), 79
Free writing, 216

Gardner, Howard, 40
Gays/lesbians, 233
Glasser, William, 122
Glossaries, 260
Goals
    academic, 51, 57–59, 62, 64, 73, 76, 319, 322
    action, 317
    assessment of, 142, 264
    athletic, 51, 54, 57, 58, 62, 65, 73, 76, 304, 308,
        319, 322
    examination of, 60
    explanation of, 57
    long-term, 58, 60, 142, 192
    methods for setting, 57–59
    mid-term, 58, 60
    realistic, 63
    short-term, 58, 60
    tasks to achieve, 69
Goldberg, Whoopi, 237
Grades, 29, 151, 307
Graphic signals, 134
Guilt, 145
Gymnasiums, 11, 276

Habits, 14–15, 116, 273
Hamm, Mia, 173
Hammerstein, Oscar, 97
Hansen, Rick, 271
Hard drives, 253
Hate crimes, 232
Hazing, 212
Head coaches, 11. *See also* Coaches
Headings, 111, 136
Health
    accident prevention and, 283
    alcohol and drugs and, 98, 289–292
    birth control and, 281–282
    eating disorders and, 275
    emotional pain and, 287
    exercise for, 276
    medical checkups and, 283
    nutrition and, 274–276, 284, 294
    self-esteem and, 285–286
    sexual assault and, 282–283
    sexually transmitted diseases and,
        279–282
    sleep and, 277
    strategies for good, 28, 98, 273, 278–279
    stress management and, 277–278, 286
    suicide and, 288
    at work, 298
Hebb, Donald, 89
Hemingway, Ernest, 176, 218
Higher education. *See also* Universities/colleges
    academic standards in, 9
    cost of, 1, 307
    knowing goals for, 16–17
    learning language of, 10
    making transition to, 1, 9–10
    sexism and sexual harassment in, 238–
        239
    technology in, 251, 252, 259–260
    value of, 31–32, 79
Highlighting, 112, 113
HIV/AIDS, 279, 280, 282
Hofstede, Geert, 246
Homophobia, 232
Humor, 30

Ideas
    information vs., 255
    journals to keep, 5
    keeping track of, 182
    methods to generate, 181–182

    support for, 178
    as tools, 44–45
Idioms, 119
"I" messages, 204, 205, 209, 238
Information, 35–36, 255
Information literacy, 263
Injuries, 64, 169, 208, 279, 283
    coping with, 169, 279, 285
Inquisitiveness, 28
Insight, 5
Instructions, 15
Instructors
    communicating with, 206, 207
    listening to fast-talking, 140
    managing your experiences with, 139–140, 165
    nonverbal cues of, 131
    paying attention to, 131, 132
    seeking assistance from, 117, 132, 140
    style of, 131
Intellectual property, 220
Intelligence, 30
Intention statements, 5–8
Interests, 31
Internet. *See also* Online documents
    job searches on, 315
    online learning on, 259–260
    research on, 220, 254
    sources of information on, 255
Interpersonal intelligence, 30
Interviews, 208, 314
Intrapersonal intelligence, 30
Introductions, 99, 221
Intuition, 185
Invisible Web, 254

Jackins, Harvey, 287
Jenner, Bruce, 97
Job placement offices, 12
Job searches, 77, 315
Johnson, "Magic," 237
Jordan, Michael, 69
Journal writing, 5–6, 304
Joyfulness, 28
Judgments, 28, 131

Key terms, 136, 137
Kinesthetic learning, 33, 34
King, Billie Jean, 146
Knowledge, 30
Kolb, David, 36

Laboratory work, 165
LaFasto, Frank, 226
Lakein, Alan, 61
Land, Edward, 97
Larson, Carl, 226
Leadership, 240–241
Learn and Serve Program, 317
Learned resignation, 144
Learning
    active, 93
    cooperative, 154–155, 170
    as cycle, 36
    cycle of, LSI-6
    distribution of, 94
    online, 259–260
    as part of community, 119
    perception and processing differences in, 35–36
    service, 317
    taking responsibility for, 139
    through your senses, 33–34
Learning disabilities, 237
Learning Style Graph, LSI-5, LSI-7
Learning Style Inventory (LSI), LSI-1 to LSI-8, 36
Learning style profile, 37
Learning styles
    application of, 37, 39, 48
    of coworkers, 46
    explanation of, 35

Lee, Dorothy, 232
Lee, Spike, 97
Leonardo da Vinci, 97
Lewis, Carl, 97
Liberal arts education, 31
Libraries, 69, 262–263
Life coaches, 328
Lifelines, 76, 84
Life skills counselors, 11
Listening, 140, 202–203, 209, 241
Lists, to-do, 61
Loci system, 100
Logic, 178, 184, 236
Lombardi, Vince, 97
Long-range budgets, 78
Long-term goals, 58, 60, 142, 192
Long-term memory, 90
Long-term planners, 59, 75–76
Louganis, Greg, 87, 237

Majors, 187–189
Maps
    concept, 143
    mind, 135–136, 138, 141
Master students
    Jim Abbott, 127
    characteristics of, 29–30
    explanation of, 27–28, 327
    Mia Hamm, 173
    Rick Hansen, 271
    Billie Jean King, 146
    Greg Louganis, 87
    Dat Nguyen, 249
    Ken Procaccianti, 49
    Dot Richardson, 107
    Oscar Robertson, 199
    Wilma Rudolph, 301
    Sheryl Swoopes, 229
    John Wooden, 331
Matching tests, 157
Math courses, 164–165, 190
Mathematical/logical intelligence, 30
Media, 208
Mediators, 209, 235
Medical checkups, 283
Meetings, 84
Memory
    explanation of, 89
    health and, 98
    method for testing, 137
    for names, 99
    paths in, 91
    types of, 90, 94
    use of body to promote, 93–94
    use of brain to promote, 94–95
Memory techniques
    associations as, 92
    mnemonics as, 100
    organization as, 92, 104
    recall as, 95, 96
    recitation as, 93
    repetition as, 93, 99
    visualization as, 90, 91
Mentors, 304–305
Metacognition, 38–39
Meta search engines, 254
Mid-term goals, 58, 60
Mind maps, 135–136, 153, 155
Mind map summary sheets, 138, 141, 153, 190
Minors, 188
Mistakes, 166–167, 240, 317
MLA source documentation, 219, 220
Mnemonics, 100
Models, 235
Modern Language Association (MLA) source
    documentation, 219, 220
Monthly budgets, 78
Monthly calendars, 74
Motivation, 42–43

Multiple-choice questions, 156
Multiple intelligences, 40
Multi-tasking, 84
Muscle Reading technique, 109, 110, 114
Musical/rhythmic intelligence, 30

Names, 99
National Association of Intercollegiate Athletics
    (NAIA), 12
National Collegiate Athletic Association (NCAA),
    12, 187, 188, 208, 212, 275, 276, 289, 290
Naturalist intelligence, 30
Networking, 210
Newton, Sir Isaac, 97
Nguyen, Dat, 249
Noise distractions, 69
Nonverbal communication
    diversity and, 246
    eye contact as, 203, 222
    by instructors, 131
    during presentations, 222
Norcross, John, 14
Notes
    abbreviations in, 134
    comparison of, 154–155
    computer use for, 134, 138, 260
    Cornell, 135
    graphic signals in, 134
    key words in, 136, 137
    labeling and dating, 134
    mind map, 135–136, 138
    for missed classes, 132
    outline form for, 136
    research, 141. See also Research notes
    review, 141
    review of, 137–138, 152–153
    shorthand system for, 140
    speaking, 222
    summary, 135, 138
Note taking
    function of, 129
    getting help with, 132
    "here and now" strategies for, 131
    setting stage for, 130–131
    strategies for, 133–134, 141
    watching for clues during, 132
    while reading, 141
    at work, 146
Novak, Joseph, 143
Nutrition, 274–276, 284, 294

Observer consciousness, 168–169
Online documents, 124, 141, 220
Open-book tests, 157
Operating systems, 253
Opinions, 177
Optical drives, 253
Optimism, 10
Organization, 104
Organizational ability, 28
Outlines, 111, 136, 158, 217
Overhead projectors, 132
Overlearning, 94

Page, Alan, 97
Paradox, 29
Paraphrasing, 220
Paterno, Joe, 97
Pauk, Walter, 135
Peg system, 100
Perception, 35
Perry, William, 179
Personal digital assistant (PDA), LSI-6, 257
Persuasion, 175
Pessimism, 10
Picasso, Pablo, 97
Pictures, 122–123, 133, 190
Pirsig, Robert, 97
Plagiarism, 220

Planners, 59, 75–76
Planning
    career, 84, 308–311
    financial, 77–81
    function of, 62
    for present, 82–83
    time management as, 51
    at work, 84
Post-reading strategies, 110, 113–114
Power-distance, 246
Practice, 15
Praise, 161
Prejudice, 183
Prereading strategies, 110
Presentations, 46, 221–222
Previews, 111
Primary sources, 263
Priorities, 61, 70, 120
Problems
    acceptance of, 103
    defining, 186
    explanation of, 102
    function of, 194–195
    getting help for, 296
Problem solving, 104, 186, 190
Procaccianti, Ken, 49
Processing, 35–36
Prochaska, James, 14
Procrastination
    explanation of, 73
    strategies to avoid, 14, 43, 66–67
    at work, 84
Professional sports, playing, 31, LSI-6, 307, 308
Progoff, Ira, 304
Projects, 46
Promises, 71, 225
Public transportation, 78
Puccini, Giacomo, 97
Purchases, 73, 78
Put It to Work. See Work

Question Cards (Q-Cards), 96, 120
Questions
    essay, 157–158
    function of, 191, 193, 205
    during lectures, 140
    on math and science material, 165
    multiple choice, 156
    predicting test, 155
    for reading materials, 111–113
Quotations, 220

Racism, 232, 233
Random access memory (RAM), 253
Rape, 282–283
Reading
    difficult material, 117–118
    increasing your speed while, 115–116
    note taking while, 141
    previewing before, 111
    questions for, 111–113
    reciting following, 113–114
    reflecting while, 112
    reviewing following, 114
    skimming when, 116
    strategies for effective, 109–114
    during traveling, 120
    underlining while, 112, 113
    using dictionary while, 117
    at work, 124
Recitation
    after reading, 113–114
    as memory strategy, 93, 99
    of notes, 137
Reflection, 112, 203
Reflective observation, 36
Registrar, 12
Relationships, 213, 214, 224–225
Relaxation, 93, 115, 162

Religion, 232
Repetition, 93, 99, 132, 222
Research
    Internet, 220, 254
    library, 262–263
    for writing assignments, 217
Research notes, 141
Resignation, 144
Resources, 11–12
Responsibility, 29, 144, 145
Résumés, 314, 315
Retroactive inhibition, 95
Review notes, 141
Reviews
    following reading, 114
    of notes, 137–138
    for tests, 152, 153
Rhymes, 100
Richardson, Dot, 107
Right-brained people, 72–73
Risks, 29, 166, 266–267
Robertson, Oscar, 199
Robin, Vicki, 78
Rogers, Carl, 203
Roman numerals, 136
Roommates, 69
Rudolph, Wilma, 301

Saccades, 115
Savings, 79
SCANS reports, 313
Schedules
    in long-term planners, 59, 75–76
    for reviews, 152
    strategies for, 63–64
Scholarships, 79, 306–307
School security agencies, 12
Science courses, 164–165, 190
Search engines, 254, 260
Seating, 130–131
Secondary sources, 263
Selective perception, 236
Self-concept, 160
Self-directed, 29
Self-discovery, 16–17, 33–34
Self-efficacy, 285
Self-esteem, 285–286
Self-fulfilling prophecy, 236
Selfishness, 316
Self-justification, 236
Seligman, Martin, 10
Senior women's administrators, 11
Serendipity, 181–182
Service learning, 317
Sexism, 238–239
Sexual assault, 282–283
Sexual harassment, 238–239
Sexually transmitted disease (STD), 279–282
Short-answer tests, 157
Shorthand, 140
Short-term goals, 58, 60
Short-term memory, 90, 94
Skills
    academic, 39, 97
    athletic, 38–39
    career, 31–32, 310
    discovering your, 309, 311
    transferable, 312–313
Skimming, 116
Skinner, B. F., 15
Slang, 119
Sleep, 95, 277
Smith, Stan, 97
Sophomore year, 319
Source cards, 141
Source documentation, 219, 220, 255
Spam, 257
Sparent, Martha, 206
Speeches, 221–222

Speed-reading, 115, 116
Sports. *See* Athletics
Stability, 10
Stereotypes, 236
Steroids, 289, 290
Stress, 14, 160, 170, 277–278, 286
Student government, 12
Student health clinics, 12
Student organizations, 12
Student unions, 12
Study groups, 95, 154–155
Studying
    distractions while, 69
    location for, 68–69
    scheduling time for, 63
    strategies for, 69–71, 96, 153, 155
    taking breaks while, 94
    time for, 59, 68, 94
    tools for, 152–153
Substance abuse, 98, 280
Suicide, 288
Summary notes, 135, 138, 141, 153, 190
Support groups, 304
Surrender, 296–297
Swoopes, Sheryl, 229

Tangrams, 180
Tasks
    to achieve goals, 69
    delegation of, 70–71
    filtering your, 64
    management of, 84
    sweetening your, 42
    on to-do lists, 61
Team doctors, 11
Team managers, 11
Teammates
    communicating with, 211
    diversity of, 231, 246
    hazing and, 212
    study time agreements with, 69
Team trainers, 11
Technology. *See also* Computers; Computer
    software; Internet
    access to, 252–253
    applications for, 64, 251, 256–258, 261
    fear of, 253
    staying current with, 261
    at work, 268
Technophobia, 253
Telephone use, 69
Test anxiety, 161–163
Tests
    cheating on, 160
    computer-graded, 157
    errors related to, 159
    essay, 157–158
    function of, 151
    getting copies of previous, 153
    matching, 157
    multiple-choice, 156
    open-book, 157
    predicting questions on, 155
    preparation for, 152–155
    short-answer/fill-in-the-blank, 157
    strategies for taking, 153, 156, 159
    true-false, 156–157
Textbooks, 112, 113, 118
Thesis statements, 216
Thinking skills, 180
Three-ring binders, 134
3x5 cards, 134, 141, 153, 182, 222
Tillich, Paul, 326
Timelines, 8
Time management
    between athletics and academics, 9, 52–56, 59,
      63–64
    creating balance in life through, 59
    eliminating procrastination through, 66–67

    for essay tests, 157–158
    explanation of, 51
    long-term planners for, 59, 75–76
    for online courses, 259
    for right-brained people, 72–73
    strategies for, 68–71
    for studying, 69
    using technology for, 64, 256
    at work, 84
Time Monitor/Time Plan Process, 52–56
Time-out, 70
Tobacco use, 98, 289
To-do lists, 61, 70, 72
Tolerance, 178
Transferable skills, 312–313
Transferring schools, 306–307
Transitions, 9–10, 12, 303
Translators, 235
Transportation, 78
Travel, 120
True/false questions, 156–157
Truth, 19, 29
Tutoring services, 12, 59, 118, 316

Underlining, 112, 113
Uniform Resource Locator (URL), 255
Universities/colleges
    choosing majors in, 187–189
    meeting people in, 10
    outstanding athletes in, 9
    technology use in, 251, 252
    transferring to other, 306–307

VAK system, 33–34
Values, 31, 72, 185, 224, 241, 320, 321
Verbal/linguistic intelligence, 30
Viewpoints, 177, 178
Visualization, 41, 89–91, 99, 161, 190, 218
Visual learning, 33, 34, 93
Visual/spatial intelligence, 30
Volunteering, 316, 317

Walpole, Horace, 181
Watson, Thomas, 328
WebCT, 259
Wernicke-Korsakoff syndrome, 98
Wooden, John, 331
Words, 132, 158
Work. *See also* Careers
    balancing schedule at, 10, 77–78
    communication at, 226
    critical thinking at, 196
    to finance education, 77–78
    health issues at, 298
    learning styles at, 46
    managing time at, 84
    note taking at, 145
    plan for change at, 328
    reading at, 124
    stress at, 170
    technology at, 268
Work-study programs, 77
World Wide Web. *See* Internet
Writing
    avoiding plagiarism in, 220
    draft, 217–219
    journal, 5–6
    as memory technique, 93–94
    methods to start, 216–217
    speech, 221–222
    at work, 226
Wurman, Richard Saul, 92

Yuen, Lenora, 67
Yukelson, David, 89

Zooming out, 162

MONDAY	TUESDAY	WEDNESDAY	THURSDAY	FRIDAY	SATURDAY	SUNDAY

Name _____   Month _____

Name _____

LONG-TERM PLANNER ___ / ___ / ___ to ___ / ___ / ___

Week of	Monday	Tuesday	Wednesday	Thursday	Friday	Saturday	Sunday
___ / ___							
___ / ___							
___ / ___							
___ / ___							
___ / ___							
___ / ___							
___ / ___							
___ / ___							
___ / ___							
___ / ___							
___ / ___							
___ / ___							
___ / ___							
___ / ___							
___ / ___							
___ / ___							
___ / ___							
___ / ___							
___ / ___							
___ / ___							
___ / ___							
___ / ___							
___ / ___							
___ / ___							
___ / ___							
___ / ___							
___ / ___							
___ / ___							
___ / ___							

Name _____

LONG-TERM PLANNER ___ / ___ / ___ to ___ / ___ / ___

Week of	Monday	Tuesday	Wednesday	Thursday	Friday	Saturday	Sunday
___ / ___							
___ / ___							
___ / ___							
___ / ___							
___ / ___							
___ / ___							
___ / ___							
___ / ___							
___ / ___							
___ / ___							
___ / ___							
___ / ___							
___ / ___							
___ / ___							
___ / ___							
___ / ___							
___ / ___							
___ / ___							
___ / ___							
___ / ___							
___ / ___							
___ / ___							
___ / ___							
___ / ___							
___ / ___							
___ / ___							
___ / ___							
___ / ___							
___ / ___							
___ / ___							
___ / ___							